George Johnston

A BIOGRAPHY

George Johnston

·····~·~·~·~ A BIOGRAPHY ·····~·~·~·~

Garry Kinnane

NELSON

FOR JO

Nelson Publishers
Thomas Nelson Australia

480 La Trobe Street
Melbourne Victoria 3000

First published in 1986
Copyright © 1986 Garry Kinnane

National Library of Australia
Cataloguing-in-Publication data:

Kinnane, Garry.
    George Johnston, a biography.

    Bibliography.
    Includes index.
    ISBN 0 17 006573 1.

    1. Johnston, George, 1912–1970 – Biography.
    2. Novelists, Australian – Biography. I. Title.

A823′.2
Typeset by Setrite Typesetters
Printed in Singapore
by Kyodo Shing Loong

CONTENTS

List of Illustrations

(Photographs are by courtesy of Martin Johnston unless otherwise acknowledged)

PREFACE

During 1984 the *Australian Book Review* in partnership with ABC radio conducted a Great Australian Novel quest, partly in fun and partly to find out just which novels and writers Australian readers valued most. There were two lists: best novel since World War II and best author in that period. George Johnston's *My Brother Jack* was the clear winner in the first category, and Johnston himself came second to Patrick White in the second category.

It comes as no surprise to find Johnston rating so highly with Australian readers. *My Brother Jack* has sold over 300,000 copies since it was first published in 1964, which certainly makes it a best-seller. But more important than the statistics is the great affection and regard that readers continue to have for Johnston's work, and for that of his wife, Charmian Clift. Two of his novels, *My Brother Jack* and *Clean Straw for Nothing*, won Miles Franklin Awards, and an early novel, *High Valley*, written in collaboration with Charmian Clift, won the *Sydney Morning Herald* prize in 1948. A pioneering television series was made of *My Brother Jack* in 1965, and a feature film of *Clean Straw for Nothing* is currently projected. With these credentials, George Johnston hardly needs an introduction to Australian readers, and indeed this biography proceeds on the assumption of a strong public interest in both his work and his life.

Critical recognition of his work has, however, been slow to arrive. Australian literary establishments are often suspicious of popularity because they presume it to be an indication of superficiality. In Johnston's case, nothing could be farther from the truth. The fact that he has been able, in at least one novel, to strike a chord in such large numbers of readers is directly attributable to his skill at putting complex ideas and states of feeling into clear, forceful characters and actions that are authentic reflections of Australian life. The writer Desmond O'Grady, who lives in Rome, recently told me that whenever he is asked to name a novel that expresses Australian life most characteristically, he recommends *My Brother Jack*. This kind of popularity is not superficial: it has been reinforced over twenty years, among readers of all ages and walks of life, and is an indication that the novel has touched upon some central myths of our peculiar urban existence in a way that feels important to us.

In recent years critics have begun to see the richness in Johnston's best work in something like its true light, and some good comment has disclosed social, literary and biographical implications of great interest. In particular, essays by A. E. Goodwin, Alan Lawson, F. H. Mares, Greer Johnson and Chris Tiffin, and Geoffrey Thurley, details of which can be found in the Bibliography of this book, all increase our understanding of those implications. In the case of Geoffrey Thurley, he goes out on a limb and argues that *My Brother Jack* is a masterpiece in the Dickens mould, and thereby opens up an interesting line of inquiry. While it does not have any of Dickens's humour, it does have a very Dickensian structure and array of characters, for it traces David Meredith's rise from obscurity and poverty through an unsympathetic family environment to worldly success, while at the same time enabling us to feel the central character's growing disillusionment with himself. Both Pip in *Great Expectations* and David in *David Copperfield* display the same kind of self-consciousness on their way to success, and the same capacity for betrayal, and the same admiration for simpler, more honest beings than themselves: compare Jack Meredith with Joe Gargery and Mr Peggotty, for instance. Take, too, the subject of love, and all three central characters make a fundamental error in their first experience of it, with Helen Midgeley, Estella and Dora Spenlow, respectively. It may well be that Johnston has touched upon the same mythic currents in our society that Dickens touched upon in his, and that this is a factor in their popularity.

However, I do not want to give the impression that Johnston was a similar writer or person to Charles Dickens: this would be quite false.* It is only in this one novel, in some respects a quite atypical novel for Johnston, that the resemblance occurs. In his other books he writes very differently, taking a variety of approaches to a wide range of subjects. The other two volumes of the Meredith trilogy, for instance, are experimental and modernistic in their structures and concentrate on the psychological state of the central character. And then there is all the writing he did for over twenty years before the trilogy — the journalism, the documentary war books, the adventure and romance fiction, and the crime novels, numbering twenty-seven books in all — representing different formulas and often under the influence of writers such as Conrad, Hemingway and Scott Fitzgerald. None of these influences was successfully absorbed by Johnston into his own style, and he had no illusions about the quality of most of his books before the trilogy. He knew they had been written too quickly and with an eye for best-sellerdom, and that this detracted from their worth. But he worked hard to change all that in his late novels, which were written with considerable care and craftsmanship, so that in the pinnacle of his literary achievement, the Meredith trilogy, he at last found his own voice and his own solutions to the problems of form, which came, not surprisingly, when he discovered what his best inspiration was: himself and his own experience.

The Meredith trilogy of novels, *My Brother Jack*, *Clean Straw for Nothing* and *A Cartload of Clay*, is an important and peculiarly Australian work. Autobiography, whether it is fictionalised or straight, is right at the heart of our literary tradition, particularly autobiography that traces the writer's development through a painful childhood. There is an interesting essay by Richard N. Coe, the details of which are in the Bibliography, which identifies the tendencies in Australian autobiography, which is a large and varied sub-genre, including such well-known works as Henry Handel Richardson's

---

* Coincidentally, Johnston was born and died exactly one hundred years after Dickens.

The Getting of Wisdom, Norman Lindsay's *Saturdee*, Alan Marshall's *I Can Jump Puddles*, Hal Porter's *The Watcher on the Cast-Iron Balcony* and Donald Horne's *The Education of Young Donald*, to name only a few that are about essentially the same dialectic between a writer and his or her nurturing culture. The common pattern is to show the child undergoing a disillusioning education, whereby it perceives the flatness and mediocrity of its cultural environment, only to find as an adult that this is the painful reality that must be adjusted to if Australia is to be accepted; otherwise it may be abandoned.

Johnston's trilogy traces this pattern also, but adds a broader and more romantic treatment of the theme of rejection and final acceptance in David Meredith's period of expatriatism in England and Greece, and his return home. This makes the trilogy very much an expression of its time, that post-war period of mass exodus from Australia of artists, writers, musicians and many others, who looked to the more sophisticated world of Europe for cultural satisfaction. This expression continues in the final volume of the trilogy, when Johnston attempts to come to terms with Australian life in the period after that exodus, when many were returning to find out whether the 1960s had brought any significant changes in the country.

It may seem unnecessary to write a biography of a man who has already written a trilogy of novels depicting his own life. But it is precisely when we know that a novel is autobiographical that we are most likely to ask questions about it. 'Is it true?' we ask, or 'Did it happen in that way?' We want our sympathy for the novelist in his role as central character to be confirmed or denied by more objective evidence. More important, we want to understand the process by which experience has been transformed into art. In this respect I have tried to show as much of the relationship between Johnston's life and his writing as possible, as a way of deepening our appreciation of his writing on the one hand, and on the other to show how his creative imagination functioned. I believe that the task of the biographer of a writer is to account for the life of his mind as well as of his body.

A biographer is also largely in the hands of his material, which he gathers from as wide a range of sources as possible.

I have had much good luck and a little bad. Those people who have been able to help have done so generously, which is testimony to a legacy of good will generated by Johnston himself. Many want to see a good biography of a man they liked and admired. On the other hand, solid personal material on Johnston is hard to find, largely because correspondence, notebooks and the like were lost in the confusion that overtook the household after his death, leaving frustrating gaps in the picture of his thoughts and movements, especially in the later years.

Mention should be made here of Charmian Clift. In the minds of many, Johnston and Clift belong together as a couple, both as writers and as husband and wife, and therefore would be best written about in a joint biography. There is, I believe, a stronger case for treating them as individuals. Of course, Clift comes into his life a very great deal, and I have attempted to devote a proportional amount of space in these pages as she occupied in actuality. But in the end their lives were their own, their thoughts, actions and beliefs unique and indivisible, as is the case with us all. Besides, the task of getting to grips with *one* personality is difficult enough, fascinating as it might be to attempt to keep two equally in focus. Charmian Clift will be receiving a biography in her own right in the near future.

Something of a legend has developed around George Johnston and Charmian Clift, who are compared often to the charismatic Scott and Zelda Fitzgerald of the Jazz Age. I cannot explain why they should attract such attention, even today, in Australians who did not know them. She was beautiful, talented, selfish and anarchistic; he was prodigiously energetic, garrulous, ambitious and sociable. And all this was mixed with a kind of 'innocence', as their friend Sidney Nolan called it, a *naiveté* that made them aspire to things they were not, in the end, up to achieving. This meant that tragedy was always in the offing, and eventually proved irresistible. In concentrating on Johnston's role in the story, I hope I have seen him fairly and respectfully, and that I have brought him closer to our understanding of who and what he was.

G.K.

ACKNOWLEDGEMENTS

My thanks to the following: David Allen, Albert Arlen, Sam Atyeo, Margaret Backhouse, Robert Beer, Toni Burgess, Didy Cameron, Sheila Carroll, Susan Clilverd, Colin Colahan, Monique Colahan, Geoff Collings, Dahl Collings, Ray Crooke, June Crooke, Bette Dixon, Lady Drysdale, Chester Eagle, Grace Edwards, Cedric Flower, Patrick Greer, Deborah Greiman, Gabriel Haire, Edward Heffernan, Rosalind Hollinrake, Donald Horne, Elizabeth Jane Howard, Neil Hutchison, Geoffrey Hutton, Greeba Jamison, Elsie Johnston, Gae Johnston, Jason Johnston, Martin Johnston, Patricia Johnston, Lucy Kerley, Anthony Kingsmill, Ray Kinnane, Harry Kippax, Lou Klepac, Bruce Kneale, Rosalind Landells, Wallace Landells, Richard Lane, Mungo MacCallum senior, Sir Sidney Nolan, Jocelyn Plate, Arthur Polkinghorne, Monica Polkinghorne, Jill Porter, John Douglas Pringle, William Pownall, Marjorie Quinton, Janette Reade, Ron Ridge, Joy Russo, John Ryland, Rachel Ryland, Charles Sriber, Susan Stokes, Anne Taylor, Wilfred Thomas, Charles Sriber, Susan Stokes, Anne Taylor, Wilfred Thomas, Hazel Tulley, Chris Wallace-Crabbe, Storry Walton, Hartley Watson, George Westcott, Nadia Wheatley, Osmar White, Anthony Whitlock, Neil Whitlock.

I am also indebted to the following libraries and institutions: Humanities Research Centre, Austin, Texas; Manuscript Department, Lilly Library, Indiana University; Periodical Section, Library of Congress, Washington; Mitchell Library, Sydney; the National Library, Canberra (with special thanks to John Thompson); La Trobe Library, Melbourne; Ballarat College of Advanced Education Library; also to David Higham and Associates Limited, Harold Ober Associates Incorporated, Angus & Robertson Publishers, Collins Publishers, Faber & Faber Limited, Horowitz Publications, Ure Smith, Sydney, and the Australian Broadcasting Corporation for permission to quote.

I am especially grateful to Martin Johnston for encouraging me into the project; to Hume Dow, who read the script so thoroughly and helpfully; and to Megan English and Joanne Barron for typing it. Naturally any errors of fact or interpretation remain my own. Finally, my wife, Jo, gave me much help and encouragement, for which I give her my thanks.

G.K.

List of Abbreviations

CofC   *A Cartload of Clay*
CSFN *Clean Straw for Nothing*
GJ   George Johnston
GK   Garry Kinnane
MBJ   *My Brother Jack*

C H A P T E R   I

Childhood and Youth

*... a final and exact if distant image of a place once lived in
and never to be returned to, like the city seen by the wife of
Lot in that last yearning moment before she became the pillar
of salt.* (MBJ 7)

The most teasing puzzle in Johnston's fictional version of his
childhood in *My Brother Jack* is the monstrous impression he
creates of his father, John George Johnston, known to everyone as 'Pop'. The first sixty pages of the novel are dominated
by the tyrannical figure of Jack Meredith senior, who strikes
terror in the hearts of his two sons, Davy and Jack, by giving
them a monthly ritual beating with a razor strop, whether
they are guilty of a transgression or not. Says Davy:

> *This went on for several years, and God knows what
> damage it did to me psychologically. I remember that from
> about the twentieth of every month I would behave with the
> innocence of a saint and the sycophancy of a French courtier
> in a desperate attempt to prove my rectitude. It made no
> difference. I was beaten anyway.* (MBJ 48–9)

When they read this, the members of the immediate Johnston family were appalled and confused by what they took to
be a totally unjust attack. Johnston's sister Marjorie and his
brother, Jack, are adamant that no such beatings took place,
and insist that while their father was a strict and at times
overbearing man, he was never a violent one.[1] When they
read the novel to their mother, whose eyesight was too poor
for her to read it herself, they deftly substituted rosier passages about the father in order to spare her feelings. Mr

Johnston was by that time dead.

Since *My Brother Jack* declared itself in so many ways to be autobiographical, it is inevitable that many readers would conclude that the head of the Johnston family was some sort of brutal psychopath. 'I had no idea the old man was such a devil!' they would declare in the street to other members of the family. 'Poor Mrs Johnston, having to put up with such a life!.'[2] The author of *My Brother Jack* made no attempt to contradict this impression, and when his brother accused him of having 'maligned the whole family', thinking especially of 'Pop', George simply evaded the issue by saying that he had never heard anything from readers other than expressions 'from all over the world saying how much they have loved the "Meredith" family', and that 'the only character maligned in it — if anybody is — is me'.[3]

George Johnston must have known he had created an unfavourable portrait of his father, notwithstanding the fictionalised name, and there are indications that this was done in a spirit of revenge. In later life he frequently and without affection referred to his father as 'the old bastard'.[4]

What was in the relationship between father and son to cause such disrespect, and eventually, from the evidence of the novel, downright malice? George undoubtedly got the occasional disciplinary whack from his father's hand, as did Jack, who took it in the spirit that was intended. Perhaps young George did not. Some members of his family thought of him as a physical coward, unable to bear pain, and he thought of himself in this way at times. I am not so convinced that he was, when I think of his involvement in sport and his later courage in coping with illness, although I bow to the family's greater knowledge of his behaviour as a child. In the father's case the source of the pain might have been verbal rather than physical. 'Pop' Johnston's worst form of cruelty was sarcasm and expressed bigotry towards anything he opposed. To other members of the family this was either funny or simply something to get used to; to young George, as sensitive to words and attitudes as to actions, this may have felt as repugnant as violence, especially if he or someone he liked happened to be on the receiving end. There was certainly a raw, over-sensitive element in his make-up that could not take admonition, for generally his mother (and sometimes his father) molly-coddled and protected him, and often favoured him over the other children. Perhaps, then, his father's cruel tongue bit deep into his feelings, and he gradually built up resentment of his father to an extent that he began to relish the idea of revenge.

Of course, we must not lose sight of the fact that *My Brother Jack* is a novel, and, whatever biographical significance it has, its fictional elements are equally important. Johnston was too experienced a writer not to believe in the value of conflict in the structure of a novel, and especially in the early pages of *My Brother Jack*, when Davy is presented as an outsider undergoing a painful childhood, it is important that the threatening forces around him are embodied in a single, powerful figure. By his violence to Davy and his mother and brother, by opposing Davy's artistic leanings, by throwing him out of the house, typewriter in arms, at the age of sixteen, Meredith senior becomes the villain of the family melodrama that dominates the early chapters of the novel, providing not only the ingredient of conflict, but also serving to impel young Davy prematurely into adulthood, where he must learn to survive by craft. The fact that little of this has anything to do with what actually happened in George Johnston's own family life is beside the point, for these events are the products of a novelist's imagination.

George Johnston's creation of Jack Meredith senior involved distortions of childhood memories, some deliberate and some probably unintentional, representations of strong feelings, and a considerable degree of pure invention. This sets before us a complex disparity between fact and fiction, between the actual and the imaginary, which is a recurring problem for the biographer of a writer, especially an autobiographical writer. And it is a recurring topic in this account of Johnston's life and work, for we will find again and again that the relationship in his writings between what he has drawn upon in his own experience and the reality discernible from different sources is far from being a simple one. His representation of his father is only one example.

'Pop' Johnston was not a man to be easily ignored. His height was 190 cm (six feet three inches) and weighed over 95 kilograms (fifteen stone), with a large dome of a head that was bald by the time he was thirty, and curved, prominent ears. He was a mixture of good-natured, sociable family man and irascible bigot, who grew more intractable as he aged. The times he lived through must have contributed to this.

'Pop' was born in Bendigo on 31 January 1876, the son of a Scottish mother, Catherine (*née* Lochied), and an Irish Presbyterian father from County Cavan, Robert George Johnston, who was Keeper of the Bendigo Powder Magazine. This was a civil service position of responsibility and security, although low-ranking and probably poorly paid, requiring only basic educational skills. Catherine may not have even had these, for she signed the birth register with a cross. John was the youngest child of four, one of whom died in infancy. He grew up in Bendigo a tall, strapping youth, and got a job as a mill worker in a local bakery, lugging sacks of flour. He also had natural intelligence and no desire to remain a labourer all his life. In his early twenties he courted and married the daughter of William Wright, the Editor of the Bendigo *Advertiser*. Her name was Minnie Riverina Wright — the family had come from Deniliquin in the Riverina in New South Wales — and she was short, stocky, sweet-tempered, played the piano and dabbled at painting. They were married in the Bayne Street Presbyterian Church on 24 May 1899. Since Minnie's family was middle class, the marriage represented a step up the social scale for young John Johnston.[5]

In April 1901 Minnie gave birth to a son, William, who lived only eighteen months. It was five years before they had another child, and this time it was a girl, Jean. Soon after this they moved to Melbourne, where John hoped to find more interesting work than Bendigo had to offer. They rented a house in Ascot Vale, where their son Jack was born in 1909. About this time John found a job as a maintenance worker with the Melbourne Tramways and Omnibus Company, which was developing the cable tram system. He was to work there until his retirement in 1941, by which time he was a foreman maintenance engineer, and the firm had changed to the Melbourne and Metropolitan Tramways Board.

Shortly before the outbreak of World War I the young Johnston family moved into a house at 11 Buxton Street, Elsternwick, which they promptly named Lochied after the maternal family line.[6] This was to be the Johnston home for more than forty years. It had been built only a few years earlier and was a bright, sunny weatherboard with a small front veranda, had five good-sized rooms, and plenty of space for a garden. Elsternwick was still a developing area then, with a great deal of vacant land about. Although it was a working-class district, its houses were not crammed into small blocks as were the terraced cottages of Collingwood and Richmond. It had all the characteristics of a prosperous, growing suburb, but with a semi-rural feel that made it an ideal stamping-ground for growing families of children. Indeed, by the time the Johnstons moved into Lochied they had added two more names to their family: George Henry, born on 20 July 1912; and Marjorie, born in 1914.

John Johnston had a lively interest in politics. He was a staunch Labor man, but like many others at that time he looked upon England as 'home', so that when the war broke out with Germany there was no doubt in his mind where his duty lay. He had been outspoken in his insistence that Australians should fight for the 'mother country', and treated nationalistic arguments, which he identified with Irish Catholicism, with contempt. He promptly enlisted in the AIF, and in 1915 was shipped off to Gallipoli. Minnie wholeheartedly shared his brand of patriotism, and was determined to play her part to the hilt, despite the demands of four young children. She therefore signed on as a Voluntary Aid Detachment nurse at the South Caulfield Hospital, which had been designated a military hospital.

Minnie's mother, Emma, who was now separated from her husband, moved into the house to care for the children. Emma had travelled a great deal, including to Spain when she was young, and had had two children by a previous marriage before she met William Wright. She was evidently a great character, a tower of strength to her seven children, and a favourite of her grandchildren, to whom she was a riveting storyteller. She is affectionately idealised in *My Brother Jack* as something of a family black sheep. Her daughter was quieter and more conventional, with a kind and sensitive disposition that was thoroughly suited to nursing.

John Johnston survived the ordeal of Gallipoli, only to be sent to France to endure three years of shelling, gassing and the horrors of trench warfare in the Somme region. He was among the last groups of soldiers to come home in 1919, and when he did it was evident that he was a changed man. There were physical changes, of course: he was partially deaf from the constant barrage of explosions, and the gas left him with a legacy of lung disorders.[7] He never talked about these things, or any other details of his war experiences. If anyone offered commiserations, he would dismiss the subject with the comment that 'there were plenty worse off' than himself.

The more significant change was temperamental. Opinions he had held idealistically before the war were now spattered about with aggression and sarcasm. His children's friends were sometimes afraid of him, and kept out of his way when they came to the house. He flew into a rage at any questioning of the value of the war, and since most public questioning came from left-wing or Catholic factions, he developed a particularly virulent hatred for both groups. When the children brought friends home, the first question he asked was whether or not they were Catholics. If they were, he would ridicule them, or loudly praise the Northern Irish or simply refuse to speak to them.[8] He was sour about what he felt was the country's lack of gratitude towards those who had fought in the War, and the portrait of Meredith senior in *My Brother Jack* as a man bitterly disillusioned with life after the war because 'the glory had curdled in the tram sheds' is perfectly appropriate to John Johnston.

For Minnie Johnston, however, the war had provided an opportunity for her particular qualities to blossom. She did not go overseas, as the Minnie Meredith of *My Brother Jack* does.[9] As part of their after-care duties at South Caulfield Hospital, the VAD nurses could take some patients home, especially to boost the morale of those men whose families may have been miles away in the country. Minnie took many such soliders to Lochied, and indeed, during the years when her husband was abroad, she seemed to have conducted a personal crusade to nurse as many repatriated wounded back to health as possible. She would play the piano while they stood around in their various states of mutilation singing popular songs of the day. Some of them stayed on for weeks, and in the case of one, Bert Thornton, for years, until eventually he married Jean and became one of the family.

This was the domestic atmosphere, then, in which the young George Johnston's awakening consciousness was developing. From the time he was three years old and his father went off to the war, and until he returned, the household was in a state of disruption. His mother was regularly on day-shifts at the hospital, and occasionally worked at weekends as well, so that he was deprived of her attention for much of the time in those crucial formative years. As a consequence he became something of a 'whinger', trailing about the house looking for comfort. Emma, for all her astuteness, was inclined to dose him with castor oil and send him out to play.[10] Whenever Minnie could, she lavished affection on him, but since this was often not enough for him, he came to place an inordinate value on it. In these early years of his childhood he was a sensitive and often unhappy boy.

The peculiarities of the household in these years had another important effect on him. The sight of all those invalids — and worse, the paraphernalia of crutches, bandages and artificial limbs that came with them — scored itself into young Johnston's psyche. Bert Thornton, for instance, had lost his lower leg in France, and repeated infection over a period of years resulted in surgery that, a piece at a time, gradually took away the whole leg. He wore an artificial limb, and the obsolete models were stored behind the hall door. Add to this the souvenir weaponry, the brass coat of arms, the ink-wells and ashtrays fashioned from shell cases, and the Johnstons' home environment takes on the character of a military museum. George drew on his remarkably clear memory of all this for the early passages in *My Brother Jack*, where he insists on the contribution it makes to David Meredith's developing personality.

> *Yet what is significant to realise now is how every corner of that little suburban house must have been impregnated for years with the very essence of some gigantic and sombre experience that had taken place thousands of miles away, and quite outside the state of my own being, yet which ultimately had come to invade my mind and stay there, growing all the time, forming into a shape.* (MBJ 17–18)

Elsewhere Meredith says that as a child he formed the impression that 'grown-up men who were complete were pretty rare beings' (*MBJ* 8).

What Johnston does in selecting these details to be the dominant environment for the whole family, but more especially for the two sons, Davy and Jack, is to show brilliantly the process by which war-consciousness is formed in young Australian males, chorused by their mothers, sisters and sweethearts, and the way in which all of them learn the roles they are expected to play in war. *My Brother Jack* is the only novel I know of that exposes this process, and the related perception that wars formed the culture of the working class for the first half of this century. In these respects the novel is not, as it has often been called, a social document so much as a vivid social *analysis*.

George was seven when his father came home from the war. Naturally, the family went down to the wharves to greet the troop ship that brought him home. For them it was a moving and happy occasion. But was it so for young George? A passage in *My Brother Jack* suggests it may have been quite the opposite:

> *I was seven then, but small for my age, and the day was charged, for me, with a huge and numbing terror. This fear was involved with the interminable blaring of brass bands, and a ceaseless roar of shouting and cheering, and the unending trampling past of gigantic legs.* (MBJ 10)

However, the worst part comes when Davy is swept up by the unknown figure of his father:

> *... without warning I was seized suddenly and engulfed in one of the gigantic, coarse-clad figures and embraced in a stifling smell of damp serge and tobacco and beer and held high in the air before a sweating apparition that was a large, ruddy face grinning at me below a back-tilted slouch hat and thin fair hair receding above a broad freckled brow, and then*

there was a roar of laughter, and I was put down, sobbing
with fear, and the thick boots marched on and on, as if they
were trampling all over me. (MBJ 10)

Even his father's attempts at affection feel to young Davy like
a physical assault. It is an extraordinary passage, marking the
beginning of the bad relationship between Davy and his
father. One can only speculate, however, on how accurate a
representation it may be of any such experience George may
have had on the wharves that day when his father returned
from the war. If it is accurate, then perhaps it is a clue to
those expressions of hatred that Johnston so freely tossed
about in later life.

After the uncertainties of early childhood, George's boyhood
settled down to be generally a happy one. Much of his time
was spent outdoors, and Marjorie recalls tagging along after
yabbies in the local creek, and up to Cox's Hill to 'muck
about', and cooking potatoes in a bonfire if there was one
going. Occasionally the children would go to the country for a
holiday, either to Dereel, near Ballarat, where Bert's uncle —
'Uncle Whittle' he was called — ran a farm, or to a place near
Wedderburn, where there was a musical family called Turley,
who had been friends of the Johnstons since Bendigo days.
The name Turley was to surface for one of the more important
characters in the Meredith trilogy. None of these normal,
healthy outdoor activities is given much place in Johnston's
fiction, and they are not drawn upon at all for the development of David Meredith's character, which is depicted in *My
Brother Jack* as being in morbid retreat from physical experience.

On the other hand, Johnston was always prepared to draw
attention to his unusual proneness to fear, as in the scene on
the wharves with his father. Marjorie testifies that this fear
was clearly in evidence throughout his childhood. He would
tell ghost stories to her in their bedroom, but it would invariably be he who would spend the night huddled beneath the
blankets in terror. When he was a little older, she would hear
him come home after dark, running as hard as he could,
slamming the side gate the bursting though the back door

like a shot: his fear was intense. And when their grand-mother's sister died and was laid out in her coffin in the lounge-room of the Johnston house, their mother, accustomed to death, insisted that as a mark of respect the children go and look at the body. Marjorie found it an unpleasant experience; but George, she is convinced, found it horrific, was visibly shocked, and was left psychically scarred by what he saw. Macabre descriptions of corpses often turn up in his novels. In *My Brother Jack*, for instance, David discovers the body of a sailor washed up on Phillip Island:

> I began to haul the dead sailor out on to the dryer part of the shore, but as soon as I exerted force the arm pulled right out of its socket, and I fell over backwards, still clinging to the corpse's arm, which had pulled away with the blue jersey sleeve and rotted threads and everything, and the stump of the limb was a ghastly transparent quick shimmer of sea-lice, that leaped and flickered and moved as if they were insane, and then I could feel them jumping and tickling all over my own hand, and I dropped the dead arm back into the sea and put my head down on the wet murmuring sand and vomited.
> (MBJ 221)

Meredith's reaction is not merely physical disgust, for he behaves afterwards like someone with a guilty secret: 'I never told anyone about the dead man's arm coming away in my hand', he confides, as if this would have been admitting to some unspeakable indecency. Johnston characteristically writes about corpses as obscenities. For example, in *The Far Road* (1962) the central action takes place against a vast land-scape of Chinese corpses that are constant reminders of the moral corruption that is part of the purpose of the novel to expose.

Johnston often refers, too, to his childhood susceptibility to fear. In *Closer to the Sun* (1960) his persona, an early version of David Meredith, recalls that 'right back to his childhood he had an odd terror of cocks crowing in the darkness',[11] and in *Journey through Tomorrow* (1947) he recalls his own fear of Chinese people: 'On the few occasions when I had to go down Little Bourke Street ... I would run with thumping heart and terror in my eyes.'[12] One feels the ring of autobiographical truth about these passages, in that Johnston certainly *felt* himself to have been a physical coward as a boy, and other members of his family have lent their support to that view.

In this respect, as in some others, George grew up feeling inferior to his brother, Jack. If Jack was afraid of anything, he would never have shown it. As well as having that enviable older brother's luck of confronting life's experiences sooner, making him seem always several jumps ahead in sophistication, Jack was also a tough and independent personality. He developed a stance as the lovable larrikin of the family, so that while he often got up to mischief, he had the charm to turn it to his own advantage. This went on into adulthood. Marjorie recalls that he would come home from work sometimes the worse for a few drinks, but would invariably have a crayfish or a juicy rock melon in his Gladstone bag as a peace offering to his mother. Like everyone else in the family, George was won over by Jack's blend of toughness and mischievous humour. George had some of that humour himself, but none of the toughness; he depended on his cleverness for attention.

Jack was much like his father, in appearance as well as in interests. He did not like school, except for the sport. The records of Brighton Technical School show that he was enrolled on the very first day it opened in 1922; but apart from winning the goal-kicking medallion for the soccer team in that year, Jack's stay was undistinguished and brief. 'Snowy' Johnston, as he was nicknamed in the school magazine, fades mysteriously from the records after 1922, when, without having gained any qualifications, he left, at the age of thirteen, to take his chances on the labour market, just as his father had done. He found a job as a plumber's assistant, with the hope of starting an apprenticeship.

Mrs Johnston was determined that George would achieve higher things. She kept a watchful eye on his progress, and was pleased to see her artistic leanings reflected in him; he was showing great promise in his sketching. Like his brother and sisters, he attended Caulfield Primary School, which he left at the age of ten to follow Jack to Brighton Technical School. When he enrolled in 1923, his prospective occupation was recorded as a 'Draughtsman', so even at this early stage the family anticipated that George would be heading for a profession. Draughting would have appealed to both parents: it was practical enough to meet with his father's approval, and required graphic skill of a kind that would enable his mother to see his artistic ability find expression.

George managed well enough at Brighton, without ever becoming a star pupil. His record in the technical subjects was average, but he was well above average in English and Civics,[13] the nearest subject to History that the school taught. In some respects he would have benefited from a more academically oriented curriculum, particularly from a subject such as History, which became a lifelong passion with him. Whenever he had money to spend on books, right through his life, he very often spent it on works of history of one kind or another, or on archaeology or ancient civilisations. High Schools were few and far between in those days, and in any case the idea of a purely academic schooling, or of going on to University, was never a consideration with Johnston's parents. There was simply not the money.

George was energetically involved in the life of the school, spreading himself over a wide range of activities. He was a regular member of the strong and successful school soccer team: local soccer was then a respectable rival to Australian Rules in Victoria, and Brighton Tech. had an impressive record. George was a fast and accurate striker, scoring nine goals in the 1925 season, and in 1926 was chosen to represent his State in the school championships in Adelaide. He suffered a broken collarbone in this year. He was also a member of the School Library Committee, and secretary of the Dramatic Club. One of his contemporaries, George Westcott, remembers him clearly as a 'fresh-faced fellow' with a 'bright personality', who tended to do the more precocious things about the place, such as act in plays and mix with the creative types.

He also wrote pieces for *Sea Spray*, the school magazine. These are brief standard schoolboy fare, but one of them, 'Night of Horror', is worth quoting in its entirety, because it is his first piece of published fiction, and because it suggests how ready his creative imagination was even then to fasten upon, in its modest way, the topic of fear:

> *The room was dark about him, and he sat, fascinated, in his chair. The boy he admired and worshipped sat bound to a chair, and the two unscrupulous ruffians, who were his friend's worst enemies, were torturing the boy. He wished that he could spring at the ruffians, but something unknown held him back to his seat. The victim was crying out 'You shall not get the plans!'. And he struggled vainly with his bonds. He looked around the room to see if anybody would help him, but nobody moved. All the people he had thought were his friends made no effort to rescue him. His beseeching eyes alighted on the boy who loved him, but turned, a moment later, for one of the ruffians was exclaiming 'I have them — the plans!'. The other villain turned, with a sneering smile, to the boy in the dark room, who wanted to jump forward, but could not. What restrained him?*
>
> *Just then a white light flashed before his eyes, and the following words appeared on a bright square: 'The next thrilling episode of this serial, "His Grandmother's Will", will be shown next week'. With a sigh, the boy turned and walked out of the theatre.*[14]

The unlikelihood of seeing his best friend and his two worst enemies in a film seems to have escaped the young author's attention, but the phrase 'His beseeching eyes alighted on the boy who loved him' is a gem.

On the evidence, then, his schooldays were vigorous and happy. He had a bunch of friends with whom he formed a Gang of Four and who stayed together throughout their teens. Bob Eagle was the eldest by a couple of years and was also a friend of Jack's. Billy Bauld was vice-captain of the soccer team in 1926. And Ron Ridge had been at Caulfield Primary with George, and walked to school with him every morning. Ridge says that Johnston's chief and most intimidating quality was his exuberance. If they went to the beach 'George would always want to wrestle on the sand, or tackle you. And on the way home in the tram he would be bumping you all the time, trying to make you fall over on some old lady. It used to irritate me. He had too much energy, and was always larking about.'[15] His abundance of energy seemed to increase as he grew up, and was usually the first thing people noticed about him.

13

The boys of the gang were not just larrikins. They would spend hours in George's room, talking, sketching, reading, building model ships, in fact generally engaging in a boyhood life-of-the-mind, with George at its centre. Marjorie says they were to some extent in retreat from the females of the house, and Jack scoffed at them, regarding their activities as a bit unhealthy. Jack Meredith's term 'sonky mates' in the novel is probably a fair expression of young Jack Johnston's feelings about them. However, their parents saw nothing wrong with them. Mr Johnston built a wall of bookshelves in George's room to house the many books he was beginning to acquire — an uncle had died and left him a number — and his mother gave him plenty of encouragement to develop his intellectual interests. Given his wide range of abilities — flair at sport, participation in drama and committees, his love of books and his outgoing personality — George gave every indication in his early teens that he was developing into a fully-rounded man. There is a photograph of him in the school soccer team for 1926 looking a little small for his age, but well built, neatly groomed and pleasantly open-faced, seemingly without a worry in the world.

How strange, therefore, it is to read Johnston's jaundiced representation of his childhood in *My Brother Jack*. The young David Meredith is an almost unrelieved failure: 'I never finished my last year at that technical school', he tells us, 'and I was failed for the Intermediate Certificate' (*MBJ* 55). He insists that it was Jack who was the cleverer of the two of them, and was 'far more concerned with sport' than he was (George was in fact a more skilful and dashing footballer than Jack, who was merely big and tough). Nor is David interested in art, for which he says he had 'remarkably little talent' (*MBJ* 55), and of the friendship with his three mates he reflects 'There was a sad, desperate innocence about it all. We shared a deep guilt at having failed at school, we had all been sent out to jobs in which we were barely interested, we had no idea where we were going . . .' (*MBJ* 64). It is out of this sense of failure that David begins to write poems and stories, but even this, he insists, was an admission of failure: 'I was setting out to try to sidestep a world I didn't have the courage to face.' He fails in his job, too, which becomes in Meredith's view of himself, a 'defection'. Perhaps the biggest and most important failure is in the breakdown of his relations with his parents, who oppose his writing, and especially with his father, who eventually forces him out of the house.

Neither in fact nor spirit is this an accurate representation of Johnston's own boyhood, which would appear to have been in generally a normal and happy one. The outline is close enough, but important details, such as his outdoor life, his participation in sport, and his enterprising, exuberant demeanour are absent from the picture given in *My Brother Jack*. In part, the reasons for this, and for the naggingly depressive tone in which Meredith so often reflects on his past, are related to Johnston's state of mind at the time *My Brother Jack* was written in 1963, but our full appreciation of this must wait until we come to that period in his life.

George completed his final year at Brighton Technical school, and in fact obtained the highest qualification that the school issued then, his Junior Technical Certificate. It is unlikely that he was sent against his will to begin an apprenticeship as a lithographer. The draughtsman plan was abandoned somewhere along the line, probably because the technical subjects were not his strength, but the position he found at one of Melbourne's most distinguished printing firms, Troedel & Cooper, as an 'Artistic apprentice' on a salary of fifteen shillings a week would hardly have disappointed him or his parents. He started work on 26 October 1926, before the school year finished, in the firm's city studio in Bank Place.[16]

George liked the work at Troedel & Cooper, and admired the skill of the craftsmen, a number of whom came from German backgrounds. In *My Brother Jack* he re-creates many of his experiences there with affection and in great detail. Some time during his first year there, he was instrumental in getting Jack a job as a storeman with the firm. Jack also must have found them amenable employers, because he stayed with them for a total of twenty-six years, excluding lay-offs during the Depression and several years of war service. (In the three years after he left school, Jack had not settled into a job, having found work as a plumber's assistant, a grocery boy and a farm hand in Horsham not to his liking.)

It was one of the requirements of his apprenticeship that George attend classes in order to improve his draughtsmanship, and so he enrolled in the evening drawing class of the National Gallery School under the tutelage of W. B. McInnes in the first term of 1927.[17] He drew from plaster casts because only the senior students were admitted to the Life classes. It was here that George met, indeed could hardly have avoided, the brilliant Sam Atyeo. They were the same age, but Atyeo was years ahead in sophistication and confidence. Even at this early stage he was full of startling ideas, which he delivered in a cocky style that someone such as George, shy and desperately unsure when it came to anything to do with art, could only listen to in dumb admiration, perhaps guessing that within a few years Atyeo would become one of the most influential avant-garde painters on the Melbourne scene.

Johnston found it difficult to get seriously involved in his art classes, and difficult to make friends among the art students, who for the most part were 'young girls waiting for the debutante ball or middle-aged women concerned as much with permanent waves as with art'.[18] The serious students, the 'embattled young intellectuals', as Richard Haese calls them, people such as Atyeo and Neil Douglas, had a precocity that made George uncomfortable, and he hung back from any active involvement with them. Increasingly he skipped classes and wandered into the Reading Room of the adjoining State Library, where he indulged his love of books. In the second term he dropped out of the class altogether, and there is no record of attendance for him at all in 1928. One wonders if his employers knew.

The books he read in the State Library were invariably on the subject that had at this time become his passion, sailing ships. How this came about is not clear, but it was all-consuming in his mid-teens. He devoured the works of Basil Lubbock, who wrote popular volumes on the history of shipping with titles such as *The Colonial Clippers, The Romance of the Clipper Ships* and *The Last of the Windjammers*, of which

George acquired a brand-new copy when it came out in 1927.[19] His other reading, too, tended to be about the sea: *Moby Dick* and the sea poems and stories of John Masefield and, above all, the writings of the author who remained Johnston's favourite throughout his life, Joseph Conrad. George shared this interest in ships with his friend Ron Ridge, who had also become an apprentice lithographer, doing his evening classes at the Melbourne Technical College (now RMIT), so that no doubt the pair of them could often be found together in the State Library when they should have been in class. Ridge and George between them built an impressive three-foot wooden model of a clipper, which Ridge still has in his possession today.

George loved to paint and draw ships, too. During his lunch hours he would wander down to the Melbourne docks (he might even have spent some time at Troedel & Cooper's Bay Street, Port Melbourne building, which was only minutes away from the docks), where he could see the old coal-hulks, — many of them cut-down clippers — which were the last sad remnants of a graceful era. Of these he made rough sketches, which he would then take home and complete, showing them as the fully-rigged, ocean-braving vessels of their prime, using as a guide the illustrations in Lubbock or some other pictorial reference. It was not the art in itself that mattered to him, but the grandeur of what the ships had been, and this excited his imagination enough to want to recreate them. Again, this suggests an instinctive passion in him for what was past — the natural tendency of a romantic or one kind of historian, and this, I believe, is very much how his mind characteristically functioned for the rest of his life.

It was in fact this interest in the bygone world of ships that started George's writing career. He discovered that he could write about it better than he could paint it, and when, in *My Brother Jack*, his writing style had fully matured, he was able to produce images of those visits to the docks that are, in their lyricism, reminiscent of the English Romantic painter J. M. W. Turner:

> ... *the slender gilt pencillings of masts declaring themselves little by little against the dark haze-banks that always in this*

> *waking time veiled the river flats, the faint images of ships far down the stream, coming in from Gellibrand, looming out of dew and light and sea mist, and then, at every bend and twist of the river, changing the shapes of beauty like a rare vase turned in the fingers of a connoisseur.*
>
> *It filled me with excitement, almost an exultation, that I could tell nobody about. I did not see it then as a way out of the wilderness, for the stuff of this material was too fragile to be considered as something that might be* used, *but I was quite sure that something important had happened to me.* (MBJ 77)

This, of course, is the middle-aged author looking back in an idealising vein with the wisdom of hindsight, but doubtless such imaginative excitement did overtake him, and fragile though the material may have been, the young George Johnston soon found a way of using it. Early in 1929, and still only sixteen years old, he wrote an informed piece titled 'Ill-Fated Voyages: Tragic Wrecks on the Australian Coast', and sent it off to the Melbourne *Argus*. To his delight it appeared in the 'Camera Supplement' on 20 April. The Editor sent him a cheque for five guineas and invited him to submit more such pieces. His journalism had begun. The next of his articles, on the area of the wharves known as 'Little Dock', came out in July. He also published similar pieces in an English magazine called *Sea Breezes*, the journal of the Pacific Steamship Navigation Company. All these, and indeed most of his early journalism, were published under his full name of George H. Johnston, and not the pseudonym of 'Stunsail' used by David Meredith in the novel. His parents and friends were proud of his newly developed talent and the sudden modest fame it was bringing him. This is in complete contrast to David Meredith's experience, where his father in particular is so enraged to discover that his son has been publishing articles, which he has been attempting to keep a secret, that he drives David, typewriter in arms, from the house. Nothing could have been farther from the minds of either of George Johnston's parents.

Writing was an enjoyable hobby, but George still had his apprenticeship to do. He re-enrolled at the Gallery in 1929, and managed to stay the whole year. This time he was not quite so intimidated by the art students, and though Sam Atyeo was not enrolled in his class in this year, the two became friendly. Atyeo had found a studio in Little Bourke Street, near the Chinese quarter, and here he would harangue fellow students with his uncompromisingly Modernist ideas on philosophy, music and painting. He was, according to Richard Haese, 'the most dynamic force among the younger painters in Melbourne during the early 1930's',[20] and his abstract paintings were to open the eyes of the following generation of painters, which included Howard Mathews, Charles Bush and Sidney Nolan.

Young Johnston often went to Atyeo's studio, where he would listen to the lively talk from the background, still saying little. Atyeo remembers him as a 'nice, well-brought-up, dullish young man', though they did often spend time together. Johnston sometimes stayed overnight at the studio (it was when he went home at nights that he had to run the fearful gauntlet of the Chinese quarter on his way to the tram stop). Atyeo tells a story about that faint-heartedness. They were walkng through the Fitzroy gardens together when they came across a man beating a woman. Atyeo intervened, and was promptly turned on by them both. Meanwhile George had run off. Afterwards he said he had known they were man and wife, and had not wanted to get involved, but Atyeo didn't believe him.[21]

He drew on this friendship with Atyeo for the memorable character of Sam Burlington in *My Brother Jack*, though many of the events surrounding him are fictitious. Johnston did not move into the studio as David Meredith does when he leaves home in the novel. Nor did Atyeo or George get involved in any murder case, as suggested by the 'Jessica Wray' case in the novel.[22] The description of Burlington in the novel does, however, bear a nicely observed resemblance to Atyeo:

> ... there was a always a perkiness and quickness of movement about him that gave him a kind of skittery, bird-like quality. (MBJ 102)

This tallies with John Reed's view of Atyeo as a 'brilliant boy, very vital, very alert, a very quick brain and a mind darting everywhere'.[23] It also fits my own perception of Atyeo when I interviewed him in January 1984.

At home George was entering a period that Jack describes as 'probably the happiest time in his life'. The three years' difference in their ages was not such a big gap in George's late teens, and the brothers were closer than they'd ever been. Jack would borrow his father's Chevrolet, and they went with mates on camping trips, usually along the Jamieson river in Central Victoria, where they would fish and shoot together. They also played Australian Rules football together for the Brighton Presbyterian Church team; Jack was a lumbering ruckman, and George a speedy wingman, though at 180 cm (five feet eleven inches) he was tall for the position. He had filled out into a well-built young man, too, and with his clear skin and blondish brown hair was, according to Marjorie, handsome and popular with the girls, to whom so far he had paid little attention.

The whole family got involved in the football team. Mr and Mrs Johnston were active in the social club, and raised funds by holding regular Saturday night parties at their house, or card evenings, or dances. Mr Johnston acted as goal umpire at the matches, though hardly an impartial one it would seem: on an occasion when George was receiving some close attention from an opposition player during a game, his father ran onto the ground to even up the score, and after a scuffle among several players the only one to be reported was Mr Johnston.[24]

George was unusually slow to take an interest in the opposite sex. Jack had been sexually precocious and had never disguised it, but, according to Ron Ridge, who was the first of the Gang of Four to marry, George still had not taken out a girl at the age of twenty-one, and was to be the last of the gang to marry. In some respects he was slow to mature, and his mother seems to have been largely responsible for this. Until he was twenty, she took all his wages and gave him back an allowance, and she chose and bought his clothes for him. Ridge recalls a time when they were out together and he tore his new suit on some wire. 'He was so afraid of what his mother would say that it ruined his evening, and he went straight home to tell her.'[25] Years of her fussing over him had left him domestically totally dependent on her, a bid for control to which working-class mothers are often prone.

Apart from his mother, there was one girl he was able to get close to, and this was Jack's girl-friend, Patricia McKean. George and Pat warmed to each other soon as they met. 'I was the first girl he could talk to,' says Pat, 'he talked to me about things he should really have talked to his mother and father about.'[26] However, his parents did not go in for sex counselling, though by that age George had probably picked up 'the facts', and sought in Pat someone who could lend a sympathetic ear and discuss the tactics of relationships. He also felt sorry for Pat, who had to bear a certain amount of rough treatment from the family, especially from Mr Johnston. She was a Catholic, of Irish descent and, although she had no family of her own, Mr Johnston was strongly opposed to her. Jack was defiant, however, and in 1930, with George's knowledge and encouragement, the couple were secretly married, although they continued to live apart for over a year while Jack saved some money and hoped for his parents to soften. Mrs Johnston gave way first, when Pat's daughter, Joy, was born, and it was George who led the conciliation by ostentatiously hugging Pat and the baby in front of the family. But it was another ten years before Mr Johnston's resistance crumbled, an event that was brought about by Jack's enlisting to fight in World War II. George felt shame and disgust at his father's behaviour, and on the evidence never forgave him. The warm relationship between George and Pat is represented with a high degree of accuracy in the friendship between David and Sheila in *My Brother Jack*.

The Johnston family fared better than a great many others when the Depression came. Mr Johnston was safe at the Tramways Board, and George's apprenticeship protected him. Jack and his family suffered on the several occasions when he was laid off by Troedel & Cooper, once for a nine months' stretch, and for a total of several years over all. Although he had the promise of being re-hired when things improved, these lay-offs caused Jack and Pat hardship. He was forced to seek work wherever he could, which included fruit-picking in northern Victoria and selling fish at the Melbourne market.

21

These setbacks did not, however, prompt him to quite the prodigious heroism of his namesake in *My Brother Jack*, who goes as far as South America in search of work, and who, penniless, walks from Sydney to Melbourne on bleeding feet to collapse into his mother's arms. George probably got the South American story from Billy Bauld, whose brother went there as a seaman.[27] As for that melodramatic trek, this was based on an occasion when Jack and a mate, having arrived in Melbourne on the train from Shepparton, where they had been fruit-picking, decided 'for the fun of it' to walk home. It was a hot day and they were certainly tired, but they also, according to Jack, 'put on a bit of an act' to make it look worse than it was.[28] When George Johnston was calling on his memories of Jack's deeds for the novel, he inflated everything about him, because he was attempting to build a larger-than-life character, an Australian mythic hero, out of the best qualities he identified in his brother. It was central to his character's heroism that he should possess massive courage in the face of adversity. Jack found the novel embarrassing and 'wrong', when he read it, because he had not done many of the things he believed were being attributed to him. He missed the point: George was not trying to 'tell it as it was', but was re-creating the past in accordance with a personal vision.

The picture one gets of Johnston in his late teens and early twenties is of a young man who was busy with and totally absorbed in his various interests. He was secretary of the football club, as well as a player, and was awarded the prize for best clubman about this time. He kept up his painting and sketching, though no longer at the Gallery. He had published more than a dozen articles in the *Argus* and elsewhere on ships, and in 1930 he helped found the Shiplovers' Society of Victoria, for which he was made its first honorary secretary. This society consisted of a group of about sixty enthusiasts from all walks of life who had a common interest in sailing ships. Johnston designed the society's emblem, which it still uses, and also managed to obtain its number one membership ticket. Ron Ridge got number two. One of the younger members, Bill Watson, owned a twelve-foot yacht, the *Veritas*, which he sailed from the Williamstown Yacht Club, and George used to catch the train to Williamstown on weekends to crew for Watson. About 1932 he painted a graceful watercolour of the *Veritas*, which hangs on Bill Watson's wall to this day.[29]

In 1933 George's sister Marjorie married, and she eventually went to South Australia to live. In that year his friend Ron Ridge married also. The year was important for George, too: a few months after his twenty-first birthday he was invited by the Editor of the *Argus*, who would have been R. L. Curthoys at that time, to become a cadet reporter on the paper. He leapt at the chance, and in October broke his apprenticeship, which was in any case almost finished, with Troedel & Cooper, and joined the Melbourne *Argus*.[30]

George was placed, appropriately, on the shipping round, which happened to be a usual starting point for cadets. This involved reporting on activities around the wharves, ship arrivals and departures, including any notables thereon, and occasionally something more adventurous, such as going with the boats that did lighthouse stores runs. In addition, he continued to write for the weekend supplement. Many of these were, again, features on ships, and he and other writers were establishing an *Argus* tradition for such articles.

George obviously loved the work, and did it brilliantly. Geoffrey Hutton was a C grade journalist on the paper then, and he recalls the impression Johnston made: 'He was a bright boy who took over the shipping round and made a tremendous thing of it. He flung himself wholeheartedly into the work, and was an extraordinarily fast writer, who could write four articles in one afternoon.'[31] George's natural exuberance seemed to explode when he used a typewriter, and words rattled forth at amazing speed. This facility, handy for meeting deadlines, was later to prove something of a danger to his writing, because it discouraged the important process of self-criticism. It was another product of his nervous energy, of which it was apparent to his journalist colleagues he had an abundance. He was usually tense too: he bit his nails mercilessly and, even at this age, was a heavy smoker.

So, George was now professional man, a journalist. He had

not had the usual education for it. Geoffrey Hutton had been to a private school and Melbourne University, and other colleagues, such as Bruce Kneale, had similar backgrounds. It bothered Johnston a little at times, and he was inclined to tell new acquaintances that he had in fact matriculated, but couldn't afford to go on to University. His mother told some people the same story.[32] The family was proud of him, and already talked of him as a success. But it was just the first stage to bigger and better things, as it was, ironically, the first stage in his establishing an unbridgeable gap between himself and the modest life of his family. This was not to become noticeable, however, until marriage actually took him out of their sphere of influence.

CHAPTER II

Marriage

*I had the thrilling feeling of having finished a long and
difficult period of probation and come at last to the beginning
of real life. (MBJ 248)*

In 1937, at the age of twenty-five, Johnston was a C grade
journalist on the good salary of £9 2s 6d per week. Unlike his
brother, he was not directly affected by the Depression, being
employed the whole time. There is a certain expectation in
working-class families that they will help each other in times
of need, and George Johnston's failure to make any such
gesture to Jack and Pat stuck in their memories, and was
recalled with a certain irony when they read in *My Brother
Jack* of David Meredith's gift of £50 to Jack and Sheila when
she is recovering from an illness. Far from lending them
money, George hardly ever went near them: 'in all the years
that we were married he would have been in our house
twice', recalled Pat.[1] What they took to be family disloyalty
was George carelessly and egocentrically following his own
interests, and these were leading him away from the traditional pastimes of working-class life. Increasingly his friends
were drawn from journalism circles or yachting people, and
he had by this time given up his involvement with the football club. He played tennis and dreamed of owning a sports
car.

He had begun to take out girls, although he was still living
at home. During the previous year he had escorted his sister
Marjorie to a ball, and found that included in their foursome

was a pretty girl-friend of Marjorie's called Elsie Taylor. She had visited the Johnston house some ten years earlier when she and Marjorie were still at school, but Johnston had not paid her the slightest attention then. Now he was impressed; he took her to another ball soon afterwards, but did not see her again for about a year.

In the meantime he had a friendship with a girl called Olga Reid,[2] who worked in a subscription library in Glenhuntly Road, just around the corner from the Johnston home. She was blonde, and though not stunningly beautiful she was interesting, well read, with leftish political leanings and she existed on the fringes of Melbourne Bohemian circles. Johnston used the library regularly and saw a great deal of Olga Reid, but however intimate the relationship may have been, it was not a steady one. He was still friendly with her when he took up with Elsie again, this time on a regular basis.

George apparently placed the two women in different categories. On the occasion of an Arts Ball, usually an unruly event attended by artists, writers and students, he told Elsie that it was an unsuitable occasion for her and refused to take her, saying that he would go alone. Elsie believes that he took Olga Reid, whom he saw as much more part of that scene, although he denied this when Elsie asked. He did take Elsie along to the library every Friday night, where they socialised in a back room with Reid and the man who ran the business, 'Wally'. The room was cosily set up with teamaking facilities, chairs and a sofa, and they would sit and talk about literature or politics or art. Elsie found these sessions disagreeable, partly because she was only twenty-one and was singularly unversed in such subjects, and partly because from time to time there was something about Reid that made her uncomfortable, particularly in the way she seemed to be giving Elsie scrutinising looks. It was only much later that she concluded that George and Olga might have been having an affair.

Elsie Taylor's family struggled during the Depression, with her father sometimes having difficulty finding work and her mother, a resourceful woman, helping to keep them afloat by making dresses. They lived in Caulfield, and Elsie was the second youngest of five children. She was a bright girl and obtained Intermediate Certificate from Prahran Technical School, after which her mother went into Myers and got her an office job.

One night, when they were walking down Glen Eira Road, George said to her: 'How would you like to become Mrs George?' She was a little stunned. 'I didn't know whether he meant it or not,' she later reflected.[3] But he did mean it, although both of them claimed afterwards that they 'didn't really want to get married'.[4] Nevertheless, they were married in St Mary's Anglican Church, East St Kilda, on 19 March 1938. They honeymooned at Warburton, then a fashionable resort in the Dandenongs, and when they returned they moved into a rented maisonette in Britten Street, Glen Iris.

Three months after the marriage, Elsie's life was clouded by the death of her mother, to whom she had been close. At a time when she needed all the support she could get, Elsie found George's mother discouraging. She kept telephoning him to ask if he was 'all right', and generally maintaining her influence over him without reference to Elsie, and in a manner that rather froze her out and did little for her confidence. When the couple went to choose furniture for the house, both his parents came too, and most of the decisions were made by George with the advice of his mother. And as the influence of Mrs Johnston over the domestic choices waned, it was George who took over as arbiter, not Elsie.[5]

Their social life, too, such as it was, was largely in his hands. Elsie would have liked to have entertained and gone out more, but George was often too busy with his interests, writing and painting mostly. What friends they had were journalist colleagues, such as Rod Maclean and Bruce Kneale. In the days before George owned a car, Kneale's wife, Lorna, would pick them up from the office at night – they worked a shift from 2 p.m. until about 11 p.m. – and they would go back to the Johnston flat and talk through half the night, 'solving the world's problems, no doubt', reflects Kneale. Maclean was a likeable young reporter on the shipping round with Johnston, and the pair of them generated much fun between them. One time they and Elsie were in Maclean's car, with George in the 'dicky' seat, urging Maclean, who was driving deliberately slowly, to go faster. Eventually George leapt out and ran alongside the car, so Maclean put his foot down and roared off up the street, stopped and waited for George to catch up, then roared off again. They kept this up for some time, with Elsie in paroxysms of laughter. One of Maclean's girl-friends, Rosalind Landells, who worked at the *Argus*, remembers Elsie as 'the dearest, prettiest, most uncomplicated person' with 'no social aspirations', and she recalls an occasion that captures some of the spirit of these early years of the marriage:

> George was a real 'fun' person — he celebrated everything! I remember going to a celebration at his villa flat at Glenhuntly[6] when he completed paying off the vacuum cleaner! I went with the late Rod Maclean (the No. 2 on the shipping round, to be killed in the RAAF not long afterwards). I recall, that night, Rod threw a rug over me as he had to park in Little Lonsdale Street to pick up 'some fool' George had asked. 'His name is Sid Nolan'. I was quite scared at being left alone in what was then a red light district. We took Sid on board and he was told firmly by Rod 'You've got to sit in the dicky seat'. And so Sid was disposed of unceremoniously.[7]

Nolan had gone to Johnston's old school, Brighton Tech., but he was five years younger, so their paths had not crossed there. Both their fathers worked for the Melbourne and Metropolitan Tramways Board, and Nolan also attended the National Gallery School, but despite this great deal of common ground their acquaintanceship in these years was slight.

George and Elsie continued to see Olga and 'Wally' from time to time after they were married, but generally their social life was modest, confined to occasional parties and dinners with close friends. Bruce Kneale recalls a recital by the famous singer George Thiele, which they attended as a foursome, which he says Elsie found boring. Another time they arranged to spend a weekend together at a beach resort, but by the Saturday night Elsie wanted to go home.[8] She seems to have found it difficult to enjoy herself socially with George, whose extrovert personality in company was in marked contrast to hers. It was not all that easy at home, either, being a non-smoker living with an increasingly heavy one; he infuriated her by leaving burning cigarettes all over the place.

Relations between Elsie and the Johnston family were never warm, although the friendship between Elsie and Marjorie would undoubtedly have continued if Marjorie had not moved to live in South Australia. There was cordiality before the marriage, but afterwards Elsie felt as though 'a curtain had been drawn, particularly with his father', and that the whole family rejected her and thought her inferior.[9] On their part, they felt Elsie was 'cold' and 'snobbish',[10] and her grief over her mother's death in the early months of the marriage might have helped that impression to form. George himself did not attempt any diplomatic role between his wife and his family, so matters never improved. The differences between them were ones of style and personality rather than of social standing, and the increasing distance between them was largely due to George, not by calculation, but simply because of his ambitions in his job. The world of his parents and brother and sisters was now less important to him, and rather than blame him for this, the family accused Elsie of dragging him away to live a life that ran against his grain. But Elsie did not have this kind of power over him. 'I couldn't tell him what to do', she insists, 'George was always right and I believed him. And he did it in such a nice way I felt I was wrong.'[11]

These matters have considerable importance to our understanding of the way in which Johnston wrote about David Meredith's first marriage in *My Brother Jack*. Just as in the case of his father, many readers have presumed that the marriage of David Meredith and Helen Midgeley is an accurate representation of Johnston's first marriage. The evidence indicates that it is not. In the first place the physical difference is quite marked: Helen is blonde and tall and exudes confidence; Elsie is dark, quite short and shy. Helen is interested in left-wing politics and literature, is sexually aggressive, four years older than Meredith, and works in a subscription library. Elsie was not in those days interested in politics or literature, was sexually defensively feminine, four years younger than Johnston, and worked as a cashier. In many respects, therefore, Elsie is almost an exact opposite of Helen in the novel.

What one cannot fail to notice is the degree of resemblance between Helen and Olga Reid. This, and the possibility that Olga Reid was the first woman with whom Johnston was sexually involved, suggests that she was very likely an important source for the character of Helen, particularly the Helen of those amorous encounters on the couch in the back room of the library, and the Helen of intellectual and political interests. It would not be fair to ascribe Helen's coldness and bitchiness, or indeed any of Helen's flaws as a wife, to Olga Reid, since she was never in that kind of relationship with Johnston; it is only their premarital friendship that provides some of the material for the Meredith/Midgeley relationship in the novel. Indeed, Helen is an inconsistently drawn character: her intelligence and serious interests before marriage are not satisfactorily compatible with her bossy stupidity and shallowness afterwards.

Elsie was quite unlike Helen, too, in the matter of the dominant partner in the marriage. Readers of the novel will recall that it is Helen who is in control there:

> *Helen naturally assumed leadership on matters of taste and sophistication; where mature judgements were needed it was usually she who made the decision. I admired her originality and vitality. I had unbounded confidence in her.* (MBJ 249)

It is Helen who chooses the house and the furnishings, just as it is Helen who dictates that they live neat, clean, tightly organised lives right down to their sexual relations, and that they will not have children. It is Helen who decides upon their social circle. As I think the evidence indicates, Elsie's role in her marriage to Johnston was not like this at all. On the contrary, it was she who had to adapt to the way of life her husband chose for them, she who was the passive one, often feeling her confidence drain as he disregarded her views. In the Johnston marriage it was George who was the dominant partner, making it the absolute reverse of the Meredith marriage in the novel.

There is no doubt that Johnston did not intend Helen to be a portrait of Elsie. He wrote her a touching letter when *My*

Brother Jack was about to be published to assure her of this:

> ... I have gone to enormous pains to make the character of
> the wife not you in every possible way, and I want you to
> understand this because I don't want you to be hurt. People
> will be hurt, I suppose. Jean and Bert probably, and Jack and
> Pat and Mum maybe — although none of them, I think, as
> much as I am hurting myself, which, if one is to be honest —
> and it's time I was — is inescapable. But you are the one I
> don't wish to hurt in any way, and I do hope you will not try
> to identify yourself with the Helen Meredith of the story.[12]

Try as he did, however, to prevent Elsie from identifying
with Helen Meredith, it was inevitable that she would be
stung in the aftermath of publication. When she read the
novel, she was not especially disturbed, because it was unlike
their marriage and she did not identify with Helen. But when
friends began to advise her that the general response, including some reviews, presumed that everything in the book,
particularly the Meredith marriage, was fact, she became confused and hurt. When she re-read the book, she began
seriously to doubt Johnston's disclaimer, and indeed to wonder if she 'really was like that'. People who knew her did not
think so, and Rosalind Landells insists that 'she could in no
way be likened to the ambitious Helen of *My Brother Jack*'.[13]

As to the question of George's role in the marriage and the
relationship it bears to Meredith's in the novel, it appears
that here again the positions are reversed. Meredith is the
passive one and suffers from Helen's frigidity and disloyalty,
and is innocent of any serious defections. It is difficult to find
in this any evidence of Johnston 'hurting himself', as he
states in his letter to Elsie, but in order to explore this in a
way that does justice to the complexity of the author's relationship to his central character, we must again wait until we
come to that time in his life when he wrote *My Brother Jack*.
By then we shall have gained a fuller knowledge of his life in
the intervening years, and be better placed to understand the
impulses behind his writing.

To return to those early years of the marriage between
George and Elsie, these were years mostly of happiness and
harmony, punctuated, however, by minor blemishes. There
was the continuing coolness between her and his family, and

there were indications of insecurity on Elsie's part. For example, Rod Maclean suggested that he, Bruce Kneale and George take a week off from what had been a particularly heavy period of work reporting the mounting tension in Europe and go to Lorne on the south coast to 'get away from it all'. Elsie was hostile to the idea from the beginning, Johnston told Kneale, and after only a couple of days away Johnston received a message from his office to ring home urgently. Kneale recalls that 'an agitated Elsie said he must return at once because a relative was suddenly terribly ill'. So Johnston returned, and when he saw Kneale again he told him that there had been no terrible illness, nothing more than a cold, and that Elsie had accused them all of going to Lorne to pick up girls.[14]

She may have had her reasons for keeping tabs on him. He was at this time extraordinarily attractive to women — Kneale can recall a woman practically pleading with him to go to bed with her — a fact that Elsie would have discerned. It was not that he was irresistibly handsome: it was his charm that drew people to him. 'He was good company, a great ranconteur, with an infectious laugh that always made him attractive,' says Kneale.

George loved to 'take the mickey' out of people, especially if it involved deflating their pomposity. Kneale recalls 'one dull gent, the quintessence of suburban man, was much put out when George, from sheer exuberance, greeted him with "H'ya, Fred, old ram! Getting any?" Fred, plainly unamused, made no reply.' On another occasion the Johnstons and the Kneales were invited to a 'musical evening' at the home of an *Argus* correspondent who liked to maintain a high tone in such matters, insisting that the men wear black tie and dinner jacket. Johnston and Kneale turned up in lounge suits. When their host greeted them at the door he was wearing a dickey (a false shirt-front); in a flash Johnston produced a lipstick and inscribed on the dicky 'we love you Rupe'. The host was furious. 'Damn you,' he said. 'You've buggered my dickey and I wanted to wear it tomorrow night!' Johnston further blotted his copy-book by escaping with Kneale to the kitchen to burst into laughter at the dismal incompetence of the musicians. Neither he nor Kneale was invited again.[15]

George and Jack Johnston in the garden of Avalon, *c.* 1933 *(Photo courtesy of Joy Russo)*

Avalon, the Johnston house in Elsternwick – a recent photograph

George and Jack Johnston in the South Caulfield Football Team, 1932. Jack is on the far right of the back row, and George is fourth from the right in the same row *(Photo courtesy of Ron Ridge)*

The Johnston family at Avalon, 1948. *Back row (left to right):* Jack, Marjorie, George. *Front row (left to right):* Minnie, Pop Johnston, Jean *(Photo courtesy of Joy Russo)*

Jack Johnston in uniform,
1940

Johnston at the *Argus* in the 1930s
(Photo courtesy of Gae Johnston)

Elsie Taylor, 1937

Overland to Alice
Springs, 1941. Johnston
is third from the left

In 1939 Johnston bought himself a new car to replace an old American Plymouth he had been driving for a short time. Evidently looking to cut a smart figure, he plumped for a small red Vauxhall tourer, for which his parents lent him the money. Bruce Kneale, who was a car enthusiast, advised him against a Vauxhall, but to no avail: style was more important than practicalities, and Johnston knew nothing about cars, nor wanted to.

There was a certain resentment in Pat and Jack over this car, not so much its purchase (though whether they would have been favoured with such a loan is doubtful), as the fact that it became yet another instrument of disassociation between them and George. 'He would drive past our house in his beautiful little car,' says Pat, 'and never even think to pay us a visit.'[16] Although George's route between home and work did not take him literally past his brother's house, the complaint is really one about neglect of family loyalties: the social world of George and Elsie was no longer that of Jack, Pat or any others of the Johnston clan.

While there was certainly a contrast in personality between George and Elsie, there was at this stage no great conflict in values between them of a kind that would foreshadow a breakdown in the marriage. When George planted three sugar-gums in the front and back garden of the house they were now renting in Mackie Grove, East Brighton, Elsie was pleased: after all, her brother had brought them as a gift and had helped to plant them. (In *My Brother Jack* Helen Meredith detests the trees, which are eucalypts, and to her taste 'drab'.) It is true that Elsie did not like living in this area, but this was because of an imprisoning effect it had on her. 'You can't see it,' she told George, 'but this house is surrounded by a high hedge of thorns. If I could pick up the house and put it somewhere else it might be better.'[17] He would laugh at this and tell friends she lived in a world of fantasy, which was insensitive and patronising, but since Elsie possessed the conventional wifely quality of complicity, serious rifts were avoided.

The relationship did change for the worse, however, as it did for so many people, with the upheavals brought on by the War. Although in 1940 the conflict was still a long way off in Europe, shipping reporters were especially well placed to see increasing evidence of its reality. From this time on things moved so quickly that relations between Johnston and Elsie were thrown out of balance. In that year Johnston went on some training cruises with Australian warships, which gave him first-hand knowledge of naval activities and techniques, and in December his *Argus* weekend features began to focus on naval subjects, the first of them bearing the title 'War Means Last of the Windjammers'. In early February 1941 he was sent to Sydney to make a report on the return of the cruiser HMAS *Sydney*, which had just spent six months covering itself in glory in the Mediterranean. On the flight to Sydney it occurred to him that there might be a good book in the subject. Later

> ... *when I was aboard the ship and heard the stories of the men, stories told bluntly and without any striving for effect, stories which brought to peaceful Sydney Harbour the indescribable spectacle of great grey ships thundering death and destruction ... and by the time I had said goodbye to the ship and the men three days later the idea for this book became fixed in my mind.*[18]

On his return to Melbourne he immediately set to work on an imaginative documentary account, and with some assistance from Naval Intelligence he was able to place the *Sydney*'s heroic exploits in an informed context of the allied Mediterranean campaign. He wrote the book at fever pitch with Elsie acting as a sounding-board and making criticisms, some of which Johnston made use of, and the typescript was in the hands of Angus & Robertson by 27 March, a mere seven weeks after the book was begun. It was called *Grey Gladiator*, and Johnston's enthusiasm in writing it is evident on every page. It is action from start to finish, making effective use of description peppered with statistics, terse dialogue, rapid shifts of focus and clipped sentences:

> *At 8.26 a.m. the crew of the* Sydney *stiffened at the cry of 'enemy sighted'. Men stood tensely behind the guns, tin helmets donned. On the bridge Captain Collins glanced at a wrist watch. In the fire control tower the gunnery officer calculated range and deflection. The range-finder operator intoned quietly: 'Twenty thousand yards'. The four forward*

guns swung grimly, the after-turrents moved steadily as the
Sydney *raced in on a converging course to close the range
... 'Nineteen thousand yards'. It was 8.28 a.m.*[19]

Notwithstanding its oversimple treatment and unrelieved breathlessness, *Grey Gladiator* is a remarkable first book. With no training in war research,[20] no experience in writing anything but short articles, no evident models to work from, Johnston by virtue of his intuitive flair managed to strike exactly the right note for the subject, and the book was immensely popular with Australian readers. It sold out in Sydney on the first day of publication, and a delighted W. G. Cousins of Angus & Robertson wrote to Johnston: 'It is strange that two of the best books of the war should be done by Australians, and *Argus* men at that. Noel Monk's *Squadrons Up* is the other book.'[21] A London edition, published by Gollancz under the title *Lioness of the Seas*, came out in June and sold equally well, despite a failed plan to have Winston Churchill write an Introduction.

The book helped win him promotion to an A grade journalist, on a salary of £13 10s per week, supplemented now by book royalties. Suddenly the whole field of war writing opened up to him, and in an extraordinary burst of activity he made rapid progress with two more books. The first was *Battle of the Seaways*, an account, he wrote to W. G. Cousins, of 'the struggle to maintain British commerce on the trade routes with U Boats and Raiders'.[22] The material for this was probably gained in the course of researching *Grey Gladiator*. The second book was *Australia at War*. Johnston had been given a job by his Managing Editor, Errol Knox (who had enormous regard for George's ability), of making a reporting tour of all Australia's defence areas and writing more than twenty articles, to be syndicated to newspapers around the country. 'It is the first time a journalist has been given permission to see the "whole works" and to write uncensored comment on it,'[23] Johnston wrote to Cousins in a proposal to make a book out of the articles. The tour, which covered 10,000 miles and extended from Wilson's Promontory to Darwin, kept him away from home for several weeks. *Battle of the Seaways* came out in July, but sales were disappointing.

In October 1941 Elsie gave birth to a daughter, Gae, named after the initials of *George and Elsie*. Their pre-War social life had come to an abrupt end: Johnston was busy reporting the growing conflict, while Elsie was tied down at home. With the future in doubt, it was difficult to make plans, and Johnston was unsure of the role he might play in the War. Should he enlist in one of the services? For people such as Jack, who had suffered insecurity and frustration in the Depression, there was suddenly security and a positive role to play by enlisting. The irony of this was not lost on Jack: 'It's the way the capitalistic system works,' he said, 'a war, Depression, time of plenty, war ...'[24] Nevertheless, there was a clear sense of duty in his joining up, although he was not as starry-eyed about it as his counterpart is in *My Brother Jack*. In the novel, Jack Meredith injures his knee while training at Puckapunyal, and is bitterly disappointed when the injury prevents him being posted overseas. The real Jack, who injured his knee while showing his daughter Joy how to high-jump, was more circumspect about missing out on going with his unit to Singapore, where most of them were taken prisoner by the Japanese. Jack Johnston felt himself lucky to have escaped that, and to have been posted to Darwin, where he 'never saw a shot fired in anger'.[25] For him, joining up was merely an obligation, not the justification of his life.

For George, however, the choice was not so simple. He certainly felt a patriotic impulse to enlist. He had long and serious conversations with Bruce Kneale about it, but a senior staff member of the *Argus* overheard them and took Johnston aside, telling him. 'Don't you get taken in by all this patriotic crap that Kneale goes on with − let him join up, but don't you be such a fool: there are going to be better things for you to do.'[26] However, he did make the decision to enlist, and arranged with Kneale and another colleague, Barney Porter, to meet at the enlistment office at the Melbourne Town Hall the following day. He also wrote to W. G. Cousins of Angus & Robertson:

> *I am clearing everything up now as quickly as possible as I will definitely be going into the A.I.F. second week in January. There is a faint possibility of a job as a war*

correspondent, but I am enlisting in the ordinary way.[27]

His Editor, Ted Doyle, had told him that the war correspondent job was in the wind, and he was torn between waiting for this and honouring his word to his mates. In the end he did not turn up at the Town Hall. The next day Kneale asked him what had happened. 'It was Elsie,' said Johnston. 'She pleaded with me, begged me with tears, not to join up. I couldn't go against her.'[28] His two mates, however, had gone ahead with their enlistment.

Elsie denies that she placed him under any such pressure. 'I said to him on frequent occasions "George, if you want to enlist, though naturally I don't want you to go to war, I wouldn't hold you back. You do what you want to do." '[29] Given the nature of the relationship, it is doubtful that Elsie could have prevented him from doing anything he really wanted to do. She might well have placed him under more subtle pressure not to leave her alone with Gae, but she would have done this on later occasions as well, when he had the chance to go abroad, and it did not keep him at home then. One must conclude that Johnston found it impossible to confide to his friends that he wanted the war correspondent job more than he wanted to go into the army. The preference is hardly surprising, considering the freedom available in one capacity compared with the restrictions of the other. Besides, it would keep him behind his beloved typewriter.

In later years he was to experience intense guilt over his decision. Towards the end of the war he was having a drink with Bruce Kneale, and unexpectedly raised the subject. 'You think I'm a coward, don't you?' he levelled at Kneale, assuming (wrongly as it happened) that this was his view of George's breach of the pact.[30] This, and the knowledge of Rod Maclean's death, as well as the decisiveness of his brother's enlistment, added to what became at times an acute sense of dereliction of duty. Much of this feeling was poured into the creation of David Meredith in *My Brother Jack*, where he castigates himself for his cowardice, insisting that it is yet another of his moral 'defections' to choose war correspondence over active service.

CHAPTER III

War Correspondent

My dispatches were admired, syndicated, published abroad. If you are given the privilege of having your name in the papers every day, and on your own terms, deception and self-aggrandisement are easy arts to practise. (MBJ 335)

After joining the *Argus* in 1933 Johnston had worked under a succession of editors: R. L. Curthoys, who had hired him, W. P. Hurst, E. G. Bonney, and from 1942 E. A. (Ted) Doyle.[1] Alec Chisholm had been Managing Director until 1937, when he was succeeded by Errol Knox. Knox presided, indeed was something of a dictator, over editorial matters for the remainder of Johnston's time on the paper. Johnston drew on several of these editorial mentors for the character of the tough-talking newspaper boss Bernard Brewster in the Meredith trilogy. According to Greeba Jamison, who had joined the paper as a reporter in 1939, Brewster bears some physical resemblance to Ted Doyle, but in terms of his relations with David Meredith there are characteristics of Curthoys, Doyle and Knox in him. Of these, it was Knox who had the greatest influence over Johnston's career. Bruce Kneale says he was Knox's clear favourite of all the journalists working under him, and it was commonly known that under his patronage Johnston was destined for higher things.[2] If he could make a success of a war correspondent's job, it would be an important step in his career.

While waiting in the last days of 1941 to hear whether the jobs would be offered to him, George hurried to finish the

38

proofs of *Australia at War*. Plans for a Christmas edition had been delayed by a dearth of binders, though Angus & Robertson, who were enthusiastic about the script and confident it would 'be a winner'[3] were eager to get the book out. Reflecting the research that had gone into it, this book was Johnston's most ambitious piece of writing so far. In Part One there is an account of the state of Australia's war preparations throughout the country and the kind of training each corps was undergoing. It also looks briefly at the contribution being made by private industry. Part Two praises the toughness and courage of Australian soldiers in action in the Middle East, and at such places as Bardia and Crete. Johnston had no qualms about inflating Australian heroism to mythic proportions. He writes of an infantryman 'having the figure of a Greek god', and of 'youngsters from the world's youngest civilization' marching 'into the land of the world's oldest civilization',[4] terms that have an intentional suggestion of epic about them. The descriptions of action have all the headlong ardour, and all the triteness, of *Boy's Own Annual* stuff:

> *Hour after hour its [the AIF's] remaining units held the ridge against the great waves of German infantry. Below them hundreds of their comrades were wading out to the waiting ships. The time limit given by the Navy had expired. The ships were beginning to move away across the blue Mediterranean. The gallant rearguard, its ranks sadly thinned now, its ammunition almost gone, did not look back. They had nothing to hope for now ... nothing but death or imprisonment. Still the guns snapped and barked at the advancing Germans. Still the ridge was held.[5]*

Repeatedly, connections with World War I are made, so that this conflict is seen as 'the story of a young nation's manhood that began at Gallipoli [and] had gone into a second volume'.[6] How well his upbringing in that patriotic house, with that obsessively war-conscious father, fitted him to write things like this! The belief was deeply instilled into him that the full status of Australian manhood was somehow tied to the dark forces of blood sacrifice, and that it was the sacred duty of the succeeding generation to attain its maturity by a re-enactment of the same heroics that initiated its fathers. Nor was this an individual rite: the whole nation, in the minds of the many Australians who were in the thrall of this myth, was being given the opportunity to prove its mettle to the world.

Johnston held these beliefs in such a way that, whatever changes he underwent in later life — and this included becoming an outspoken pacifist in his last years, when the Vietnam war was on — he was never able to view those succeeding generations of World War I and II participants with anything but awe. He never became ironical about them. In his most serious moments, such as his writing of *My Brother Jack*, in which the whole vision of the novel is framed by the two wars, his respect for those who fought is profound. In 1956, in long, serious conversations with Sidney Nolan, he was to talk with such eloquence about the war and its mythic significance that he inspired Nolan to paint his Gallipoli series.[7]

Yet Johnston did not choose to place himself in that heroic role. Again, this was always a matter for self-denigration with him. That praise of Australian heroism is invariably accompanied by the kind of painful sense of failure that is so characteristic of David Meredith when he is confronted by the reality of the initiation that men like his brother are undergoing, but which he has, to his own cost, forgone, as he confesses in *My Brother Jack*:

> And the anguish inside me had twisted and turned into an awful and irremediable sense of loss, and I thought of Dad and the putteed men coming off the Ceramic, and I thought of Jack when I had seen him at Puckapunyal five long years before, looking just like these men, hard and strong and confident and with his brown legs planted in the Seymour dust as if the whole world was his to conquer, a man fulfilled in his own rightness, and suddenly and terribly I knew that all the Jacks were marching past me, all the Jacks were still marching.... (MBJ 378)

This sort of writing is, of course, a lifetime away from *Australia at War*, which contains almost nothing of Johnston's personal experience, and thus nothing of this anguish, which in any case took years to accumulate. It does have the same respect for the Australian soldier, and the same tendency to place him in the kind of mythic context that echoed the feelings of a whole era of Australians struggling to establish the nation's identity. Moreover, the fact that Johnston did not participate in the sacrificial aspect of that struggle probably became a compelling reason for his talking and writing about it in such glorified terms.

Johnston did get the war correspondent job. Errol Knox appointed him in late January 1942, and on 4 February he was issued with the first accredited war correspondent's licence for a newspaperman to cover a war in Australia. Osmar White, who wrote for the Melbourne *Herald*, remembers: 'He beat me to the barracks and got number one licence, and I got number two.'[8] Johnston's dispatches were to be published by the *Argus, Adelaide Advertiser* and *Sydney Morning Herald* group, though articles of his were also to be published from time to time in the *Age*, the *London Daily Telegraph* and *Time* and *Life* magazines in New York. Five days after his licence was issued, he was handed a uniform, given an honorary ranking as captain, paid £59 15s 9d in lieu of holidays and posted to Port Moresby. He was to receive a briefing at HQ in Townsville before flying in.[9]

The Japanese attack on New Guinea had begun about a month before this. By the time Johnston arrived, Rabaul had fallen and Port Moresby was the only defence base standing between the Japanese and the Australian mainland. Singapore fell only a few days after he landed. There was, therefore, plenty of action to report and considerable danger in doing so. His arrival date was Friday, 13 February, and he wrote in the notebook, which he immediately began to keep: 'Ominous date, but arrived safely.'[10] He might well have thanked his luck: the Lockheed aircraft that had flown him and Osmar White to New Guinea crashed in a Cairns swamp on the way back, killing both pilots.

The scene that confronted him in Port Moresby was chaotic. There had just been a bombing raid, and most of the Europeans had been evacuated. Not content with enemy damage, Australian troops had just looted the town, including the local museum, from which they had 'souvenired' valuable artefacts. The Australian 39th and 53rd battalions, poorly equipped and untrained for the kind of warfare they were about to wage against a well-equipped and successful Japanese army, inspired little confidence. On top of all this, the heat, sandflies, appalling mosquitoes, bad water and food, all conspired to give war correspondents such as Johnston a testing baptism.[11]

He could not relate such dismal information back to his paper. Censorship was strict, often unnecessarily so, a matter of constant annoyance to the correspondents. Johnston recorded in his notebook many details that the censor would not have passed: incidents of desertion, for instance, and troop and artillery statistics and movements, as well as the destructive effects of Japanese air raids. He also recorded the shooting of a Lutheran missionary by an Australian soldier, after it was discovered that the missionary had helped the Japanese. In fact this notebook had a strict purpose. It was not a true diary, although it was recently published as such; it contains no personal information, and many of its entries are not of witnessed events, but are based on hearsay, and frequently of doubtful accuracy.

It is likely that Johnston intended to get a book out of New Guinea from the moment he knew he was going there, and that the 'diary' was simply the formula upon which to base it. Much space is given to colourful anecdote: stories of heroism, humour and mateship among the men, and horror tales of shocking injuries and mutilated bodies. A common one, which stuck in his mind for years afterwards, involved troops moving along the Kokoda trail giving a shake to a severed hand wedged in a tree beside the track. Another incident, which he remembered in his last months of life, was hearing that Japanese soldiers kept their fingernail clippings in tiny urns to be sent back to their relatives if they were killed. Odd details such as these he remembered long after the standard wartime heroics had faded from his mind.[12] Many of them went into the notebook in preparation for his *New Guinea Diary* book.

During the first four months in New Guinea he sent back more than seventy articles, mostly on the rescue work of pilots, the heroism of ground staff, relations with the natives and between Australian and American troops. He also wrote pieces on the enemy that are notable for their grasp of

Japanese competence at a time when a fatuous brand of racism among the Australian public caused many to underrate dangerously the ability of the Japanese. Nevertheless, like most correspondents, he deliberately painted a rosier picture of the allied campaign than was true at the time in the interests of maintaining morale at home.

Johnston returned to Melbourne in June, and was temporarily replaced in New Guinea by Geoffrey Hutton. Elsie may have put pressure either on him or the office for his return, for relations between them were under some strain. According to Bruce Kneale, it was becoming increasingly obvious that the Johnstons were drifting apart. 'George was taking giant strides in developing himself, while Elsie was standing still,' he observes.[13] Rumours were flying about the *Argus* office that Johnston was having an affair with one of the office girls.

When Johnston returned to Moresby in September it was obvious to Osmar White that he was withdrawn and tense. He confided to White that he had grown bored with his marriage. His popularity among the other correspondents was low, too, although this was more to do with his attitude to the work than anything else. His undisguised ambition and competitiveness engendered wariness among his colleagues in the correspondents' mess. 'He was not', says White, 'a good sharer of information. If George went off to see the General [whereas] most of the other blokes would say what the hell he was saying, George wouldn't tell you: he was not prepared to. He was after the beat, which made him a damn good newspaperman.'[14]

White had been to the Kokoda area with photographer Damien Parer and correspondent Chester Wilmot, and, despite the danger of such a mission, they did not mind keeping up the tradition of sharing information with those correspondents who, like Johnston, preferred to operate from base. According to White there was no resentment or charges of cowardice levelled at Johnston for adopting this approach:

> *He decided to play it that way, and I think he was probably quite right to play it that way ... I think he felt he could serve his newspaper better by staying far enough away from*

it to get the whole picture. It was a point of view that I came around to very much later in Europe — that sometimes when you got terribly close to it you couldn't see the wood for the trees. You had to spend at least part of the time back where the intelligence people could tell you what was going on.[15]

Nevertheless, the possibility that he could be rightly accused of cowardice was one that haunted Johnston for years after the war. The corollary to not enlisting was that war correspondence work would always have the stigma of evasion attached to it, and later in his life he became a harsh critic, not only of his own role as a war correspondent, but of the very nature of the exercise.

In the latter half of 1942 the allied forces had a number of successes in New Guinea, and Johnston, like his colleagues, gave a glorified account of the Australian and American campaigns. In his notebook, however, he again recorded comments that would not have passed the censors, particularly about the Americans. When General Douglas MacArthur arrived in October, Johnston wrote:

> Oct. 3rd. *MacArthur up on the track (Kokoda) today; only as far as the road went through!*
>
> Oct. 16th. *Everyone is incensed with the new censorship bans, including MacArthur's personal censorship of stories of his visit here which have been slashed to convey the impression (a) that he went right up to the front line (which he certainly did NOT) and (b) that this was NOT his first visit to New Guinea. Censorship now is just plain Gestapo stuff!*

Along with many Australians who knew the truth, Johnston was angered by American attempts to take full credit for saving Australia from the Japanese:

> Nov. 12th. *The fact remains that no American ground soldier has fired a shot in this campaign so far, but there is a widespread tendency for many Americans to decry the Australian efforts and perpetrate rumours that the A.I.F. is only opposed by a handful of Japanese — 90 or 250.*
>
> *One American was asked today if the hundreds of wounded Australians coming in had been in traffic accidents!*

In fact American efforts were often marked by confusion and incompetence:

> Dec. 12th. *Yesterday, for the sixth time, American bombers dropped bombs on their own positions, killing two and wounding six.*

Johnston omitted incidents of this kind when he put together the book based on his notebook, called *New Guinea Diary*, which he set to work on immediately when he got back to Melbourne. Like its predecessors, this book was aimed at the popular market, confining itself almost entirely to action and feats of heroism.

George returned from his New Guinea duties five days before Christmas 1942, and was immediately granted a month's leave. To Elsie he seemed tired and unsettled, as if he always wanted to be somewhere other than where he was. The strain between them was not helped by an unwelcome surprise that came in the mail for Elsie one day. A letter arrived containing an opened love-letter from Johnston, posted from Brisbane to the girl in the *Argus* office. Some third person in the office had intercepted the letter and redirected it to Elsie, by way of informing on Johnston. Elsie confronted him with it, but he shrugged it off as a trivial flirtation. Intent on saving her marriage, Elsie phoned the girl, arranged a meeting, which ended amicably, and the affair petered out.[16] Johnston still seemed unsettled, however, and agreed to every office request to travel about. He relieved Geoffrey Hutton in Brisbane for six weeks in February. When he returned in March, he was back barely a week when he agreed to another assignment, this time a substantial one. He was to accompany the Federal Attorney-General and Minister for External Affairs, Dr H. V. Evatt, on a diplomatic tour of the United States. Elsie greeted the news with dismay: again she would be left on her own with Gae, and with few indications of support from Johnston's family. Amid the bustle of getting away, Johnston telegraphed Angus & Robertson 'unable to complete galleys of *New Guinea Diary*'. Cousins managed the corrections, and the book came out in mid-1943, while Johnston was away. He left Melbourne on 1 April, arriving in San Francisco with the Evatt entourage on 8 April.

Johnston's movements over the following eight months are unfortunately obscure. He wrote few letters home and seems to have been deliberately secretive about much that happened during this time. He was certainly in Washington in May, and either there or in New York had a warm reunion with his old friend Sam Atyeo, in the company of Evatt. The improbable Atyeo had been appointed personally by Evatt to the Australian War Supplies Procurement Office in Washington, and whenever Evatt visited the States he spent some time with Atyeo, whose company delighted him. Johnston and Atyeo talked over old times as Gallery students, and generally got along well together. Unfortunately, Evatt and Johnston did not. At some stage they had a 'furious row', says Geoffrey Hutton,[17] and when the Evatt party left the country in June, Johnston was no longer with it. Elsie believes it had something to do with an American woman called Jane, with whom Johnston had become involved to the point of neglecting his journalistic duties. Up until that point, relations between Evatt and Johnston had been good: Evatt had written an Introduction to his latest book, *The Toughest Fighting in the World*, an American version of *New Guinea Diary*, in which he gives high praise to Johnston's work in New Guinea. The details of what went wrong between them have not yet come to light.

Johnston wrote to Elsie on 20 August, saying that he had 'stayed on ... writing a book on Australia, including the effects of Americans on Australians'. This book was eventually published in 1944 exclusively in the United States as *Pacific Partner*. He was also producing articles for *Saturday Evening Post, Life* and *Collier's* magazines, mostly on New Guinea subjects, including a portrait of MacArthur for *Life* that amounts to an astonishing piece of whitewashing, after the comments he recorded in his New Guinea notebook. Among other things, he excuses MacArthur's failure to give proper recognition to the Australian fighting efforts:

> There was some resentment among several war correspondents who insisted that MacArthur was trying to convert what was a purely Australian ground victory into a combined success. This was actually unjust. At that time it was

important to prevent the Japanese from knowing that the Americans were being kept intact as a separate force to be flown into the north-coast areas for the final assault on Buna.[18]

This might have warmed American hearts, but it would have made some Australian blood boil. Johnston had been, after all, one of those correspondents who objected to the way in which MacArthur promoted the image of American troops at the expense of the Australians.

The glossy American journals were, according to Geoffrey Hutton, 'mad keen to get him',[19] and since he was writing for them as a freelance, the fees, generous by Australian standards, were going into his own pocket. He told colleagues that he had made thousands of dollars in America, and spent them all in the New York night clubs, presumably with Jane. Certainly Elsie knew nothing about such money. Johnston's relationship with Jane was hardly covert, although her surname is unknown. He introduced friends and colleagues to her as his girl-friend, and Geoffrey Hutton recalls that she was 'exactly like his wife', although 'not overloaded with intellect'.[20] Johnston later used her name for the heroine of the novel *The Far Face of the Moon* (1964), but whether there is any further resemblance between them it is not possible to say. The fictional Jane is a virtual nymphomaniac.

During the last half of 1943 Johnston's letters home became so rare that Elsie sought an explanation from the Diplomatic Service. They had none, but agreed to include her mail in the official bag to ensure their safe arrival. Still she received no replies to her letters. She went to Ted Doyle at the *Argus* office, but he had no news either. Doyle had expected Johnston home in September, along with Errol Knox (now a Brigadier) and his son-in-law, Major Henry Steele, who had been visiting the States. Finally, Elsie received a letter in November from him saying that Knox and Steele had been transferred to a faster ship in Panama, and that he had been forced to remain 'still ploughing along' in a cargo ship. But Elsie believed that the real reason for his delay was his reluctance to leave Jane.

Indeed, when he finally arrived home in December, he

could talk of nothing but Jane. He assailed Elsie 'on the couch one morning, and told me about this Jane, and that he wanted to divorce me and go back to her'.[21] Rows and bitter accusations followed, and Johnston went into moods of black depression. He even threatened suicide, and left a note in his trouser pocket for Elsie to discover to the effect that he had been found dead somewhere. His despair grew partly out of the knowledge that the affair, which had been as much with America itself as with Jane, could not be renewed. Nevertheless, it brought matters to a climax with Elsie, and within days after his return he decided that they should separate. He terminated the lease at Mackie Grove, and found a flat in East St Kilda for Elsie and Gae. For the time being he was going to stay at a hotel.

He didn't last long, however. Three days before Christmas he moved into the flat with them, and so the turmoil of uncertainty continued.

If he was unhappy at home, Johnston was more exuberant and popular than ever at the office. He sought the centre of attention, and played the raconteur at every opportunity, as Greeba Jamison recalls:

> *He would burst into the big reporter's room, described in perfect detail in* My Brother Jack, *and the whole place was turned on end, particularly for the girl reporters. He would snatch up the best-looking one he saw, grab her on his knee or swing her up towards the ceiling and catch her in his arms; everyone, men and women, would cluster round and George would tell us with tremendous gusto, a spate of exaggerated adjectives generously sprinkled with bloody (one of his favourite words), great gusts of laughter, of his exploits in the war, Very Important People he had met, women he had made love to. Usually we would repair to the Duke of Kent hotel across the road in LaTrobe Street and the story would continue over many rounds of beer.*[22]

This was very much the Johnston that his colleagues saw: 'the complete extrovert', wrote Geoffrey Hutton, with whom he was sharing an office, 'with inexhaustable talent for making friends'.[23] It was about this time, too, that he began acquiring the tag 'golden boy', in reference to his fair colouring and the favour of the *Argus* hierarchy. Bruce Kneale says that it was he who gave him the name, not least because everything

Johnston in New Guinea, 1942

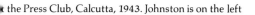
the Press Club, Calcutta, 1943. Johnston is on the left

Johnston with an American correspondent,
somewhere in Asia, 1943

Johnston on leave from China, with Gae, 1945

Johnston, left, outside the tent of T'se Ch'i, with the Tibetan's
wife and daughter, July 1945 *(Photo courtesy of the Australasian Post)*

Lieutenant Clift, AWAS

Clift modelling a hat, early 1940s

Clift, aged seventeen, posing as a courtesan,
photographed by her sister, Margaret

A study portrait of Charmian Clift, by her sister, Margaret, 1945

Sid Clift, father of Charmian

Amy Clift, mother of Charmian *(Photo courtesy Margaret Backhou*

he touched seemed to turn to success.[24] His marriage was an obvious exception to this.

From America Johnston had sent Angus & Robertson the typescript of his first attempt at a novel, entitled 'The Sun Rose Twice', but when he got back he requested its return, with the intention of rewriting it. It never reappeared. Instead, he worked on a new book, about his American experiences, which turned out to be a problematical homage to Jane, provisionally titled 'Hey Listen, Jezebel!' This sets out to be a humorous sequence of anecdotes of an ingenuous Australian's encounter with the sophisticated world of wartime New York. The script was finished by February 1944, and Angus & Roberston agreed to publish it under the alternative title of *Skyscrapers in the Mist*, although it was to be another two years before it finally came out, after a great deal of equivocation One story it contains has a premonitory touch:

> It is said, though I cannot corroborate the story, that the bar [of a New York restaurant] carried a sign copied from a London taproom announcement of the early eighteenth century: 'Drunk for a cent, Dead drunk for two cents, Clean straw for nothing'.[25]

Twenty years later this grim little epigram would have a special significance for him.

Johnston discovered early in 1944 that he would be going abroad again, and wrote a rather depressed note to W. G. Cousins on 28 January, saying, 'pushing off in a month . . . to India, Burma, Africa and then to the U.S., and will be away probably two years or so'. For some reason he wanted his absence 'to be kept confidential as far as Sydney newspaper circles go'.[26] He added that he hoped to get 'real rip-snorter of a book' out of this trip.

Once more Johnston's departure was in haste. He wrote to Cousins from Perth requesting that all royalty cheques be paid to Elsie, and also to send her the proofs of *Skyscrapers in the Mist* for correction. This was an odd thing to do. She had never proofread anything before, and had no idea what was required. More important, as she read through the proofs she discovered that she did not like the book in the least, neither its subject-matter nor its flippant tone. So she simply sent it back to Angus & Robertson, telling them as much and leaving the corrections to them. Elsie wondered, however, whether the gesture of giving her some part to play in the book might not have been George's way of making a peace offering, of putting the whole Jane affair in the context of his great discovery of America, so that it might at least seem more understandable to her, if not more forgivable. In her circumstances, optimism was Elsie's best refuge.

Again Johnston's movements abroad are difficult to trace; he travelled about so frequently that it is possible to give only an outline for most of the time, though occasionally specific details of his activities in Asia are clear. His first address was the Army Public Relations Office at South-East Command in New Delhi, and from this base he was to make regular trips by air and road to surrounding regions affected by the war during most of 1944. His official brief was a roving commission, which meant that he could generally decide for himself the areas from which he would correspond. The many articles (over 150) that he sent back to the *Argus* and other publications from the Asian region formed the basis of a comprehensive book, which he was to put together at the end of the war and call *Journey through Tomorrow*. This book provides the best guide to the events in his life during 1944—45. It was an important two years for Johnston, because of the range and newness of experience that Asia was to provide him with.

Johnston spent March and April in Ceylon and India relaxing, after which he went to Burma to report on the bitter fighting in the northern town of Myitkyina and the Mogaung Valley area generally, where the bid to recapture Burma was under way. Reading his reports, one is struck by his broad view of the correspondent's role. Unlike the war books he had so far written, he did not confine himself to racy descriptions of action and heroism. In fact he did little of this from now on. Instead, he wrote on the many human touches he observed, such as the effects on the civilian population, or the behaviour of soldiers when they were *not* fighting. He sent back to the *Argus* pieces on the Kachins (the native head-hunters of North Burma), on Burmese national pride, on Australian soldiers playing two-up, and on the way the arrival of a monsoon brought the fighting to a halt. He was appalled by the wanton destruction of local culture, and especially the brutal disregard by Americans for Burmese sacred objects:

> When I first arrived at Namkam, not far from the Chinese border, it was almost noon and I stopped to eat my luncheon ration alongside a large temple, almost completely destroyed by bombing. Like most Burmese places of worship it was a gimcrack structure of corrugated iron and hideous fretwork, now jumbled into a heap of tangled wreckage. Curiously, the holy images were untouched — a number of miniature Buddhas and three huge Buddhas sitting back to back. An hour later the Americans arrived and went to work with tyre levers and hammers. By nightfall the three large Buddhas had been beheaded and all the smaller Buddhas ripped from their pedestals.[27]

Elsewhere he makes the point that the Japanese during their occupation of Burma showed considerable respect for the local culture, and did not generally practise this kind of desecration.

In June Johnston flew to China for the first time, travelling via the dangerous route across the Himalayas in northern Assam known as 'the hump'. He entered a description of it in his notebook as 'A mass of twisting ravines and sharp-fanged peaks, it had always been something real and personal, and oddly malignant, to hundreds of pilots flying into China'.[28] He was to fly 'the hump' many times in the next sixteen months, and was always to find it frightening.

Most of his time in China was spent in the western provinces of Szechwan and Yunnan, specifically in the cities of Kunming and Chungking. Kunming, on a high plateau at the end of the Burma Road, had so far managed to escape the ravages of the war and to preserve its beautiful medieval character. By contrast, Chungking consisted almost entirely of newly built temporary shacks, and had a particularly uncomfortable climate. It was the wartime capital of Republican China, and had been bombed so often that the authorities had given up attempts at permanent reconstruction. It was here that Chiang Kai-shek made his headquarters for his direction of the Chinese war effort. Johnston writes about unexpectedly coming across him one day:

... towards evening I saw a huge sedan black and glistening, draw up beside a dried-up parkland which extended from one of Chungking's dusty streets to a similar dusty street on a higher level. A small man stepped out. He was wearing a simple khaki suit of some light material with flat buttons of brass. The big car drove away, and the little man strolled alone in the park with his head bent thoughtfully and his hands clasped behind his back. I knew who he was, although I had never seen him before, and he looked much smaller and older than I would have imagined. Moreover, he did not look like a soldier; more like a scholar or a professor worried by taxation demands. He had a quiet, intelligent face heavily lined. I looked at the lonely little figure as he walked gently uphill and stepped into the shining car again at the higher road. It was my first sight of Generalissimo Chiang Kai-shek.[29]

The incident prompted Johnston to think about Chinese politics. He sent the *Argus* a piece titled 'China's Political Problems',[30] in which he discusses Chiang's peculiar grip on power, and his obsessiveness and obstinacy, while at the same time defending his dictatorship as a necessary means of uniting China against Japan. He also points out the considerable support for Chiang among the Chinese people and their provincial leaders. This was the first time Johnston had attempted to write seriously on political matters, and it is interesting that it was not politics as such that triggered his interest but the incongruous sight of that small frail figure commanding such immense power. The novelist in him was responding to the human aspect of the drama he was observing.

In September Johnston witnessed an event that touched him deeply. The people of Kweilin learned of a Japanese advance on their city, and they fled in their hundreds of thousands south along the road to Liuchow. As it happened there was also a famine in the country, and thousands of refugees died along the way. Johnston took a jeep along the Kweilin/Liuchow road and was staggered. 'Imagine', he wired the *Argus*:

the entire population of Melbourne abandoning their homes and taking to the roads in flight from the city....On the road south to Liuchow struggles a constant procession of wooden-wheeled pony carts, water buffaloes, decrepit trucks, wheelbarrows, rickshaws and sedan chairs. Already thousands of refugees have died by the sides of the road, where the bodies of old men and women, cripples and children are rotting in the hot sun.[31]

As a child, the sight of the single corpse in the lounge-room of his home had disturbed him. Consider the effect of seeing thousands of them in such terrible circumstances. Throughout his life he was to talk and write of this event.

In October 1944 Johnston set out on a three-month trip to Europe — his first. This turned out to be a 12,000-mile tour that began in the Middle East and took in Italy, Greece and Jugoslavia, transport by courtesy of the US Air Force. He did not write much about this trip, indeed the only piece published by the *Argus* at this time was a defence of communism in southern Europe. 'Almost always', he wrote, 'it is a spontaneous expression of feeling that comes from people who have suffered and are suffering still, rather than emanating from a clever, calculated indoctrination.'[32] He spiced this with a swipe at democracy for its indifference to the poor. Five years later, in the Cold War climate, the *Argus* would not have printed such views, but during the war the communists were on our side, so it was allowed to stand. He wrote, too, that when he was in Athens he could see 'hints of future bitterness and unrest' between the Greek political factions. He could hardly have imagined at this time how significant this country would become later in his life.

Most of the three months of this trip of Johnston's was spent in Rome, where he was loosely attached to a US Press contingent, with accommodation provided by the US Air Force. He probably was not happy there. No articles appeared by him at this time, but he did write a story that suggests he was lonely and homesick. His central character, Barrington, has a brief affair with an Italian woman whom he meets in a jewellery shop while buying a mosaic bracelet for his wife back home. The language barrier between Barrington and the woman intensifies his feelings of alienation in Rome. He considers writing to his wife about the affair, but in the end decides that she would not understand, and keeps it from her. Johnston gave the story the title 'Roman Mosaic', but he did not send it off for publication straight away. Possibly he thought of it as a draft, and wanted to tinker with it some more.

Johnston left Rome in January 1945, and flew back to Burma, arriving in time to report on the Allied advance to reopen the Burma Road. His articles tell of the huge quantities of war supplies that could now be pushed into China along the Burma Road, and the successful repulse of the Japanese forces that followed. K. E. I. Wallace-Crabbe, who was then a squadron leader in the RAF, recalls seeing him in Burma about this time:

> [it was] at a place called Maymyo, about one third of the way up the Burma Road to the Chinese border of Wanting . . . The night before, our location had been severely bombed in an attempt by the Japanese to 'collect' either Generalissimo Kai-shek or the U.S. General 'vinegar Joe' Stillwell. In our partly wrecked building, and the few remaining bungalows in the smashed courtyard, we were a strange, mixed collection. Suddenly a superbly uniformed U.S. war correspondent intruded. To my surprise it was George Johnston. He said he had come by air from Chungking, and had with him a staggering collection of watercolours he had painted in different war areas of China.[33]

None of these pictures seems to have survived. He evidently kept up his sketching and painting wherever he was, and he used some to illustrate feature articles on New Guinea and Asian topics in American magazines, such as *Collier's* and *Saturday Evening Post*.

By March 1945 the Burma campaign had been successfully completed and Burma and India made safe for the Allies. As things cooled down, Johnston's interest wandered increasingly away from war matters. He had not seen much of India to this stage, so he rectified this by making an extraordinary tour by train across the northern breadth of the country, taking in Calcutta, Delhi, Benares, Jaipur, the Punjab, and then on to Kashmir and Afghanistan. This journey gave him the chance to write the sort of journalism he most liked: feature articles, which the *Argus* placed in the Weekend Supplement. In these he writes with great enthusiasm for the country and its people, and covers such matters as the influence of the English, poverty and the caste system, Indian bureaucracy, and a conversation about cricket with the Maharajah of Patiala. Fascinating though it all was, he ended the tour thoroughly exhausted, and when he returned to HQ in April he was sent home on a month's leave. He was in Melbourne by 20 April, fourteen months after his departure.

At home, Elsie was still nagged by the problem, now assuming the proportions of a saga, of the proofs of *Skyscrapers in the Mist*. Angus & Robertson had refused to correct them and had redirected them to her. She then wrote to W. G. Cousins, making her views on the book clear:

> Dear Mr. Cousins,
> May I write frankly to you? I do NOT like Skyscrapers in the Mist! In my opinion it is not right to waste precious paper on such a subject ... Australia does not want second-rate novels, and to my way of thinking Skyscrapers in the Mist is one. Also, after the reputation Mr. Johnston has built for himself, I think he would be very foolish to spoil it with this book ...[34]

She added that Johnston had himself expressed doubts about the book (which is not a novel) in a letter to her. Even so, in his tiredness he was hardly in a mood to quibble or to carry out a substantial rewrite of something so far in the past, so he simply corrected the proofs himself and returned them to Angus & Robertson for publication. It would take another year for it to come out.

Up until this point Johnston had published no fiction, though he clearly was eager to do something with 'Roman Mosaic'. Bruce Kneale, who was now magazine editor of the *Argus*, tells how Johnston asked him in the office one day about the stories Kneale wrote and published in various magazines. 'Hey, sport,' he said to Kneale, 'tell us how you go about writing a story, what do you do?' They talked about it, and next day Kneale was astonished when Johnston slapped a story on his desk and said: 'There you are — read that and tell me if it's any good.' Kneale read it and was impressed. Indeed, he thought it was too good for the *Argus* magazine, and advised him to send it to one of the big American journals.[35] What Johnston did not tell him was that he had written a draft of the story in Rome over the winter, though he did tell Kneale that it was based on an experience he had had. Kneale still thinks of the occasion as an example of Johnston's remarkable facility — asking how to write a story one day, and offering the finished product for publication the next! 'Roman Mosaic' appeared sixteen months later in *Collier's* magazine, and was his first piece of published fiction since his school-magazine days.

Relations with Elsie seem to have been cordial enough during this month of leave, but the fact that Johnston would soon be off again may have prompted a kind of truce between them. Before he departed, however, an event occurred which, though nobody could have known it at the time, was profoundly to change the course of his life. One lunchtime he was holding forth to a group of friends and colleagues in the Australia Hotel, when Bruce Kneale came up to him and said: 'I've got someone here who wants to meet you.'[36] There, beaming at him, was the most astonishingly beautiful AWAS lieutenant he had ever seen. Her name was Charmian Clift, she was interested in writing, she knew exactly who Johnston was and what he had done as a war correspondent, and she was herself the Editor of the Ordnance Corps magazine, *For Your Information*, at the Albert Park barracks. The three of them, Kneale, Johnston and Clift, all in Army uniform, sat in the Australia Hotel all afternoon talking. It was not long before Kneale could see sparks of mutual attraction flying between Johnston and Clift. However, it went no farther at that time. Whatever feelings they may have felt had to be suppressed, because Johnston was leaving shortly for Asia again. He departed on 19 May 1945, but no doubt he had carefully filed away in his memory the name and whereabouts of Lieutenant Clift for future reference.

Johnston flew to India, and almost immediately went back into China. For the next two months he shuttled frequently between his familiar haunts of Kunming and Chungking. He knew them both so well by this time that he could write detailed descriptions that vividly evoked the contrasting characters of the two cities. Of Chungking, with its extremes of climate and terrain, he wrote:

*Huge cellars open up from the footpaths of the main streets
and looking down one sees precipitous warrens of clustered
huts and hovels falling away hundreds of feet down the
boulder-strewn slopes on which the pavements surprisingly
rest. It is like opening up a trapdoor in a street that outwardly
appears normal and seeing down below, instead of a cellar, a
whole suburban area standing on end!*

*During the ghastly period of the air-raids, Chungking's
clammy fogs gave the city protection for seven months of the
year, and the terrain for the remaining five months provided
the sheltering tunnels and the cave shelters burrowed for
miles beneath the great crags — provided also the cave hospitals, cave schools, cave factories, cave arsenals. Here for
years of suffering and hardship such as even London never
knew the battered population lived like troglodytes.*[37]

Kunming, on the other hand, the centre of business and
situated on a fertile plateau, is personified as:

*... a fat voluptuary, sensuous, rouged, heavy with jewels
and sprawling on a sheet of fine satin that had become soiled
and frayed.*

*Few, if any, cities in all China so swiftly absorbed modern-
ism and the paraphernalia of the Western World. The Burma
Road and the smuggler's trails out of Tibet, the roads fre-
quented by the secret operators of the opium ring, all led to
Kunming ... One would see the fat profiteers and parasites
and the men in beggar's rags dying or dead in the muddied
streets.*[38]

Johnston's style of writing here has reached a degree of
definition. There is a confidence and energy that communi-
cates itself to the reader immediately, and the long sentences
avoid confusion or tedium by containing vivid and clearly
realised images. It is a good, descriptive journalistic style that
would have pleased his editors because it is highly readable.
Admittedly he is also wholly concerned with surfaces, and so
there is little evidence of a capacity, in point of view or in
terminology, to get beneath what is visible and analyse. Johnston was not an intellectual; his writing at this stage reflected
the way in which his job demanded that he report the world,
and that was to convey the experience without going far into
the meaning. Not only is this good reporting, but it is also a
sound training for a novelist.

Later in his life he was able in his writing to draw meaning from his experiences, including some he had in Kunming. He once walked along the main canal of the Pan Lung river where he came upon some Australian eucalypts, which contained, wedged in their lower forks, the bodies of dead babies 'clad in fine clothes and with their tiny, cold feet hanging from the scented foliage, neat in shiny slippers of bright new satin. They were there to placate the evil spirits and to prevent the next child from dying.'[39] He was to recall this experience in the last months of his life, while writing the novel *A Cartload of Clay*. There he places it in the context of David Meredith's struggle to find meaning in his life by establishing connections that will transcend differences of time and place. The result is a peculiar suggestion of personal destiny in the events of Meredith's past:

> So Meredith kept his eyes lowered and sought for links, and now he could pin down one important point in the arabesque, because little Emma, the maternal grandmother who had looked after him while their parents were away in the First World War, had been an orphaned girl in Bendigo during the gold rush, and for a time had lived with the Chinese miners in the diggings at Eaglehawk ... And when these Chinese had grown older and had prospered or failed or been driven out by the hardening and stupid racism of the awkwardly growing country, they had gone back to their homeland, to Canton and Foochow and some of them farther out west to the Yunnan plateau, and they had taken with them as gifts little exotic trees in pots to demonstrate to the stay-at-homes the bizarre distance of their journeyings, and these were the stately trees, massively flourishing in an unfamiliar soil, that overhung the Pan Lung river, where once upon a time he had walked and talked with Wen Yi-tuo. It was not altogether unreasonable to imagine that they might have been the very trees planted by one of the Chinese diggers who had befriended his grandmother in Bendigo. (There had been one evening, a tranquil dusk of velvet violet, smelling of damp moss and dust laid by rain, when the poet had pointed out to him the dark bundles jammed into the forks of the trees, the bodies of the dead babies...) (CofC 39—40)

Johnston met the Chinese poet Wen Yi-tuo around this time, in Kunming. They were probably introduced by the subject of another of his experiences in that city, a woman whose name is unknown but who appears in *A Cartload of*

Clay as 'Phoebe'. She seems to have been an American who had gone to China as a Methodist missionary before the war, but when Johnston met her she had taken a job buying pig's bristles and shipping them back to the States for paint brushes. In an album covering his time in China there is a photograph that is likely to be of her, for her appearance loosely fits the description of Phoebe in *A Cartload of Clay* as 'small and shy, with freckles and auburn hair and a childish snub nose, and of a rather scholarly bent' (*CofC* 41). In the novel Meredith talks in a callous way of his affair with Phoebe. She was, he says, 'an ardent and accomplished mistress, which rather surprised him, knowing her earlier prim background and her Methodist upbringing' (*CofC* 41). He goes on to say that he rented a tiny doll's house of a cottage in the grounds of a hospital and kept it for months as a 'place of assignation'. The affair ended, he says, because of a combination of her possessiveness and his guilt at not telling her about his wife in Australia. Elsie recalls Johnston telling her about a woman in China he was involved with, but doesn't remember any of the details. One thing that Johnston could not resist about the woman was her occupation, and he used it several times in his fiction.

By mid-1945 the war in China was no longer headline news in Australia, and Johnston's reports were now usually found on the back page of the *Argus*, whereas the year before they had been consistently in a position of prominence. Headline space was now increasingly given to pieces by Geoffrey Hutton and David McNicoll on the European conflict and its aftermath, or to Axel Olsen and James O'Connor on the continuing struggle against the Japanese in the Philippines. In fact the war in China was rapidly cooling down. This gave Johnston an excuse to take a break. In what sounds like a plot for a comic movie, a group of US Cavalry people were taking a plane-load of Australian slouch hats into the high country of Tibet in order to trade them for hardy Tibetan mountain ponies. The Tibetan nomads were apparently very partial to digger hats. The colonel in charge of the operation invited Johnston and *Liberty* magazine photographer James Burke, who spoke fluent Chinese, along for the ride, though it turned out to be somewhat more testing than they expected.

The party flew from Kunming to an airstrip near the town of Yung Kwan Chai, which was some 3600 metres (12,000 feet) above sea level, 'the highest airfield in the world', wrote Johnston.[40] As he stepped from the plane he was breathless, and not just from the lack of oxygen:

> Here was a valley of breathtaking colour and beauty ... a valley of a million flowers glittering in bright warm sunshine ... And dominating the far end of the valley, in peerless, shimmering majesty, stood the white, 25,000 ft. peak of Minya Konka, appearing to cover half the sky ...[41]

He pressed some of those glittering flowers into a letter back to Elsie. It was the beauty of this valley, and others like it, that inspired the setting for the novel *High Valley* (1948); Johnston never tired of enthusing lyrically about the valleys of Tibet.

Together with Burke, Johnston went with a pack train into the higher peaks around Minya Konka, where blizzards, freezing temperatures and precipitous ledges made progress extremely hazardous. They camped with Tibetan nomads, sleeping in their yurts (tents), eating tsamba (a heavy barley-meal bread) and drinking Tibetan tea with lumps of yak butter floating in it. One nomad, an extraordinary cowboy (or yakboy) called T'se Ch'i, accommodated them, along with his family, for three days and nights. T'se Ch'i had introduced himself in an auspicious way when Johnston was instructing some lama priests in the use of a rifle:

> I looked up and saw a tall, slim man watching us, a pic-turesquely handsome man with the face and bearing and dignity of a red Indian chieftain. I handed him the rifle. He took a quick aim — there was almost no difference in his movement to accept the weapon and his actual firing — and he plugged the tobacco tin clean in the centre.[42]

Here, enjoying a strange hospitality, Johnston had his thirty-third birthday. He was one of the very few Australians, perhaps even the first, to have visited the high regions of Tibet up to that time. He reflected with a hint of nostalgia on how, beneath the unfamiliar exterior, life in the Tibetan community was not unlike life on an Australian farm. 'There were the children', he wrote, *playing at evening, throwing stones at the sheep. There was the constant stream of neighbours and visitors dropping in for afternoon tea, or to borrow a cylinder of yak cheese, or to compare jewellery and babies — I doubt if any people in all the world are more affectionate towards children than the Tibetans — or just to gossip as women do at afternoon tea gatherings the world over . . . There was T'se Ch'i striding along with us in the afternoons when we went to shoot rabbits and pheasants . . . There was an old man and his two sons returning with his yak train to the little nomads' camp, and being welcomed by shouting children and barking, tail-wagging dogs, and the old man lifting the smallest boy to the back of his horse for the ride into the horse lines. There was so much of warm living and kindness and humanity . . .*[43]*

It was during this time that Johnston had an unforgettable meeting with the leader of the white sect of lamas known to his followers as the Living Buddha. It was known that the great man's proudest possession was an old phonograph, so Johnston and Burke had gone prepared with a gift recording. It happened that the only one they could lay hands on was of a popular song called 'It Must Be Jelly 'Cause Jam Don't Shake Like That', so it was with some anxiety that they awaited the Living Buddha's reaction. They need not have feared: 'The tune was received with tremendous approval, the Living Buddha nodding his head rhythmically to the beat of the hot jazz, his eyes closed, and a beatific expression on his face. Then he played for us his two records. One was Mei Lan Fan singing a Chinese operatic piece. The other was Noel Coward's 'Don't put your daughter on the stage, Mrs Worthington'![44]

After the entertainment, Johnston and the Living Buddha settled down to a serious debate on reincarnation and the comparative merits of Christian and Buddhist beliefs. 'Christianity has a childish logic that appeals to large groups of simple people', asserted the sage, 'but to an intelligent man it is unsatisfactory. Logic in religion should not be easy to find. Ours is a religion for the individual scholar or thinker, yours is a good enough religion for the masses.'[45] There could hardly have been an Australian precedent for such a lofty conference, nor hardly an Australian less qualified to participate. Johnston had no religious faith at all, and no professed respect for Christianity. On the other hand, he had acquired some appreciation of Eastern philosophical views. He did not, however, record his own responses to the Living Buddha's opinions.

Johnston's time in Tibet did nothing for his respect for the general lama population. With Burke he spent some time in a lamasery called Konka Gomba, reputedly the setting of Shangri-La, the retreat in James Hilton's novel *Lost Horizons*. Johnston found the reality to be far from the ideal refuge of the fiction, for within the lamasery walls the lamas showed all the jealousy and avarice that characterised the war-torn world outside. They were not even particularly devout, being more preoccupied with the dollar exchange rate than with prayer. Johnston and Burke were relieved to get away from the place.

The final days of the Tibetan interlude came close to being tragic. As they descended from the higher regions, Burke developed a severe kidney infection. The pain was such that he grew delirious, and one night attempted his own life with the colt .45 they were carrying. Johnston injected him with morphine and nursed him back to a state fit for travel, although, with Burke continually falling off his horse, progress was slow and painful. They arrived back at base camp later than had been arranged, only to find everything cleared away and the DC3 that was to fly them home standing at the end of the runway revving for take-off. As it made its run, Johnston's heart sank: they would never get out of such a remote place, he thought, and would die before anyone found them. Miraculously, at that moment the aeroplane's starboard engine cut out, and the pilot was unable to complete the take-off. Johnston fired his revolver, and they were rescued. Burke recovered and stayed on in Asia for many years after the war, and he and Johnston managed to maintain their friendship, although their lives went in widely different directions. There is a brief but affectionate sketch of him under his own name in *A Cartload of Clay*, where the rescue incident is described, and is concluded by a reference to Burke's fatal fall in the Himalayas in the early 1960s.

> It was the right ending for Jim. And a damn sight better than dying in the squalor and cold and rat-stench and misery and

pain of that terrible chorten eighteen years earlier. (CofC 100)

Although the visit to Tibet lasted only about five weeks, it was an important time in Johnston's imaginative life. He was to write six novels and one factually based book out of his Asian experiences, and two of these, *High Valley* and *Journey through Tomorrow*, make substantial use of his knowledge of Tibet. Tibet had not only provided a break from the war, it had also put him through something of a mind-expanding experience of a kind he could never have had by staying back at base. Indeed, Asia generally was an important educational and imaginative stimulant, and he was to write about it often in the next decade. Specifically, his prolonged contact with Asian cultures planted a seed of respect for an attitude to life that is not obsessed with a successful career, though it would be years yet before that seed would germinate.

In August Johnston was back in Kunming in his role of war correspondent. One of his first reports after Tibet was on the pitiable return of those masses of exiles from Kweilin almost exactly a year earlier. They were struggling along that same road, in the opposite direction now, but just as overwhelmingly lamentable as before, with just as many collapsing to die along the way beside the littered remains of last year's victims. Certain images, especially ones that expressed the will to survive, stuck in Johnston's mind for a lifetime: 'an old woman in faded coolie blue with a treadle sewing machine strapped to her back, and a wispily-bearded man with one trachoma-whitened eye who was bent double by the great weight of the sow he was carrying' (*CSFN* 22).

There were also moments of levity. In Kunming, Johnston and Sydney journalist Nigel Palethorpe along with the townspeople celebrated (slightly prematurely) the end of the war by setting off fireworks. When they went back to the store for more fireworks, they found, Johnston wrote, that 'with shrewd oriental realization of the principles of supply and demand the price had already trebled'.[46]

Late in August the wind-up of the war quickened. Johnston joined James O'Connor in Manila to cover talks between General MacArthur and Japanese envoys about the terms of surrender. Then in September this pair followed MacArthur to Japan for the last stages. On the way Johnston was able briefly to go to the now recaptured Shanghai to report the Chinese acceptance of surrender from Field Marshal Oka-mura. It was his last look at China, where he had seen so many new and extraordinary things.

In the weeks leading up to the surrender ceremony, Johnston and O'Connor sent back reports on the turmoil of life in Japan immediately after the dropping of the atomic bomb. Johnston's pieces concentrated, again, on matters of human rather than military interest, which were left to O'Connor. He was appalled by what he saw of Hiroshima and Nagasaki. He stood on the rubble (alarmingly ignorant of the radiation effects) and reflected 'dazed, uncomprehending . . . fearful' on the implications of what had occurred, and concluded that

> The pent-up forces of India, heaving and tumultuous; the unpredictable power and violence of China, where civil war blazed again even as I stood in a shabby mission garden near Hiroshima; the strange mysticism of Tibet, which had not known this war; the soft, misleading apathy of a ravaged Burma — all these things were no longer as important as the dead birds and the blasted flowers.[47]

The saturation bombing, too, had left its mark on the people of Yokohama, Kawasaki and Tokyo:

> . . . children hiding their eyes or fleeing in panic, girls turning their backs and cringing as if expecting blows, men just looking at us without expression. Sometimes a little boy would poke out his tongue and then flee wildly across the fields. In most of the faces there was a dull apathy, in some dismay, in some bewilderment, in many a sullen hostility. One had the sensation of walking precariously along the crumbling lip of a smouldering volcano, but nothing happened.[48]

As well as the victims, there were those who had benefited from the war. Johnston interviewed a group of nine Japanese millionaires at their plush hotel — bankers and industrialists who had made massive profits. It was a sour and uncomfortable interview, as the businessmen, immaculately dressed and, according to Johnston, eating lobster from silver plates, deplored the effects of the war on the Japanese working man. He sent the *Argus* a suitably sarcastic piece on this, and another on the luxury in which Axis diplomats were living in

Tokyo at this time. Another piece conveyed the atmosphere of fear and suspicion as MacArthur's men began the search for war criminals:

> We walked back to the sumptuous dining hall, panelled in teakwood, and two Germans came hurriedly towards us, the leading man breathlessly announcing that he was not a Nazi but the man following him was, and the second man stared at him malevolently and snarled 'Pig!'
>
> There was a constant whispering in the gardens of bamboo and decorative pines, and in the dim corridors of the cream-coloured building there were the shadowy figures of fear and intrigue and treachery and distrust. It was a scented place, but we were glad to get away from it.[49]

Then there was the group of right-wing dandies — a mixture of Russian, French, German and Swedish men and women, mostly young — who had been living in the hills of Karuizawa as parasites on the country they had expected would win the war, but who now turned collaborators. Now that the Americans were in control, they expressed hatred for the Germans and Japanese, and complained bitterly that they had refused to share their luxuries with them. 'Will we have to become Soviet citizens now?' one of them weakly asked Johnston, who wrote: 'They had filled their glasses with the last of the vodka and they were toasting a picture on the wall — a framed yellowed photograph of the last Tsar of all the Russians . . .'[50]

The last phase of his war correspondence duties took place on 3 September, when he attended the surrender ceremony between Japan and the Allied forces on board the USS *Missouri*. Johnston and O'Connor sent the *Argus* a joint report, which occupied the whole of the front page, giving full details of the signing of the treaty and conveying the atmosphere of a moving and spectacular occasion. After this there was only the business of tidying up and preparing to go home. He did not do this immediately, however, but stayed on for a few weeks putting together his material for the book on Asia that was to become *Journey through Tomorrow*.

How is his contribution to war journalism to be valued? He undoubtedly played his part in keeping the Australian public informed and quite possibly in sustaining its morale. This was what every conscientious war correspondent hoped for, and it is difficult to find anything wrong in that. Many of Australia's best journalists, Geoffrey Hutton, David McNicoll, John Hetherington, Osmar White, Wilfred Burchett, to name but a few, earned distinction in the role, and Johnston firmly established himself among their ranks. Furthermore, he did this without alienating himself from their comradeship. On the contrary, he was generally well liked, despite a certain wariness at times of his magpie approach to gathering information. It is true that in New Guinea some correspondents had reservations about him; but others, such as Osmar White and Geoffrey Hutton, defended him warmly. Geoffrey Hutton wrote that he had the gift of 'dissolving personal and social barriers, giving cheek to politicians, editors and generals. Nobody ever resented it. He could charm the birds out of the trees.'[51] Bruce Kneale tells a story that illustrates this. When Johnston came back from Asia, Errol Knox said to him one day in the office: 'You'll have to come back and start work again on the paper soon.' Knox was a figure whose dignity nobody on the paper except Johnston dared to lower. 'Christ, Knokka, I can't come back yet,' he retorted. 'I've still got six hundred quid of yours in expenses to spend!'[52] Greeba Jamison insists that Johnston had a kind and sensitive side that was endearing: 'To some of the younger journalists who were taking their work frightfully seriously, he was always helpful, encouraging; he was never the "distinguished war correspondent" when he came back on leave − just one of the gang in the reporter's room.'[53] With testimonies such as these from his colleagues he had every reason to feel pleased with the way he had conducted himself as a journalist and war correspondent.

Yet Johnston was to look back on this time of his life, and the work, with scorn. At least, this is so if we take his autobiographical fiction as representing his actual views on the matter. It is difficult not to feel that the following passage from *My Brother Jack* is self-reproach of the harshest kind, and that this is one of the moments in the novel when David Meredith is closest to his creator:

> *. . . the falsity I built, or allowed to be built, around myself is*
> *perhaps less excusable. I wrote copiously and I wrote bril-*
> *liantly and I wrote with all the practised 'flairs' for which*
> *Gavin Turley had commended me, and I skulked and dodged*
> *and I was desperately afraid, and I wrote myself into my own*
> *lie, the lie I* had *to create, so that it was taken for granted*
> *that I was there,* right there, *in the thin red line of heroes,*
> *and gradually I picked up all the tricks of evasion and avoi-*
> *dance and wove them into an almost fool-proof pattern. I*
> *suffered nothing more than a spurious, self-inflicted heroism.*
> (MBJ 330)

One wonders if anyone ever did accuse Johnston of this kind of deception, because there is nothing in his war correspondence or his war books that deliberately attempts to give the impression that the writer is 'right there' in the front line of the action. As has already been pointed out, most of Johnston's war articles concentrate on human interest subjects away from the actual conflict. Why then did he suppose that people did infer this, making him a liar by default?

The reasons seem to have been both professional and personal. He had always felt that the very situation of the war correspondent was parasitical, and that the only authentic roles in war were the soldier's and the victim's. One recalls with what conviction he wrote about Australian heroism and 'blood sacrifice' in the war books (and later in *My Brother Jack*). He was to devote a whole novel, *The Far Road*, to exposing the essential self-interest, not only of the role of the war correspondent, but of journalists in general. David Meredith says in the latter novel that 'Duplicity was inextricably woven into the *modus operandi* of the game',[54] and that 'In a later age, Judas would have been a journalist'.[55]

As well as this disillusionment with the profession, Johnston came to hate himself for having chosen it. He must have thought of that failure to join his mates at the enlistment centre, of Rod Maclean, of his brother and indeed of his father in World War I, and believed that he had taken the less honourable course. One perceives that his question to Bruce Kneale 'You think I'm a coward, don't you?' suggests that it was really Johnston who thought of *himself* as a coward, and that his choice to serve out the war in the capacity of a war

correspondent was an act of shameful self-interest and evasion. When he came to write about that sense of personal and
professional dereliction in *The Far Road* and the Meredith
trilogy, it formed part of his tortuous purpose to expose that
particular George Johnston he once had been, and to annihi-
late him.

C H A P T E R I V

Charmian

Nor, in those days, was anything quite under control, neither eyes nor mouth, nor the contralto voice that was also too big and with a husky lilt to it, nor the body in that ridiculous stained battle-dress, still with a child's gawkiness about it . . . she seemed to have no breasts at all, but her shoulders were broad and her hips lean, and with the gawkiness she had a certain quick, boyish grace. Boy's hands, too, square and brown and muscular and grubby. And even if nothing of all this was under control then, there was a sense of vital power about her, as if she were practising with everything all at once and on any person available. (MBJ 342)

Johnston was back in Melbourne on 15 October 1945. The problem confronting him now would be adjusting to the dull routine of peacetime. As well as this, there was the uncertainty about the future of his marriage. Elsie was no longer sure of what she wanted: part of her was dreading his return, which would bring with it his tension and volatile temper, his ceaseless smoking and now frequent drinking. And yet she wanted the marriage to work. It had been a lonely and anxious war for her; and she hated the St Kilda flat and wanted a house with a garden and a normal family life for Gae.

The St Kilda flat had originally been an instrument of separation between George and Elsie; she was to live there with Gae, he was to pay the rent and support them, and find a place of his own. But this he never did. As soon as he returned from Asia he acted as he had done on those earlier periods of leave, and moved in with his wife and daughter. The permanency or otherwise of the arrangement was not discussed, and Elsie continued to keep house and play the role of wife. In this way, perhaps, she saw a chance of getting the marriage back on a good footing.

Johnston himself did not know what he wanted to do. Over Christmas 1945 he was making plans to go to Central and South America, and the only thing holding him up, he said, was that he could not get a berth on a ship, because he was 'not a war bride'.[1] In February he was hurrying to finish the last pages of *Journey through Tomorrow*, in anticipation of leaving any day. The purpose of the trip is something of a mystery: it was not an official assignment for the *Argus*. He mentioned at times that he wanted to pick up with Jane again,[2] so the trip might have been his own idea, as a way of finally breaking from Elsie, or it might just have been a vague aspiration that he did not really expect to put to the test.

Johnston had told Angus & Robertson that they would not be getting *Journey through Tomorrow*, because with restrictions on paper they could not promise to get it out as soon as he wanted. When they first heard of it, it was a book about Tibet only, but Johnston expanded it to include all his Asian areas of operation. Cheshire's promise to get it out quickly turned out to be extravagant, however, for it was to take them eighteen months. Cousins later wrote to Johnston that he could have beaten that time, and added indignantly: 'I don't want Cheshire to get your next book.'[3]

Despite being noticeably tired and unsettled, Johnston was, as ever, the 'golden boy' in the office, though a certain unreliability in him did not go unnoticed. 'George would say almost anything to keep people happy at the time — happy, that is, until he broke his word to them,' says Greeba Jamison.[4] But such faults, if they were perceived by Errol Knox, did not stand in the way of his promotion, which everyone regarded as inevitable. The board of directors had decided that the old *Australasian* was due for a facelift, and Knox had sought Johnston's views, which were to transform it into a livelier news and current affairs journal with good features and the occasional items of fiction and poetry. He also had connections to obtain material from *Time* magazine in the US. This might not have impressed Knox so much, but Johnston's performance as a journalist over the years certainly had, and it was no surprise to anyone when he was given an editor's job. On 18 March he was appointed first Editor of the new weekly, called *Australasian Post*. Although many of the articles came from the general news staff, he had a small staff of his own doing much of the work, including Howard Palmer, Hume Dow, Keith Attiwill and photographer Bernie Bailey. Geoffrey Hutton and John Hetherington contributed features on a regular basis, and Bruce Kneale was the part-time fiction editor. Johnston threw himself into the job with characteristic gusto, and according to Hume Dow made an immediate success of it.[5]

The new job meant, of course, that the proposed trip to Central and South America was off. Exactly how it came about is uncertain, but around this time he made contact with Charmian Clift again. In *Clean Straw for Nothing* Meredith telephones Cressida Morley at the army barracks after having a prolonged and bitter row with his wife, Helen. Perhaps this is what Johnston did. In any case, they got together again, and this time, according to Bruce Kneale, it simply 'exploded between them'.[6] They saw each other every day, and it was soon obvious to all Johnston's friends and colleagues that it was, in Greeba Jamison's term, 'on' between them.

For her twenty-three years, Charmian Clift was unusually worldly. There was nothing coy about her: she was confident, straight-backed, and certain of her attractiveness to men. She had gained considerable experience of life, including several passionate affairs, although there remained a fresh, natural vitality about her that seemed unspoilable. Everyone who knew her in those days testifies to her extraordinary beauty. Greeba Jamison recalls: 'She was the most beautiful, the most sexy young woman I've ever seen. She knew she was and she revelled in it, flaunted it.' Her green eyes, dark hair, generous and mobile mouth and clear, rich skin suggested foreignness. Who was she? Where was she from?

Her father, Sidney Clift, was born and raised in Derbyshire, England, and had classical northern English features:

dark, stocky build, large squarish head, strong, capable hands and a look of gentle defiance about him. He had trained as an engineer, though had never become fully qualified. In a spirit of adventure he came to Australia before World War I, and quickly warmed to the independent outlook he found in many Australians. He refused to fight for the English in that War, and loved to refer to them as 'bloody poms'.[7]

After wandering about Australia for a time, he met Amy Curry in a King's Cross boarding house. Amy, too, was endowed with an independent spirit and had run away from home. They married and went to live in Kiama on the New South Wales coast, where Sid had found a job as a mining engineer in charge of the blue metal quarry. In their small weatherboard cottage on the highway just north of the town proper, overlooking Bombo Beach, they had three children: Margaret, born in 1919; a son, Barré, in 1922; and Charmian, in 1923. Margaret, four years older than her sister, was always a little aloof, which earned her the family nickname of 'the duchess'. Barré developed rheumatic fever when small and this held him back a little, and he tended to look to his sisters for protection. And adequate protectors they were, too, robust and talented girls, who were as cheeky and aggressive and could swim and surf as well as any boy in the district. Indeed, they often rescued strapping males from the treacherous undertows off Bombo beach.

Sid and Amy Clift were liberal-minded parents, though there was never the money for expensive education for the children. Since they were avid and intelligent readers, especially of literature, their interest was passed on to the children. Both parents could quote Shakespeare or Byron at the slightest provocation, and Amy, throughout her life, wrote poetry, some of which was published in the local paper. Later, Charmian was to pay considerable homage to her mother's great character and literary example, and to recall how natural it seemed to her as an eight-year-old to sit out on the woodpile and write or read poetry. Sid had a curious taste for sceptics: Montaigne, Cervantes, Rabelais, Voltaire and, above all, Laurence Sterne. Like Amy, he loved Shakespeare: thus Charmian was named after Cleopatra's attendant. There was in their house a spirit of freedom, in a low-key sort of way, which encouraged the children to dip into what they liked of the volumes on the bookshelves or, if they wished, to play outdoors.

School, of course, was another matter, and Charmian in particular hated it. Both girls preferred to use their freedom at Bombo Beach. A large part of the girls' childhood was spent roaming the rocks, or surfing, fossicking for crabs or sleeping in the sun. All this developed a deep love of nature in Charmian, which lasted all her life. Indeed, she was never happy unless living within sight of the sea. She loved being out, on the move, in action, whatever the weather, indeed the stormier the better. She stifled in offices, closed spaces, or anything that reeked of security.

The Clifts had little to do with the town of Kiama. They were a closeknit, proudly independent family, who thought themselves rather better than the rest of the town, though they would never have made it apparent. Sid Clift voted Labor, and according to Margaret would have voted communist if there had been a candidate. When the Railway Commission decided to close the quarry during the Depression, Sid insisted on keeping it going by doing all the maintenance himself and by putting in extra, unpaid hours. Years later, at his funeral, the many men whom the quarry had kept in employment during that time came from miles around to pay their respects. The Clift family was astonished and deeply moved to see that their father, who had lived such a quiet and asocial life, had attracted such loyalty and affection from the community.

During her teens Charmian developed an appetite for adventure and excitement that dull, remote Kiama could not possibly satisfy. She longed for fame and glamour, which she identified with the big city — Sydney. Her mother wanted her to be a teacher, but she was dreaming of becoming a film star.[8] Her impatience for experience got her into some risky situations, such as hitching rides on the highway with travelling salesmen and taxi drivers, and having to battle her way out of trouble. At some point during her teenage years it seems likely that she had an illegitimate child, which she regretfully had adopted out, though whether this was with the knowledge of all her family is uncertain.[9] When Margaret went to Sydney in the mid 1930s to study art, Charmian jealously itched to follow her, but her parents insisted she stay at school, where she was clever but bored. She tried a business-school course, where she at least learned to type, but after a time went back to Wollongong High School. Later she tried nursing in Lithgow, but hated it and came home to Kiama, where she worked as a petrol-pump attendant. Then a picture of her on a beach won her £50 as 'Miss *Pix* Magazine', with her picture on the cover, and she finally persuaded her parents to let her join Margaret in Sydney, with the vaguest of plans of becoming famous in the theatre. The nearest she came to it was a job as an usherette at the Minerva Theatre, after which she got a job in the Bjelke-Petersen physical culture studio, and this led to some photographic modelling. Her movements are shadowy at this time. She had boyfriends, but she was drifting aimlessly when the rest of the world was purposefully gearing for war.

Margaret, too, had not fared as well as she had hoped, and was dissatisfied with her job in a photographic studio, and so the sisters decided in 1942 to join the Australian Women's Army Service. They chose the Artillery Corps, to be trained as anti-aircraft gunners: Margaret as a Heightfinder, Charmian as a Predictor. In 1944 Charmian was transferred to LHQ (Land Headquarters) in Melbourne, where she was to work in the office. Here her literary ability was discovered, probably by the Director of Ordnance Services, Howard Kingham, and she was placed in charge of the Ordnance Corps monthly magazine, *For Your Information*, given a commission and allowed to live out in accommodation of her own. It was odd, as Clift later pointed out, that it was the army that gave her the first real opportunity to write, for which she always remained grateful. She not only edited and wrote for *For Your Information*, but she began to write short stories and send them off to civilian magazines as well. Some of these appeared in the *Australia Weekend Book* and in *Australia National Journal*. By one of those coincidences that make life itself sometimes feel like a novel, it was Bruce Kneale who helped her in these first publishing ventures. He had occasion to visit the Ordnance office at the Albert Park barracks, and got into conversation with her about writing. Since he had published stories of his own, he was able to suggest a few names as publishing contacts, and their friendship progressed from there. Kneale was, therefore, a friend of both Johnston and Clift for some months without ever having reason to bring them together. When he did, it was not by design. Clift rang him at work one day to say that one of the contacts he had given her, Gwen Morton Spencer, editor of *Australia National Journal*, which had taken one of her stories, was giving a party at Menzies Hotel for her Melbourne authors. Clift had been invited, but being a little nervous of meeting a crowd of literati, asked Kneale to go with her. When the party dispersed, he chanced to say that he was going to meet George Johnston at the Australia Hotel. Clift inquired: 'George Johnston the war correspondent? I'd love to meet him.' So they made for the Australia Hotel, where they found Johnston surrounded by his usual group of listeners.

The time of this first meeting was May 1945, while Johnston was on a month's leave from Asia. Whatever interest they might have inspired in each other at that meeting came to nothing, because he was heading back to China. Nor is there any indication that they contacted each other during the following year. Indeed, in the latter half of 1945 Clift took up with a young air force officer called Leo Kenney, about whom she grew serious enough to become engaged. He gave her a copy of *The Oxford Book of English Verse* inscribed: 'Cliftie's book. All we writers have large libraries. Portsea again. L.K.'[10] Kenney had been a novice priest, but joined the air force when war came. He idolised his fiancée, and arranged to have her portrait painted by Edward Heffernan, a young product of the Gallery school, who happened to be a neighbour of Kenney's father. The sitting proved to be a little unnerving for Heffernan — Clift turned up in her uniform on the first day and had no hesitation in removing it to stand topless before him while they considered suitable blouses.[11] During the course of the painting, in May 1946, Kenney had to leave for Singapore to take an advertising job, while waiting to be taken onto the staff of Malaysian-American Plantations as a plantation manager, after which Charmian would join him and they would be married. He wrote to Heffernan that Charmian liked the portrait, and that he'd arranged payment for it, and added: 'I think Charmian is a bit lonely in Melbourne. Will you shout her a beer for me some time?'[12] But if she was lonely, it was not for long, for around this time Johnston, who had been back from abroad for several months, made contact with her again. What prompted it? Perhaps he saw her somewhere, or heard her name mentioned. Perhaps he had been holding off until he knew something more definite about the South America trip. Now that this was settled and he was Editor of the *Post*, perhaps he decided that that astonishing beauty from a year ago could no longer be ignored.

Edward Heffernan, still believing her engaged to his client Kenney, was astonished to find, when Clift turned up at his Heidelberg residence to examine the finished portrait, that she had brought along a new escort — a tall, blonde *Argus* journalist, who professed some knowledge of art. He inspected the picture with the destructive eye of a successor and declared emphatically that 'it did not do her justice'.[13] In the end, poor Heffernan was left with the picture, for the new lover did not want it, and the old lover, now that the original had found herself another, lost interest in the copy as well.

Both Johnston and Clift were later to write fictional accounts of their first meeting. In *My Brother Jack* David Meredith meets Cressida Morley on a visit to the golf course where Cressida's AWAS unit is practising anti-aircraft gunnery. Cressida carries a copy of *Tristram Shandy* everywhere she goes. The two meet briefly and leave it at that until they meet again at Mario's restaurant in Melbourne after Meredith returns from Asia. Meredith has gone to the restaurant by himself, and there he is surprised to see Cressida with his old colleague Gavin Turley. It is from this meeting that their relationship really begins, and it is this meeting, of course, that corresponds closely to Bruce Kneale's account of having introduced Clift to Johnston. It is doubtful that Johnston ever saw her practising gunnery as in the novel, and Cressida's age, eighteen, is three years younger than Clift was when she was transferred to Melbourne. It is true that Clift was, like her father, extremely fond of *Tristram Shandy*.

Clift herself wrote a version of their meeting in an unfinished and unpublished work titled 'Greener Grows the Grass'. Clift's heroine is called *Christine* Morley (totally shunning all the literary and moral connotations of the name Cressida), and an important difference between her and Johnston's Cressida is that Christine Morley is a writer who works for the same newspaper as Martin Smith, who is Clift's version of Johnston. Clift has a scene in which Christine Morley utters a brief word of welcome to Smith when he comes into the office on his return from Asia. Smith does not remember that they had been introduced on an earlier occasion, when he was back on a brief period of leave, and he has to be reminded of it by his colleague Bill Eaton, who had in fact been the one who had made the introduction. Clift gives Eaton a strong resemblance to Bruce Kneale as

a little man, with a little man's vanity in his personal appearance. He wore good suits and stiff collars ... there was something of the gremlin in his bright black eyes, in the dominant hook of his bony nose, in the sudden ecstatic quivering of his neat moustache when he was amused. He did not look like a newspaperman, but then he didn't look particularly like anything else either.[14]

When Christine Morley leaves the room, Smith and Eaton hold a revealingly suggestive conversation, which is worth quoting at length.

'Tell me, Marty ... if you want to, if you don't want to, tell me to mind my own business ... are relations still ... strained? ... between you and Leonie?'

Martin slouched to the high grimed window and looked down into the street, at the shiny beetletops of parked cars, at the mess of clotted humanity the green light had vomited across the intersection. 'Yes' he said simply, and then turned back to Bill, with his face twisted into puzzlement and tiredness. 'It won't work, Bill. I feel like a heel, but it's no good. She can't give me the things I want. She supplies certain of the necessary commodities expected from a wife, but there are so many things lacking. I'm looking for something, Bill. I don't know what I'm looking for, and I don't know where I'll find it, but I know Leonie can't ever give it to me. That's why

*I want to go away again. To China or India or Italy some-
where to hell out [of] it.'*

*Eaton looked nowhere in particular, with no particular
expression. The pencil went chink, chink, chink against his
teeth. 'Why don't you have an affair with Christine Morley?'
he said.*

*There was complete revulsion in Martin's stomach. He had
a sudden mental flashback to Christine Morley's eyes as she
had met him in the corridor. Vibrant eyes, lightly green and
warm with pleasure. And her mouth curling crookedly from
big white teeth. 'Welcome home' she had said, and he'd felt
every movement of her back as she walked on to the women's
room.*

*'Is it the normal thing for unhappy writers to take a dose of
Christine Morley?' he asked. 'A green-eyed purgative, eh?'
But he could feel a tingling under his shoulder blades.*

*Bill Eaton's eyebrows quirked satanically. 'I'll tell you
about her,' he said, 'She's a bitch. She's the mother of all
wantons. But she's also one of the nicest, most intelligent,
most honest women I've met. In fact she's the only honest
bitch I've ever met. She's also a friend of mine and I'm very
proud of it. I'm probably the only friend she has. She's been
here about two years now, and she's the best woman writer
we've got. She came from nowhere in the back-blocks with
some unimportant tragedy that seemed very important to her.
I think she could probably be a very great writer if she didn't
let men get at her so much. She's too good-looking, and it's
always easier to go dancing and drinking than sit at home and
work. I think she's pretty lonely just now. She got herself
engaged to a Malayan planter, but he's been gone two
months, and I have an idea that respectability is beginning to
pall. She'd do you good Marty, because she'd never ask
anything from you, and she'd give you more than a nice
body.' He twirled the pencil point into the table and it snap-
ped with a vicious crack. 'But don't, for Christ's sake, fall in
love with her.' His mouth lifted in a sudden sardonic grin.
'Ain't I the generous guy? Procurer. Except that I think you
two need each other.'*

*Martin looked at him curiously. 'Why don't you save her
up for yourself?', he asked.*

*Then Bill Eaton, for Bill Eaton, said a very strange thing.
'Because I value her friendship too much. You see, I'm the
only man she knows who hasn't an axe to grind.'*[15]

When Morley and Smith do get together, their thoughts
about each other are again revealing, in that they depict the

coming together of two people who are both in their own way bruised and looking for a way out of an unsatisfactory entanglement.

> *Martin Smith looked very tall in Bill's room. Very tall and very untidy and very tired. He has a dreadful nose, she thought. And a sulky bottom lip. It's a boyish face grown old. I wish I hadn't said that stupid thing to him in the corridor. He probably thinks I'm a complete moron. He's in a dreadful state of nerves. His nails are chewed. They're revolting. She smiled at them both. 'My tongue is hanging out,' she said.*
>
> *'Good old Christine,' Bill murmured in despair, 'I can't remember a time when it wasn't.'*
>
> *Martin said 'Mine is too. Let's go.' And he thought, she doesn't look like a bitch. I know bitches. They have a bitchy aura hovering around them. She's beautiful and vibrant and young. And her eyes are hurt. I wish I could get this.*
>
> *The lift plunged down. They were pressed together by some cameramen. Then they were out in the sun-chequered marble of the entrance hall and Christine walked between the two men into the street. She's tall. Martin thought. She's almost as tall as I am. Maybe that's high heels. But she walks as though she were barefoot and carried a basket on her head. She walks as though she owned the earth. She knows she owns the earth. She doesn't walk like a bitch.*
>
> *And Christine thought, Oh for God's sake. You're dirty. You're cheap. Try to remember you're engaged to Leonard. Think of Leonard. Think Leonard I love you. Just because Martin Smith is an author and a correspondent and looks interesting, you don't have to get your filthy claws into him. But she felt the looseness of his body moving beside her, and she sensed, rather than saw, the sardonic amusement of Bill at her other side. The excitement kept thumping behind her eyes.*[16]

There is some nice writing here, even though it is only a first draft. Thinking each other to be tall links Christine and Martin in their thoughts. Another link is made by giving the two rejected partners, Leonard and Leonie, names with the same root.

The typescript of 'Greener Grows the Grass' bears no date, but it was probably written in 1969, and forms part of an autobiographical novel that Clift was working on in the year of her death. A more substantial portion of it exists under the title 'The End of the Morning'. Much of the extracts quoted above provide an insight into the emotional beginnings of the Johnston/Clift relationship, in a way that is different from, but nevertheless complements, Johnston's version in *My Brother Jack*. Bill Eaton plays a similar role to Gavin Turley, but is much more singly based on Bruce Kneale's personality than Turley, who is always a composite of several of Johnston's colleagues. Martin Smith's frayed edginess, and his dissatisfaction with his wife, are different from David Meredith's self-lacerations and accusations against Helen, but they do not contradict Meredith's character; rather they add another dimension to it, and in doing so bring us closer to a complete picture of Johnston himself at the time of his return from abroad and his involvement with Clift. And the character of Christine Morley is less idealised than the Cressida of *My Brother Jack*.

The biggest difference between Christine Morley and Cressida Morley is that Cressida is never, at any stage of the Meredith trilogy, shown to be a writer. And this, of course, is the thing that most separates Cressida from Charmian Clift. Exactly why Johnston chose not to portray Clift's craft, her artistic commitment, the thing that was probably her greatest passion, is a matter that has generated interest, and will be discussed in a later chapter.

If Johnston misleads us by not representing Clift's craft, Clift also misleads us in 'Greener Grows the Grass' in placing Christine Morley on the staff of Martin Smith's paper for a period of two years before they start their relationship. Clift did not join the *Argus* staff before she met Johnston. It was not until after the war that she moved, along with her superior officer, Howard Kingham, who may have had a hand in it, when Errol Knox himself invited her onto the paper. He had seen a copy of *For Your Information* and had been impressed by her work, so much so that despite her lack of formal training he placed her on the Women's Supplement, probably as a secretary at first, but with a writing position in mind. '. . . there wasn't ever going to anything else ever, ever, except being a writer,' she believed of herself.[17]

From the beginning, their love was more than physical. They took their own and each other's writing aspirations seriously, and talked to each other excitedly about literature. She probably talked as much about poetry as about fiction at this stage, but it is likely even in these early days of their relationship that they hatched plans to write novels together. Clift told Greeba Jamison in the office that she desperately wanted to become a serious writer. Johnston probably saw the writing of books more as a happy alternative to a lifetime of hack journalism, or for that matter editorial work. Their dream was that they could make those two aspirations complementary, and write their way to success as a team. But the blatancy of their passion obscured for some the imaginative and intellectual side of their relationship, and people talked as though sex was their only interest. Bruce Kneale himself made the mistake of treating their relationship lightly when he saw Clift sitting at a hotel bar one day looking a little the worse for drink and a late night, and said to Johnston: 'Look at her sitting there looking like the mother of all whores.'[18] Johnston visibly froze, and Kneale suddenly saw that what was between them was deadly serious, and that not all the years of their friendship were as important to Johnston as this relationship. Kneale could have bitten off his tongue.

In the office, their behaviour was a scandal. Some of the disapproval was out of sympathy for Elsie. Greeba Jamison recalls that 'they were both serenely indifferent, callous, careless about the fact that George was married, still living with Elsie, with a young daughter. We all knew and liked Elsie, and most of us were a bit disenchanted with George because of his treatment of Elsie — but we all liked Charmian too and she was an irresistible force.'[19] Some senior staff were more than disenchanted: here was a thirty-four-year-old Editor and twenty-three-year-old assistant behaving like teenage lovers in the precincts of a newspaper that prided itself on its dignified private and public image, and no one doing anything about it. The Chief of Staff, Jack Rasmussen, a devout Catholic, vehemently disapproved, as did Ted Doyle, who had recently become Managing Editor, and had been against Clift's appointment from the start, probably because she had not undergone a normal cadetship. The women on the staff of the social pages disapproved, too. Even Howard Kingham, her benefactor, turned against her. Kingham was particularly incensed one evening when Johnston, Clift, Kneale and one or two others stayed back after work drinking and making a noise in Johnston's office, and he muttered some scarcely veiled threat.[20] Most of the vitriol of the staff members was directed against Clift; it may have been felt that Johnston's position on the paper was unassailable.

Unhappily, Johnston continued to try to deceive Elsie. But she was astute enough to perceive that something was wrong, even if he was refusing to admit it, and even if he was still using the flat as his home, adding further to her dismal uncertainty. She became aware of Charmian's existence one day when she went to the *Argus* office and accompanied Johnston and a group of the staff to a pub across the road for lunch. Elsie and Charmian sat opposite each other. There were candles on the table, and Johnston leaned across and said to Charmian: 'Your eyes look beautiful by candlelight.' Elsie began to feel edged out, and to see what she was up against.[21]

Soon after, Johnston took Elsie to a party at the home of Dorothy Stevens, the ballerina. All evening Elsie could sense that people were putting themselves out to be pleasant to her. She took a taxi home, and Johnston drove Clift back to her apartment in South Yarra.[22] He even brought Clift to a party at the St Kilda flat, where she got drunk and was messily sick in the toilet. Elsie cleaned up after her. Meanwhile Johnston drove Clift home, and did not return until the morning. A few days later Elsie received a note of apology and a posy of violets from Charmian.[23] All the violets in the world, however, could not have driven off the stink of humiliation that Elsie felt clung to her.

So the prolonged agony of ending one relationship in the midst of the tumult of another went on, made worse by Johnston's tortuous vacillation. Admittedly his situation was difficult. He was not, by the laws of the time, in any position to sue for divorce. That course was up to Elsie, and so far the matter had not been seriously discussed. On the other hand, for a couple to go off and simply live together was a bold move, again in those days rarely contemplated. It would be especially difficult for Johnston and Clift, when so many people would know what their situation was. There was also the question of Gae to be considered, and Johnston already had some cause to feel guilty over her. He had hardly been a model father. His long absences abroad and his lack of commitment to her and her mother at home had made him something of a stranger, which meant of course that the child greatly idealised him, and yet it was an ideal that he never lived up to. One of her earliest memories of this time, when she was about five, is of being struck angrily across the face by the tie her father was attempting to put on when she was clinging to his leg in the bedroom.[24] Much of the time he lavished attention on her; but his moods and his uncertainties and his scenes with her mother made him an unpredictable and disturbing presence.

There might also have been a degree of uncertainty in Johnston's mind about how long he and Clift would last together. He had known beautiful and clever women before, but never one so brilliantly unfetterable. Years later, when putting together the first outlines for his Meredith trilogy, Johnston brought his extraordinary memory to bear on these early days of his relationship with Clift in order to lay the foundations for the eventual breakdown of Meredith's marriage to Cressida. The surviving notes make moving reading, for they have a distinct feeling of autobiographical truth about them. About Cressida, he observes 'her need to be courted and admired, her everlasting wistfulness for a wanton freedom, [to] swim up out of the mile long beach of childhood, out of the running freedom of her own solitudes, the miseries of playing second fiddle to somebody else, the pressures to escape from binding family tyrannies into a bigger and unrestricted world of gaiety and glamour and excitement'.[25] The word Meredith most often uses to describe Cressida is 'pagan', suggesting her uncivilised character. It is both his fortune and his misfortune to love her, for

> *She represents the unattainable prize, something more than he can ever hope to have achieved.* And she is his. *The most precious thing he has ever owned. To lose her would be to lose everything. Still struggling onward from the dreary little*

*house in Elsternwick, he has gained much, but nothing so
precious as this. He cannot afford to lose it. His jealousy,
however indefensible in cold-blooded logical terms, is just as
natural and as deeply embedded in his formative past as
Cressida's original honesty. For Cressida is Golden Boy's* real
laurel wreath.[26]

It is true that these notes were made almost twenty years
later, when Johnston was struggling to come to terms with
what had by then become an intense jealousy of Clift's
'pagan' ways. But it is also true that he is drawing upon his
memory of what they were both like when they first met, and
his suspicion, even then, that he might not be able to handle
Clift's irrepressible desire for freedom. This quality in her
raised deep-seated doubts in his view of himself, a view that
went back to his working-class background. Charmian was a
great prize, a prize awarded for his sudden success in the
newspaper world. But that success was to a large extent a
trick, a slice of luck dealt to him by the war and by his own
capacity to 'sell himself' to the right people. Underneath he
believed he was not the brilliant journalist he was taken to
be, and that the tag 'golden boy' sometimes had a disquieting
note of irony about it. It is often the working-class boy's
legacy to feel that however high he climbs the ladder of
success, he is never the rightful owner of the prizes, that he
has gained them by default, and that at any moment his fraud
will be discovered and he will be back on his arse where he
belongs. He possessed Charmian Clift for the moment, but
would he be able to hang onto her?

Meanwhile Johnston continued on with what he, and his
staff, felt was the right course with the *Australasian Post*. But
here, too, he was having his difficulties. The board of directors was constantly insisting on greater circulation for the
journal, and yet Errol Knox was constantly resisting Johnston's attempts to enliven its image. Opinions differ as to
what Knox wanted. Bruce Kneale believes that Knox's temperamental conservatism made him oppose anything he considered 'American' or 'cheap', whereas Hume Dow points out
that later on, when the journal came under Knox's total control, the magazine plunged immediately into the mindless
depths where it has been ever since. What Johnston wanted

was to include serious current affairs, good features and fiction, along with pictures of bathing-suited girls and other commercial ploys in order to give the *Post* wider appeal, but Knox seemed to be opposing him in both aims. So they began to have heated rows — and both had fearful tempers — over the direction the *Post* should take. The favourite son was beginning to fall from grace. At the same time those influential figures on the staff began to pressurise Knox for Clift's dismissal. The enemies were closing in. Johnston told Hume Dow and others of his staff to begin looking for another job because he was intending to resign.[27]

One weekend Johnston and Clift went off to Portsea together (expurgating Leo Kenney?), and when they returned things came to a head with Elsie. He entered the flat once again as if it was his home, expecting a meal and a clean shirt, and finally Elsie's patience ran out. They had a row, she told him to get out, and he angrily roared off down the street in his car.[28] That night Johnston and Clift moved into the Post Office Hotel next to the 'old tin shed' in Elizabeth Street, and the pretence was over. Except for the legalities, the marriage between George and Elsie was finished.

It was soon obvious to everyone in the office what had happened, and the consequences were not long in coming. One day in July 1946 Johnston left the building on some duty or other, and in his absence Knox called Clift into his office. He told her that her behaviour with a married member of staff was intolerable, and she was summarily dismissed. Distraught, she went to Howard Kingham and pleaded with him to intervene on her behalf, but he refused. When Johnston returned to the office later that day, he was told what had happened. Such was his fury that despite the fact that Knox was in the middle of a board meeting, Johnston scrawled out his resignation, crashed into the meeting, flung the paper at Knox and snarled: 'This is the last time the woman pays — if she goes I go!'[29]

Bruce Kneale believes that Johnston did not, for one moment, expect Knox to accept his resignation. 'His golden boy, his own creation, whom he had, like Pygmalion, brought up from raw material and fashioned into the very journalist and war

85

correspondent that he wanted — George could never believe Knox would let him go.'[30] But Knox said that if that was the way Johnston wanted it, then he had better go. His resignation would take effect from 30 July 1946. Johnston was thunderstruck, says Kneale, and emerged from Knox's office ashenfaced. He and Clift left the office outcasts, but hardly from Paradise. A part of them was, on reflection, privately happy and proud of their defiance.

It was an act of great importance for Johnston, because it was the nearest thing to an heroic declaration he could make. What better way to lay claim to the prize than through a demonstration that she was more important than his career? What better way to keep her in his debt and ensure her faithfulness than by acting as her protector? He probably had no need to resort to such gallantries, for she was as besotted with him as he was with her. But it is difficult not to conclude that it had an effect of binding her to him even more securely, especially when in later years their marriage weathered storms that would have wrecked most others.

Both now unemployed, they retreated for some weeks to the bayside town of Sorrento, where they stayed in a bungalow owned by Sol McDermott, the proprietor of the Post Office Hotel in Melbourne. Here they went boating, considered their future, and began to write. Clift worked on short stories of her own, and Johnston had much to come to terms with, especially all that experience in Asia. He had already made a beginning on what was to be his first published novel, and had released the first chapter as a short story entitled 'Gharri-Wallah' in the 25 April issue of the *Post*. As the title suggests, it is about India, using the nationalist upheavals as background in a way that, while authentically depicted and well-informed, never becomes the stuff of a serious political novel. Its central character, Michael Casey, presents something of a credibility problem. He is a painter who has lived in India for twelve years, and, we discover early in the story, has a murky past, including a prison sentence for raping the young wife of his commanding officer (he turns out to be innocent). At the beginning of the novel Casey is deeply embittered and shows his hatred for the

English and Indians alike, so that he is a classic outsider figure. He is rescued from his malaise by his love for an American girl, Kylie York, who has Charmian Clift's green eyes and the job of exporting pig's bristles from China to make brushes, taken of course from Johnston's ex-missionary girl-friend from Kunming days. Through his affair with Kylie York, Casey is drawn into political intrigues that are reaching boiling point, and so his reinstatement into the world of human problems is complete. As a novel it is something of a missed opportunity, for Johnston's experiences in India did equip him with the knowledge to put together a serious work on Anglo-Indian relations from an outsider's point of view. But the writing is too often cliched and superficial, and there are too many stretches of descriptive padding. It was published by Angus & Robertson in 1948 – difficulty in getting paper would have slowed it up – under the title of *Moon at Perigee*, and then as *Monsoon* by Dodd, Mead in the USA in 1950 and Faber in the UK in 1951. It never achieved high sales anywhere, nor critical praise.

Sorrento was a breathing space and little more. It had apparently few idyllic moments for them – indeed they seem to have been tense and ratty with each other. Johnston writes about these weeks very briefly in *Clean Straw for Nothing* as a time when Meredith conducts himself 'foolishly, with unnecessary angers, and with a good deal of emotional instability' (*CSFN* 55). Even at this early stage he reveals his inclination to jealousy, accusing Cressida of flirting with Archie Calverton, and 'in a bar along the coast from the cottage, where we had both been drinking, she bit my finger to the bone while I was wagging it at her' (*CSFN* 55). How much biographical truth may be in this incident is impossible to say, but the Archie Calverton character here is unlikely to be drawn from Peter Finch, as he is in later parts of the novel. They probably did not meet Finch until they went to Sydney. What does feel authentic about the passage, however, is the strain that relations between Johnston and Clift were coming under in this time of refuge and uncertainty. Freedom is a two-edged sword.

Despite the fact that Johnston's reputation would easily get

him another job, and that they must have foreseen these
events to some degree, they had acted without plan, entirely
from impulse. This was characteristic of them both, and of the
effect they had on each other; again and again in their lives
they would spur each other on into situations of risk. It was
their way of escaping from circumstances that threatened to
trap them, or were seemingly unresolvable. The limb on
which they now found themselves seems to have been exactly
what they wanted, as if all Johnston's vacillations over the
previous months with Elsie were intended to create a situation that could be resolved only by an explosion. In that way
casualties can be justified as victims of uncontrollable forces,
rather than of calculation or moral evasion. And Charmian,
who was by temperament the calmer and more farsighted of
the two, allowed this to happen; she might easily, for instance, have steered George into more discretion around the
office, or suggested he look for another job before he resigned
from the *Argus*. But such was not their way. The break with
Elsie and Gae, with Leo Kenney, with the *Argus*, with Johnston's family (whom Charmian had only briefly met), with
moral censure, and indeed with Melbourne itself, were all
achieved in one decisive rupture. It meant that they could not
stay around Melbourne, where their circumstances were
known. Nor did they want to, for this was not their spiritual
home: George had outgrown it, Charmian had never belonged to it. They needed a looser, freer environment in
which to start afresh.

~·~·~·~·~·~·~·~·~·· C H A P T E R V ~··~··~·~··~·~·~·~·

Northern Pastures

*If there is any particular area of one's life which nostalgically
one would like to live through again without any change
whatever — and there are few that beckon back — I am pretty
sure this would be it. (CSFN 58)*

The move to Sydney was another impulsive choice. Johnston
and Clift had given an army friend of Clift, Janice Benta, a lift
to Spencer Street station to catch the train to Sydney, where
she was returning after her discharge. As she left, Johnston
and Clift were touched with envy, and suddenly they saw no
reason why they should not head for Sydney, too. They
quickly packed their belongings into Johnston's car, said the
most perfunctory goodbyes to family and friends, and drove
north. On the way they decided they would stop off at Kiama
to visit Charmian's parents.

If Johnston harboured any apprehension about the reception he might get from the Clifts — he was after all a married
man living 'in sin' with their daughter — it was soon dispel-
led. After a strong dose of the Johnston charm they warmed
greatly to him. Sid Clift was impressed by his knowledge and
experience of the world, and Amy, with whom George flirted
and nicknamed 'hubba', liked his humour and openness.[1]
Moreover, Amy was delighted with his being a writer, which
probably counted more with her than his being an unemployed journalist. The Clifts were not the sort to adopt lofty
moral postures about the relationship; they saw the situation
for what it was, accepted it immediately, and indeed gave the

couple every encouragement to stay together. All this created an atmosphere of such warmth that Johnston and Clift extended their stay in Kiama by some weeks, turning it, in effect, into a honeymoon. It was spring, and they spent most of their time lazing on Bombo Beach, or making tours of Clift's childhood playgrounds.

They were often to look back on these days with deep fondness. In *Clean Straw for Nothing* Johnston becomes at times excessively lyrical in his attempts to recapture their intoxication with the place, with each other, indeed with life itself in those golden weeks. In the passage titled 'Lebanon Bay' (a reference to the Lebanese cedars that are a feature of Kiama), Johnston makes David Meredith reflect: 'during this time in Lebanon Bay we have been given our own small vision of Paradise, and this share of Paradise has been contained and complete in itself . . . it will mark both of our futures indelibly, but we are not to know it yet.' What he means by this reference to the future is that whenever things were going badly between them, and the marriage looked like foundering, the depths they touched in each other at Kiama enabled it to survive. It was not just the memory of that time: it was that a bond had been formed that proved stronger than any threat from outside, and stronger than any incidents of betrayal, keeping them together even when common sense may have dictated that it would have been wiser to separate and go their own ways. 'You two would destroy each other,' says Gavin Turley in *Clean Straw for Nothing* (p.28), by which Johnston is, much later in their lives, giving expression to his belief that whatever tragic fate may be in store for them, they would undergo it together, that they would bring each other down rather than separate. Such Brontëan extremes may seem like self-indulgent fantasies, until one observes the evidence of their final years.

It was not long before reality began to encroach upon their Kiama paradise. They had some savings, but it was obvious that eventually they would need an income. More pressing was a place to live and work, and when they arrived in Sydney in the late months of 1946 apartments were rare and expensive. Eventually they found a tiny furnished flat in

Manly, which took a crippling bite out of their savings in key money — an exploitation that flourishes in hard times — even though it was a dismal place in which to live. In October the long saga of *Skyscrapers in the Mist* climaxed when it finally appeared in print, but it sold too badly to make any improvement in the bank balance, and did nothing for Johnston's reputation; the book had been a misconception from the beginning, despite some lively pages.

Johnston had asked Elsie for a divorce, but she was resisting. He wrote to her demanding the return of some of the gifts he had brought her from Asia — jewellery, ornaments, clothing materials — so that he could give them to Charmian.[2] No doubt this did not help to soften Elsie's attitude.

Broke as they were, Johnston delayed making moves to get a job. Instead, typically, he began a new novel, tearing into it with fury. This time it was a thriller with the arresting title of *Death Takes Small Bites*, and he was clearly looking to make some quick money from it. Drawing freely on his experiences in China, especially of Yunnan province and the roads to and from Tibet, Johnston weaves a confusing story of intrigue between corrupt Chinese and American capitalistis interested in opium and Tibetan oil. The novel also re-enacts Johnston's triumph over Leo Kenney: the heroine, a strong-minded American nurse called Charmian, is wooed away from her dedicated doctor fiancé by the somewhat ineffectual hero, a newspaperman called — in the novel's one moment of comic flair — Cavendish Cavendish. *Death Takes Small Bites* contains stretches of competent formula writing, but generally it is spurious and poorly plotted, and is plagued with some of the worst prose Johnston ever wrote. He knew it, and later told his agent he thought it was 'a pretty lousy book'.[3] Others thought so too: if he did offer it to Angus & Robertson, which is likely, they turned it down — an unprecedented move in their relations. But perhaps the recent experience with *Skyscrapers in the Mist* had prompted them to a little wariness about Johnston's 'quickies'. He sent the novel to the Curtis Brown agency in London, and they managed to sell it to Gollancz for publication in 1948. In the end it paid its way: Dodd, Mead published it in the United States also in 1948, and then in 1959 it was re-issued in Penguin. In 1951 it was translated into French and published under the puzzling title of *A Petit Feu*, selling over 100,000 copies.[4]

For the moment, however, Johnston was scratching about for projects that would pay the rent. By not taking jobs, he and Clift were evidently giving themselves a taste of living as full-time writers. More important, they were giving themselves the chance to write something more serious than previous efforts, and furthermore to do it together. Either very late in 1946 or early in 1947 they set to work on their first joint novel, using once again his Tibetan experiences, but this time with the story provided by Clift.

Some time early in 1947 Johnston attended a luncheon at the Rhinecastle cellars in Sydney, and found himself in conversation with a young man called Albert Arlen. They talked about wine, and about writing. Arlen was still in the RAAF, stationed at Singapore, and was enthusiastic about writing a musical. Johnston said he would like to collaborate in the venture, but they decided to postpone it until Arlen got his discharge the following year. This could have suited Johnston, because by this time he was flat out working on the new novel, which was progressing well. Clift did not work by his side the whole time: the flat was so dingy and cramped that she took her typewriter down to Kiama on occasions and did her writing there. Sometimes Johnston went too — Margaret can remember them working together on the veranda of her parents' home, buried in pages of typescript and clouded in cigarette smoke, busy and happily collaborating.[5]

In April, Charmian found she was pregnant. Johnston immediately began to use this to put pressure on Elsie for the divorce, and this time she relented. The decree nisi came through on 28 April, but Johnston was not permitted to remarry before the expiry of a further three months. Elsie, being the innocent party in the terms of divorce of those times, was granted custody of Gae, but George did not contest this. Johnston and Clift married in the Manly registry on 7 August amid a small group of friends. Clift was looking 'radiant and unashamedly with child',[6] and both of them apparently treated the occasion as something of a joke. Afterwards they went back to the apartment of journalist friend, Arthur Polkinghorne, and his wife, Monica, who had arranged a party without telling most of the guests that it was a wedding celebration. For the Johnstons and the Polking-hornes it was an 'hilarious day'. Not long after the marriage they found a better flat in Simpson Street, Bondi; not grand, but with two bedrooms and a sitting-room, which George transformed into something of their own by painting several murals on the walls.

The joint novel was completed in the latter half of 1947, and its title, after that breathless scene that had confronted John-ston up in the Tibetan mountains two years earlier, was *High Valley*. Once again the central character is made to be something of an outsider figure. Salom, whose parents have been killed in the Chinese civil war of the 1920s, in the first communist uprisings, is adopted and raised by Tibetans. When he is grown to manhood, he goes down into China to live with his own people, but he is unhappy because the Chinese make fun of his Tibetan clothes and his outlandish speech. A wise old Chinese advises him to return to Tibet and seek happiness in a place called the Valley of the Dream-ing Phoenix. For all its beauty, this high valley is a place of hard work and cruel winters, and, while remote from the strife that plagues the rest of the world, it is at the same time a closed society dominated by narrow customs and religious corruption. Salom falls in love with Veshti, the daughter of the valley's headman, but Veshti is promised to another, and Salom is warned off. The couple disregard the warnings and the threats of a corrupt lama, and attempt to escape from the valley in the midst of one of its worst winters, only to die tragically.

As popular romance, *High Valley* is engaging, well written and was easily the best thing either of them had done to that stage. The clear, lyrical descriptions of the landscape and way of life are brimming with Johnston's Tibetan experience, and similarly the affecting love story between Salom and Veshti is a correlative of an intensity of feeling which, of course, the authors themselves knew more than a little about at that time. Their enthusiasm for the task is evident on almost every page. Before it was offered for publication, however, the script was sent off to the *Sydney Morning Herald* as an entry in their recently established £2000 Literary Competition. Entries had to be unpublished and submitted under a *nom de plume*.

With the book finished and the child due very soon, Johnston decided it was time to take a job. He had friends such as Arthur Polkinghorne and Mungo MacCallum senior (whom he'd met in Melbourne during the war) working on the *Sun*, so he applied for and was instantly given a feature-writing role. The *Sun* had some good writers then, and several — Alan Reid, John Hetherington, Kenneth Slessor — were to make significant names in Australian writing. Within a couple of months of his appointment Johnston was given a by-line, which appeared every day under 'Sydney Diary'. This 'Diary' was soon an enormous success. As well as the usual sport and crime stories, it ran items of general cultural and political interest that were lively and informative. In some respects it was the newspaper version of a radio talkback show, inviting opinions and stories from readers, and replying to their questions.

One issue Johnston raised takes on a certain irony in retrospect. He deplored the need for so much of Australia's artistic talent to find better pastures abroad. 'Most of them are youngsters,' he wrote, 'all of them are intelligent, and all are bitter about the frustrations and stultifications about our current national way of life. Artists, writers, musicians, scholars, are finding that Australia offers them insufficient encouragement ...' for Australian life, he complains, is 'dominated by Randwick, Bradman and the White Australia Policy'.[7] This stream represented the cultural cream of that post-war generation, all bent on expatriating themselves to Europe. Johnston mentions no names in the article, but he would have had no trouble in compiling an impressive list that included Peter Finch, Joan Sutherland, Robert Helpmann, Paul Brickhill, Cedric Flower, Sidney Nolan, Albert Tucker, Arthur Boyd, Len Williams and his guitarist son, John, and many others. At the time of writing the article Johnston could hardly have known that he and Clift were also to join the stream in a couple of years, and would eventually become identified in the

Australian imagination with everything that expatriation signifies.

'Sydney Diary' was in some respects Johnston's best journalistic creation. Its energy and wide-ranging concerns, from tracing lost pets and the price of food right up to loftier matters, such as fears about the discovery of uranium in the Northern Territory — 'wouldn't it be awful if one of the Great Powers decided we have to be "protected"?'[8] he wrote in 1948 — all contributed to the development of his education as a writer. Specifically, it engaged him in a dialogue with his readership that was free from the narrow constraints of shipping reporting and the temptations of war correspondence, requiring him to recognise and write about a broad spectrum of matters that concerned Australian readers.

Continuing his Melbourne tradition, now that he was back in the newspaper world, Johnston became a gregarious member of the Sydney fraternity, meeting either at Cahill's Coffee House in Castlereagh Street or at the Long Bar of the Australia Hotel. There he was at his most garrulous, always assuming the centre of attention, telling stories of his war adventures or provoking arguments over politics, often infuriating people to distraction, but rarely boring them. He began to acquire, too, in those days of Cold War paranoia, something of a reputation for being a communist. Because of his knowledge of China, and the topicality of the struggles continuing between the communists and the Kuomintang, Johnston talked often and sweepingly about his belief that communism would rid China of its political corruption. Frank Brown, who wrote the column 'Things I Hear' for the *Sun*, complained to the chiefs that Johnston was a communist supporter and should be sacked.[9] There is a passage in *Clean Straw for Nothing* in which Meredith is prevented from publishing a series of articles expressing sympathy with the Chinese communists by his Editor, Bernard Brewster. The passage represents Johnston's time on the Melbourne *Argus*, and it may well be drawn from an actual experience on that paper. Certainly Errol Knox would have opposed any such pieces appearing under *his* imprimatur. Equally, Johnston may have run into some admonition for similar reasons on the *Sun*, especially as Mao's side pushed closer to the Revolution during 1948, and the prospects of Australia being overrun by the 'yellow peril' appeared to some people to be a growing reality. Anyone who knew Johnston could not have taken him seriously as a political agitator, nor as a general promoter of left-wing causes. Nor, for that matter, did he have much working-class loyalty. He told journalist Charles Sriber on more than one occasion 'my father drove a tram in Carlton, and I got out of the bloody working-class and I don't ever want to get back to it'.[10] Johnston would never have put politics before his personal interests.

It was in the Long Bar that he met up with Albert Arlen again, and this time they got down to something definite about a musical. Arlen had begun setting *The Sentimental Bloke* to music and wanted Johnston to do the libretto. 'George was so excited about it that he took me round to George Ferguson of Angus & Robertson the very next day to secure a contract for the performing rights,' recalled Arlen.[11] For all his enthusiasm, Johnston discovered that his natural fluency was something of a handicap for stage-writing: when he went to Arlen's house for dinner a couple of months later, taking Charmian and Cedric and Pat Flower along to let them hear what they had done so far, Johnston said he would first read his synopsis. The result was a little alarming. 'After George had been reading for an hour,' recalls Arlen, 'Nancy [Arlen's wife] stopped him, saying "George, this synopsis will run for four nights, and there's still all the music to fit in!" He did not understand the theatrical form. We outlined and suggested a story line, and he said he would follow this.'[12] His confidence was somewhat damaged by the occasion, however, and he found it hard to sustain interest in the project.

Despite having the reputation, along with Mungo MacCallum, of now being the highest paid journalist in Sydney,[13] money was still a problem. He had always spent it as fast as it came — on books, wine, eating out — and, considering his earnings both by means of good salaries and the royalties on books and overseas articles since the war, he had little in material terms to show for it. He and Charmian had lived on his savings while he was unemployed, but any dreams of financial independence were now out of the question. Charmian had given birth to their son Martin in November of 1947, and this meant that Johnston's wages now had to support a Sydney household, as well as the one in Melbourne.

Johnston's difficulties may have been brought home to him more strongly by his friendship with MacCallum, who had married into the wealthy Wentworth family. MacCallum himself was aware of the contrast,[14] and whenever the Johnstons went to dinner at MacCallum's large home at Point Piper, one of the more expensive areas on the harbour, there was an unspoken but distinct sense of class difference in the air. Perhaps nowhere else did Johnston feel his working-class background more than here, although it did not in any way make him resentful of MacCallum. On the contrary, he had an admiration to the point of snobbery for things he considered 'substantial' or 'genuine', and this could mean anything from a good education to owning silver cutlery and original paintings rather than prints. It was not just money that made MacCallum different, but the fact that he came from a noted family distinguished in scholarship, and was surrounded by heirlooms that one did not even discuss in terms of money. This seemed to Johnston to make all the obsession with tasteful decor of the Australian middle class seem hollow and despicable. His feelings about these matters are very clearly indicated in *My Brother Jack*, where David and Helen Meredith go to dinner at the rambling Victorian mansion of Gavin Turley and his wife, Peggy. Turley is Australian *noblesse*, and there is a shabby grandeur about the way he lives, surrounded by valuable things, all of which have an impressively 'heavy' and 'substantial' (terms which Meredith frequently uses) feel about them. The dinner is a 'simple and wonderful' steak-and-kidney pie and vegetables brought to the table in an enamel dish, and added to all this is Turley's own easy and unhurried social confidence, stemming from his not needing to claw his way up any social ladders. All of this is shown to be in stark contrast with the way in which the Merediths are living under Helen's constricting reign, where coloured candles and fussy dinner parties are part of a set of suburban aspirations that Meredith is finding increasingly phoney and claustrophobic.

That dinner with the Turleys is based on one MacCallum remembers at his house quite well, even down to the steak-and-kidney pie, although it was not Johnston's first wife who accompanied him, but Charmian. And it was not, as the novel states, in the Melbourne suburb of Toorak that it took place, but at Point Piper in Sydney. As an expression of Johnston's sense of social inferiority, Turley is an interesting character, because he represents everything that David Meredith (and Johnston) was not. Of course he is not simply a representation of Mungo MacCallum: there are three journalist colleagues drawn upon for the creation of Turley: MacCallum, Geoffrey Hutton and Bruce Kneale.[15] Different as they all were from one another, they had certain things in common that contrasted with Johnston himself, and for him that contrast was a telling one. Each had received a private school education; each had taken a University degree; each had, outwardly at least, an appearance of having a right to his place in the world, which, to Johnston, gave them an enviable confidence, at least in their young days. Compared with them, Johnston felt uneducated, insecure, and that he was something of an impostor. Consequently, in a perfectly understandable attempt to compensate for these failings, his behaviour in front of others was often know-all, ultra-confident and self-important. He would, in other words, determinedly out-do them in areas where they had an advantage. This included writing, since they all wrote seriously quite apart from their standard journalism, and it was part of Johnston's ambition, too, to be a better and more successful writer than any of them. There was always, therefore, a sense in which his relations with these and other journalists had, in its very gregariousness, a competitive edge to it. Thus Charles Sriber, who was often one of the group of journalists at Cahill's Coffee House or the Long Bar, felt that 'he was always playing the big man ... always on stage ... always had to be the man who dominated the conversation ... and to lesser known journalists he could be very patronising'.[16]

One of the ironies of Johnston's envy of MacCallum was

that in certain respects MacCallum had cause to envy him. Neil Hutchison, head of Features at ABC radio then, and to whom Johnston had recently been introduced by MacCallum, perceived a love/hate relationship between the two colleagues, who were not only friends and drinking companions, but rivals as well. Their personalities were in total contrast. Mac-Callum, says Hutchison, was one of those people who said 'no' to life, whereas 'George said "yes" to everything ... Here was MacCallum, the intellectual, unpopular but profound, and there were Charmian and George, unprofound but surrounded by people who loved them'.[17] Specifically, Hutchison is thinking of the open house that the Johnstons kept at the flat every Saturday night. The first time he went there to that 'squalid little Bondi flat', Hutchison found the place swarming with literati and budding notables, including William Dobell, Kenneth Slessor, Paul Brickhill, John Thompson the poet, Ruth Park and D'Arcy Niland, as well as newspaper and radio people such as Wilfred Thomas, Arthur Polkinghorne, Danny Speight (who had been in China with Johnston), Norman Eristone and Richard Lane. According to Lane, Peter Finch had been an occasional attender, but by mid-1948 he had left for England. The point Hutchison is making is that MacCallum, and indeed several other people, for all their better-informed, more incisive minds, could never match the magnetic capacity to attract people to them in the way that the Johnstons consistently did. They may have been nobodies in terms of social status, and they were from the cultural back-blocks so far as Sydney was concerned, but they had a vitality and a generosity that people found irresistible. They sought attention, of course, and thrived on it, despite the fact that it was not always good for their work.

Their financial situation was considerably improved in May 1948 when *High Valley* won the *Sydney Morning Herald* prize. The £2000 purse was the price of a three-bedroomed home at that time, though of course they did not think for one moment of doing anything so security-minded with the money. No doubt most of it went on books, good living and paying off debts. A more important result of winning the prize was the effect it had on their reputations as writers. It put Clift's name on the map, and for Johnston it did more than any previous works to establish him in the public's mind as a novelist, rather than as a journalist who produced the occasional book. Angus & Robertson were rather slow in getting it out, but when it did appear in mid-1949 it was warmly reviewed. Sadly, W. G. Cousins, who had been Johnston's devoted editor right from the start of his relationship with Angus & Robertson, died before he could know the full extent of the success of this, their most successful venture together. The *Sydney Morning Herald* judges had praised it for 'writing of real distinction', and the *Argus* reviewer for its 'brilliant descriptive style'. Later, when it was published abroad, the terms were equally complimentary. Such success made them, during 1949 at least, the literary toasts of Sydney.

It was, perhaps, the fact that they wrote as a team that caught people's imaginations. There were other well-known writing couples, such as Ruth Park and D'Arcy Niland, but somehow the fact of marriage partners succeeding in a single artistic venture raised feelings about the perfect relationship, combining all those usually incompatible professional, imaginative and domestic elements into a harmony that cut right across socially determined roles. People assumed that, against all the odds, they must have had a perfect understanding, and there is no evidence from those days that they did not. Zelda, the wife of American novelist F. Scott Fitzgerald, was once asked what she did to help in the writing of his books. 'I just fuck,' she replied, with the bitter honesty of the satellite wife. Johnston and Clift did more: they fed ideas to each other, read and criticised each other's work, and loyally sustained each other's commitment to the task in hand. The writing of *High Valley*, said Johnston, was a 'fair fifty-fifty . . . she is the better writer, I the better journalist'. Charmian told a publisher that her education was 'negligible until taken over by my husband'.[18] As for their love life, they both shocked Neil Hutchison by openly declaring that they 'made love together every night',[19] often the consummation of an evening's writing together. It was a formula, at least in those spring days of their relationship, that worked wonderfully well for them both.

Towards the end of 1948 Johnston was promoted to the position of Features Editor on the *Sun*, and Arthur Polkinghorne took over the writing of 'Sydney Diary'. By this time the Johnstons had begun to write dramatised features for radio, a development that came about through their contact with Neil Hutchison. They might even have begun these early in that year, because there is a photograph of them both with Peter Finch at 2UE, and he had departed for England by mid-1948. In any case it made a change from writing only for readers, and it was a change that they both made, but especially Clift, with enjoyment and easy facility. Evidently they were now alert to the demand for succinctness in writing dramatised material, and so good were their ideas and scripts that Hutchison was able to build a whole ABC production team around them, and in the ensuing two years produced many excellent programmes that were to form a platform for what was arguably the finest era in Australian radio. The features they wrote were on a wide range of topics, from 'Nefertiti of Egypt' to problems of migrants in Australia in the 1940s and on the revolution in China. Another topic was a 'diary' series, which included titles such as 'Diary of an Unhappy Marriage', 'Diary of a Cad' and 'Diary of a Modern Woman', by Clift on her own, which shows an advanced interest in problems faced by a woman divided between career and home. The word 'facility' is meant to be a two-edged one in describing their approach to these radio features, because they seemed to Hutchison to toss them off with an amazing speed, having done extremely little research for them. They once told him that for a programme on the Greek poet Sappho they now 'knew everything because they had spent the whole day in the Public Library reading up'![20] And yet, despite their magpie approach to gathering material, and their reliance on imagination more than information, they produced, according to Hutchison, 'well-written, bright' scripts that made excellent radio features of just the kind he wanted.

They continued writing for radio throughout 1949, but there were signs that novel-writing was becoming too much of a struggle, especially if George was going to remain in the newspaper game. When their daughter, Shane, was born in February, Charmian's capacity to write was even further curtailed. The demands of family life were beginning to make inroads into the dream of becoming full-time writers, a dream they often mentioned to friends. In this year it seems they had, for the first time since they had met, no substantial writing project in hand. With two small children to care for, Charmian was, in that familiar way, frustratingly restricted. She had a good friend and confidante in Toni Burgess, who occupied a neighbouring flat with her child, and the two women spent a good deal of time together, keeping each other cheerful and holding long, spirited conversations. They shared an interest in poetry, of which, recalls Burgess, Clift could recite reams by heart: Chinese verse, T. S. Eliot, Donne, Louis MacNeice, Auden and Dylan Thomas, 'whom we both thought we had discovered'.[21] Despite the frustrations, Clift seemed happy, and was a conscientious mother, with 'a marvellous sense of hope and expectancy about her,' says Burgess, who also felt that at times George was less than a perfect husband. On one occasion the two women spent the day getting drunk on home brew they had made, and when Johnston came home they were falling about with laughter and sticking pins into an effigy of their landlady. Johnston flew into a needless rage and then retreated into cold silence for the rest of the evening.

In fact coldness, and a certain edginess, is something Burgess remembers as common in Johnston during this time. There are reasons to suppose he was going through bouts of unhappiness, not with Charmian, but with himself. He was certainly drinking a great deal, and not just socially, and chain-smoking as much as ever. Mungo MacCallum recalls that after Johnston began on the *Sun* he was dogged by doubts about himself, especially as a writer. He knew that his inveterate facility was a danger, but he was unable to curb it. 'It just pours out,' he told MacCallum, with an air of apology.[22] The fact that he was assertive in public among his journalist friends, as has been indicated before, was no indication of real confidence within himself. On the contrary, it was necessary for him to be 'interesting', to be the centre of attention, to be the 'tough, trench-coated reporter',[23] as John Moses once wrote about his image in the eyes of some young reporters, and it was necessary for him to impress this upon the world. And yet it barely masked an element of congenital *naïveté* in him, an innocence about the world that laid him open to being occasionally surprised by the way it works. Charles Sriber recalls how he researched a story about prostitution in King's Cross, for which he had to obtain permission from the Chief Commissioner of Police to publish. When that permission was refused, Johnston protested in the office with a shocked indignation that even the junior reporters found hard to believe, 'It looks as if *they* are in it too!'[24]

The edginess was also a sign that he was getting itchy feet, anxious for a complete change. What he really wanted was to get out of journalism altogether, but of course lack of money prevented it. Besides, even to come up with a best-seller would not, in the limited Australian market, bring in enough funds to enable him to give up his job. As far as he could see, he would always have to be a part-time novelist. (There was little to be had from the Commonwealth Literary Fund in those days.) Johnston complained bitterly about the plight of Australian writers in a *Sun* article titled 'Why Write A Book?', pointing out that a win at the races or a 'find-the-ball' competition attracted no tax at all, whereas a writer such as himself or Ruth Park, who was struggling to subsist in a Sydney slum, lost more than half of their £2000 *Sydney Morning Herald* prize to the tax man. The government, he complained, looked more favourably on gambling than on talent and years of hard work. 'In Australia', he writes, 'the author is ground down immediately beneath the crushing inelasticity of a system which could − and often does − drive him to some other country or even into some other less imaginative and less frustrating profession'.[25] Clearly, thoughts of expatriation were already crossing his mind.

Late in 1949 he received the good news that the American publishers Bobbs-Merrill had agreed to do a US edition of *High Valley*, for which they were prepared to undertake a $10,000 promotion campaign, and they were anticipating good sales. The news must have raised the Johnstons' hopes of financial independence. It also inspired them to start a new novel: Bobbs-Merrill had asked them to supply a biographical sketch of themselves, and when they sent it off early in 1950 it included the comment: 'At the moment we are collaborating on a second and more ambitious novel, "The Piping Cry", which I hope you will have the opportunity of seeing.'[26] Once they had got started, this new project took up all their energy and writing time; Albert Arlen was still pressing Johnston for his contribution to *The Sentimental Bloke* musical, but was told that it would have to wait until the new project was completed.

It is worth spending a little time here on the details of 'The Piping Cry', because it represents Johnston and Clift's first attempt at an Australian novel, and because the manuscript disappeared mysteriously without trace, and it is unlikely that it will ever be recovered. They had been criticised for choosing exotic subjects in their novels, and one review of *High Valley* had complained that 'their admirers will wish that George Johnston and Charmian Clift had decided to give them the Great Australian Novel with one of our own aboriginal race as hero',[27] a piece of advice that one is grateful they did not take. But while they did want to write on an Australian subject, they depended so much on actual experience for their subject-matter that they were waiting until sufficient new experience came readily into focus. Once they got it under way — by about January 1950 — they began drawing on recent material close to their own lives. What little is known about 'The Piping Cry' at this stage is obtainable from three publisher's readers' reports that were made to Bobbs-Merrill in the United States. These reports indicate that it was a serious attempt to write about Australian philistinism in the late 1940s.

'The Piping Cry' has five main characters: Adam Reeves, an artist; his model and mistress, Lily; Kettering, an artist who has 'sold out' to become an advertising executive, and is Reeves's rival for Lily; Julie, one-time fiancée of Reeves and the daughter of a big advertising executive; and, finally, Harris Ogilvey, an alcoholic ex-writer.

Reeves and Kettering were at art school together, the two star pupils, but Kettering has the greater assurance, possibly the greater talent, and is more successful with women. Kettering wins a foreign scholarship and goes off to Europe; Reeves goes into the army when the war breaks out. After the war, Kettering returns and goes into advertising. The two men meet, and their old rivalry resumes, with Reeves struggling to be a serious painter and Kettering always assuming superiority. Reeves acquires a model and a mistress in Lily, but he soon begins to suspect that Kettering is trying to take her from him. When she mysteriously stops coming to see him, Reeves is convinced that she has gone to Kettering.

Meanwhile, Julie and Kettering have arranged a one-man exhibition for Reeves, which is to be his big opportunity to make his mark on the art world. He works furiously, taking risks in his painting prompted by his anger at losing Lily and the brandy to which he increasingly resorts. The exhibition is less than a resounding success: the pictures sell well at first, but this is because of the excellent promotional work of Julie and Kettering. When the reviews come out the critics are unenthusiastic; they praise his technical skill, but accuse him of uncertainty, immaturity and of having nothing to say. Reeves is devastated, believing he has lost everything. Wrongly presuming that Lily has gone to Kettering, when she has in fact been reluctantly involved with another man in order to protect her sister, Reeves challenges Kettering to a fight, which he promptly loses. The novel closes with Reeves alone with Harris Ogilvey, the broken-down writer, each drowning his sorrows in brandy.

Bobbs-Merrill's readers praised the style of the writing and its power to evoke Sydney Bohemian life. 'No other book or manuscript that I have encountered has brought out for me the life and appearance of a big Australian city as this one does', writes one of them. But they all found the story of the bruised artist, misunderstood by critics and society in general, trite and uninteresting. One wonders what Australian readers would have made of it, since the theme has a special local relevance, in that Johnston and Clift were obviously attempting to make a point about the relation of artists to

Australian society at the time.

Certain details in the reports suggest fascinating similarities with *My Brother Jack*. Consider that Reeves suffered from 'an unhappy and narrowing early environment' and was 'misunderstood by his parents', was an art student who befriended a more confident and successful colleague, was riddled with 'doubts and self-distrust', is tied to a female who wants to make him respectable, and is seduced away from her by a beautiful and precocious girl, and one cannot help noticing the similarity to David Meredith's rejection by his parents, his self-disparagement, and his relationships with Sam Burlington, Helen Midgeley and Cressida Morley. It all suggests, of course, that even at this early stage Johnston had planned that his first *Australian* novel would be autobiographical, and would follow the pattern of his own emergence from working-class obscurity to relative prominence, focusing closely on his own uncertainties, as he eventually did in *My Brother Jack*.

Moreover, what we can glean of 'The Piping Cry' suggests that Johnston, with the help of Clift, was attempting to dramatise a crisis in his life at that time. Indeed, it may well have been a crisis for both of them. The characters of Reeves and Kettering polarise the question: 'What kind of artist (writer) am I going to be, a serious one or a commercial one?' Further, if he was to fail as a serious one would he become a broken-down wreck like Harris Ogilvey?' Johnston and Clift may have been putting these questions to themselves, for they were undoubtedly feeling that they had come to crossroads in their writing lives. It all hinged on money, and Johnston's remaining in journalism. With two children and Elsie and Gae to support, Johnston and Clift felt trapped and frustrated. He was, according to Neil Hutchison, consistently drinking too much, and spoke of being concerned about his health. And being now thirty-eight years old, he was reaching that familiar stage of personal crisis when it was beginning to seem that most of his days of challenge and excitement were behind him. Much of this crisis seems to have been seriously expressed in 'The Piping Cry', and it is a great pity that the manuscript was lost, and that no publisher, in the end, either wanted or had the chance to publish it.

The biographical sketches of themselves that the Johnstons sent to Bobbs-Merrill in early 1950 contain the interesting comment that they would 'leave for London at the end of this year and should be there for three years or so'. So as early as a year in advance they knew they were going to be living abroad, although it was clearly envisaged that it was for a specific period of time, after which they would return home. Their opportunity came through Johnston receiving yet another promotion, this time by being put in charge of the London office of Associated Newspaper Services, the group that owned the *Sun*. The news could hardly have come at a better time, and enabled them to forget their frustrations for the time being at least, and to look forward to something that they both had always wanted so much: to see Europe.

In July 1950 a phone call came through to Johnston's office from Pat Johnston in Melbourne saying that his father was seriously ill and might not have long to live. How quickly he received the message is unknown, but the family were dismayed at the length of time it took him to arrive at Buxton Street.[28] When Pat Johnston rang again, she was told that George had left for Melbourne the day before. Pat believes that he went directly to see Elsie and took her out to dinner, but Elsie flatly denies that they were together. Mr Johnston died two hours before George arrived, on 7 July. His sister Marjorie, who had come all the way from South Australia, and his brother and sister-in-law were bitterly disappointed with him, especially since they had had to listen to his father asking whether or not George had come yet. Indeed, so eager were they to satisfy Mr Johnston's desire to see his son that, according to Pat, they took the extraordinary measure of dressing Jean's eldest son, who was roughly George's build, in George's old war correspondent's uniform and telling the almost blind Mr Johnston that it was in fact his son. He hugged the figure, believing it to be George, and died deceived.[29]

Afterwards Pat berated George angrily. In his defence he protested that he had been unable to face the sight of his father suffering. He was about to wear a red tie to the funeral, until Pat demanded he put on one more appropriate. When he returned to Sydney he told Hazel Tulley, one of the reporters in the office, that he had 'cursed [his father] into his grave'.[30] If there was not deliberate malice in any of this, it amounted to a particularly callous form of disrespect.

Busy though they must have been in the remaining months of 1950, planning for the move to London, Johnston and Clift kept writing as always. No doubt they wanted the coffers to be as full as possible when they left, so they wrote several more radio features between August and November, and Johnston completed a new pot-boiler, provisionally titled 'Murder by Horoscope', which he sent off to his newly acquired London agent, Pearn, Pollinger & Higham. At the time they were still wrestling with 'The Piping Cry', which was proving difficult, probably because it demanded more concentration than it was now possible for them to give it. They decided they would have to work properly on it when they got to London. There was, too, the persisting problem of *The Sentimental Bloke* musical, for which Albert Arlen, and no doubt Angus & Robertson, were growing impatient. This also was postponed until London. At least they would not arrive with nothing to do!

With flats so hard to come by in Sydney, Charmian promised her friend Toni Burgess that she could take over their slightly bigger and better one when they left. And there was a row when it was discovered that George had promised it to somebody else, indeed to two separate people, without saying anything to Charmian. Charmian was adamant, and the flat went to Burgess.[31] After getting through the Christmas and New Year turmoil, they had the task of packing up everything, including their now prodigious quantity of books, for though they certainly envisaged coming back to Sydney, their stay in London would be long enough to require them to set up home in a virtually permanent way.

It is important to keep that projected return in mind. In recent years Johnston and Clift are commonly thought of as part of that stream of expatriates who left Australia not merely to gain experience in the more sophisticated cultural pond abroad, but also to forsake the narrowness and philistinism at home. Expatriatism is in its full sense a form of rejection of one's own culture, and an act of self-exile that implies a perhaps painful, and often final, criticism of one's own nurturing. Many Australians expatriated themselves in this sense, and indeed never have returned to Australia to live. Johnston and Clift were not expatriates in this sense. Johnston had rarely used the term until he was writing *My Brother Jack* in 1963, when he was thinking of returning to Australia. 'Three years or so'[32] was all the time he envisaged being away, when he was preparing to go to London, and it was to a promotion in the *Sun* office; he was not leaving as an act of rejection of his country, despite his public criticism of its treatment of writers, and it is clear that he did not envisage his long-term future being anywhere but in Australia.

Johnston and Clift and their children departed from Sydney on the P&O liner *Orcades* in mid-February 1951. By coincidence, Greeba Jamison, on twelve months' leave from the *Age*, had boarded the ship in Melbourne, and was also off to England. They spent a good deal of time together on the journey, of which Jamison has vivid recollections:

It was the first time overseas for Charm and myself, and we were both excited, goggle-eyed, exhilarated by everything — Colombo, views of camels in the desert by moonlight as we went through the Suez canal, Port Said, Cairo, Marseilles, all ports of call.

Beautiful as ever, but more mature, Charmian attracted a lot of attention in the ship — but she was much the responsible mother and wife and no longer 'flaunting' herself as in earlier days. She and George were still very much lovers, and often myself and another friend of the Johnstons travelling in the same ship would purposely leave them to themselves sometimes, or watch the children so that they could have a little time alone together. George was the same as ever.

Charm and the children were distinctive always for their dressing — hard to describe, but Charm always extremely smart, chic, but with enough of the bizarre to make her dressing interesting above average. The children too, were dressed a little toward the bizarre, and were considered, for want of a better word, 'quaint'. They were spectacularly beautiful children — Charm, with a child holding onto each hand, turned all heads as she walked along the deck.

One episode stands out. For the children's fancy dress

> *party Charm decided Martin and Shane would go as Adam and Eve (she would!). In the parade round the deck they walked hand-in-hand, Shane naked, Martin with a hastily improvised fig-leaf in the appropriate place. Beforehand, George was a little worried about Shane parading with no clothes on — Charm could not understand why he should have been concerned and went on airily making the fig-leaf for Martin. The Johnston children won the prize for the best pair![33]*

That tinge of bohemianism, maintained along with their well-dressed, successful-professional look during their four years in Sydney, disappeared almost the moment the ship docked at Tilbury on 15 March 1951. There, waiting for them, was a chauffeur-driven car sent by the office of Associated Newspaper Services to convey them to London in a style befitting its new Chief. This was their first taste of the way things were done in England. Greeba Jamison went by humble train. But as the road and railway line ran parallel for part of the journey the dignity was momentarily lowered as the two parties waved gaily to each other[34] — all but shouting in boisterous unity 'London, here we come!'

CHAPTER VI

London

It was, in fact, quite some time before London itself grew to be disappointing, which was not the fault of the great metropolis itself but a dawning realization that I had been blundering around in circles for more than six years, ever since coming back from the war and leaving Helen. I was still trapped in the squirrel cage, spinning an interminable meangless tread-mill, still torn by conflicting ambitions and desires, unwilling to commit either to one thing or the other — the precarious-ness of belief or the safeness of conformity. (CSFN 159)

A large, plush apartment at 4 Palace Court, Bayswater Road, was provided by Associated Newspapers. It was not quite redecorated when they arrived in March 1951, so they had an uncomfortable few days in a hotel before they could settle in. London was still in the last weeks of winter, and presented a dismal scene in its cold, war-torn dreariness. The children came down with colds.

Johnston only gradually took over the reins from his prede-cessor, Frederick Peterson, who stayed around the office for most of the remainder of that year. Already working in the office were Victor Valentine, his old friend from China days Nigel Palethorpe, and Jack Pollard. In the following months Hazel Tulley and Donald Horne, who was then about thirty, joined the staff.

Only a fortnight after their arrival the Johnstons spent a few days in Paris. This was to be the pattern of their life in England — to escape from the routine of work as often as possible, and to see as much of Europe as they could in the

time available. Charmian in particular was constantly pressing for visits to the Continent.

Apart from all this, there was much to do on various books
in hand. Correspondence was frequent between their agents,
Pearn, Pollinger & Higham, their US publishers and themselves. 'Murder by Horoscope' had been returned for revi-
sion, though it was never published, and George still had *The
Sentimental Bloke* hanging over him. Both were postponed,
however, in favour of rewriting 'The Piping Cry', which
seemed more important. They promised their agent that it
would be ready in time for a spring 1952 publication by
Bobbs-Merrill in the US, as well as a simultaneous publication of a UK edition by Faber and an Australian one by Angus
& Robertson.[1] Johnston wrote to George Ferguson of Angus &
Robertson that he was 'confident that this time we shall be
delivering to you a *real* Australian novel, which might cause
quite a stir out there'.[2] This is another confirmation of the
high hopes that were investing in 'The Piping Cry'.

As well as this they had other plans, of staggering, indeed
unrealistic, proportions. Johnston told his agents that he was
going to write an 80,000-word novel called 'Pagoda', and Clift
a 60,000-word novel called *Walk to the Paradise Gardens*,
both within the foreseeable future.[3] Where they would find
the time seemed hardly considered, but it all sounded very
impressive when they told it to David Higham, one of the
directors of their new agency. Higham found them 'very
pleasant indeed',[4] and was hardly inclined to doubt their
abilities, given their record so far. On the day he met them he
was bearing the good news that the paperback rights to *High
Valley* had been bought in the US, and they were to receive a
handy advance of $US 1750.[5]

All their hectic social life in these first couple of years in
London was conducted in style. George played the newspaper executive in neat suits and spotted bow-ties, while Charmian went in for elegant outfits and long cigarette-holders.
Johnston's position got them to many opening nights at London theatres, book launchings and celebrity-crowded parties,
where they swaggered among the famous. There is a picture
of Johnston solemnly wagging a finger at Laurence Olivier,

who seems about to head for the nearest exit. They renewed their friendship with Peter Finch, who though fully occupied with his own blossoming career, continued to see them from time to time, and Johnston wrote the odd article about him in the London press. Charmian wrote home to Toni Burgess that she had met Louis MacNeice and T. S. Eliot. MacNeice, whose poetry she had always enjoyed, was a bitter disappointment, after he sneered something superior to her about 'awful colonials'.[6] The Eliot meeting was comic. As head of Faber & Faber, Eliot liked to meet his authors socially at least once, usually for afternoon tea, and this he did with Johnston and Clift. They turned up at his office a bit panicky, Charmian hastily pulling on a fresh pair of white gloves she had kept in her handbag especially. They knocked, and a voice said 'Come in'. They saw, at one end of the room, a lectern, from which Eliot apparently read his verse, but no poet. A movement from under a desk drew their attention, and there, greeting them, was Eliot's posterior — their first glimpse of the great man. 'I beg your pardon,' he said from the floor, 'I dropped my pencil.'[7]

They had many Australian friends about them, some regulars, such as the Flowers, who were often roped into babysitting. Others were visitors on brief stays or extended working trips, and among these in 1951 were Richard Lane, Hume and Gwyneth Dow, and Geoffrey and Nan Hutton. Many years later Nan Hutton was to write about visiting them, and she described something of the Johnston rationing of life into work and play:

> Dinner at the Johnstons' flat in Bayswater was always a good meal, and Charmian conjured it out of the bare larder London offered at the time.
> But, at 9 o'clock, the table was swept bare and out came their typewriters and George shouted 'Everybody out', and before the door closed you could hear them hammering away, beating out another collaboration . . .
> . . . They were not gentle, sympathetic friends. They were lively, moody or gay, fantastically energetic, they seemed to devour time and life, and they always did exactly what they wanted to do.[8]

Charmian, too, recalled what it was like to be an Australian

in London in that year of the Festival of Britain, and in doing
so describes very much the circle in which they moved:

> There were a lot of other Australians being excited in
> London that year. Paul Brickhill had finished The Great
> Escape *and was waiting for publication, knowing already, I*
> *think, that he was going to crack the best-seller lists. Peter*
> *Finch was over in Dolphin Square, not quite yet daring to*
> *believe what everybody was saying about his talent, and*
> *sometimes needing reassurance.... Loudon Sainthill hadn't*
> *then designed those magical sets and costumes for* The Tem-
> pest *that would take us down to Stratford later, in a blizzard,*
> *behind a snow-plough, the car waltzing on the iced roads (but*
> *worth it to cheer Loudon for a success so spectacular), but he*
> *was there, and Cedric Flower was there, doing the rounds of*
> *the theatres and painting buses and bridges and guardsmen*
> *and the Round Pond and posters for the London Under-*
> *ground, and Pat Flower was there, writing her first thriller,*
> *and Albert Arlen was there, talking about the music for* The
> Sentimental Bloke,[9] *and Sidney Nolan's drought paintings*
> *were receiving attention although the buyers weren't*
> *stampeding in those days, and more fools they.*
>
> *I used to think that the most desirable state of being that*
> *could be imagined was to be a young and talented Australian*
> *in London.*[10]

Johnston valued his friendships with painters more than
with journalists or even with writers, of whom he knew very
few. In these years he was particularly close with three painters – Cedric Flower, Sidney Nolan and an ex-pupil of Max
Meldrum in Melbourne back in the 1930s, Colin Colahan.
Cedric and Pat Flower were friends from Sydney days. The
friendship with Sid and Cynthia Nolan probably dated from
this time in London, though Nolan has the dimmest of recollections of meeting Johnston in Melbourne before the war,
perhaps at that party to which he was taken by Rod Maclean
and Rosalind Landells.[11] One thing Johnston might have discovered while talking to Cynthia was that they had a common
friend in Sam Atyeo. In the 1930s Atyeo and Cynthia, who
was then Cynthia Reed, sister of John Reed, had been close
friends. This was in Melbourne, before she met Nolan. She
had been a great admirer of Atyeo's advanced ideas on art,
and indeed she had organised his first exhibition in her Little
Collins Street shop and gallery in 1933. Moreover, it was

through Cynthia Reed that Atyeo first met H. V. Evatt,[12] with whom, as we have seen, he formed an unlikely friendship. It was during the process of distancing himself from the Gallery School, and with it from contact with the young George Johnston, that Atyeo got to know Cynthia Reed; the two friendships probably had little overlap. Nor would Johnston have met her in those days. But when he met her as Cynthia Nolan in 1951, it is likely that they were able to trace back these connections, and that she would have been able to fill him in on Atyeo's doings since the war, including the news that he had gone to live in Vence, in the south of France, where he grew flowers for a living. At that stage he had given up painting altogether. Interestingly, this is exactly how Sam Burlington ends up in *My Brother Jack*.

As for Johnston's friendship with the painter Colin Colahan and his wife, Ursula, that proved productive on both sides. Colahan was a witty and engaging man, smallish, spry and extremely knowledgeable about art, music and archaeology, and also about wine. Since the Johnstons wanted to see Europe, and the Colahans knew it well, they planned a summer trip together. They worked out a scheme whereby they would combine work with pleasure. 'One night at dinner,' recalls Colahan, 'George had a most genial idea – that the four of us should drive down to the Bordelais, "do" all the great vineyards, he would write a copious article, I'd do lots of drawings, he would syndicate the article, and we'd make lots of money.'[13] Johnston bought himself a new car for the trip – the latest model Standard Vanguard – and the children were bundled off to a holiday farm in Hertfordshire, which they did not much like. The trip was a huge success, as an adventure, if not in the financial terms they had hoped, and set a precedent for similar forays over the next couple of years.

Colahan was always surprised by Clift's tendency to burst into tears. She did this on the day they said goodbye to the Mayor of Bordeaux, she was so overcome with joy.[14] In 1953 Colahan painted her portrait in the studio of his London house, where he liked to play recorded music while he worked. During Charmian's sittings he played Mozart's *Requiem*

Mass, with the result that she was always on the verge of tears, and on at least one occasion ran from the studio in floods.[15] The portrait itself is a fine one, and catches wonderfully well Clift's dramatic beauty in these years, and her particular sophisticated style.

What Johnston found most intriguing about Colahan was the story of how he came to leave Australia to live in London. In November 1930 Melbourne had been shocked by the brutal murder of a young art teacher called Mollie (Mary) Dean: she was well known in art circles, and had for a time taught art to the young Sid Nolan. Colahan had been one of her boyfriends for some months, and one of the peculiar features of all her relationships was that she would never allow any of her friends to see her home. On the night of 20 November, she went to the cinema to see *Pygmalion* with Colahan and the artist Percy Leason and his wife, after which she went home, as usual, alone. At 1 a.m. in the morning she was attacked in an Elwood lane, was sexually mutilated, one of her stockings tied round her neck and her underwear tied round her arm. She died the following day of a fractured skull. The police treated Colahan as the prime suspect, for although he told them that Mollie had rung him from a public box at about 12.30 to apologise for a tiff they were having, there was no record of such a call at the telephone exchange. He was therefore held in custody, while the Press had a field day about artists and Bohemians and their degraded lifestyles (Mollie Dean had done some art modelling, requiring her to pose nude). After four days the operator who had been on duty on the night of the murder returned from a holiday in the country and produced the record of Mollie Dean's call. So Colahan's story was verified and he was released,[16] but he was so devastated by the ordeal that he got away from Australia as quickly as he could.[17]

Colahan had better luck in England, where he painted a couple of portraits of Bernard Shaw, and when the war broke out he was made an official war artist, which guaranteed him a steady and lucrative income. After the war he bought Whistler's old White House, cheap because it was bomb-damaged, in Tite Street, near the Embankment, and continued to paint busily. Johnston listened with great intent to his story,[18] and possibly with a dim memory of the Mollie Dean case, which attracted so much publicity in his youth. The fact that Colahan left Australia in dismay at its readiness to smear artists at any opportunity must have reminded Johnston of Sam Atyeo's 'escape' from the narrow provincialism that dominated the Melbourne art scene during the 1930s, and the two expatriate painters became linked in his mind with a rejection of Australian philistinism. This was to develop into an important theme in his later writing, especially in the Meredith trilogy, and, of course, Colahan's and Atyeo's stories were fused to form the Sam Burlington episode in *My Brother Jack*.

This was not the only time Johnston was stimulated in his writing by Colahan. His short story 'Requiem Mass', written around 1952, clearly draws on his relationship with the Australian painter, and even suggests that he might have harboured a certain ambivalence, either about Colahan, or about the sort of high-toned living he represented. The central character of the story, Halliday, is a charming artist and collector, not just of *objects* but also of people, including his young actress wife, Erica, whom he uses as background for his performance as a *connoisseur*. Erica weeps whenever the Mozart *Requiem Mass* is played. At the end of the story the bodies of Halliday and Erica are discovered in their apartment in what looks like a death-pact, but is more likely a wife-killing and suicide. Johnston's narrator is an educated Englishman, interested in archaeology and intrigue, and is in some respects a more serious predecessor of Professor Ronald Challis, the amateur detective later invented by Johnston for his series of 'Shane Martin' crime novels. 'Requiem Mass' is a strange story, not I believe intending to make any connection between Halliday and Colahan, but simply making use of the air of mystery that surrounded Colahan, and certain details of their lives — the connoisseur's interest in art and wine, the effect of the music on Charmian — to give imaginative expression to Johnston's fears about the life-killing capacity of too much dedication to art. It is one of Johnston's best pieces of writing, and probably his most serious-minded achievement to that time. Strangely, he did not offer it for publication for another two years, and it was not published until after his death.

Johnston's task as head of the London office was a demanding one, and he often put in long hours, arriving home exhausted late at night. He did not always eat well, and kept himself going too often on cigarettes and alcohol. He was, however, an agreeable and lenient boss with his staff. 'He didn't care what we did,' insists Hazel Tulley, 'as long as we got our work done.'[19] He usually led the joviality, often took the staff down to the pub for drinks, and was totally casual about such matters as hours of work and administrative niceties. He was unapologetic about doing his own writing in the firm's time, and about using the office stationery, equipment and secretaries for it. Nevertheless, he worked conscientiously, kept a happy office, and the *Sun* chiefs had no cause to be dissatisfied with him.

Charmian's life was less convivial. Even though the children were at the Kensington Montessori school 'learning to draw ancient battles and grow mustard cress', recalls Martin, she was still stuck in the flat for much of the time doing housework or else taking them to Hyde Park once they were home. Occasionally she was able to get some research on China done for George's novel 'Pagoda' by going to the British Museum Reading Room. Writing generally had to be done in the evenings. In the winter of 1951—52 they worked flat out to complete 'The Piping Cry', which Bobbs-Merrill had deadlined for 1 November, 'a very good thing', wrote Johnston, 'because the deadline really forced us to attack the problem, and the book itself is going along marvellously'.[20] Whether they made it or not may never be known, for this was the last reference that has come to light on 'The Piping Cry'. By one of those maddening sequences of coincidences that haunt researchers, the correspondence for 1952 of Johnston's three publishers and his literary agent is missing, and with it all further references to 'The Piping Cry'. Johnston intended to airfreight a copy to Angus & Robertson for publication in Australia at the same time as he sent one to Bobbs-Merrill in the US.[21] Neither script is traceable, nor is the Faber copy, nor the one the Johnstons kept for themselves. Whether it was actually sent, or ever even completed, remains a mystery.

The missing publishers' correspondence also makes it difficult to trace their movements and writing plans for 1952. These might not have been very complicated, however, because one thing that is certain about their writing in that year is that it was dominated by a new, grand collaborative project for a novel about seventeenth-century China, which they planned to call *The Big Chariot*. Everything else took second place to this. Albert Arlen wrote from Sydney suggesting that if he came to London they might get the interminable libretto for *The Sentimental Bloke* finished between them, but Johnston quickly and a little brutally wrote back advising Arlen not to come and to find someone else because he and Charmian were totally immersed in work on *The Big Chariot*, which at the moment, he wrote, 'represents all our aspirations, and could change our lives completely'.[22] The reason for this excitement was that the few advance chapters that he sent to Higham had generated ideas that this might be 'the big one' that would make the best-seller list, and someone in the agency had already contacted 'Hollywood Moguls' about film rights.[23] Johnston wrote to George Ferguson of Angus & Robertson that he would be looking for good terms because they needed all the money they could get. 'Sorry to sound so business-like, but *The Big Chariot* may be very important to us both, and may be the means of getting out of journalism at last and devoting myself to full time authorship.'[24]

In order to get some advice on the historical background for *The Big Chariot*, Johnston visited Arthur Waley, the translator of Chinese classics, in his Bloomsbury flat.[25] The novel's title had in fact been taken from a Han Dynasty poem translated by Waley, and Johnston was eager to trade yarns about China with the great man. Waley was cool and uncommunicative at first, and mocked his Australianness. 'Impossible to think of a place so horribly far away,' he told Johnston. Eventually Waley thawed and gave him some help, and they became friends. Johnston was astonished to learn that Waley had never been to either China or Japan, and guessed that he did not want the modern reality of those countries to destroy his

119

picture of the ancient magnificence of their civilisations. Johnston was lucky in being able to appreciate both.

Johnston and Clift worked together furiously on *The Big Chariot* and got it to the publishers early enough in 1952 to allow publication in March 1953. In the USA Bobbs-Merrill decided on a promotion campaign of similarly generous proportions to the one they had conducted for *High Valley*, despite the fact that that novel's sales, whilst healthy enough, never did reach the American best-seller lists. One senses more than a hint of desperation in the Johnstons' hopes for *The Big Chariot*: it was almost four years since they had published a novel — *High Valley* was the last — and the dream of becoming full-time writers was disappearing in the welter of newspaper commitments, family-raising and social life. London was beginning to have its sour moments — the weather, apart from anything else, was, with its appalling winter smog in those years, depressing and unhealthy — and they felt a growing need radically to alter their lives. After all, Johnston was now in his fortieth year, and Clift was almost thirty, so labels such as 'young' or 'promising' authors were starting to wear a bit thin. Friends noticed them talking with increasing vehemence about getting out of the rat-race and living on an island somewhere, possibly Greece. If such hopes were to be realised, they would need a financial windfall, and they felt that *The Big Chariot* might just be the book to do the trick.

In that summer of 1952 they took another Continental holiday, by themselves this time, and with a view, partly at least, to gathering some fresh material for their writing. They drove through France, Luxemburg, Germany, Austria and Italy, joyfully soaking up every feature of the landscape, every village, every little restaurant, every peasant-clad figure. Though the tour was to yield them only a few short stories, it is clear that many incidents proved affecting and memorable. Charmian kept a notebook in which she recorded observations for later reference, and a wonderful testimony it is to her sharp eye for detail and her determination to let no experience escape. In France she saw:

> *An old woman picking dandelions by the roadside. She*

gathered them into a basket. She was dressed in black, with a blue apron, and black stockings and boots, and when she bent over you could see how her stockings were rolled just above the knee . . . You could see all the tops of her bare legs — they were skinny and knotted into ropes of sinew. She stooped very slowly, as though it hurt. But she had a lot of dandelions in the basket. I wonder how old she was really? Do the peasant women work until they drop, or is it the work that makes them look so old? They are beside every road, gathering faggots, or something, I don't know what. And they all move so patiently, so tiredly, and don't look up when the car goes past. The men do, leaning on their hoes. If you wave, sometimes they wave back. Not often.[26]

In Germany:

It was the first time we had slept in German beds, and we couldn't understand the eiderdown things. They kept slipping off all night. I remember at Bondi that the continentals who lived in the block of flats always had strange buttoning linen cover things hanging out on wash days. Toni and I used to giggle about them.[27]

In Italy, in the small town of Lerici, on the Bay of Spezia, where Shelley drowned, they had an oddly haunting experience, which they both remembered and wrote about. Their hotel room overlooked a square, and there was a restaurant underneath them. One evening they were in bed while a noisy party was taking place below. Suddenly the laughter was silenced by the sound of strange music, thin and high-pitched. They opened the shutters to see that the music was being played in the square by three very old men in round-crowned hats and long shabby coats, playing two violins and a high-pitched pipe. Charmian recorded in her notebook:

Later, when we had returned to our beds, they played again, and now it was a gay tune that persisted in my sleep, endlessly repetitive yet constantly refreshing. The bells were somehow mixed up in it, pealing with laughter at the ironical pipe, ever higher, ever clearer, leading them on with such joyful absurdities that they crashed out demented, discordant chimes and were suddenly quiet. We awoke together. The music was fading lightly, lightly, the strings thrummed and the pipe danced on six notes that were the distillation of youth and spring and crushed flowers, and when we crept to the window we saw that the table below was quite empty, and across the square the three old musicians were walking away (still

121

we did not see their faces). The very tall old man was still in the middle, and as they played they bent their knees and shuffled from one side to the other in time, but their legs looked very thin and very infirm, old men's legs, and I stood at the window and wept as they slowly shuffled into the dark shadows past the clock tower and were gone from us. Still we stood, listening, until we could no longer be sure whether we still heard the vibration of a thin, high note . . . a reed . . . Pan in the moonlight . . . all youth . . . all beauty . . . and I was still weeping when I returned to my bed.[28]

In these notebook observations, Charmian's account is a little self-consciously romantic in a quasi-Keatsian kind of way, especially her repetition of 'lightly', and her introduction of 'Pan, moonlight, youth and beauty' into the scene. She is thinking, and weeping, about herself and her own joy in witnessing such a delightful sight, but when she later wrote a story about the incident, calling it 'Three Old Men of Lerici', she used the material to a different end. That strange music becomes a means of bringing about a realisation in her central character, Ursula, that she has been cruelly misjudging her husband, Freiburg (named after a German town they had just passed through), during their motoring tour. She has been constantly treating his enthusiasm for everything they see as the worst kind of tourist vulgarity. But when she discovers, standing at the window, that the music has a peculiar discordant beauty, she also realises that Freiburg's openness to even the harshest music of life is the secret to his happy and uncritical disposition, and she suddenly understands what is lovable about him. Ursula's moment of joy is like a Joycean epiphany, or revelation, and the self-indulgence of the notebook observation has been transformed into a gesture of generosity by the woman towards her husband. The theme of openness to life is an appropriately Shelleyan one, a literary echo that could well have been deliberate on Clift's part.

It is tempting to see in Ursula's sudden perception of her husband's virtue a biographical insight into relations between Johnston and Clift at the time of this holiday. This would be supported by the importance that they both attached to that night in Lerici, which Johnston placed alongside the Merediths' 'honeymoon' at Lebanon Bay, when he writes in *Clean Straw for Nothing* that Cressida had the same look of love in her eyes in both places (*CSFN* 134). Lerici represented one of those moments that stayed with them for the rest of their lives.

There is, however, something further to be said about Clift's notebook for that holiday, which is that the surviving pages of it turn up almost word for word in Johnston's *Clean Straw for Nothing* without any acknowledgement that they were originally written by Clift. Simply described as 'Notes From an Expatriate's Journal' (*CSFN* 101–16), they contain exactly the observations that Clift made about exactly the same places that she recorded as they drove through Europe in 1952. Because it is not publicly acknowledged, this appears to be plagiarism, which would be a disturbing thing indeed to find in Johnston's work. But plagiarism would be a hasty conclusion. It is almost impossible that Clift did not know he was making use of it. Even if she did not see that part of the typescript, which is possibly the case, Johnston himself fully expected her to read it in published form, and almost certainly asked her to help him with it between 1964 and 1969. It is unlikely he could have been expecting to deceive her, so that common sense dictates that the passages from Clift's notebook went in under his name with her blessing. Nor would such sharing between them have been unusual. Incidentally, there is a pithy epigram penned in Charmian's handwriting on the back of one of the notebook pages that will please feminists: 'She also has a life in the vertical position.' As, indeed, she always had.

Other stories came out of that motor tour. One by Johnston, titled 'The Dying Day of Francis Bainsbridge', is a kind of morality tale about a tourist who steals a little wooden crucifix from a wayside shrine in the Tyrol, an act that brings about his death. The idea came from seeing exquisitely carved figures in shrines decorated with flowers beside the roads in the Mosel Valley and in Austria. Clift wrote a story called 'Wild Emperor', about two people, Doris, an Englishwoman, and Josef, a German, who are struggling to come to terms with their repressed feelings. The setting is a Tyrolean

village, with the mountainous landscape playing an important part in the story's theme. These and other stories from
around 1952 were given to Higham in 1954, but he was
unable to persuade a publisher to take them, and they simply
got stuffed in drawers until they came out in the 1984 anthol-
ogy of their stories, *Strong Man from Piraeus*. In some respects,
however, they contained their best writing so far, and certainly their most revealing.

During the remainder of 1952 Clift busied herself in the
British Museum researching into the history of Mesopotamian and Babylonian culture for a novel she was tentatively
calling 'Barbarian'. What was happening with the projected
Walk to the Paradise Gardens is uncertain, but she was
evidently having trouble with it. Johnston could see a fearful-
ly busy year coming up in the office in 1953, with all attention
directed towards the Coronation in June.

They had probably come back from the Continent full of
ideas and optimism, fingers crossed for the success of *The Big
Chariot*, which was due to appear in the USA in April 1953.
What they had done in this novel, which is far too complex to
summarise here, is to construct a tale of two brothers and a
father set against the historical background of seventeenth-
century China, during the last nineteen years of the Ming
Dynasty. There is a hint of a comparison with modern China
in the idea of a new, aggressively efficient leadership ousting
a traditional one, which has become decadent, but no sustained political or historical parallels are seriously attempted.
What is interesting is the contrast between the two brothers,
Cheng Wei and Cheng Yuan, and their relationship with
their father, Cheng Li-jen. The narrative describes Wei as 'the
stronger, more assertive character. The strength and bulk of
his figure had given him self-confidence; he was already a
young man, forthright and probably brave. The next step,
unless he were watched, was towards arrogance and perhaps
brutality.' Yuan, on the other hand, is 'shy and slim, with
nervous mannerisms that frequently concealed the intelligence and sensitivity he seemed to possess. He had inherited
the delicacy of his mother with no compensation of his
father's strength.'[29] Wei is a soldier and a leader; Yuan is a

poet and scholar, and is apprenticed to a printer. Their father is a wise and authoritive figure, combining the qualities of both sons.

This contrasting of the two brothers makes *The Big Chariot* an interesting precursor to *My Brother Jack*, which of course uses much the same pattern, with Jack Meredith and Wei linked as the brave ones, and David Meredith and Yuan as the clever ones. Yuan is even given David's profession as an apprenticed printer, and is closer to his mother than to his father. *The Big Chariot* may have drawn on the same sources, in that Johnston's sense of difference between Jack and himself formed, perhaps even unconsciously, a model in his mind for two distinct kinds of male personalities, linked by family ties, but poles apart in their physical and spiritual make-up. This connection is the only truly interesting feature of *The Big Chariot*. The father is a fictional stereotype, quite unconnected with Johnston's father, though he is perhaps an idealisation of qualities Johnston might have liked his father to possess; but that is speculation. There is no important female character, so it is difficult to imagine that Clift played a large part in its writing. It is a novel that badly lacks the power to sustain interest. Events, and an enormous number of minor characters, are presented in page after page of lifeless prose, which provides a confused, ill-focused and inconsequential narrative. One of the most astute comments on the novel was passed by the mother of Johnston's colleague Vic Valentine, who had lent her the copy Johnston gave him. She found it unreadable, and (with apologies for the racist connotations) shook her head. 'Too many chows,' she said, 'too many chows.'[30]

The reviews gave no inkling of its failure – on the contrary, they promised the success the Johnstons were waiting for. 'Power, beauty and understanding' were the terms of praise used by the *New York Herald Tribune* reviewer, who concluded that 'the authors have combined all the essentials of a good historical novel to produce one of the best in many a long day'. The *New York Times* reached for clichéd superlatives such as 'memorable' and 'flawlessly written'.[31] Johnston sent copies of these notices to Morley Kennerley of Faber in an attempt to encourage Faber to promote the UK edition, which was a month or so behind the US edition in production. Faber had agreed without hesitation to publish the novel, but did have some reservations, and wanted to make substantial cuts in order to reduce the padded feel of much of it. George and Charmian forbade the cuts. Despite the heavy promotion campaigns and excellent reviews in both countries, the sales of *The Big Chariot* never took off. Nor did anything come of the Hollywood film negotiations. Simply, when it got out amongst the readers, they did not like it. And one cannot blame them, for this was a case where the public was right and the reviewers wrong, as the Johnstons themselves came to admit years later. Perhaps the factor that most dissuaded ordinary readers was the impression that not a word of the story comes from any deep conviction in the authors; it is all off the top of their heads, and therefore not believable. Given their hopes and expectations, right up until it hit the bookshops, this failure of *The Big Chariot* must have been a bitter blow. In the end it made only $400 profit for Bobbs-Merrill and the Faber sales were equally dismal.[32] So this was not the book that would change their lives.

The failure of *The Big Chariot* seemed to knock the confidence out of them for a time. They produced no published work in 1953, apart from Johnston's occasional features and the 'London Diary' column he wrote for the *Sun* in Sydney; but it was not just the writing that was going wrong. Johnston's health was beginning to show worrying signs, and a tendency to chest complaints was becoming apparent. He was on drugs while completing *The Big Chariot*, and the doctor warned him that he was overdoing things by trying to do two jobs. What was just as bad as the work load was his brooding over the way in which the newspaper work was at total odds with his own writing, robbing him of the time and energy to do it properly. This, the heavy smoking and drinking, plus those poisonous London smogs, were hardly a recipe for good health.

When Johnston's annual leave came in April, he and Clift were able to get off on another holiday, this time for two weeks in the Bordeaux and Dordogne regions, somehow 'at the expense of the French Government'.[33] They used as a guide a recently published book by Freda White called *Three Rivers of France*, and as usual had 'a wonderful time'. Johnston later stressed the importance of these Continental excursions as sources of rejuvenation. In *Clean Straw for Nothing* he writes that for Cressida it was 'spiritually like some pagan vegetation rite of regeneration and renewal. In the sunburnt pepper-and-salt of Provencal landscape, in the sunny bright blue of the Mediterranean . . . she seemed reborn'. For Meredith, holidays became a sheer physical necessity — 'for tonic and therapeutic rather than for spiritual values' (*CSFN* 134–5). There can be little doubt that the trips were a restorative for Clift and Johnston in exactly the same way.

One interesting development occurred when they got back from France; Johnston asked Faber for a copy of *Hellenic Travel* by W. A. Wigram, which they had published, and which, he wrote, 'we desperately need because Charmian and I are planning a trip to Greece within the next twelve months for the purpose of getting additional material for another novel'.[34] So the Continent regenerated their creative energies, too. All they needed was a visit, and they were fired up with new ideas and inspiration. Johnston started reading up on Greek myths as well, and had one or two discussions about them with Sidney Nolan.[35]

The idea of going to Greece might well have come indirectly through Nolan. A year or so earlier he had taken the Johnstons to the Pimlico flat of Clarisse Zander, mother-in-law of the Sydney painter Carl Plate. Mrs Zander had been on an archaeological tour to Greece, which included a visit to Hydra, which she found not only beautiful but cheap, and she pointed out that it would make an ideal retreat for a writer to go to and 'write something worthwhile.'[36] The Johnstons had taken note of this, and were now fully intending to investigate the place for themselves.

The Coronation lived up to its promise to keep Johnston busy at the office, where he put in long hours and wrote pages of gossip about the royal family. He was present at the ceremony, at one stage standing near the Queen Mother, 'Staring', he told Hazel Tulley, 'right into the Royal pores'.[37]

He later wrote to Gae in Melbourne — she was now twelve — that he would never forget the Coronation 'because just as I arrived at the Abbey my braces broke, and all through the ceremony I had to hold my trousers up with one hand, and then walk back to Fleet Street in full evening dress still holding my pants up!'[38] At least he could still joke, despite the 'appalling confusion' that the Coronation created in his life. It also meant that they were unable to get away for a holiday that summer, which would have made the traumatic events of the next few months even harder to bear.

In September 1953 Associated Newspapers Limited was taken over by the Fairfax family, owners of the *Sydney Morning Herald*. What took place was a merger, in which Denison, the owner of Associated Newspapers, and Fairfax bought shares in each other's firm, with editorial management of the *Sun*, which had been losing money, passing over to the *Sydney Morning Herald*. At first Johnston referred to it lightly as 'the great merger',[39] seeming not to anticipate significant changes. When he learned that he would soon be replaced as head of the London office, he began to see the seriousness of the situation. It was a demotion, and probably meant that he had gone as high as he would go in the newspaper world: he could certainly not expect much favour from the new regime, given their current treatment of him. But with no other way to make a living, he would have to put up with it, for the time being at least, and this rankled. He met his successor, Anthony Whitlock, who was already under instructions from the *Herald* chiefs to move swiftly, and before September was out Johnston was no longer in charge. He was not ungracious in defeat, and pressed a copy of *The Big Chariot* on Whitlock, inscribing it 'all the best'. Charmian stood less on ceremony: 'Damn you!'[40] she scribbled on the flyleaf. Whitlock and his wife, Neil, did their diplomatic best to remain on good terms and, socially at least, this was the case.

As it happened, the winter of 1953–54 was a particularly bitter one, and Johnston came down with a bout of bilateral pneumonia that laid him low for some months.[41] He was cheered by a Christmas card from Gae, followed by a letter — her first to him — to which he replied late in January with

Margaret Clift *(Photo courtesy of Margaret Backhouse)*   Johnston and Clift on the rocks at Kiama, 1946

Barré Clift, brother of Charmian, with his wife

Clift with Johnston and Peter Finch at the 2UE studios in Sydney, 1947

Successful Londoners in their Kensington flat, *c.* 1952

Johnston, the newspaper executive, *c.* 1952

Johnston with Martin and Shane, in Hyde Park, 1953

Cedric and Pat Flower

Colin Colahan's portrait of Charmian Clift
(Photo: Colin Colahan)

Johnston gives advice to Laurence Olivier, *c.* 1952

some warm chat about his planned trip to Greece, the Coronation, and a promise to send stamps for her collection. He sent these a few days later with a note saying how much he was feeling the cold. 'It is snowing again today – and the temperature has been six degrees below freezing point night and day for the last three days. Brr.!!'[42] Elsie had sent him sporadic news over the years of Gae's progress, but now that she was taking up the lines of communication for herself, Johnston was delighted and eager, for the moment at least, to respond. He had been instructing Angus & Robertson to send Elsie money from Australian book royalties from time to time – £100 here, £25 there, which generally only balanced out the outstanding alimony payments; there was no systematic arrangement.

In April 1954 Johnston and Clift were off on the long anticipated holiday to Greece. Before they left, Johnston sent David Higham the manuscript for a first novel 'by a friend of mine, Miss Patricia Bullen',[43] who was in fact Cedric Flower's wife, asking Higham to try to get it published. (This was only one example of Johnston's willingness to help launch a friend's writing career.) He also said that they were leaving the next day for five weeks in Athens. In fact they moved around various parts of Greece, using Athens only as a base. They visited the islands of Crete, Rhodes and Paros, taking many colour slides, so that when they go back to London they could moon over such sights as 'little islands floating magically on an indigo sea, the cypresses stiff against early morning oyster skies . . .'[44] There is a fine photograph of them both on Paros wearing striped trousers made by an Athenian tailor who is reputed to have made clothes for Garbo; unfortunately the poor quality of the print prevents its reproduction in this book. And of course they went to Hydra, where Meredith and Cressida in *Clean Straw for Nothing* stay in a crumbling waterfront hotel, and the proprietor delights them both by asking for their passports, so much like illicit lovers do they seem in their happiness (*CSFN* 135) – and, to a Greek, in their seeming childlessness. From their window the Johnstons could watch the slow commerce of the *caiques* in the tiny Hydra port, like spectators at some theatrical event. As they had expected, as they had *wanted*, they were at last under the spell of Greece.

When they returned to London, they had some new writing plans. For some reason they decided 'to write separately from now on'.[45] No big best-seller schemes, no ideas of Hollywood films; perhaps the let-downs were too painful. Johnston had a Greek novel mapped out in his head, and got straight to work on it and Clift decided to make another attempt at *Walk to the Paradise Gardens*. All other writing projects — the bits of 'Pagoda' and 'Barbarian' that had been researched and written but had not worked out — were scrapped, except that George incorporated some of the 'Pagoda' material into the new novel, which he was calling *The Cyprian Woman*.[46] He told Higham it would be ready by November.

The following months also produced some rough moments in George and Charmian's relationship. One suspects a falling out, in terms of work at least, in the decision to keep their writing separate, but there might have been more to it. Johnston had always sought attention from attractive women, and over the years Charmian must have observed him flirting. In Sydney, according to Neil Hutchison, he may have gone farther than that. In any case, some time during these months of mid-1954, there was much talk in the office about an affair with an extremely attractive and very young typist called Patricia Simione. Charmian had taken the children to Cornwall for a week or so, and one Monday morning Simione said she had gone home with Johnston for the weekend, and, moreover, infamised herself round the office with stories of the gaudiness of Johnston's underwear.[47] Since everyone in the office knew about the affair, it is possible that Clift did too. There are several references that suggest she was particularly unhappy around this time, such as Cynthia Nolan's comment on Hydra that she 'had a bad time of resentment and rage behind her',[48] and the allusion in *Clean Straw for Nothing*, in the chapter 'London, 1954', that 'it had been in London that the seeds of pain were sown, that the breach in the personal relationship, never at that time expressed or even hinted at, began to encroach upon their love' (*CSFN* 130). In this novel Johnston never makes mention of his own infidelity as a factor in this, but he does go into some of the complexities that were beginning 'to encroach' upon their relationship, such as his old tendency to jealousy of Clift's assertions of independence, and her intensifying hatred of the life she was forced to live – that of little more than the pretty wife and mother – in London.

The section in which Meredith suspects Cressida of having an affair with Calverton has given rise to much speculation about Clift and Peter Finch. All one can say about this is that there is no evidence of any kind to support such speculation, and that if one reads the London chapters in *Clean Straw for Nothing* closely, one finds that Johnston has included the scenes with Cressida and Calverton in order to show Meredith's crippling jealousy at work, and that that jealousy is ruining his life: 'It was not so much that I detected, or even suspected, weakness in Cressida, but that I mistrusted life itself' (*CSFN* 162). Even if Clift had been unfaithful, Johnston, if the office story is true, was hardly in a position to play the wronged husband, for he was guilty too; but specific sexual matters do not seem to be as important as other, more psychological ones, which, once again, are convincingly analysed in *Clean Straw for Nothing*. For instance, Meredith's resentment of Cressida's occasional retreats into her own thoughts: '. . . my possessive jealousies and Cressida's own possessiveness of that silent uncommunicated private world in which her own myth was harboured . . .' (*CSFN* 154). What Meredith is admitting to is that displays of independence *of any kind* from Cressida, physical or mental, are difficult for him to cope with because they take her out of his reach and out of his control. This, I believe, gets to the heart of the problem between Johnston and Clift: displays of independence from her created jealousy and resentment in him, essentially because right from the beginning of their relationship he was never completely secure in his own capacity to retain her love. In this situation in 1954, when London was placing increasing restrictions on Clift's life, she was probably inclined to be more assertive about her independence, especially her independent-mindedness, such as wanting to write only on her own from now on, and perhaps have friendships that were entirely her own, and this caused Johnston to react with increased resentment and doubt, in turn driving her to dig her heels in. So a vicious circle developed, and given all the other things going wrong in London, it would hardly have been possible to avoid unhappiness. Not that it was as intensely bad in 1954 as *Clean Straw for Nothing* suggests: that novel was written in the 1960s, after many other events had taken place that were to influence Johnston's attitudes. In 1954 they were discovering unpalatable features in each other, but there was no continuing stand-off between them. In any case, if they were going to do anything about the future, there was not the slightest doubt in either of them that they would do it together, and that whatever the problems, they had only each other to rely on.

The situation in the office was getting worse. Anthony Whitlock did his best to ease the awkwardness of Johnston's position, but there were nevertheless numerous quarrels, and much shouting from both sides. Whitlock's task was made difficult by the resentment of some of the staff, who generally were loyal to Johnston. Donald Horne simply couldn't bear the whole business and resigned.[49] Most of those who remained were dismayed, and had, according to Whitlock, an 'air of failure' about them because they had been taken over.[50] Nor did they like the businesslike approach of the new regime. For example, Johnston had allowed them a £6 per week 'slush fund', which was a general entertainment allowance, and this, despite Johnston's efforts to preserve it, was cut. No doubt his irritability was partly frustration at having to stay in the newspaper industry at all, but nevertheless it was hard for him to take the ignominy of demotion in the sight of those he had led, and hard for him to accept that he had reached the limits of his career. It was one thing to reject the rat-race; to be rejected *by* the rat-race was an entirely different matter.

Johnston never made it plain in his writing that this was a factor in his abandonment of journalism. On the contrary, he always gave the impression that it was the profession's shortcomings that drove him out. This implication occurs twice at least in later novels, where he has David Meredith attack the lack of moral and intellectual standards in journalism. The first time is in *The Far Road*, where he attacks the indifference to human suffering on the part of war correspondents such as Conover. The second time is in *Clean Straw for Nothing*, where he deplores the newspaper industry's failure to stand against Cold War politics, the nuclear spectre and mindlessness. 'We're letting them turn the world into a rat-race and a jungle and nobody gives a bugger!' Meredith tells Cressida, adding 'You try to write anything intelligent and important and they won't wear it' (*CSFN* 137). This outburst is a prelude to Meredith's decision to get out of journalism altogether. Such reasons are interesting guides to Johnston's later reflections on the newspaper game, but they do not bear much relation to the actual circumstances under which he left it in 1954. These have much more to do with his long-held aspirations for a different way of life, as well as the more immediate events in 1953 and 1954, which include his loss of status on the *Sun*.

However, Johnston was not getting out yet. At least, he saw no way to at this stage. He and Clift were still playing their London roles to the hilt, and although their social circle had diminished to a few colleagues, such as Vic Valentine and Nigel Palethorpe, and artist friends, such as Finch and the Nolans, the Flowers and the Colahans, they remained generally their cheerful selves, still on the look-out for their big chance to escape. Martin and Shane, still at the Montessori school, had grown exceedingly English, with their organised birthday parties, their duffle coats and impeccable accents. Both were fair-haired, clear-skinned and strikingly beautiful children. Shane was still chubby and preoccupied with her dolls, whereas Martin was beginning to sprout tall and slim, played incessantly with his prodigious collection of tin soldiers and was exceptionally bright. Johnston nauseated friends by constantly calling him 'Professor', and he was only half-joking – another piece of working-class 'compensation'. When he said it in front of Neil Whitlock, she noticed Charmian fling a look at the heavens.[51]

Meanwhile, he plunged headlong into writing *The Cyprian Woman*, and finished it by October, a month earlier than planned. He did not succeed in putting much of Greece into it, apart from some rather forced classical references (the 'Cyprian Woman' was Euripides' name for Aphrodite). The names of the Greek characters don't always sound convincingly Greek — Davaris, Porontios, Nikki (instead of Nikko) — and the country itself is a vague back-drop that could be anywhere. Basically it is a crime novel in which the main story turns on the involvement of Stephen Colvin with two women, Christine Lambert and Erica Kostandis. Lambert is a married writer with surprisingly liberated sexual views, and Kostandis is a beautiful Greek whom Colvin virtuously declines to seduce. Johnston's handling of the sex is coy and moralistic, and is further evidence that such matters were preying on his mind in these months of mid-1954. Lambert is a woman writer, intelligent, beautiful, thirty years old and insistent on her right to independence from her husband's control, to the point of sexual promiscuity, and she is the crudest possible expression of his worst fears about independent-mindedness in Clift. Colvin is just as crude an example of how a gentleman should behave: indeed, there is not a central character in any of Johnston's books who is sexually aggressive or who seduces the 'wrong' woman; that part of himself is simply left out of Johnston's fiction. And his dislike of it in women crops up again and again: in Christine Lambert, in Grace Adams in *The Darkness Outside*, in Helen Midgeley in *My Brother Jack*, and in Cressida Meredith in *Clean Straw for Nothing*. His views on sex were thoroughly conventional, and thoroughly male-biased; eventually he came to see this and take himself to task for it.

Not surprisingly, *The Cyprian Woman* is a poor novel, the second one in a row. Johnston knew it and did not want it taken seriously, or so one assumes from his comment that it was 'lighter, on a more popular plane' than previous novels.[52] He later said it was reviewed 'better than the book deserved'.[53] American publishers rejected it, and Faber & Faber were not keen, but would accept it to keep him in their stable. However, he had recently met the publisher Sir William Collins, and they had taken to each other instantly. Johnston told him about the novel he was writing and about

plans for future novels about Greece, all with such enthusiasm that Collins, who insisted that George call him 'Billy',
was infected and demanded to see the manuscript of *The
Cyprian Woman* personally.[54] He said he thought the novel
would do well, and offered generous terms, but one gets the
impression that it was Johnston and the future he was
buying, more than that obviously unimpressive novel. In any
case Johnston was glad to be free of Faber, who, he felt, had
not sold his books particularly well.

Johnston's interest in matters at the office was failing
rapidly, prompting him to little bursts of spite, especially
towards his new superiors at the *Sydney Morning Herald* office
in Sydney. They apparently asked him for a story that involved comparing the size of two film stars' breasts — they
were probably attempting to 'ginger up' the *Sun.* Johnston
cabled back a picture of two large grapefruit.[55] On another
occasion, when the Wolfenden Royal Commission was creating a wave of interest in homosexuality, Johnston sent a
feature that attempted to put both sides of the question. A
note came back from Rupert Henderson, the Managing Editor
of the *Sydney Morning Herald,* saying that the article was
'unacceptable'. Johnston hastily flung them back a piece on
London sewers and sewerage workers, with the comment to
Sydney, and to Anthony Whitlock, that 'if they don't like
what I write for them I'll give them shit'.[56] Relations between
Johnston and his new bosses were deteriorating fast.

The situation was affecting Johnston's health, which had
not fully recovered since the pneumonia early in the year.
Also the late nights spent in writing *The Cyprian Woman* took
it out of him, not to mention 'drinking pretty heavily between the two tasks' of writing and journalism. He says in
Clean Straw for Nothing that Meredith had by 1954 'pushed
himself very close to a breakdown', and had had further
warning from his doctor: there is every reason to think that
Johnston is accurately describing his own state here. His
colleague Hazel Tulley marked the change that had taken
place in him since she first saw him:

> *If you met George when he first came to London, as I met
> him one day just walking along the street, he was bubbling*

with life: 'Hello Haze!', and we had a talk, and a joke, and a
laugh, and here was George handsome, interested, ambitious
. . . and that was the George I had known in Sydney.
    But when George left London he was angry, he was de-
pressed, his pink and white had gone and he was this dreadful
yellow colour. I saw him on a bus not long before he left for
Greece; he didn't know I saw him this day. He was sitting
back, his mouth was open and his eyes were closed, and he
looked a different man from the one I'd seen before: he looked
ill. He looked beaten.[57]

Johnston was not beaten. He was down, and he and Charmian knew what they both needed. But how could they live
as a family if he gave up journalism? So far, the gods had
smiled on them, and had reprieved them from two sticky
situations. When Johnston's months of unemployment
brought them into debt in Sydney, the £2000 prize had bailed
them out. When they were ready, indeed anxious, to go
abroad, the London job had come up. Now they were about
to receive their third stroke of luck.

Johnston was walking down Regent Street one September
day in 1954 when he saw an old friend, Wilfred Thomas the
radio broadcaster, walking towards him with some tapes
under his arm. Thomas said he was going to the BBC studios
in order to edit a radio programme he had put together on the
plight of the sponge-diving community on the little-known
Greek island of Kalymnos. At the mention of Greece, Johnston pricked up his ears and asked if he could come along and
listen. So they went together to the studios.[58]

Thomas and his actress wife, Bettina Dixon, had been
friends of the Johnstons since Sydney days, when they worked in ABC radio together. In fact Dixon had played the lead
in Clift's feature play 'The Diary of a Modern Woman' in 1949.
The four continued to see each other in London, where Thomas was currently making programmes for the ABC on the
subject of refugees and displaced persons, with a particular
interest in people wanting to migrate to Australia. Thomas's
immediate project had been the brainchild of the Greek Con-
sul in Melbourne at the time, Eugene Gorman, who had
learned that the sponge-diving industry on Kalymnos was
failing. Synthetics were making natural sponges increasingly

hard to sell, and since there was no other source of income, the economy and life of the island was in trouble. The plan was to bring the divers to Darwin as a means of reviving the ailing pearl industry, since the war had made it no longer feasible to use Japanese divers. The Kalymnian divers would, it was thought, be able to earn enough money to bring their families to Australia, and two problems would be solved in the one stroke. It was a bold and imaginative plan, and it was Thomas's job to make a programme called 'Plan For Survival', aimed at exciting general interest in the idea back in Australia.

When Johnston learned all this, he could hardly contain himself. 'Do you know,' he said to Thomas, 'I've been looking for a book to write that would get me out of Fleet Street, and this is the one!'[59] Exactly what kind of book he saw in the story at this time is not clear, but it might not have been a novel. The story itself would be, as both he and Thomas saw, an unusual and fascinating enough one, and for Johnston it had the added attraction of linking Greece with Australia. He could take his family where they wanted to go, and publish something about Australia, as well as *in* Australia, where of course he was well known. It looked to be a great recipe for success.

Johnston and Clift listened excitedly to the programme when it was broadcast, and immediately began to make plans. Money, all of a sudden, loomed large. All those years on a comfortable income, a generous expense account, a free flat and royalties from books, and they had saved almost nothing. Now they needed to scrape together and treasure every penny. As a beginning, they would have to sell many of their possessions.

Johnston would have felt some pleasure in cabling his resignation to Rupert Henderson in Sydney. He had recently heard a rumour that Henderson was fed up with his unco-operative attitude, and was planning to call him home.[60] The many quarrels he had had with the new regime had brought several resignations from him in the past year, only to end in his abject withdrawal when he cooled down. He was not without apprehension even now, as it dawned on him that this was the final break, but Clift was magnificently firm in her support for his action. Once it was done, they decided to waste no time hanging about London. The resignation was probably tendered in October, and all the arrangements that followed were directed towards getting them to Greece before November was finished.

The suddenness of the decision made it difficult to get money together. There was nothing in the creative pipeline that would pay: they sent Higham the three stories written about their 1952 trip plus 'Requiem Mass', but the agent was unable to sell any of them.[61] Charmian was continuing to have difficulty with *Walk to the Paradise Gardens*, so that was in no shape to send off. They sold the car. They held an auction of books, records, odds-and-ends at the flat, to which most of their friends came, but they ended up presenting much of it to them as gifts.[62] However, Johnston pulled off one bold success: with Anthony Whitlock's support he brazenly requested Rupert Henderson, since he was wanting to bring him home anyway, to give him the return fare in cash rather than a ticket from England to Australia. To his delight, it was agreed to. Whitlock ensured that Johnston got as much out of his employer as was possible by way of expenses and contributory funds, and in the end the Johnstons were able to leave with something over £1000 plus their return fare to England.

As the date of departure neared, they could talk of nothing else – how it would be a new beginning, how the money they would make from the book would set them up as full-time writers, how wonderful it would be, in Johnston's words, 'to take the children back to the source of civilisation'.[63] These were familiar extravagances, and this was familiar optimism, and their friends smiled with them but kept silent about the unrealistic fervour that lay so perceptibly behind it.

A farewell party at the flat was arranged, and friends and well-wishers crowded in everywhere. From the office there were journalists Anthea Batten, Nigel Palethorpe, Michael Webster, Hazel Tulley and Victor Valentine (to whom he had dedicated *The Cyprian Woman*). Anthony and Neil Whitlock were there, and Harry Kippax, who had just arrived from

Sydney to take Johnston's place, and Patricia Simione, flashing her eyes about the room, though no doubt not in Charmian's direction, and Mary Buck, Johnston's personal secretary and office wife, who had typed his manuscripts in the firm's time and had been rewarded with the dedication of *The Big Chariot*. When Johnston called for silence so that he could speak her praises, Clift whispered through clenched teeth: 'Bloody Mary; if another person mentions to me how marvellous she is I'm going to throw up on their feet!'[64]

Paul Brickhill the writer was there, and Colin Colahan the painter, and Cedric and Pat Flower, who were themselves anxious to leave England. The Nolans had already gone to Italy. English guests and Australian expatriates who had gravitated to the Johnstons mingled together famous or unknown, squatting on the floor when the chairs were all occupied. Very late, and apologetic, Peter Finch turned up and announced that he had just signed a contract with J. Arthur Rank for £70,000 a year, but he was so broke at the time that Neil Whitlock had to trim his frayed shirt cuffs for him.[65] In *Clean Straw for Nothing* Finch's characterisation, Archie Calverton, turns up at four in the morning drunk and dishevelled, refusing an invitation to come inside, but pressing into Meredith's hand a St Christopher medal for luck before pushing off into the London fog like some Dickensian outcast. This is fictitious, because Finch was observed circulating among the guests at the party.

A shadow was cast over the good cheer when Wilfred Thomas and Bettina Dixon arrived, somewhat late, with a solemn announcement. Thomas had received a phone call from Canberra just as he was leaving, saying that the Kalymnian scheme was off.[66] The divers had decided not to go after all — the prospect of deep waters, sharks, and leaving their familiar way of life proved too daunting, and they felt it would be better to look for work on the Greek mainland. Thomas had been dreading breaking the news, and there was a moment of gloomy silence after he spoke. It was broken by Johnston, who piped up 'What the hell — we'll go anyway: it's too late to change — we'll just have to see what happens.' 'We can't go back on it now,' rejoined Clift, 'I've already cancelled the order for the winter coal!'[67]

In the morning, as they sat amid the debris of the party, such defiance perhaps felt reckless and a little scary. In *Clean Straw for Nothing*, Johnston makes Meredith recall 'this racking apprehension in my guts about what we were committing ourselves to. And the knowledge that it was too late to do anything about it. Whatever the doubt or fear or despair, there was no turning back. We were committed. Irrevocably' (*CSFN* 124).

So on 25 November 1954 they left England for Kalymnos. The fact that their specific purpose in going had evaporated was beside the point; if one excuse to get free failed, they would simply invent another. The plan now was to go to Kalymnos for about a year, or however long it took to write a book of some kind about the island itself, depending on what turned up. After that, life was to be an open question, and this was exactly how both of them wanted it.

CHAPTER VII

Kalymnos

'Oh it's awful, *Mum!' Martin sobbed. 'I haven't had any peanut butter since London and I don't know what* anyone *is saying.'* (Mermaid Singing 13)

The Johnstons spent about a week in Athens, during which time they were able to arrange to rent a small house on the sea-front on Kalymnos. In a letter to Higham finalising the details of publication of *The Cyprian Woman*, which had dragged on because of the change-over from Faber to Collins, Johnston added, 'Everything goes well. The sun is bright, the children are settling in magnificently (they are swimming today!), and Charmian and I are both happy and confident.'[1] On 2 December 1954 they set sail for Kalymnos via the island of Kos, both of which lay just off the Turkish coast, a journey of over two hundred miles across the Aegean from Piraeus. It was a rough crossing. If they had been expecting cloudless skies and Mediterranean blue everywhere, they did not know about Greek winters: icy winds and gunmetal waves lashed their small *caique*, a fitting introduction to the winter months ahead.

Nor could the Johnstons have chosen a less inviting part of Greece than this rocky, treeless outpost that 'not even the Greeks visited if they could help it', according to Cedric Flower, who with his wife joined the Johnstons there later. There were no hospitals, doctors or dentists, no running water, no sewerage. Many Kalymnian families were subsisting, and not all that well, on money sent them from their menfolk

141

working abroad; the word 'Australie' was scrawled on several Kalymnian walls. Flower remembers 'the distressing sight of crippled ex-divers, legatees of the "bends", who got about the streets in billy-carts, or were propped in corners for all to see. The general feeling of the place was one of isolation and depression.'[2]

Despite all this, the Johnstons remained cheerful and determined to make their Greek adventure a success. The house they had rented from Athens turned out to be a narrow, yellow, unfurnished, unheated affair with a leaky roof. It did have a toilet cistern, but this was utterly functionless because there was no water or sewerage to connect it to. And the rent of six hundred drachmas per month was exorbitant. But their Greek neighbours welcomed them warmly, gave them furniture, cooked them meals and, despite the language gap, helped them to settle in.[3]

Notwithstanding George's assurances, the children did in fact have their difficulties in making the change from a comfortable and familiar London existence. There were frequent displays of insecurity and dejection; Shane, just six, was clingy and surly and defiant, while seven-year-old Martin seemed panicky, and flew between extremes of showing-off and bursting into tears. Unable to communicate with the Kalymnian children, Martin was desperate enough for friendship to resort to bribery: Clift noticed his precious collection of soldiers was missing, and when she asked him he confessed that he'd given them all to the Greek children 'because they didn't have any', but Clift understood him to be buying popularity. The irony was that the Kalymnian children had no use for such toys, which were not part of their life.[4] Eventually the difficulties sorted themselves out, especially when they began at the Primary School — the 'Black School' it was called — and began their rapid acquisition of the language. Also, the Kaylmnian adults made a great fuss over them, often showing them favour over their own. They had trouble with the names, distorting them to 'O Matis! Say!', a strange invocation, which rang above the waterfront activities whenever their presence was in demand.

Johnston and Clift got straight down to work on the book,

which they decided should be a novel, and another collaboration, despite their vow of a year earlier that they would not collaborate again. Only three weeks after their arrival Johnston wrote optimistically to Higham,

> We have settled very happily into Kalymnos and the book has begun and is well under way. We are both tremendously excited about it. It is far better than we had even dared to hope, and we both feel that we are on a winner. The big problem is to make our writing justify the theme, which really is one of epic dimensions.[5]

The first title conceived for it was 'The Kalymnian', after its hero, Manoli, a tough sponge-boat captain whose fortunes affect those of the island itself. He is probably a composite of several such figures on Kalymnos, embodying the strength of spirit that the Johnstons saw in them all, and never ceased to admire: for years after they left the island they talked repeatedly of the magnificent qualities of the sponge divers and crews. Many of the other characters in the book, too, are named and modelled on the Kalymnian neighbours and friends they were getting to know: Irini, Mina, Sevasti, Mikali, Manoli. They were always quick to use the material immediately to hand.

Internal evidence suggests that Johnston did most of the writing of this novel: the central foreign character, Morgan Leigh, is something of an *alter ego*, and the story is mostly concerned with male adventure, both sexual and heroic. There is no female character who would represent Clift's authorial viewpoint. Johnston later claimed that it was really his book, 'the two names having been left there as an obligation of contract',[6] so it seems that the collaboration was only nominal. When the script reached Bobbs-Merrill in March they went into raptures, convinced they had at last got a money-spinner out of Johnston and Clift, though they did suggest that the title be changed to *The Sea and the Stone*. One of the editors, Herman Ziegner, wrote a self-congratulatory internal memorandum implying that much of the credit should go to themselves for backing 'a pair of authors with big talent, something very close to genius':

> ... we have carried on with these authors in the hope of getting a book with the intense dramatic power of High

Valley, *written with all the skill and artistry Charmian Clift*
and George Johnston have at their command, and much closer
in its people and setting to the experience and interest of
American readers. Published at a favourable season, such a
book could turn out to be a major success. It took five years,
but I believe we have the book we have been building for in
The Sea and the Stone.[7]

Ziegner's colleague, Ross Baker, replied with the sobering
reminder that while they certainly should go ahead and publish, they had so far received small returns for their lavish
promotions of Johnston books.

In England, Higham felt they should keep their options
open and offer the novel to both Faber and Collins, but
Johnston had had enough of Faber: money was more important to him now than status, and Faber were 'the deadest of
dead losses as far as our novels are concerned'.[8] They had
pinned a great deal of hope on the success of this book, which
could determine whether they could buy another year or two
living in Greece, or give it all up. Until they knew of Bobbs-
Merrill's enthusiasm, they must have waited for the mail with
unconcealed impatience. The suspense niggled them into
almost weekly changes of plan, whether they would go to
Hydra — still in their thoughts from April — or to somewhere
equally beautiful, such as Mykonos or Spetsai, and for how
long. One scheme, should the book make enough money, was
to stay on Hydra 'for two years and then back to Australia'.[9]

Here is further evidence that Johnston was not consciously
'expatriating' himself from Australia. Even at this stage being
away was still a kind of extended working holiday, especially
now that he had left England. Of course they wanted to stay
on as long as possible, though they still had no intention of
putting down European roots. As soon as anything went
wrong they were obviously prepared to scuttle back home
immediately. Australia was there, warm and familiar, should
it be needed: he never published nor was heard to express a
word of criticism against Australia the whole time he was
away, although he did begin to think about it more critically in
1963, during the writing of *My Brother Jack*.

Another reason for Clift not being deeply involved in the
writing of 'The Kalymnian' was that she had a book of her

Farewell party at the Kensington flat. *From left to right:* Anthea Batten, Patricia Simione, Harry Kippax, Johnston, Michael Webster, Mary Buck, Victor Valentine, Anthony Whitlock

...rd from Sidney Nolan, 1957

Mr + Mrs George Johnston
Poste Restante
HYDRA
GREECE

02 AUG 57

30
BERGAMA

Canakkale.

...re it is that famed
...t. We took a taxi
...ere.
...t to Anzac today so
record is complete.
Thought of you both.
Love. Sid.

A bedroom in the
Johnston house,
Hydra

Katsikas store (at
left), Hydra

Clift at work, Hydra

Clift shopping with Martin, Hydra

house by the well, Hydra

On the quayside, Hydra. *Left to right:*
Marianne Jensen, Clift, Wolf
Cardomatis, unknown, Johnston,
1959

A card from Leonard Cohen, 1962

Hydra, early 1960s,
with Johnston's loss
of weight in painful
evidence

own under way. The business of organising school for the children and getting to know the neighbours, acquiring some help in the house and generally coping with the domestic chores had fallen to her, and since these matters in the Kalymnian context presented themselves as a total change from the life she had been used to, they stimulated her into putting it down in a kind of personal diary-cum-travel book which she dedicated to her mother and decided to call *Mermaid Singing*, after Eliot's Prufrockian dreamer:

> *I have heard the mermaids singing, each to each.*
> *I do not think that they will sing to me.*

While Johnston was indulging himself in hot-blooded fictions, Clift slowly and painstakingly put together an imaginative and lyrical record of their day-to-day adaptation to the new way of life. She details the primitive customs and ceremonies of the island's near-peasant population, including portraits of people such as the one of their domestic help, Sevasti:

> ... *the leathery folds of her cheek emphasised the beautiful modelling of her thin fine nose and the flat plane of her brow. Her smile, for all the broken stumps of teeth and spaces of shiny pink gum, is enchanting, her hands truly marvellous. And in spite of the marks of obvious suffering — a pattern in flesh of the looting of her home by the Germans, its ultimate destruction by British bombs, the near starvation and flight to Turkey, the nomad life of a refugee in Palestine and Egypt — in spite of an inherent gentleness that is calm and lovely, Sevasti carries within her an inextinguishable spark of raffishness. It is apparent in the very way she wears her coif, not folded severely about brow and chin like the other women's, but rather loose and slipping on top, with ends always coming untied and flapping around her shoulders. It is this raffishness that leads her to dispose of the empty tins of the household in a mad hurling game played from the balcony, with George as her partner and harbour buoys, caiques, and even passing pedestrians as targets.*[10]

Its attention to detail gives *Mermaid Singing* substance, and Clift's genuine absorption in the subject gives it conviction. She had to ward off Johnston's attempts to make it more 'colourful' by gingering up the adjectives, according to Cedric Flower, who arrived in time to witness some embarrassing scenes as Clift successfully resisted her husband's attempts to 'correct' her style.[11] The result is arguably her best book.

With 'The Kalymnian' finished, Johnston cast about for material among local legends and gossip, some of which he turned into stories, such as 'The Anatolian Turk' and 'The Good Gorgona', which never found a publisher, and 'Strong Man from Piraeus' and 'The Astypalaian Knife', which did. A fisherman had given Johnston a striking horn-handled knife studded with discs of coloured bone, which had come from Astypalaia, and its beauty had stimulated him into weaving a love story around it. He sent these four stories to Higham to try to sell, but the agent replied with the discouraging view that they were not publishable, and though he would send them off he thought Johnston was 'not as happy in the short story medium as in the novel'.[12] Other bits of knowledge Johnston picked up on Kalymnos had to wait around in his mental filing cabinet (he certainly did not keep actual records or notebooks) until he found a use for them. One was that Kalymnos gets a mention in *The Odyssey*, and the other was a story someone told him about Phidias, the great sculptor of the Parthenon, who was said to have been buried on Kalymnos with a large quantity of his best works, enough to make an archaeologist lose sleep. Both items eventually turn up in Johnston novels.

With the arrival of summer they relaxed a little, swimming every day and soaking up the sun, taking picnics. The children were on school holidays and were quickly turning brown, though their blond heads distinguished them from the Greeks. Johnston revived an old pastime, cruising about in Kalymnian boats. 'If ever I make a fortune', he wrote to George Ferguson, 'I'll buy one and bring it out to Sydney. Lovely, chunky, graceful nine-metre boats that spin around like a London taxi.'[13] In July, Cedric and Pat Flower arrived, and though they had painful moments listening to the rows over *Mermaid Singing*, the thing that most struck them was the absolute accord that existed between Johnston and Clift about what they were doing in Greece, and about the importance of staying on for a while. 'They were like a double-act,' says Flower, 'except that it wasn't an act: they would feed each other lines — Charmian would give George a cue, he would respond. They would support each other all the time.'[14] During that month, news came that Bobbs-Merrill in the USA, and Collins and Faber in the UK had all made offers for *The Sea and the Stone*, although Faber wanted some 'obscene' passages cut, which they felt 'wouldn't be safe to publish'.[15] This was the chance to break with Faber, and the contract was signed with Collins, who had UK and Australian rights, so would replace Angus & Robertson as Johnston's Australian publisher. Collins also wanted a change of title to *The Sponge Divers*, which was agreed.

The Flowers did not like Kalymnos much, and gradually persuaded the Johnstons to see it for the desolate pile it was. Having achieved this, they suggested that they would mind the children for a couple of weeks while George and Charmian travelled about to find a more congenial island, with special regard to Hydra, which had come up repeatedly in conversation. While they were gone, the Flowers were not granted a quiet life, being placed on the receiving end of a plague of bed-lice, an earthquake and two important-looking telegrams for Johnston. One was from his old office in London asking him to write up a report for them on the earthquake's devastation of the town of Volos, and the other was from the US literary agency Harold Ober Inc., to say that *Cosmopolitan* magazine had bought the story 'The Astypalaian Knife' for the staggering sum of $850. When Johnston returned, the news made him very cocky indeed. He flatly refused to do the Volos assignment 'on principle', if we take *Clean Straw for Nothing* as a guide, the 'principle' of course being to demonstrate to everyone, including himself, that his ties with the newspaper world were severed for good. He then delivered a patronising rebuke to Higham for lack of faith in his stories:

> ... you may be interested in telling your readers that my short story 'The Astypalaian Knife', which they considered not worthwhile showing to anybody, has been bought in New York by 'Cosmopolitan' for 850 dollars. It is to appear in their December issue. Earlier, Collier's saw the story and although they finally turned it down, they praised its 'warmth and style' and expressed an eagerness to see any future stories I write.

> This does, I feel, endorse my belief that an author's mate-
> rial should be submitted around and not merely held for a
> critical examination. I'm sure you see my point. Had I
> accepted the opinion expressed by your readers on the manu-
> script I might have felt it not worthwhile to submit the stories
> elsewhere. I would thus have been 850 dollars worse off
> (which is roughly equivalent to the advance paid by Collins
> on my novels) and would have made no headway with other
> magazines, such as Collier's and the Post, both of which have
> asked to see future material simply on the grounds of having
> read the material upon which your readers based their some-
> what disheartening reports.
>
> > With best wishes,
> > Yours,
> > George Johnston.[16]

Another problem reared its head at this time, and this was
the discovery that he would have to pay tax on his English
and American earnings at the rate payable by residents of
those countries, even though he was not receiving the benefits of that tax. This was in addition to his Greek tax.
Johnston was to wage a long, bitter and largely unsuccessful
struggle against the stupefying unfairness of this, which was
to make substantial reductions in his and Clift's income over
many years.

However, the immediately important matter, now that the
Johnstons had seen and decided upon Hydra, was to shift
camp as soon as possible. They had already rented a house
close to the waterfront, and with the Flowers to help with the
moving, there was nothing standing in their way. Nevertheless, the farewells were prolonged and tearful. The children in
particular had grown fond of the life on Kalymnos, and the
local people were for their part sad to see their adopted
foreign family depart.[17] It had in fact been a successful experiment. The break with the rat-race had been achieved, two
books and several stories had been written, boosting their
writing reputations, and Greece was throwing new material
and ideas to them all the time. Most important, Johnston and
Clift were happy, and Clift publicly reflected on this:

> George and I were very happy too. If something of the
> dramatic quality of our first months had been dulled with the
> coming of spring and our growing familiarity with the island

and its people, we had found a new sense of consolidation and belonging. We had lost the feverish desperation that had marked both our flight from London and our arrival in Greece, and if the Fleet Street spectre still gibbered sometimes we did not let it worry us too much.[18]

Clift had another reason for feeling optimistic that August: just as the nine months on Kalymnos had brought about a rebirth of spirit in her, she found she was to bear a child the following April. It was a family joke that the child was conceived one night during an earthquake, when they slept on the beach for safety. Johnston said it ought to have a classical name, because it was fathered under the auspices of Poseidon, god of earthquakes and the sea, so they asked Martin what name he thought most suitable. 'Agamemnon,' replied Martin.[19] Not relishing the thought of the baby being called 'Aggie' if the family returned to Australia, a compromise was reached that if it was a boy he should be called Jason. George and Charmian were delighted with the prospect of a third child, although he had strong reservations about island medical facilities and insisted that a bed should be booked in an Athens hospital. The success of 'The Astypalaian Knife' meant they could afford it.

~~~~~~~~ C H A P T E R   V I I I ~~~~~~~~

HYDRA: The House by the Well

There is no rush here where no wheel turns and everything
moves to the gentler pace of the plodding mule or pattering
donkey, where hours rest easily on the couch of peace, and
the calendar is a slow ratchet of unfretful customs and sanc-
tified days and innocent festivals. (CSFN 172)

The island of Hydra is barren and uninteresting, but the town
is small and beautiful in the scale of a theatrical set. The
mostly white houses spill down from a steep back-drop of
hills and collect in a jumble around the port, which is secluded behind a tall gateway of rocks. The view eastward from
the top of these rocks is of a pattern of islands, which stretch
away to the horizon like lilies on a pond. Although it is only
some forty miles from Athens, and within sight of the Pelo-
ponnese, Hydra (pronounced 'eethra') is in several respects
peculiarly remote from the technological age: it continues to
disallow the presence of motor vehicles, and in the Johnstons'
time there was only a locally generated electricity supply,
which closed down for part of the day, and well water only.
Building controls have prevented any modern architectural
developments, so that in its essential appearance the town
has hardly changed since the nineteenth century. In summer
these days the place swarms with tourists, but when the
Johnstons arrived it was still relatively unknown to foreigners.

The locals were astonished to see a foreign family, complete
with children, suitcases and domestic odds and ends. Usually

150

foreigners were either tourists passing quickly through, or else strange, artistic types, with whom the islanders could have no discourse. People with children are more accessible, and for that matter more respected, by Greeks in small towns and villages, so the Johnstons were soon treated as familiars, which made their settling-in process easier. There was one foreign couple already living on the island — Christian Heidsieck, from a well-known Reims champagne family, and his Russian wife, Lily Mack. Heidsieck was a potter, and lived inland behind the hills, so he had only an occasional relationship with the town. Nor did he have much of one with the Johnstons immediately, for at the end of that year he was drafted into the army to serve in Algeria for two years.[1]

Michael Cacoyannis, the Greek film director, had been making *A Girl in Black* on Hydra during 1955, and the Johnstons got to know him and the actress Ellie Lambetti during the later months of that year. There were also cultural nomads coming and going, some leaving after a few days, others declaring an intention of staying on and living the good life. Cedric Flower said they tended to talk too much about what they were going to do, and he could see the dangers for the Johnstons even at that early stage. Flower and his wife had no wish to stay, and had put in an application to be repatriated to Australia on a Greek migrant ship.

Patrick Greer, an Irish teacher who had been at the British Institute in Spain, arrived with his Australian wife, Nancy Dignan, after someone in Athens had told them about the Johnstons. Greer wanted to be a writer, too. He was nervous about approaching Johnston at first,[2] but then he came upon him in a small grocery shop on the port run by two brothers called Nick and Tony Katsikas, who, by way of creating a convivial atmosphere for customers in the shop, served out cognac or wine in small metal measuring cups. A group would gather, chairs would be brought from the living quarters, and the talk would begin in halting mixtures of Greek and English, invariably with Johnston at the centre, just like old days in the Long Bar of the Australia Hotel. If the weather was warm enough, they would move the chairs out onto the quay in front of the shop, and Nick and Tony would serve the drinks, with perhaps a little food from their own kitchen, on rough wooden tables. This place became the frequent haunt of Johnston and Clift when they were not working. After his initial conversation in the shop with George about writing, Greer became a regular member of the coterie. The Greers were able to use the Heidsiecks' house while they were away, and they become more or less permanent Hydriots. In this way the beginnings of a foreign colony were established.

The news from publishers continued to be good. Johnston's American agent, Harold Ober Inc., was negotiating film rights for *The Sea and the Stone*, and *Argosy* magazine in England had accepted the story 'Strong Man from Piraeus'. Johnston was again provoked into a small reprimand for his London agents for tardiness in their dealings with Ober and in getting his work sold generally: he had received no word for two months about Collins's plans for the British edition of *The Sponge Divers*. Meanwhile, the American version was getting good reviews.

In November 1955 Sid and Cynthia Nolan arrived for a prolonged stay. Johnston had urged them to come, stressing the quiet and cheapness, and most of all the wonderful light. Nolan was actually meant to be painting in Italy, having received an Italian fellowship specifically to make paintings of the war-damaged Mantegna frescoes in the Capella Ovetari in Padua. 'A rather grandiose conception', reflected Nolan, 'as a comment on war, which I am still going to go back and do.'[3] At that time the task was getting the better of him, so he decided to use the fellowship money to take up Johnston's invitation. It took them some time to find a house, but when they finally did it was worth the wait. The Greek painter Ghika (Nikos Hadjikiriakos) owned his family's seventeenth-century mansion, perched on the hill behind the town, with breathtaking views in almost every direction. Ghika lived there only part of the time, and so had made the house – a virtual palace – available to approved painters in his absence. Cynthia Nolan learned of this and managed to get it for the remainder of their stay on Hydra, some seven or eight months.

After the Flowers left to return to Australia, the Johnstons, the Greers and the Nolans were the only resident foreigners. Through the winter of 1955–56 they spent a good deal of time together, often talking about art and writing, and at times, especially when Johnston and Nolan were alone together, about Australia and the past. They shared, of course, a Melbourne background, which in that exotic setting drew them closer together. They mused on their fathers working in the tramsheds, and on Australian Rules football, which had once been important to them both, and on cycling, which had been Nolan's sport as a teenager. Johnston, for some reason, began to talk a lot about the war to Nolan: the bad things he had seen and heard, the terrible sacrifices. 'Rough stuff, some of it,' recalled Nolan. Then the subject would get around to classical myths; they were both constantly diving into Johnston's copies of *The Iliad* and Graves's *Greek Mythology*. Nolan claims he was less respectful towards the Greek myths than Johnston, who 'took them for granted' in a knowledgeable and reverential way. 'I take nothing for granted,' asserted Nolan when talking about the difference in their attitudes, 'I had no more respect for them than for St Kilda football club. All the same to me, in that it was all grist to my mill.'[4] In fact Nolan's mill was already at work, as he made numerous sketches for a series of paintings that would fuse both Australian and classical images of war.

It was not just the talk with Johnston that stimulated this. Alan Moorehead had been living on the neighbouring island of Spetsai, writing his book *Gallipoli*, and Johnston had read, and passed on to Nolan, a deeply felt piece by Moorehead in the *New Yorker* dealing with the Anzacs. 'It was like unlocking a door,' Johnston later wrote.

> From then on, when the retsina circled and wild winter buffeted at the shutters of the waterfront taverns, we would talk far into the small hours about this other myth of our own, so uniquely Australian and yet so close to that much more ancient myth of Homer's. Nolan's poetic imagination saw them as one, saw many things fused into a single poetic truth lying, as the true myth should, outside time.[5]

If often occurred to them, too, how geographically close both Troy and Gallipoli were to each other, and indeed to themselves, lying just a few hours away across the Aegean. Out of all this came the inspiration for Nolan's 'Gallipoli' paintings, for which the sketches done on Hydra were a preparatory 'working through' of ideas. The actual paintings were not begun, however, until several years later in London.

In January of the new year, 1956, a golden opportunity to buy a house came up. It was a three-storeyed, nine-roomed stone house, near a well, built in 1788 by a sea captain who had successfully run Nelson's blockade of French-held ports and made himself rich. Johnston often commented on the coincidence of the house's birth with the date of the arrival of the first fleet to Australia. At times he even tried to see it as fateful. The going price to the Johnstons of 120 gold pounds (about £500 sterling at the time) was remarkably low, since apart from needing some minor renovation the building was in good condition. It being a bargain gave them no time to waste, so they had to consider and decide almost immediately. To buy it would take all the money they had put away for the hospital in Athens and the fare home if things did not work out, and also would mean making a long-term commitment to living on Hydra, and for Charmian to give birth at home without professional medical assistance. Never able to resist a risk when they saw it, they of course bought the house. It was the first piece of property they had owned, either of them in their lives.

With Clift in the final months of her pregnancy, there was a lot to be done in a short space of time. Apart from writing and moving, Johnston had to get some renovations done. They decided to knock down the wall between the two top rooms, creating a large sunny studio that led out onto a roof terrace. From here was a spectacular view across the sea to the mainland. Johnston found it no easy task to make his wishes clear to the Greek workmen, and in the end the alterations took some months to complete. This meant that his writing slowed down, and in fact he did not send anything off for publication between July 1955, when he sold 'The Astypalaian Knife', and about March 1956, a long gap for Johnston.

It was at this time that he began a whole new authorial venture. Perhaps the domestic preoccupations prevented him undertaking anything very serious or requiring deep re-

search. Whatever the reasons behind it, he soon became enthusiastic about the idea itself. His plan was to write a series
of crime novels, popular 'thrillers', featuring a professor of
archaeology-cum-amateur-detective called Professor Ronald
Challis, a sort of rival to Simenon's Maigret and Agatha
Christie's Poirot.[6] Instead of using his own name, Johnston
decided to borrow the children's names in order to create the
pseudonym 'Shane Martin'. The first of the series, *Twelve
Girls in the Garden*, was completed by March, and both Collins
in the UK and William Morrow in the USA, a new publishing
house for Johnston, bought it unhesitatingly and with enthusiasm for the idea of a series. Meanwhile, Penguin bought the
paperback rights to the old *Death Takes Small Bites*, paying an
advance of £100.[7] Clift at this stage was hurrying with the
finishing touches to *Mermaid Singing* before her baby arrived
to take over her time.

These busy and productive months of early 1956 are most
vividly described in a letter from Cynthia Nolan to Pat Flower
in late March. The two women had been friends since the war
years, when they had worked together organising hostels for
munition workers.[8] As Patrick White has written, Cynthia
Nolan wrote 'extravagant, sometimes crazy letters which
would open all of a sudden into passages of great sense'.[9]
This letter is a good example.

> My Dear Pat,
> So delighted to hear all goes well and you are both content
> to be back. I always fear a moment of revulsion, but you seem
> to have avoided this. No wonder you both loathed Greece, I
> understand this completely. It's the most difficult country and
> the strangest to adjust to of any I've been in. Apart from this
> your anxiety dear was enough to turn your stomach what
> utter misery. And living with other people is a penance, a
> mortification, an impossibility. Then Hydra in summer, full of
> myths I could never raise more than a yawn over, preferring
> my case histories contemporary, with the name of Brown.
> Nor do I swoon over shards, pieces or pillars. Nor readily
> accept fleas, lice and bugs. But it is winter and we live in this
> great house that stands alone, rising three storeys out of the
> bare hill behind Carmini. Everything is charming, the beds
> heavenly comfort, a puller when one bothers to pump water,
> a basin and taps here in my bedroom, from every window

scenes from some book of hours, eight with plate cacti, blue hyacinth, single stock, geraniums, cyclamine, white daisies and scarlet poppies. All surrounded by great thirty foot high stone walls. It's dead quiet. Only sometimes in the evening goat bells, or the sound of a distant mouth organ. We have had, true, the tail end of some of the blizzards, but many days to sit outside in, and two last week when I sunbathed naked. You know what this means after London also I regret to admit it, but after all the small rooms, the discomfort, the other people's houses, the stove by the la and the bath under the bed, I am happy, content, relaxed, at home as I haven't been since eighteen. There is no hope. I thought I'd beaten all that, it's just waiting till I had a taste to stick out its tongue. Unworthy am I, and that's the way I am. As to local food, its quite all right now, fresh fish of several varieties every night except storm times, good salads as they come round, lamb that melts. The citrus better than I've had anywhere, extraordinary. I tell you I like it all, the white two storey houses that have a blue haze for that twenty evening minutes, the kites that jerk up into the blue and white sky, the brilliant mainland that you can touch across the satin ribbon blue, or pewter or yes wine red aegean, the naked mountains that glow and stand up like cardboard cut out against a primrose cloud. Sorry, I am in love again, besotted, swooning, unable to embrace enough. Every day madness grows. It is true I have no ambition, I have always wanted to pull out, not to give it a go. Cities, unless one can live in sheltered luxury, disturb me. Walking along those crowded pavements, into those pushing shops, the noise of the gutters and horns, the smell of petrol and people, the anxiety on every face. JJJJJJJJJJ go my rhythms. Buses, undergrounds, smoke, voices. JJJJJJJJJJ. But not S. who is a city man, stimulated, as one should be I'm sure, by all the sights and sounds, longing to get in, to compete, to give it a go. No matter how flyblown the café-table, he will want to sit with me, for one or two or more hours, over some piece of something, watching and thinking and perhaps expounding. I long to flee. So although he has enjoyed his bits of Greece (God and Delos singing out of the sea, Delos with its carven lions, frail pillars, and scent laden dew. We had the whole island entirely to ourselves) and finds the myths utterly fascinating, not to say hilarious, he would die of boredom if he was confined to any island, while I could spend my days within just such walls as would fill my hours with meditative scrapings and weedings, with all the great steps that have uncovered from their years old overgrowth, with creating a garden that would become one of the wonders of the world. And I mean this. Undoubtedly what talent and desire I have lies here. Such a garden is my thing. One over which I dwelt a lifetime, and which would take other lifetimes to grow entirely to perfection. Quoth the raven, not only nevermore but never, never, never. Little bits I'll do, scraps, a tree here or there — nothing. But I stand and contemplate and think what could go where, slowly putting the place together. Woniora Ave of course one could only do so much with. But this place is something else.

As to the Johnstons. Charm is admirable truly. As her hour approaches I think some or most of the bitterness and frustration and anguish have gone. She swings along, shoulders back, great smile working, although I know she must be deadly tired, by now. I've seen thousands of pregnant women, and strong ones who delighted to be bearing a baby, but I can't remember one who bore herself with such verve, with such an air. I view her having it here with the local midwife with the greatest timidity. Fine, if all goes well. Or not all that fine, with no drug whatever. You know how she is on the Greek way of life — without, I may say knowing a lot about it — and it's been a joke to see her horror as more and more Greek dames she's met in shops or side street tell her not to worry, they will be along from the first pain, they will sit with her, and keep her company, throughout! Yes one feels this is as it should be, but we, want to never so much, can't act natural within another culture.

The Johnstons new house is the last bargain in Hydra, and really quite a dream. I expect they have told you of it. But whatever their usual exaggerations, this is tops. I fear George will bugger it as nearly as he can as I note his preparations with his treasures from the trunks — sets of prints beautifully framed by himself in black pas pt. etc. George and I have certain qualities in common, that he would not admit to. We both are in a way gregarious but detest most people. George more than I, dislikes, I would say, everyone outside his immediate family, and this in spite of wanting awfully to love the whole world and more so, have the whole world find him the greatest mate going. We both like to talk. And if we lived in the same house it would be a matter of who could get to the carving knife quickest. I can say this with you still understanding that I like George, he's good fun in short doses. I think he probably dislikes me intensely. Certainly we have often to maintain great control not to attack the other. I don't know but can guess what he has stopped himself from telling me. I know I have just managed not to say that the Sea and the Stone is the most revolting rehash of Steinbeck and

157

Hemingway, and the Greek characters as unreal as Heming-ways Spanish ones in For Whom the Bell Tolls, without the book having any of its merits. One doesn't care what is done in this way, it's a good way to live and make a living, writing what one can sell well and decently and having a pleasant life. But I will not say what he wants to hear, that he is a brilliant writer. And if asked I will say that if he wants to write something a bit better he'll have to go to what he knows — Elwood, Melbourne, and the shoddy flats of third-rate journalists, the newspaper rackets, the big time boys. Austra-lia. And NOT be afraid of treading on the toes of some mate who will one day cut him in the hotel Australia bar — and who really hates him like shit anyhow.

Well all this because there is, I suppose, a lot of writing talk in the air. The other couple, living in Lily's house, are Irish writer and aus-jewish painter or anything you please (Nancy has infinite ability for making dough, she could I know take a restaurant or photography business and turn it over almost immediately, has done in the past). Anyhow, Patrick the husband is Protestant Irish, an orphan, educated at a school for distressed gentlefolk. He is I should think a good teacher — they have made a mint between them at British Institute abroad — but will kill himself, Nancy told me (I don't see any signs) if he doesn't write. He's been writing short stories for years on the side, I mean about six short stories and six articles and one turned down novel. And not only will he not be the great writer he thinks he is, he won't even be a writer who will sell, if he doesn't pull his head in. I get frank even though I have the best intentions, because everyone gives everyone else their things to read and wants to know what they think (thank God there is nothing of mine or Mr. Nolan would be passing that round) and each in turn says Wonder-ful out of one side of their mouths and Crap out the other. I got tight the other night and told Patrick his was one long whine, and complaining was good if you could do it like Faulkner, Dostoyevski, Kafka, but a whine was neither good nor saleable. How can I get out of that one? When S. and I are sitting at a large table in one of the cafes and the others come in to join us I always notice a rush as they hasten to bring their chairs and place them jammed tight around S. while I sit in a lonely state with three quarters of the table to myself. As S. says, they're in a panic. However, we really all get on rather well. It's fine not having any more. Did you know that horror English painter Vere? Frightful troublemak-er, almost managed to get S. and George at each other's throats. And Carol I didn't go for really, the foreign accent and upturned eyes − a nuisance with men around. Sooner or later there would always be trouble where she was, as S. said, because that's what she wants.

I think I have said too much now. Love and to Cedric. S. gets madly homesick for Aus. I shall really wither if I get my roots pulled up much oftener. Hugs.

PS April. *Have left this open until now to give news of the baby. Jason arrived at 6 a.m. within three quarters of an hour and with the aid of Zoe and the midwife. The latter crooned over Charm. and rubbed her stomach with alcohol during the event, and gave her two tumblers full of ouzo after. The time must have been hell without any drug, nevertheless she is a damn lucky girl and I tell you I heave a great sigh of relief. Fortunately all this family seem so strong (spit spit). This way seems so much the best under the circumstances. Jason is very like Charm., same build, and big mouth and bone formation of face − but the longest fingers I've ever seen − what does this portend? and I'm not sure he isn't going to catch George's nose − George reports also, with what satisfaction you can imagine, that he has a large cock. Knowing what an adoring mama Charm. is I think she is now all pride in this third wonder.The poor girl has certainly had a bad time of resentment and rage behind her. George is absolutely thrilled. Shane so relieved it's not another girl . . . and Martin watching over his mother, sitting beside her all the first afternoon while G. was elsewhere, and reading five chapters of The Iliad without stop − aloud. The old crone − once procuress, remember, insisting on coming in the second day and spitting − and I mean spitting, three times first on Charm. and then on Jason. You can imagine this old nursies blood pressure.*

We were terribly thrilled to hear your wonderful news Cedric! May it go on better and better. And that you both have a good flat quick. More and more good times and beautiful money! and quick building with your cottage at T. address is co Bank of NSW, Berkeley Sq., Wl.

love C.[10]

There is an addition to the letter which, in retrospect, casts an ominous shadow into the future. Scribbled in hand up the margin of the page Cynthia Nolan has written: 'I find one can get as much of every kind of Berbital etc. at the chemist as one asks for!' Considering that all three of these talented women − Cynthia Nolan, Pat Flower and Clift − were eventually to take their own lives by means of overdoses of barbiturates, this gleeful reference to its ease of purchase in

Greece has a chilling effect on one.

Nolan himself conceded that 'Cynthia didn't quite like George's relationship with me ... she thought he drank too much, smoked too much and talked too much'.[11] The feeling was on both sides — Johnston thought her supercilious, and resented her protective reign over Nolan's time and movements. This made things difficult for a close relationship between the four of them, and was probably a disincentive to the Nolans to stay beyond that year. Not that they necessarily would have, given his itchy feet. In fact things got so soured towards the end that in her next book, *Peel me a Lotus*, Clift painted an unsympathetic portrait of Cynthia as the bitchy, aloof Ursula Donovan, which she did probably, according to Cedric Flower, 'out of loyalty to Johnston'.[12] When she read it, Cynthia 'never wanted anything to do with the Johnstons again'.[13] The two men remained on good terms, despite Cynthia's disapproval, and later Johnston drew on his affection for Nolan for the likeable character of Tom Kiernan in *Clean Straw for Nothing*. Interestingly, Kiernan seems to have no partner in his life — 'an unattached man — an asexual man, too' (*CSFN* 187–8), who is totally and ruthlessly dedicated to his painting. The characterisation puzzled, but did not offend, Nolan.

With Jason born and the house changes in hand, the Johnston's continued the busy task of settling. Not much money was coming in, and even that was still being reduced by tax. They heard from Peter Finch in May that he so liked *The Sponge Divers* that he was going to see what he could do to negotiate a film contract. Films were a subject of much conversation over the summer because an American crew had brought Sophia Loren and her entourage to Hydra to make *Boy on a Dolphin*, an event that brought a sudden invasion of visitors, many in sumptuous yachts, to disrupt the peace and quiet of the island. In effect this marked the moment of 'discovery' of Hydra by the international set of the day, many of whom would continue to drop in every summer in order to see and be seen. The Johnstons, in this first year, tried to ignore all this, and concentrate on the business of living as a family and adapting to the local community. Martin and

Shane were attending the 'Down' Primary school, which juts out from a steep cliff overlooking the Johnston house. It is called this presumably to distinguish it from the 'Up' school, situated high-up the eastern hill. It was something of a strain for them to be immersed in Greek culture and its language in the mornings, and at midday return to an English-speaking environment with quite different cultural interests. But in these early years on Hydra this was, according to Martin, 'a good thing because it taught us to question in a way that the other kids did not'.[14] In fact, so long as the family was happy, this bi-cultural situation was an enriching one. Their friendships with the local children were important to them all, not least because they smoothed relations between the adults. Their Hydriot neighbours proved, like the Kalymnians, to be extremely kind and helpful. The Katsikas brothers were especially important in this respect, for it is hard to imagine how the Johnstons would have survived the times when no money was coming in if Nick and Tony Katsikas had not allowed them considerable amounts of credit on supplies to tide them over. If the Johnstons ultimately failed to merge fully into the Greek way of living, it was no fault of the Greeks. Johnston and Clift often claimed that they were merging in because, they insisted, they were 'fully accepted by the locals'.[15] But this was not the problem. It was more that they both already had a cultural identity as Australians, in their own and the Greeks' eyes, and this could not be shed simply by a change of location. Nolan could perceive this. 'George made desperate efforts to become part of Greek culture,' recalled Nolan, 'but I watched this with amusement.'[16] It was some years before George came to see the fundamental difference between being a resident in a country and being part of that country's culture; until he did, he allowed himself to be caught up in a sometimes absurd self-deception. For instance, it was often embarrassing to them both to admit in front of visitors, even after years of living there, their dismal failure to speak Greek. Johnston went into a store one day to buy what he thought he was describing in Greek as 'a large hairy brush'. When everyone in the store began to fall about with laughter, he was worried, and looked foolish when quietly told that he'd just asked for 'a large hairy cunt'.[17]

In September 1956 the Nolans departed, to visit other European places and then back to England. Johnston got down to work on his second 'Shane Martin' book, and Clift began, in what time she could find, on *Peel me a Lotus. Mermaid Singing* came out in the USA to some good reviews, raising hopes for good sales. Over the ensuing winter the publishing news was almost constantly good. Michael Joseph accepted *Mermaid Singing* for an English edition and paid an advance of £100, and an advance of £300 was expected from a British film company for the rights to *The Sponge Divers*.[18] These sums did not in themselves amount to much income for a family of five, but they augured well for the future.

Christmas, however, brought a serious setback. Greek winters, as they had found on Kalymnos, can be bitterly cold. This winter of 1956—57 saw snow, and the Hydra houses were not well heated. Johnston came down with another bad dose of pneumonia over Christmas, and his condition sank to an alarming level. In fact the local doctor — an incompetent drunkard — examined him and gave him up, saying there was no point in doing anything because he was going to die anyway. Clift threw the doctor out and determinedly nursed Johnston herself until he was over it.[19] But he was left with the legacy of a frightful cough, which often brought up blood. Doubtless at this time he knew he had a chronic lung problem, and probably suspected it to be cancer. It did not, however, make him change his smoking and drinking habits.

Nor did it change his capacity for hard work. Johnston completed his second 'Shane Martin' novel, giving it the awful title of 'Press the Rue for Wine', and immediately launched into a third. Then in April came the culmination of all the recent good publishing news when *Twelve Girls in the Garden* was taken by the Dollar Book Club in the USA, with a guarantee of $10,000. Although this was to be split fifty-fifty between author and publisher, even $5000 was far more than they had earned from any previous work. Nor could it have come at a better time, for, as Johnston said in a letter to Higham, asking for a £500 advance on the Book Club money, 'in a few months time we shall have (for us) a great deal of money, whereas at the moment we are broke'.[20] In fact, they had £3 10s in the bank, so the situation was indeed desperate.

Once again fortune had smiled just as Johnston and Clift were on the brink of disaster. Now that money was not an immediate worry, the mixed fortunes of their new books could be borne. Harold Ober Inc. in the US, who subjected all their typescripts to an oddly irrelevant form of literary criticism, did not like 'Press the Rue for Wine', and was trying to hold off sending it to William Morrow in the hope that the third 'Shane Martin' book, which Johnston said was almost finished, could be published instead of it. In the meantime Collins in England read a script of 'Press the Rue for Wine' and liked it, although they suggested a change of title to *The Saracen Shadow*. Their decision to publish it more or less pressured Ober and Morrow into doing the same thing, proving that the complex relations between the UK and US agents and publishers could be turned to Johnston's advantage. Clift also was getting good news and bad news: despite warm reviews and some reports from US college bookstores that she was 'building a place among the young intellectuals and artists',[21] *Mermaid Singing* was not selling well. On top of this, the film negotiations for *The Sponge Divers* fell through. Still, neither illness nor bad news ever stopped them working hard, and before the winter was out Johnston had finished the third 'Shane Martin', titled *The Man Made of Tin*, and Clift had completed a first version of *Peel me a Lotus*, and both typescripts were bundled off.

In *Peel me a Lotus* Clift tried to write a mixture of travel book and diary, partly fictionalised, and less documentary than *Mermaid Singing*. The names of the characters, apart from the Johnstons, are fictive, but those characters are closely based on the actual people: the Nolans, the Greers and others who were an important part of that first eighteen months on Hydra. The book is more self-absorbed that its predecessor, and many of the events and much of the dialogue revolve around a central question put by a 'Mrs Knip', who asks of the author and her husband: 'But what are you doing it *for*?' This was a question that the Johnstons themselves felt important to face now that they had committed themselves to living as a family there indefinitely, and because it had been put to them from time to time that what they were doing was impractical, futile, escapist and harmful to the children. The worst part of this was that they did feel the need to provide some justification to themselves as well as to others. In *Peel me a Lotus* the author's answer to Mrs Knip's question is to say that Greece feels 'more real' to her than anywhere else. This answer is unsatisfactory, except as a subjective affirmation that Clift simply likes it more than anywhere else. What she might have pointed out in her reply is that most people live where they live because of a geographical accident of birth, and do not even question whether or not it suits them. At least the Johnstons were trying to make an intelligent choice based on a combination of factors, including work, interests and economics. After all, they could hardly have survived as full-time writers in England or Australia. In the end, *Peel me a Lotus*, by raising issues that it does not seriously attempt to explore, is not as satisfying a book as *Mermaid Singing*. It is less about relations between a foreign family and Greeks than the earlier work, and its concentration on relationships among the foreign community gives it a gossipy and superficial feel. The publishers may have thought so too, because they did not much like the first version, and returned it for substantial changes.

With four new books behind them, a third child, and the purchase and renovation of a house, Johnston and Clift could look back on their first eighteen months on Hydra with some sense of achievement. With money now in the bank and the debts paid, they relaxed over that 1957 summer. It was noticeable how Hydra was changing — the tourists were arriving in ever-increasing numbers, no doubt partly due to the release of *Boy on a Dolphin*. Certain early representatives of the 'beat' generation, the 'disillusioned' youth of the post-war years, as they were often called, were also discovering Hydra's advantages of cheapness and a pre-twentieth-century way of life. These youths mostly came from the more affluent countries, such as West Germany, Sweden, France or America, and usually they adopted the role of a poet, or painter or philosopher (or all three), and they were all into Zen and detested anything that was done to make money. With its wonderful climate, the warmth and tolerance of its people, and its still depressed economy, Greece was the ideal place to harbour themselves.

More foreigners had taken up residence on the island by this time. There was David Goschen, an English poet, and his wife, Angela; a Swedish writer, Axel Jensen, and his wife, Marianne, later to have an affair with Leonard Cohen and give the title to one of his better-known songs ('Farewell Marianne'); an American writer, Gill Schwartz, and his wife, Loetitia; and, to round off this virtual little United Nations of expatriates, a striking-looking French *roué*-cum-painter called Jean-Claude Maurice, in patched jeans and wearing one gold ear-ring, who came spouting existentialist philosophy, with the credentials of having had several conversations in a Paris café with Jean-Paul Sartre.[22] Maurice liked to show off his handsome body, and women, not least among them Charmian Clift, found him attractive. Not all the arrivals were strangers. Charles Sriber, from Johnston's Sydney journalist days, came around this time with his wife, Ruth, to live in Athens, and occasionally they and the Johnstons would stay at each other's houses. However, Johnston found many of the newcomers on Hydra to be a source of irritation, particularly when they poured scorn on his work for being 'commercial' one day and borrowed money from him the next. 'It isn't that I'm mean,' Clift has him complain in *Peel me a Lotus*, 'or even that I mind being thought respectable, but I'm just beginning to wonder if I'm expected to bloody well subsidize them *all!*'[23] He was of the wrong generation to appreciate the habitual sponging that was part of 'beat' philosophy; and he had seen too much of Depression and war to go along with their simple-minded forms of anti-materialism and pacifism. He got along well with older refugees from civilisation, such as Greer and Sriber, and also with those local Greeks of his own generation with whom he could get into conversation.

Invaders apart, the family enjoyed that summer. They swam day after day in the clear water around from the port, where they dived from the rocks and where Clift, in particular, with her fine Australian crawl and her naturalness in the water, showed everyone the benefits of a Kiama childhood. Johnston finally managed to buy a boat from a Greek fisherman, and felt a little guilty at taking it because it represented the fisherman's livelihood. He changed his tune, however, when the boat, which had been named *Agios Bunyip*, promptly sank soon after it was taken out.[24] He bought another, however, this time calling it the *Slithey Tove*, which proved a successful source of fun, as they sailed and fished out in the straits.

The children continued to be more deeply involved in the local life than their parents. This was the time of intense anti-British feeling over Cyprus, and the teacher in Martin's class was taking a few free hits at the British when Martin stood up and complained that *his* friends in London were very nice people and shouldn't be called names; the consequence was that Martin was given the honour of laying the school wreath on the local memorial on Greece's National Day in that year.[25] The development of the children in Greece was one thing that Clift, in particular, had no second thoughts about, being convinced of its positive advantages. She reflected in *Peel me a Lotus:*

> *I thought today how beautiful my children have become in this deeply natural world, thin, brown, hard creatures, still unconscious of their own grace or even of the extravagance of beauty in which they move and have their being: for them it is no more more to be observed than the number of times their sharp little breasts rise and fall breathing it in.*[26]

The domestic side to life had consolidated nicely. They went to Athens and bought some good furniture, and a new porta-gas cooker to replace the old oil-burner that had flared up and singed Charmian's eyebrows. She had managed to create a galley-type kitchen, which was the envy of every house-owner who saw it — not for its modern facilities, of which it had few, but for its austere, peasant-like atmosphere, which somehow made it a room extremely comforting to sit in and talk while the chores were being done.[27] In all, the house by the well was a successful acquisition, both as a good practical family home, and as an expression of the Johnston style of living. Before the year was out a card came from Sidney Nolan (who had visited Troy earlier) saying, 'Got to

Anzac today, so the record is complete. Thought of you both.' Nolan had always said to them 'Fly with Icarus', and that was the philosophy he adopted for himself as he travelled light about the world, pursuing his own imaginative risks. The Johnstons, however, with three small children anchoring them to the ground were forced to look mostly to the household gods for help and inspiration.

~~~~~~~~~~ **C H A P T E R   I X** ~~~~~~~~~~

HYDRA: The Serpent in the Rock

*Sailing those waters we were once wise in what had to be
done in a night of storm, should a beautiful woman rise on the
tempestuous waves lashing at the boat and cry her aching
question: 'Where is Alexander the Great?' Quick as a flash
one had to be ready with the reply: 'Alexander the Great lives
and reigns!' If this were shouted out the woman would vanish, the storm-wind quieten, the seas subside, and sunrise
would come over an Aegean innocent again. To neglect that
response, that cry of affirmation, was to be doomed. We knew
that. We were warned about it, Cressida and I, the first time
sailing off Santorin, another time coming into Patmos, with
the sun rising behind Samos like the gold embellishment on an
ikon.*

    *Greece's, of course, is a fatal beauty. It always has been, I
suppose. So how important it is to understand the hazardous
breathtaking mysteries, to grasp at wisdoms in the moment of
peril, to stand upright and shout with loud and confident
authority into the very howling mouth of danger, 'Alexander
the Great lives and reigns!'* (CSFN 310—11)

If things had continued to go the way they had to the end of
1957, Johnston and Clift might have established the secure
economic base on which so many other factors, emotional and
physical, depended. Up until this time it must have seemed
to them that if they continued working hard at their writing
in the way that they had been, then a reasonable degree of
success must follow as a matter of course. But this overlooks
the crucial factor of luck. It is, after all, this as much as
anything that allows an author to find the right formula for a
best-seller, or decides a Book Club to take up a particular

work as its monthly choice. It had happened once, but a second time was to prove most elusive. If they expected 1958 to be as good a year generally as the previous two, they were to be disappointed. Moreover, many later, serious problems can be traced back to events in 1958.

They were as diligent as ever: Johnston started work on a new novel under his own name this time, which he was calling 'The Horde'. Clift got back the script of *Peel me a Lotus*, and proceeded to rewrite it. But the problem was that none of their books was really making much money. The two further 'Shane Martin' novels, *The Saracen Shadow* and *The Man Made of Tin*, did not bring the series into the kind of popularity either in England or America that had been hoped for. The only funds coming in were a $200 advance on 'The Horde' and a dribble of royalties. The $5000 from *Twelve Girls in the Garden* was already nearly all gone. Worse, the Greek authorities now demanded a hefty tax settlement.

As if these bread-and-butter problems were not enough, serious signs of marital strain between them began to appear. Clift wrote in *Peel me a Lotus* that Johnston was at times suffering from some deep personal anxiety, which was a consequence of the summer heat and irritating visitors:

> He broods about them (the heat, foreigners, the island), in the sweaty windblown watches of the night, and threatens to sell the house and go back to London. From being a gregarious, warm-hearted, talkative, generous and romantic fellow he has become suspicious, moody, unfriendly, irritable and despairing. His work, too, is causing him concern. Nothing seems to go right with it, although he works harder than ever, patiently exploring every avenue, every corridor of possibility that might lead to some sort of security ...[1]

Of course he worried about security − ironically the very thing they had fled from in London. He was understandably concerned about such things as the children's secondary schooling, particularly where it could be had and how it could be paid for. His illness, too, was undoubtedly a cause of irritability. But Clift is not giving the whole picture of the problem, which to a considerable degree implicated her. His 'suspicious' and 'despairing' frame of mind owed something to her own behaviour in responding to the interest shown in

169

her by other men. One such culprit was Jean-Claude Maurice, who had paid her considerable attention when he arrived during that summer of 1957.[2] Probably nothing came of it at this stage, but there were sufficient obvious signs for Johnston to sense trouble, and for all his old insecurities about Clift to come once again to the surface. Patrick Greer's observation of it prompted him to lay part of the blame on Johnston. 'It took about a year of their company before both of us [i.e. Greer and his wife, Nancy] realized that interference was exactly what they wanted. They needed the conjugal drama, preferably a public, quayside enactment of it.'[3] This is a cynical view, but for someone who may not have known the background to the relationship, a perfectly understandable one, especially at times when, if Greer is to be believed, he was himself 'encouraged to have a thing about Charmian' by none other than Johnston.[4] Such behaviour, though neurotic, was quite consistent with his fear of losing Clift. It threw out the challenge to her to demonstrate her loyalty; and if she did not reject the offer, then it only confirmed to Johnston what he suspected all along – that he was not capable of holding onto her.

Maurice, like others who talked about existentialism and bandied about fashionable names, managed often to enrage Johnston, who thought of existentialists and their ilk on the whole, in the language of his Melbourne upbringing, as 'bludgers'. Patrick Greer remembers his pet hates: 'Kafka, Rilke or Robbe-Grillet were then mode names, signs of culture, introduced by the would-be literati who came seasonably to the island. Any of these names, as well as [those of] such painters as Jackson Pollock, could and were used as red rags to provoke an anti-Psyche outburst from George.'[5] Another of his hates was Dostoevsky, but there was a strong anti-modernist attitude in Johnston, whose own preferred writers were essentially traditional realists in the nineteenth-century mould, although no conscious theories guided his writing. This was complicated by the fact that he admired, and understood well, Sidney Nolan's abstractionist work, and would have often heard, without making objection, Nolan's modernist views on art, including his love of poets such as

Rimbaud and Verlaine. That was different: Nolan was a friend; Maurice was an enemy and a threat. One can imagine, therefore, with what revulsion he contemplated the idea of an affair between him and Clift.

Greer sympathised with Johnston, and detested the 'literati' just as much. To get back at them he invented a philosopher called Blorgh, 'and for a while Johnston and I had fun dropping his name in such company, offering his esoteric notions on life, art, love and death'.[6] Years later Johnston seized upon their little joke and developed it into a satirical short story, changing the fictional philosopher's name to Pollini and calling it 'Vale, Pollini!' He took further literary revenge on Maurice, in particular, by using him as the basis for several unsympathetic characters in novels he was to write in the next few years.

As in the previous year, Hydra had many visitors over the summer of 1958. It was now an established stopover on the tourist routes, partly for its beauty, and partly because people had heard of the foreign colony and now wanted a look at it. Maurice Bowra, the Oxford don, went on a 'Hellenic cruise', and was encouraged by a friend, Neil Hutchison, Johnston's old Director of Features at ABC radio, to drop in on the Johnstons.[7] Despite a mindless prejudice against what Patrick Greer heard him call 'the Oxford thing' (some conspiracy theory that he and Nolan shared to the effect that Oxford somehow contrived to dominate World Culture), Johnston found Bowra good company, and Bowra 'thought he was terrific', and in particular was 'absolutely charmed' by Martin, who he thought was bright enough, and deserved the opportunity, eventually, to go to Oxford University.[8]

Indeed, Martin was constantly charming the visitors. The English novelist Elizabeth Jane Howard spend several weeks on the island during that summer, and befriended Martin, who had developed by this time into a talented sketcher, a chess-player and a meticulous amateur zoologist. Shane, incidentally, had formed an entirely different personality — tough, wild and physical, contrasting utterly with Martin's serious intellectuality.

Howard was writing her novel *The Sea Change* at the time,

and found she could not resist writing Martin into it,[9] in the character of Julius Lawson; and a thoroughly affectionate portrait it is. She also talked about Martin's education to Johnston, who confessed his concern. In fact Howard and Johnston were in agreement about a number of things, including Hydra itself, which they were both disliking at the time — she for its terrible food and claustrophobic atmosphere, he for the way in which it was changing. Clift, on the other hand, 'loved the place',[10] according to Howard, who also noted her tendency towards exhibitionism in front of visitors, men in particular. This observation is supported by Grace Edwards, an American who was taken to Hydra and introduced to the Johnstons about this time by the American painter Norris Embry. Edwards grew very fond of George, and recoiled from what she saw as sexual aggression in Clift right from their first meeting. 'She came straight off the boat and arrived right in the middle of a conversation we were having on the port, and immediately took charge with an awesome confidence and female aggression, directing her attention solely at the men present.'[11]

Charles Sriber, who was seeing the Johnstons at infrequent intervals, noticed a change in their relationship, and especially in Clift, who often went to Athens alone. He observed an increasing need in her to be liked by men, and that when she'd had too much to drink she tended to get herself into compromising, even dangerous, situations. One night when she stayed with the Sribers, Charles heard a commotion coming from her bedroom after she had come home in the early hours of the morning. When he investigated, she was being beaten by a Greek man she had brought back, and whom Sriber had to throw out. In her cups and in tears, she confessed to Sriber: 'I have always been a bad girl, since I was thirteen and went with taxi-drivers.'[12] Clearly some deep unhappiness was troubling her. The attention-seeking, the need to impress men, the self-punishment that followed if she gave in to these tendencies, point to a dissatisfaction that went back through her whole life. Johnston's reaction, predictable as it was, did not help: he was suspicious and vindictive, often in public, usually to the embarrassment of everyone present. At this stage he may have had no actual grounds on which to accuse her: he had no evidence, and she was making no admissions. He was not the only one to be suspicious, however. Sid Nolan arrived in the late months of 1958, just for a three-day visit with some friends. He, too, noticed a change in the atmosphere between Johnston and Clift: tension and depression prevailed. Clift insisted that he go with her to view the work of a painter friend of hers at his house. 'He wasn't much of a painter,' said Nolan, 'but I could sense what was really going on: she wanted to show me "her painter", and she wanted me to admire him.'[13] Nolan does not remember much about the man: it might have been Maurice, it might not. That there was 'something on' between him and Clift seemed to Nolan very likely. George was different, too, Nolan felt — displaying an uncharacteristic tendency to a jokey kind of bitterness and self-disparagement. His health, too, was obviously not good, and Nolan noted with some alarm his physical deterioration.

These problems, real as they were, undoubtedly were aggravated by too much drinking. The daily routine was that after the children had gone off to school, Johnston and Clift would work at their typewriters until about midday, when the mail boat came in. Jason would be left with a neighbour or with the children when they came home from school for the siesta period, and George and Charmian would head for the port, check the mail, and then meet other members of the foreign community either in or outside the Katsikas store, depending on the weather. Here the talk, and the drinking, would begin and last maybe well into the afternoon.[14] After this they would go home and sleep, perhaps do a little more work in the evening, eat and then have friends round or go out, and the drinking and talking would pick up again and last until late in the night. Regularly they would fall into bed with skinfuls of wine or brandy, regularly they had smoked prodigiously, regularly they had called on a great deal of nervous energy. They did not always fight with each other, of course: more often the fights, or arguments is more accurate, were with visitors or newcomers. The foreign community on Hydra, according to Martin, only rarely tangled with each other; on the whole they tended to support each other and close ranks against interlopers. Johnston often got into excited debates — some of which Martin recalls as stimulating — which under the influence of alcohol ran out of control. And often, even when arguing, there was still plenty of good humour between Johnston and Clift. After a night of the bitterest conflict they could surprise and exasperate everyone the next day with displays of affection and good-natured loyalty.

Despite the drain on their energy of this, they doggedly kept up their work as always. If there was one quality that distinguished them totally from most of the other foreigners on the island, it was this. Whatever the situation, rain, shine, ill-health or bad blood between them, they never shirked that morning's slog at the machine. Underneath, they both realised only too well that without this the whole point of them being there was gone; without this they were drifters and self-deceivers, who might as well go back to the rat-race as drink and argue each other into oblivion. The occasional glance into this black pit was enough to drive them to the typewriter each morning, regardless of hangovers.

Oddly, Johnston seemed to lose a little confidence in his latest work. He got the script of 'The Horde' off to William Morrow, and when they suggested severe cuts he readily agreed, and when they suggested a change of title to *The Darkness Outside* he also agreed, and soon after, when he sent them a new 'Shane Martin' script, they suggested a change in title of this from 'The Long Walls' to *The Myth is Murder*, to which he also agreed. The publishers were probably right, but on earlier occasions he had always insisted he knew best; now he was noticeably unassertive. His imaginative life too, on the evidence of his current work, was shrinking back from its previous sole preoccupation with the 'external' world of history and adventure to being more expressive of personal concerns. The effect of this on his writing was no bad thing. *The Darkness Outside* marks the change in imaginative orientation and is a better novel than any of the previous efforts.

The setting is an archaeological dig in southern Iraq, which continues his interest in ancient civilisations that began with the Professor Challis crime novels. Indeed, while he was writing *The Darkness Outside* he was also working on *The Myth is Murder*, which was specifically concerned with the story of Phidias's legendary burial on Kalymnos. To be sure, Johnston was in these books still indulging his hobby as an amateur historian, but *The Darkness Outside* goes beyond this. His central character, an American Professor of Archaeology called Eliot Purcell, has been conducting a ten-year campaign to find an ancient Mesopotamian city. He has collected together a small team, plus some Arab workers, who have all been operating in secrecy and isolation from the rest of the world for three years. Their isolation is unexpectedly penetrated when they discover near their camp an Englishman, old and near death from starvation. As they nurse him back to health he rambles deliriously about some cataclysmic event that has taken place in the world 'outside'. This triggers off a current of fear in the scientific party, which extends to the Arab workers, who flee. Finally, the group disintegrates because of its internal conflicts, which bring disaster for all but two of its members.

The novel's theme of isolation from the rest of the world bears an interesting relation to Johnston's feelings about the small group of foreigners living on Hydra. A frequent term in the novel is 'propinquity', a key word in Johnston's thinking at this time, for it is a label for all the distrust and claustrophobia that can come from being confined for too long — three years, as it is in the novel — in a limited place such as Hydra with too few people. It should be remembered that until this time Johnston had been an inveterate traveller to all parts of the world by all manner of means, from aircraft to yaks, and even when in London a year had never gone by without a trip to the Continent. Now, suddenly, all this was over; the only trip he could afford was the occasional three-hour ferry boat ride to Athens. *The Darkness Outside* suggests, then, that he regretted losing touch with the 'outside' world, and was feeling increasingly frustrated and irritated by the incestuous foreign society of Hydra.

Another feature of *The Darkness Outside* that marks its

serious intention is the use Johnston has made, after many years of admiration, of Joseph Conrad as some sort of model. He knew well *The Nigger of the 'Narcissus'*, and its famous Preface was the one piece of literary criticism in which he showed any sustained interest.[15] The central idea in *The Darkness Outside* of a mysterious stranger acting as a source of destructive fear on an isolated crew shows a distinct similarity to Conrad's novel. Moreover, there is a passage of comment on Conrad's philosophy that begins with a passing reference to *Heart of Darkness* and allows Purcell, the first-person narrator, to make an explicit connection between his own thoughts and Conrad's stringent pessimism:

> Always, with Conrad, the same obsessive theme — the veneer-thin skin that civilization gave us, a protective covering so fragile and so vulnerable that under the pressures of physical isolation, feeling the last breath of the unseen and the unexplained, the moral pattern warped, the skin broke, the most sophisticated and civilized among us reverted to primal impulses, became responsive to the instincts of the savage.[16]

The effect of using Conrad as a model, slight and occasional though that use is, helps to steady the narrative of *The Darkness Outside*, and to raise the level of treatment of the ideas. Both J. B. Priestley and Muriel Spark had some high praise for it in reviews, and others pointed favourably to the Conradian features. This was all real literary progress for Johnston, signifying that he had managed for the first time to express intense, personal preoccupations in an indirect and artistically satisfying way. It is not a great novel, but it is an honest one.

Johnston got the script for this and *The Myth is Murder* to the publishers by October 1958, an impressive eight-month effort, considering he had written *The Darkness Outside* twice. In fact he had become obsessive about his work, and this may partly have been a means of escaping from a situation that was becoming increasingly unbearable. Absent during the winter, Jean-Claude Maurice returned that 1958 summer, and this time it became 'obvious to everyone on the island'[17] that he and Clift were involved in an affair. Whatever public rows took place over this situation, and these were numerous, there was no denouement. It dragged furtively and painfully along, the subject of gossip and cause of humiliation to all. Johnston's only practical reaction was to bury himself in his work. At the same time he was planning a way to get on top of this new enormity: he would take his revenge in his next novel.

At this time the financial situation had become desperate, and Johnston detailed to Higham the pathetic figures for 1958, including tax deductions:

> In English earnings, so far as they are accounted for, you will see that out of an earning of £257.18.10 I receive £61.3.9, while out of an earning of £102.19.7 Charmian receives £64.14.7. This meagre return comes from five books in circulation or accepted, two foreign translations, one sale of foreign serial rights, an earlier novel, and certain magazine extracts. For this, and all the work it represents, the return in total is £125.18.4, which I'm sure you'll agree is hardly worthwhile.[18]

He pleaded with Higham not to deduct tax from the advances due, totalling £475, on recently completed books, adding: 'If this is not done our situation here will become quite impossible and we shall have to sell up and get out.'[19] In another letter in the same month, January 1959, he told Higham in despair 'we have come to the end of our financial tether'. Unfortunately, Higham's hands were tied in the matter – British law required him to deduct income tax before payment. However, he did promise Johnston he would try to gain approval for a reciprocal scheme whereby tax paid in Greece would give him at least partial exemption from British tax. In the circumstances he felt he had to do something.

Johnston's extraordinary burst of creative activity continued. Clift wrote to Higham that 'he just started a new novel, so is at his happiest'.[20] Under the circumstances 'happiest' was a relative term, because much of the writing must have been done under stress. His provisional title was 'The Islanders', and here he was for the first time turning his attention directly on the Hydra foreign colony. He had a few things to come to terms with, a few debts to pay, and some spleen to work off, in particular about Clift's behaviour with Maurice over the summer, so large sections of the novel were written in a spirit of anger mixed with dejection.

Since it was to be autobiographical, Johnston's first task was to find a way of placing himself in the picture. For this he needed an *alter ego*, and he searched about until he came up with a name out of his childhood — Meredith, after the little town near 'Uncle Whittle's' farm at Dereel, near Ballarat. That time was fresh in his mind as he wrote the opening pages, which are sprinkled with scraps of Meredith's memories such as his 'old terror of the sounds of cocks crowing in the darkness'[21] and how 'he used to be sent away on school summer holidays to a little mixed farm in the scraggy gully country west of Ballarat',[22] images that refer directly to Johnston's own childhood, and probably coincided with his memory of the town of Meredith. He may have had a second reason for choosing the name, and that was its literary connection with the English novelist, whose first name also happened to be George.

As well as describing the Hydra situation, the novel demonstrates Johnston's increasing tendency to express his thoughts about home. For the first time, and on several occasions, he uses the term 'expatriate' in the novel; he even quotes Laurence Sterne using it, in a prefatory extract from *A Sentimental Journey*: '. . . the balance of sentimental commerce is always against the expatriate adventurer'.[23] Here, then, were the beginnings of a realisation that what he had done, almost unawares, since coming to Greece was to become an expatriate. He was not sure of the implications of this, nor was he ready to explore it thoroughly. He had put his finger on it, and it was to keep surfacing over the following years.

'The Islanders', which was published as *Closer to the Sun*, was Johnston's second 'serious' novel in a row. It has no historical outlook and no adventure story, indeed no plot to speak of, but has instead a thematic structure: the clash of two lifestyles. The Meredith family, David, Kate and two children, are attempting to survive on the island of Silenos by means of Meredith's writing (Kate, like her later counterpart Cressida, has no artistic or professional dimension to her life). Like the Johnstons, they are finding the going tough. When they are visited by Meredith's elder brother, Mark,

David's lifestyle is called into question. Mark Meredith has no significant autobiographical basis – he bears no relation to Jack Meredith of the trilogy – and is probably loosely based on an English playwright, Gilbert Horobin, who often visited Hydra. As a successful London playwright, Mark represents the success that David might have been if he had not 'dropped out'. This gives him a role similar to the one played by Gavin Turley in *My Brother Jack* and Archie Calverton in *Clean Straw for Nothing*, and that is to act as a foil for David Meredith, thereby bringing into sharper focus his unstable character and the dangerous degree of over-reaching that his way of life represents. Mark Meredith is given the same question that Mrs Knip puts in *Peel me a Lotus*: 'But what are you doing it *for*?'

Mark arrives on Silenos with a party of rich friends brought by the millionaire Suvora on his yacht. The time corresponds to the summer of 1958, when Hydra saw that massive invasion of tourists. Johnston's attempt to integrate the exotic visitors into the theme of comparative lifestyles is unfortunately inept and, because he gives it too much space, finally harmful to the novel, since David Meredith's eventual defence of his chosen manner of living owes nothing to the presence of the rich visitors, or for that matter to some of the foreign regulars. It is hard to find any reason for their continuous presence in the novel other than to provide a kind of bizarre glamour, which is presented in an uncritical way, and is not successfully integrated with the other elements in the novel.

Far more intense is the handling of events that have a close connection with actual circumstances on Hydra during 1957 and 1958. Foremost in this is the triangle of David Meredith, Kate and the Frenchman Achilles Mouliet, for which Johnston drew on his own feelings about Clift's affair with Jean-Claude Maurice. Maurice had already made an appearance as Jacques in *Peel me a Lotus*, where Clift describes her responses to him during his first time on Hydra, over the summer of 1957, when she found him fascinating but was not involved with him, and shows that she was not at all blind to his self-conscious posturings:

> *How offensive, how artifical and silly his provocative, shuf-*
> *fling walk, his skin-tight pants, his jasmine flower, and that*
> *damned earring. How intentional it all is — the slow eyelids,*
> *the enigmatic smile, the shirt arranged to display the better*
> *the golden mat of hair on breast and belly, the irresistible*
> *glance that flicks on and off like a traffic light, the interesting*
> *touch of* angst. *Not Dionysos after all, the fleet, the free, the*
> *beautiful, the ever-young — but only a little curly dog in*
> *season, whose imperative it is to sniff after any and every*
> *lady dog.*[24]

In *Closer to the Sun* Mouliet has the same golden curls, the earring and the beautifully proportioned and constantly near-naked body as Jacques. Meredith, however, is even more hostile to him and experiences 'a sudden odd pleasure in recollecting how two of the Frenchman's teeth had been knocked out by a fisherman in a tavern brawl the previous August, and how astonished and disturbed everyone had been at the revelation that the teeth were false'.[25] Jacques suffers the same ignominy in *Peel me a Lotus*, when he reveals that the beautiful white teeth that everyone so admires are actually screw-ins.[26] Later in *Closer to the Sun* Meredith's hatred of Mouliet is more bitter as he becomes aware of Kate's affair with him, a fact he cannot reconcile with the kinds of women usually attracted to Mouliet: 'breasty girls with horse-tail hair-dos and willing legs sheathed in black pants waiting their turn at the semenal wellspring'.[27]

Incidentally, Maurice turns up yet again under the name of Jacques in *Clean Straw for Nothing*, though this time Johnston treats him a little more circumspectly, allowing a certain integrity to his existentialist philosophy — 'To be free, it is all there is' (*CSFN* 179) — and his friendship with Cressida. Moreover, in that novel Jacques insists that he has not slept with Cressida, and Meredith's jealousy makes him seem small-minded and unnecessarily distrusting of Cressida.

In *Closer to the Sun* Johnston was in no such generous mood. Establishing Mouliet as a decidedly unsympathetic character, he then describes in detail a prolonged sexual encounter between him and Kate Meredith, who is unable to resist his somewhat transparent seduction techniques. The encounter is artistically weakened by being described by

Johnston acting as an omniscient narrator — he presents it as factual, yet makes Kate refuse to admit that it even happened — but there is a feverish intensity to it that is rare in Johnston's work before this. What he was doing, of course, was masochistic. Indeed, if his intention was to hurt Clift and Maurice by exposing them, as it probably was, consider the suffering he was experiencing by putting himself through the torture of imagining what they were up to. There is something pathetic in this jealousy-motivated attempt to use fiction as an instrument of retaliation, just as there is in the last chapters of the novel, when Johnston shows Meredith tempted by Erica Barrington, only to keep him consistent with all his male protagonists by having him retain his virtue to the end, thereby giving him a moral victory over Kate, who is both liar and betrayer.

Not content with this, he rubs Kate's nose in the dirt, for David Meredith learns of the affair from the island garbage man, Dionysos, who has seen her with Mouliet. The point of this is that Meredith is the last to discover what is so publicly known that the dustman, still in his role as a purveyor of 'rubbish', has to be the one to tell him. This theme of degradation applies to the Hydra foreign community generally, when, right at the beginning of the novel, Dionysos is said to be 'the most important man on the island', and images of waste and squalor are used to describe his nightly round of collecting the garbage. While it is clear that Johnston entered into the novel in a spirit of intense ill-will, and sustains this in relation to some aspects of the Hydra expatriate community right up to the end, he does, nevertheless, provide an optimistic outcome for David and Kate by establishing a truce between them. Meredith reflects:

> He and Kate had built something. He could see that now. They had built something that was better than either of them had realized, and they had built it with the things that were to hand, here, now ... with the materials available ... he had brought off his own stand for the right to hold the tiller in his own hand, and, by God! this was something.[28]

Johnston probably assumed that their friends would believe the novel to be true. Most of them knew about Clift and

181

Maurice: Grace Edwards, Patrick Greer, Charles Sriber, Anthony Kingsmill, who heard about it from Clift afterwards. Just what did he expect Clift herself to make of *Closer to the Sun*? She later commented that 'it was a very important [novel] to me because it was half-way honest — that is, honest for half its length, when obviously uncertainty engulfed him and he retreated into storyline and the old trick of dazzling observation',[29] which is frustrating because we do not know which half she meant was honest and which not. Essentially she is suggesting that the novel is honest in so far as it is dealing with matters of real concern to Johnston, 'feeling out the ground', said Clift, 'for one that was to come so many years later, *Clean Straw for Nothing*'.[30] Whether she felt as detached at the time from the personal animosity and moral one-upmanship that went into *Closer to the Sun* is a matter for conjecture.

During the months of writing this novel — January to August 1959 — Johnston became ill again. A bout of Asian flu in March weakened him physically,[31] and the emotional nature of the task contributed to a growing crisis. The evidence for this in his writing went back a number of months: the whole nightmare quality and the singling out of irrational fear as the central force behind *The Darkness Outside* was an early sign of trouble. *Closer to the Sun* displays several signs of it in the way already discussed, but also, and most tellingly, in a passage in which Meredith experiences premonitory hallucinations of his own death:

> Only now was the actual fact of failure there in front of him, right under his eyes, as visible and as tangible as the fact of death represented by the dry, black, brittle, stiff-legged beetle up-ended on the cover of his notebook! He had a swift strange image of the beetle swollen to the size of a man, the dead, bent legs rigid in mid-air, the black carapace emptying itself to nothing . . .[32]

The indications were there that the strongest forces occupying his mind were fear, dejection, resentment and failure. And it was all sapping his health. Even when the summer came he could not get back to full strength after that bout of flu. His weight began to drop alarmingly, and the blood spitting got worse along with the cough. Still, he drove himself mercilessly to finish *Closer to the Sun* by August, clinging to the conviction that it was 'the most ambitious thing I've yet attempted'.[33]

If Johnston was well on the way to a breakdown by mid-1959, Clift was finding life just the opposite: after years of frustrations, success was now beginning to come. *Mermaid Singing*, her best book to this stage, was written before she had given birth to Jason. Then she had gone through 1956, 1957 and 1958 struggling unsatisfactorily with the novel *Walk to the Paradise Gardens*. *Peel me a Lotus* required two attempts before it was finally ready in 1958. As Jason grew less demanding of her time, she gradually got back into form, and with the publishers making good noises about *Peel me a Lotus* she worked confidently, and had the script of *Walk to the Paradise Gardens* in the publishers' hands by April 1959. The response from Harper in America was just what she needed, for she was offered a $1500 advance, good royalty terms and an option on her next novel. 'I am, of course, immoderately happy,' she wrote to Higham on 30 May. Whatever his personal unhappiness, Johnston gave no indications of professional jealousy, and it was entirely characteristic when he wrote proudly to Higham 'Charmian's beginning to do nicely under her own steam, isn't she? I'm overjoyed.'[34] In fact, the success made her a little cocky at times:

> I have all sorts of writing plans and shall probably go on producing a novel a year for many years to come. I think 'Lotus' was better than 'Mermaid', and 'Paradise Gardens' better than 'Lotus', and I know the next one, 'Honour's Mimic', is going to be better than 'Paradise Gardens'. I have, you see, enough confidence in myself at least ...[35]

Clift was undoubtedly pleased with the idea of being the breadwinner for a change, so things were going better for her at this time than at any other stage since they had left Sydney. Unlike Johnston, she was not enraged by the foreign community, and even when critical of it, as she was at times in *Peel me a Lotus*, it was never with Johnston's savagery.

Indeed, Clift liked living on Hydra just as much as she had at first, and in 1957, when Elizabeth Jane Howard noticed how much she loved it there. To her it was always an opportunity to live differently from respectable suburbia and to give expression to her strong sense of personal freedom. These were not ideas Clift was prepared to examine, for they were more matters of belief. She once said of herself that she was a 'Yes sayer'[36] to life, and it was in this spirit that she was determined to remain on Hydra: such an attitude is open to exploitation, and in sexual matters this might have happened in her relations with one or two men, Maurice especially. Not that she was a passive object in this: she generally did what she wanted to do. But different people saw her behaviour in different ways. Grace Edwards, as on that first meeting on the Hydra port, saw her as a sexual aggressor who would blossom fully into life only if men were present, but would shrink back into passivity if she were with women only. Charles Sriber felt that it was not specifically sexual attention she sought, but she had a need to be liked and admired by men, not just for her looks but for her mind as well. A number of women have said that Clift made it obvious that she was bored by women. The testimony from almost everyone who knew her was always that she loved attracting men, and would take it farther if she wanted to, sometimes with members of their social circle.

This is not to say that she ceased to love Johnston or ever seriously threatened to abandon him for another man; no affair could replace her commitment to him and the children. Also the talk on Hydra about her promiscuity was, according to Grace Edwards, greatly exaggerated and, to her knowledge, Clift's affairs were limited to three men: Maurice, an American called 'Chip' (or 'Chick') Chadwick and Anthony Kingsmill, with whom she openly lived on Hydra in 1964. The biggest indulger in loose talk about her seems to have been Johnston himself, who, if he had drunk too much, would at times allow his bitterness and jealousy to come to the surface, and gabble publicly about his wife's 'wampum belt'[37] of male scalps. This would lead to scenes, sometimes ugly, sometimes comic: some Hydriots still recall the sight of Clift hurling furniture at Johnston from a taverna window, to the amusement of everyone, including, after a moment's reflection, the Johnstons themselves.[38] At other times they could become violent with each other, and the ill-feeling would simmer for days. The children were at times unfortunate witnesses to their worst rows, and Martin, then about twelve, has painful memories of burying his head in his pillow at night to shut out the fury coming from the next room.[39] Such moments would pass, but from about this time in 1959 onwards, the frequency and intensity of their brawling steadily increased. Charles Sriber recalls a time in Athens when Clift came to visit after a day's shopping. The weather turned rough and Sriber suggested it would not be wise to go back on the ferry, and to stay the night with him and his wife. Clift became agitated and insisted that she could do so only if Sriber would give her a note explaining the situation to Johnston, who 'would beat her',[40] she said, if she stayed away overnight without a legitimate reason. She suffered from abuse by Johnston and other men, physically and verbally. Sriber saw her mortified once by Michael Cacoyannis, the Greek film director. Cacoyannis was making a film of Frederic Wakeman's novel *The Wastrel*, and Clift suggested that Jason be given a role and that she could go to Bermuda as his chaperone for the filming. Cacoyannis felt that Clift was already taking too lively an interest in Wakeman, and said loudly in front of a number of people: 'Charmian, you must remember that you are no longer young, no longer beautiful.'[41] Clift was visibly hurt. Of all people to humiliate her, a Greek artist of the stature of Cacoyannis would have cut deepest. Johnston would have been the same: they were both inordinately proud of their friendship with Greeks, and especially of important ones such as Cacoyannis and Melina Mercouri, whom they had recently met.

Higham sent news in September 1959 that, despite the good reviews by such names as Muriel Spark and J. B. Priestley, *The Darkness Outside* was not selling well. Nor had Harold Ober Inc. in the USA been able to get it accepted by a publisher yet. But there was a worse development. As Johnston struggled with the tortuous closing chapters to *Closer to the Sun*, and sent the typescript off, and, as if addicted to churning out words on his machine, launched into yet another 'Shane Martin' novel, his health took an alarming turn. Clift had been nagging him for months to see a doctor in Athens about his weight loss — he had gone down from his normal 75 kilograms (11 stone 12 pounds) to 55 kilograms (8 stone 10 pounds) since January[42] — and now he was overcome by serious breathing difficulties. No doubt his reluctance was fear of learning that he had cancer; he told Grace Edwards he was convinced that he did. Finally, he agreed to go. In mid-October he left on the early morning ferry to be examined by a friend of Edwards, Dr George Anastosopoulos, in his Athens surgery, after first having X-rays at a clinic. Anastosopoulos examined him, but said he could not complete his diagnosis until the X-rays arrived from the clinic, and to come back in the evening, after the siesta period. Johnston therefore spent the whole of the afternoon in the city, wandering about alone, fighting his growing terror of what 'the verdict' would be.

As soon as it was all over, he wrote a fine story about that day, called 'The Verdict'. Once again he adopted the approach he was now taking in all his serious writing by making use of David and Kate Meredith, though when the story was published, in re-written form, which was not until several years later, Kate's name was changed to Cressida, the name she had by that time acquired in *My Brother Jack*. In 'The Verdict' Meredith grows a little farther away from his prototype in *Closer to the Sun*, and closer to the Meredith of the trilogy, especially in the rigour of his self-analysis. The story is dominated by his grim situation — that of waiting for a virtual death sentence, a situation that creates a sudden sense in him of alienation from life, and an overwhelming awareness of mortality. As he walks through the city, everything he sees becomes a nightmarish reflection of his own sense of death and waste:

> trodden lumps of clay, half completed excavations which held yellow water from the rain the night before ... The black rods of the reinforcing steel writhed out of the concrete pillars like huge worms trying to release themselves and escape into the pools below.[43]

There are the familiar references to his childhood and to his relationship with Kate, and to his own part in the souring of their relationship in that 'he, in his weakening physical condition, had cringed away from any physical contact with her out of sheer fear of inadequacy and humiliation, loving her desperately, yet afraid to touch her'.[44] The past slowly drifts through his mind, but as well as the inevitable tinges of regret he also feels a peculiar sense of release from the need to 'keep on trying' with his burden of life, as he anticipates what he feels will be the inescapable finding of the doctor. The beauty of the story lies in its images of flickering life: 'a flock of sparrows chittering up from the wasteland', and 'two desiccated pepper trees' resisting, in that city-scape, the forces of destruction; and also, in Nitza, the Greek air-hostess to whom he chats in the street, and who cannot stay to have a drink with him because one of her airline's planes had crashed the day before, and she must be at work to put on the bright face of life in order to wipe away the memory of death and disaster. These and other brave images of life recur through the story, and are finally brought together in the tender conclusion, which achieves a symmetrical return to the images of childhood and pepper trees described early on:

> The smell of the crushed peppercorns was still on his fingers, and it brought back all his childhood, and he knew that nothing had been resolved and that he had to begin all over again. He felt so miserable that he could have cried. He put his head down in his hands and wished that he was dead.[45]

Although Meredith has received a reprieve in that his illness is not cancer, but tuberculosis of the lung, he is not happy, because it means that he has to continue his Sisyphean task of living just at a point when he has become resigned to the release of death. Now he must shoulder his responsibilities — family, writing, life — all over again, as if he were being sentenced to begin at childhood and live it all over for a second time. The prospect seems intolerable.

It is a well-composed and satisfying story, and no doubt a clear reflection of Johnston's own state of mind on that day when his tuberculosis was diagnosed. Oddly, he made no attempt to publish it, but kept it hidden away for eight years, until he decided to absorb it into *Clean Straw for Nothing*. Its depiction of the sexual distance between Meredith and his wife is a revealing one, corresponding to what Johnston himself had been telling friends of late — that his illness had made him all but impotent. 'A one time a year man,' he told Grace Edwards. His lack of potency could hardly have made Clift, at the age of thirty-six, happy about their future together.

The doctor insisted that Johnston could beat the TB only if he changed his way of living. The first thing he had to do was to get right away from the destructive situation on Hydra. He was to have rest, good food, carry out a strict antibiotic programme and give up alcohol and cigarettes. Grace Edwards invited him to stay with her in her flat in the Metz in Athens, which proved to be a good arrangement: 'a quiet six weeks living with a man without sex, and we got along well together', says Edwards.[46] It was during this time that he wrote 'The Verdict'. Edwards was a good listener, so Johnston talked to her a great deal: about his past, about archaeology, an interest they shared (he told her the Kalymnos story about Phidias, which he had, since writing it all down in *The Myth is Murder*, come to believe), and, of course, he talked about his marriage. He swore to Edwards that when he got back to Hydra 'he was never going to play the role of jealous husband again'.[47] Both he and Edwards agreed that Hydra was the most destructive place for human relationships that they'd ever known. 'There is a legend on Hydra that a huge serpent is said to lurk in the upper rocks,' he told her. 'But I know now that the serpent is the foreign community.'[48] He believed that the presence of this community had poisoned his marriage.

Clift visited Johnston at the Edwards flat, and seems even to have displayed a little jealousy herself that Johnston's recuperation was taking place outside her sphere of influence. She turned up one day and announced pointedly to Johnston that she had Chadwick waiting for her in the street, ready to escort her back to Hydra, an invasion of his sanctuary that brought back all the old nagging doubts and jealousies.

Nor would the demands of everyday responsibilities leave him alone, especially the financial ones. He wrote to Higham telling him of his illness, but making light of it and insisting that it would soon pass and not interfere with his work, but that he was desperately short of funds and needed any outstanding moneys that may have been due to him, including '£6 from Collins (my God! why do we even bother)' and to pay it without deducting tax, which he would pay later 'when we have the money — at the moment we have nothing'.[49] In this state of desperation, and feeling on familiar enough terms to ask for a loan, he wrote to Sir William Collins, making his situation plain. Collins, moved by the news, as were all his London friends and publishing contacts, sent £250 immediately,[50] without any formal requirement that it be repaid.

Johnston's period of rest with Edwards was to have been for at least three months, but he missed the children, and was plagued by thoughts of Clift and Chadwick. After six weeks he could stand it no longer, and decided to return to Hydra. When Clift fetched him, she was shown by the doctor how to administer his daily injections of streptomycin, and was advised that he still needed rest and, above all, peace of mind. On 8 December he cheerfully wrote to Higham that he was 'back from Athens and well on the way to a full recovery, I hope, and I am now able to continue what remains of my treatment at home'. In the early months of 1960 Charles Sriber came across him in the office of Chandris Shipping Lines, arranging to have his books sold on board their ships, which did regular runs to Australia. According to Sriber he was back to his old chirpy self, and said his health was 'clean' and he was 'feeling marvellous'. He had also made a start on a new novel with the projected title of *The Far Face of the Moon*.

In Melbourne also, friends and family had been shocked by the news of his illness. Letters came expressing sympathy and concern, one of the warmest being from Elsie. Johnston wrote to Gae in February that he had been 'very, very touched by her [Elsie's] concern', and that their good wishes had done him 'very much good'.[51] Gae was at this time a second-year Arts student at Melbourne University, and according to Bruce Kneale, who had been one of the recent sympathetic correspondents, she was 'an exceedingly attractive and highly intelligent redhead'.[52] Johnston sent her some copies of his recent books, and wrote that he had 'a feeling of being on the verge of writing something really worthwhile', but was hampered by the effects of the drugs he was taking. He added, 'If we can hold out a little longer I think we'll see brighter times ahead.'[53] This optimism might have been prompted by some good early responses from Ober to 'The Islanders', the title being changed at this time, at their suggestion, to *Closer to the Sun*.

Over the early months of 1960 Johnston worked steadily but at a considerably reduced speed and intensity. *The Far Face of the Moon* represented a return to what Clift called his 'faction-fiction'.[54] In some respects this was a safer kind of subject in his fragile condition, eschewing as it did the harrowing and potentially explosive matter of Clift's behaviour, though it is possible that it was still on his mind sufficiently to influence his writing. In this novel Johnston made free use of his old adventures in flying 'the hump' out of Assam into China during the war, and used his familiarity with the route to create a background of dangerous missions for the pilots stationed at the fictional 'Zone Q-4'. The main story, however, is concerned with the effects on the men of the arrival of a group of Hollywood entertainers, headed by a sex symbol called Jane Carson. The central male character, Jacob Strickland, is impotent, and the central female character is a nymphomaniac who makes herself available to almost anyone at the air force station. For female names Johnston dug back into his past love-life: 'Jane' connects with her American namesake from around that time in Johnston's life, though she has Clift's 'malachite green eyes', as did most of his heroines. Jacob Strickland reveals towards the end of the novel that he has some years earlier killed his wife in a fit of sexual revulsion. *Her* name — Olga Renneck — is remarkably close to that of Johnston's first probable sexual partner, Olga Reid, a likely model for certain aspects of the character of Helen in *My Brother Jack*. So, even if he was not dealing directly with current events in *The Far Face of the Moon*, there is a clear indication that the *subject* of impotence and promiscuity, the two extremes of his own sexual problem, was occupying his mind and giving him some material that was at least useful for fiction. Clift later disingenuously said: 'where he dredged that lot up from God alone knows (since he has no truck with psychiatrists, mistrusting that profession soundly)',[55] but she was too intelligent not to know where he'd 'dredged' that material from.

When the publishers read the typescript, however, they turned up their noses, and insisted that it was so bad that he must, for the sake of his reputation, withdraw it. They made it clear to him, according to Clift, that after the poor sales of *The Darkness Outside* 'He couldn't afford another failure'.[56] This did not seem to worry Johnston; he didn't care too much about this novel. Without a fuss he complied with the publishers' wishes, and gave some thought as to how it might be rewritten.

Among their visitors that summer was Mungo MacCallum junior, the son of his old colleague. Young MacCallum arrived with his fiancée, Susan, but they were unfortunate to strike the Johnstons at a time when there was a great deal of tension in the air, with friends of Johnston and Clift not helping much by taking sides.[57] Other visitors included an English couple called Peter and Didy Cameron, who had been urged by Elizabeth Jane Howard to look up the Johnstons. The four hit it off exceptionally well, and again Martin was the good PR man in acting as a guide to all the best things on the island. Comfortably upper-middle class, the Camerons were shocked by the poverty in which the Johnstons were living, observing that 'a tin of corned beef was a rare treat, and Charmian ran anxiously to the vegetable boat when it came into port in order to get fresh, cheap vegetables, with cabbage forming a large part of their diet'.[58] They were shocked, too, by George's frail condition. The problem of Martin's education (which seems to have been more important to everyone than Shane's, who was after all only a year younger) came up in discussion, as did money difficulties and the possibility of better medical treatment for Johnston. Out of all this came an idea for a trial return to England. The Camerons owned a hobby farm at Stanton, near Broadway in Worcestershire, which they used only occasionally. They offered the Johnstons the use of it for up to twelve months, and they in turn would live for part of that time, at least, in the house on Hydra. Perhaps, they reasoned, Johnston could look up some of his old contacts in London and see if he could get back into journalism. In any case, it would be an escape from the 'propinquity' of Hydra and its effect on their relationship, which was still under stress, both from Clift's continued interest in the opposite sex and from alcohol, which had re-established something of its former hold. 'I could see the dangers,' said Didy Cameron, who saw Clift break down in the kitchen one day and weep 'because they'd lost their spirit'.[59] So the subject was mulled over in those summer months, and finally they decided to give it a try, though for some reason they did not plan to make the move until late in the year — October, perhaps.

In the meantime Johnston had hit upon a new subject for a serious novel, and rather than rewrite *The Far Face of the Moon* he got straight down to work on this. He might have talked about it to Leonard Cohen, who was then a little-published poet writing his first novel, and was visiting Hydra for the first time. The Johnstons put him up in a spare room for a while. Johnston had often related to Clift the story of his grim drive along the Kweilin road in 1945, through all those dying refugees, about which he had at the time sent back vivid despatches to the *Argus*. Continuing his recently acquired interest in death, his imagination took up the horror of it all once again, seeing in it an opportunity to make points about war, journalism and his own past. Clift claimed that she 'nagged him into' creating the novel out of an event that 'had shattered him', and that he undertook to set it down 'as truly as he could, fictionalized but no less true for that'.[60] He knew from the beginning that he would call it *The Far Road*, and also he seemed to know, more surely than in any previous novel, exactly what the span of events, the central characters and the purpose of the novel were to be.

Once again, he uses David Meredith as his protagonist. Once again, he creates a male foil for him, this time an American journalist called Bruce Conover, as a means of contrasting the values that lay at the centre of the novel. He had done this in two previous novels — *The Big Chariot* and *Closer to the Sun* — as he was to do in the Meredith trilogy; in all except *The Far Road* the contrasting pair are brothers. Conover may be based on a war correspondent of Johnston's acquaintance, but more important than biographical accuracy is that he represents the morally indifferent, ambitious young journalist who is a striking contrast to the morally scrupulous, disillusioned Meredith.

Johnston makes the flight from Kweilin the outcome of a communiqué saying that the Japanese are about to attack the city, which is issued by officials who have been bribed by the capitalist speculator Fabian Ling. Ling's purpose, which is successful, is to cause a currency devaluation so that he can buy cheap and sell dear when the market recovers. Because this happens in the middle of a famine, thousands of Chinese refugees die along the road to Liuchow. Meredith and Conover go in pursuit of the story, in the course of which they reveal much about themselves. Conover is physically brave, unmoved by the suffering he sees, is brute enough to rape a victim, and professional enough to count the masses of dead and not to attempt to tell the whole story of Ling's part in the catastrophe, which, he points out, would not get past the censor anyway. Meredith, older, discovers he is a physical coward, is devastated by the death and suffering about him, admits his own culpability in not giving water to a dying man, and in the end is so overwhelmed by his inability to reconcile his ineffectuality with his moral outrage that he suffers a breakdown. The point made several times throughout the novel is that the attempt by the war correspondent to play the role of the detached observer is fundamentally immoral.

The most powerful moment in the novel comes when the brutally professional Conover takes a photograph of a starving Chinese child on the Liuchow road:

> *Conover was squatting there, not six paces away from him, focusing his camera on the sprawled figure of a child. The Leica that he held in his strong, gilt-fuzzed hands was as black as the muzzle of a Luger.*
>
> *The child was a little girl of six or seven in a ragged scrap of a dress who looked as if she had been tossed across a heap of baggage. There was something ridiculously doll-like in the*

abandoned, inhuman posture of the skinny little figure. The arms and legs stuck out at curious angles, and the head lolled sideways on the pale stalk of the neck, and the bare legs and arms were stick-thin and so colourless that they seemed to be made of bones (the bones of a bird, thought Meredith, with a stab of sharp pain, the bones of some tiny fragile creature which the air might support).

Conover slid back a few careful inches, then squatted again, and refocused the Leica.

'Malnutrition,' he muttered.[61]

When the child dies soon afterwards, Meredith suffers a mental breakdown and begins to believe that the Leica camera had in fact been a Luger pistol, and that Conover had 'shot' the child in a very different sense. The scene brilliantly captures the essence of the moral dilemma of the journalist: whether to remain uninvolved or whether to take sides. Conover's professional insistence on the former position is one that Meredith — and Johnston — comes ultimately to reject.

What made Johnston suddenly launch into an attack on his old profession? The seriousness of mood in the novel suggests it was more than just another good idea for a yarn. The novel's dedication reads 'For Charmian, in earnest', and indeed she was proud of it: 'I loved that novel,' she affirmed, 'I stood up and cheered for it.'[62] Johnston himself was pleased with it, too, despite the fact that it was the most dismal failure on the market of all his books. 'It sold all of 82 copies in Australia,' said Clift,[63] and not many more anywhere else. But why did he suddenly feel so 'earnest' about journalism? It may have been that the subject had recently come up in conversation with the Camerons, and George was turning over in his mind the dreaded prospect of returning to it if he asked for and was given a job. Strange, then, that he should attack and not defend a game he was going to rejoin. Perhaps he was trying to resist going back at all, and was trying to persuade himself out of it. If the latter was the reason, he was not to succeed, for within a few months he would be turning up, cap in hand, in Fleet Street, no doubt choking down whatever remnants of pride he had salvaged from the admission that he could not survive as a full-time writer. In any case, whether he was looking this far ahead or not, the attack on journalism in *The Far Road* represents a forceful assertion of principles from Johnston in what is a fine novel, deserving of more attention than it has so far received. Yet how puzzling it is that its writing almost coincides with his abject attempt to return to the very profession he was condemning.

So around October 1960 the Johnstons prepared to leave for England. What a time of the year to go back! Yet so much was wrong in their lives that some kind of break was necessary, even if it was merely removing themselves from the site of their troubles. There are passages in *Clean Straw for Nothing* that reflect on the factors that persuaded them to go. Meredith fears it is a confession of the failure of their dream: their English friend Miriam argues that accepting 'Beatrice's' offer to change houses will give them a chance to get back into the 'real' world. Reluctantly, David and Cressida agree that she may be right, and that her charge that their experiment on the island has not come off is true. In a melancholy passage Meredith reflects on the past sixteen years of their life together, and perceives the forces of disintegration at work, bringing him to a desperate realisation:

> It was only when we drank too much that the constraints of habit and mutual decency and consideration dropped away and we abandoned evasions with each other, only then that the complicated facade so painstakingly erected and preserved over so many years crumbled into dusty desolate ruin.
>
> But looking back on it there is no clear black or white about anything. It is all a hopeless tangle of the good and the bad, the serene and the savage, the brutal and the beautiful, of love and hate and loyalty and betrayal. It is hope and despair, and magical experiences that become soiled and smutty, and delicacies that jar, and murderous attacks delivered with the gentlest of touches. The priceless things are all mixed up with the cheap trash and junk. It is a trap from which there is no escape, a thicket in which we can find no path. Sometimes when I look back to see the way we have come it is all overgrown again, and even the memory of what we have passed through is blurred and distorted. The clear pure spring we drank at long ago is tainted, and I can no longer separate the gayest and happiest of festivals from the bitterness of quarrels.
>
> Is it the island that has done this to us? Or only ourselves? If we could find some way out of the thicket, the tangle, the

clashing rocks. Some way out. One is almost desperate enough to ask for any way out. I don't think we can find redemption here. It must be elsewhere. (CSFN 144-5)

The Merediths give in to despair, but the Johnstons did not. *Clean Straw for Nothing* makes it seem worse than it was, because, once again, that novel was written when things *were* worse. The Johnstons in 1960 were battered, but, according to the Camerons and their letters to friends, cheerful and optimistic about the England idea. Where they got the money for the fare is a mystery; they did, however, leave Hydra in debt by a considerable sum of drachmas to the Katsikas store.

CHAPTER X

My Brother Jack

... it was she who first advanced the disturbing thought that they might have subjected themselves to a kind of subtle social dismantling, that gradually their life on the island had unfitted them for any other sort of life. (CSFN 284)

Stanton near Broadway lies on the border between Worcestershire and Gloucestershire. It is a beautiful village almost wholly of seventeenth-century cottages, built in the distinctive ochre-coloured Cotswold stone. The house in which the Johnstons stayed is a magnificent Tudor farmhouse perched high behind the village proper, with a view across the Gloucestershire plains to Tewkesbury. It has about a hundred acres of land, and was (and still is) called Charity Farm. Its owner, Peter Cameron, made only occasional use of the place, and that was as a holiday and weekend resort for himself, Didy and their four children. It was not then operated as a farm, though nowadays it is. The house exchange took place as arranged, although Cameron did not accompany his family on their stay in the Johnston house on Hydra, because his job as a legal officer for the United Nations required him to be in New Guinea.

Fine as it was, Charity Farm was not the most convenient of places for the Johnstons, who really needed to be near London. They could not afford a car, so their relatively frequent journeys had to be done by train. Their life, therefore, was once again a confined one, just as it had been on Hydra, especially for Charmian and the children. Stanton, in that snowy part of the country in an English winter, not to mention the pecking order and other trappings of the class system in Engish village life, was a far cry from Hydra. Occupying as they did a house connected with the British gentry, a certain kind of role was offered them, and expected of them by some, which they would have to make an effort to reject. Clearly, the sort of freedom they had grown used to on Hydra was not possible here.

There were big problems facing Martin and Shane in their schooling. Because they had not sat for the special examination set for eleven-year-olds, commonly called the 'eleven plus', they were automatically forced to attend the Secondary Modern School at nearby Winchcombe. Secondary Modern schools were second-class high schools, and were such an educational failure that they have since been discontinued in favour of the Comprehensive system. Martin and Shane hated Winchcombe school, and were thoroughly miserable for the two terms they were there, although the headmaster did perceive their unsuitability and arranged a place at Cheltenham Grammar for Martin for the following year, 1961.[1] Jason, then four years old, found a new interest in the world of modern electrical applicances, of which there were none on Hydra, and could not resist cookers, vacuum cleaners or washing machines, with their magical buttons and noises. Luckily the Camerons lived in fairly shabby domestic comfort anyway, so would not be very concerned about minor damage by small children to furniture or applicances.

The local pub became something of a satisfactory substitute for the Katsikas store, and the Johnstons soon formed a number of friendships. John Ryland, now the owner of Charity Farm, remembers that they were 'tense but joined in with life in the village',[2] and that they gave several lively parties, the first of which was a fireworks party on Guy Fawkes night. Nevertheless, they found it difficult to be wholehearted about their life there. The very temporary nature of the house swap was an inhibiting factor, quite apart from the sense of alienation they now felt from English customs and values.

There was to be no dramatic improvement in Johnston's health. No 'miracle' drug would cure him if he was not prepared to give up smoking, heavy drinking and worrying, and begin living in a relaxed and healthy fashion. The London doctors could do no more than tell him this, which he already knew; the new antibiotics they gave him could work only if he gave them the chance. To make radical changes in his living habits would have required a complete change in his attitude to work: what he wanted, and got tense about, was a major success to bring him a fortune, because he craved financial security and the freedom from the necessity to work constantly and commercially. He was beginning to think that that success would never come, and that he would have to seek security elsewhere. A conventional existence now seemed to be the only way to be free of the constant threat of poverty, and thereby free from the anxiety that was proving so destructive to his physical and emotional well-being. So he went to London in an attempt to return to the field of journalism, which he had abandoned only six years earlier. And, as he later told the Australian writer Colin Simpson, the attempt turned out to be a disaster:

> I thought I could easily get back into newspaper work. After all, I'd run a newspaper service in London, I had lots of mates in Fleet Street — or I thought I had. It was 'Wonderful to see you again, George!' and then 'Haven't been too well, I hear. What are you now — forty nine? Let me have a word with the editor. Phone you Monday'. You know, 'Don't call us, we'll call you'. It was a young man's world, and let's face it, I did have a spot of TB.[3]

By Christmas their financial situation was desperate once again, and they were surviving on a £300 advance for *The Far Road*. Johnston had begun another 'Shane Martin', his fifth, but that would not be in a state to bring in money until after January. It was winter, they were broke, and the unhappiness of the last few years on Hydra hung over them like a dark cloud. They could have been forgiven if they had sunk into a state of deep despair. Certainly they were depressed, but at least the anger and blame-laying between them seemed to have ceased; indeed, they bore each other up stoically. There is a most moving passage in *Clean Straw for Nothing*, which represents faithfully the Johnston/Clift generosity of spirit in attempting to sustain each other's morale. Broke as he is,

199

Meredith, while in London for his job interview, uses the remainder of his money — 30 guineas — to buy Cressida a suede coat, a 'kind of bribery' to get her out of her depressed unwillingness to leave the house and meet the villagers, or visit friends in London. Meredith's impulsive act is partly to cheer himself up, and partly a gesture of love to Cressida, whose mental state is causing him concern:

> One thing to be thankful for was that Cressida and I seldom quarrelled any more. But she was more withdrawn than I ever remembered her to be, with her emotions held on a tight rein. She seemed desperate for solitude. During the day, when the children had gone off to the rural secondary modern school to which officialdom had allocated them, she would take a book and shut herself off in the old study for hours. Going past the window of the room to fetch firewood, I would sometimes catch a glimpse of her seated at the big desk staring at nothing, her book unopened in front of her. Or she would take long, solitary walks in the high woods with Harry the dog we had temporarily inherited, and sometimes at night she would go out under the frosty chink of stars to help the farmhands with the lambing on the cold hills. She was friendly with the farmhands and an old wizened gardener and a gamekeeper and the shepherd at Chestnut Farm, as if the only real accord she could find was with simple people living to simple elemental rituals. She had not turned her face to the wall exactly, but she had turned it away from one kind of reality and seemed to seek for some other reassurance elsewhere. She was not happy. Neither of us was. (CSFN 240)

It is with these matters in mind that Meredith buys the coat. When he gets home to the farm, he discovers that she has done a similar thing by spending the last of the housekeeping money on a number of bottles of expensive liquor as a spontaneous gift to cheer him up. Both suddenly see the funny side of it:

> It had been a long time since we had laughed together. Really laughed. 'It is terribly corny, isn't it', I said, 'Like that awful O. Henry story. Hell, never mind. What does it matter? Something is bound to turn up'.
> 'Micawber!', she said, but we were very close then, happier with each other, I think, than we had been for a good many years, just the two of us together again and isolated once more from worlds that were intrusive and brutal and destructive. (CSFN 241)

Something does turn up. As with the Micawbers, their determination to meet their misfortunes with defiant optimism is rewarded with a lucky last-minute reprieve. Their painter friend Tom Kiernan, the character based on Sidney Nolan, writes them a letter saying: 'Heard you were back in old Dart and having a bit of a rough trot. Had intended contacting you to tell you how impressed I was with your novel . . .' (*CSFN* 241). With the letter is a gift of a sumptuous book on Chinese culture, which when they open it they find contains among its pages forty five-pound notes.

Dickensian it was, but it actually happened to the Johnstons. Their wheel of fortune was as dramatically timed as if it were under the control of a writer of popular fiction. Sidney Nolan did in fact send them a gift of money in precisely this way, after learning of how desperately it was needed.[4]

They had been rescued before, and they would be again, but never from quite so deep in the jaws of disaster. Cedric Flower had said they were in the care of the gods, but it was a friend this time who came to the rescue. 'They were innocents,' said Nolan. Certainly there were times when friends thought of them as wayward children, needing the protection of wiser beings who were never as far away as the Johnstons liked to pretend.

After Christmas, Johnston tracked Nolan down in his studio in Putney. Their reunion brimmed with feeling. In the three years since they last met, Nolan had put considerable work into the Gallipoli series, and Johnston was impressed:

> He had gone beyond the stage of sketches now and was painting big. He was very busy at this stage with other shows, commissions, decor for the theatre, but whenever he could find time he returned feverishly to the Gallipoli pictures. The studio was stacked with them — those haunting, ageless heads that seemed neither dead nor alive, neither of the past nor the present, eerie centaur figures half submerged in lethe-like waters . . . I remember one howling meltemi-swept night when all the kerosene lamps had been dancing in a jump of shadows, and in a rare outburst of emotional passion he had flung his sketches down and cried 'you can't paint it! You need metal and a forge. It's got to clang!' But he had painted it.[5]

Apart from visiting Nolan, Johnston stayed away from London after Christmas. With Clift, he confined his life to Stanton for a while, dealt with David Higham by mail mostly, and got on with his current 'Shane Martin' book. Higham wrote early in January, thanking him for introducing Leonard Cohen, who, he said, 'may be a useful acquisition', though it was to eventuate that Higham would make the mistake of turning down Cohen's business because he thought his first novel, *The Favourite Game*, was a failure. The 'Shane Martin' book, dreadfully titled *A Wake for Mourning*, was finished by early February, no doubt in anticipation of an advance. But Collins's new reader, Lord Hardinge, thought the book 'was awful' and insisted on changes, which further delayed any payment. Frantic, Johnston 'sent out an S.O.S.'[6] to Collins asking for £300 to be credited to his account, and this was done in the form of a loan for reasons of tax avoidance.

Despite the constant struggle to keep their heads above water, and the other things that made it more difficult than Hydra, they were not wholly resigned to giving England up. On the one hand, they saw educational advantages to the children in staying on, and there were times when they concluded that this was what they should do. On the other hand, they felt they would all be happier on Hydra. Their uncertainty lasted some months. At one stage, in February 1961, there was a plan for Charmian to return to Hydra to sell the house, but by 1 April Johnston wrote to Higham: 'Such a time of doubts, decisions, changes of plans, indecisions etc., that it's only now we have something definite to tell you. We are now definitely going back to Greece on April 15th.'[7] In the end, lack of money had forced the decision on them, for events were soon to prove that, if they had been able to afford it, they would have stayed on in England. Against this, however, was their unwillingness to sell the Hydra house: they did not want to stay in England badly enough to do this. It was unthinkable to sever their ties with Greece completely. Also, whatever the educational disadvantages, Shane and Martin were dying to get back home to Hydra, to their friends and their pets.

In her biography of Peter Finch, *Finch, Bloody Finch*, Elaine

Dundy writes that Finch gave Johnston and Clift £1000 for the fares back to Greece.[8] This is doubtful. They might well have seen Finch on more than one occasion in England, but Dundy's only evidence for the hand-out is taken, word for word, from the fictional *Clean Straw for Nothing*. Johnston told two people, Elsie and the writer Colin Simpson, that he had had to 'borrow' their fares back to Greece, and he told Simpson that the lender had been his old mate Vic Valentine, from the *Sun* office. This is more plausible, and sits better with his story to Elsie and Simpson to the effect that by the time they got back to Hydra they were £1500 in debt. They could not, even with the money they owed the Katsikas brothers (about £25), have got into this much debt in such a short time if they had also received a 'gift' of £1000 from Finch. Before they left England, Johnston received a commission from Peter Graham Scott of Associated Rediffusion to write a TV play called *Beachhead*. Scott had already done an adaptation of *The Darkness Outside*, which was shown on ITV a year or so earlier. George would not have time to write *Beachhead* now until he returned to Greece, he told Scott, and would send it from Hydra. He seems never to have written it.

'Our trip to England', he wrote to Elsie some time later, 'was a ghastly flop', and he added that he returned to Hydra 'totally scared, without any work in the truck [he seems to have wanted to banish the TV play from his mind], lung shadows persisting, absolutely depressed, and by this time in debt to the extent of £1500'.[9] Clift regretted the whole ill-conceived venture. She wrote a piece years later for the *Sydney Morning Herald* called 'Other People's Houses', recalling the impossibility of attempting to lead 'somebody else's life pattern', insisting that it 'all ended badly', and that there had even been a falling-out with the Camerons over some personal possessions.[10] Didy Cameron did not quite see it that way: she admitted that they had a small row over a Hogarth print that was slightly damaged by the Johnstons, and that they broke a Chinese vase in Hydra, but replaced it.[11] Didy Cameron visited them on Hydra in 1962 and again in 1963, and relations between them were fine. The fact that it 'all ended badly' in England was no fault of the Camerons, but more to do with the Johnston's unwisdom of attempting to go back to a life they had rejected in 1954.

Approaching Hydra, their depression turned to fear of facing debtors and critics, and they urgently rehearsed all the justifications they might give. Clift later told Colin Simpson 'As the ship came in towards the wharf I could see a crowd of people. I thought "Who's on board, I wonder?" and "Probably some politican", because people were holding up placards. When we got nearer I could read the placards, and I started to blubber. They said "Welcome home to the Johnstons" and "You've never been away!" '[12]

There was a party that night on the quayside in front of the Katsikas store. Tables were brought out, though it was not yet summer, and the festivities lasted the whole night. At one stage, one of the Katsikas brothers drew Johnston aside and, obviously embarrassed, said he wanted a word. 'This is it,' thought Johnston, 'he's going to be nice about it but he's going to ask about his 2000 drachmas', which, of course, he did not have. But instead of asking for money, the kindly Greek drew a wad of notes from his pocket and shoved it into Johnston's hand, saying 'You take this and pay us when you can . . . a man like you he can't not have money. You take it, you order whatever you want from us . . . we know everything will soon be all right. You must take it, because you are our friend.'[13] 'You couldn't not take it,' said Johnston. Indeed he had no choice, but it hardly made him happy: the prospect of repaying his debts had grown impossible.

It is tedious to talk of luck all the time playing such an important role in Johnston's life, because simply by choosing the life he did he was inevitably throwing himself and his family to the mercy of fortune. Under these circumstances, everything that came his way, good or bad, could to some extend be attributed to luck. Any freelance worker puts up with the same thing. Let us just say then that chances were reasonable that a long run of meagre pickings would be likely to be followed by a sudden bonanza. And now it happened again. Only a few days after this abject return from England in April 1961, a letter from Higham followed them to Hydra saying that *Closer to the Sun* had been chosen as the October

Literary Guild selection in New York, and that they would be forwarding soon an advance of $25,000, to be divided equally between publisher and author. Harold Ober Inc. had actually cabled the news to Charity Farm, and did not realise it had missed them. Growing concerned at hearing no response, they contacted Higham, who eventually got the message through two weeks later. An ecstatic Johnston replied to Higham, indicating just how undecided he had been right up until the last moment: 'Strange to think that had the news come a fortnight earlier we should probably have stayed on in England. Now we shall be able to visit regularly.'[14] Why they should want to do this is puzzling – they had only a few close friends there, most of whom could better afford to pay a visit to them. In the flush of excitement Johnston might have thought himself richer than he in fact was: $12,500 seemed like a fortune at that moment. At least they could breathe again. Higham put it move strongly than this: 'You've worked very hard to reach the corner now turned,'[15] he wrote. Which corner did he mean, one wonders? Financial or literary? Or both?

In the following months of 1961 the Johnstons were happy to be back in Greece and full of confidence. This went for the children, too. Shane went back to the 'Down' school, while Martin, after his two terms at the Secondary Modern School, went into Form One at the Hydra High School. The summer brought more tourists than ever before, and Clift revelled in them, selling copies of their books to tourists at the quayside. She complained to Higham that *Peel me a Lotus* had been allowed to go out of print:

> *Fantastic things are happening to this island, which by next year may well be one of the most fashionable resorts in the world, and* Lotus *is the only book about it. I am asked a dozen times a week by tourists where they can buy a copy, and the owner of the new Marine Club, which is also a book store – or will be when it opens next week – says he can get rid of as many copies as he can get hold of.*[16]

Fashionable Hydra certainly was: Jacqueline Kennedy had visited, Jules Dassin and Melina Mercouri had announced they would make a film of *Phaedra* there in September, and Tony

Perkins sat in the Johnston kitchen that summer, drooled over by Shane and Charmian. Clift was especially pleased about the publicity stirred up by such big names, not only because she wanted to sell her books, but also because she, and Johnston too, at times indulged in a degree of celebrity-collecting of their own. This represented a shift of ground, of course, from their beginnings on Hydra, when they had wanted a quiet retreat in order to 'write something worth-while'. That ideal was fading almost unnoticed, as they attempted more and more to derive some sort of benefit from the invasion of sophisticated tourists. George still felt, along with some of the other permanents, that the tourists were mostly a nuisance, and if he'd had enough to drink was prone to get into heated arguments with them outside the Katsikas store, only to end up trading insults.

Peter Finch was in Athens during that summer making the film *In the Cool of the Day* with Jane Fonda, and at one stage took time off briefly to visit the Johnstons. This visit probably inspired the passage in *Clean Straw for Nothing* where Archie Calverton confides his deep cynicism about the world of success that he inhabits with such violent competitiveness, insisting that it is Meredith's life that is the enviable one, because 'success is all bullshit'.

> All I want is to have it my way, man, and in big lights. I just want to fuck the other bastards because it's me that's fucking them. I believe in the Twentieth Century Fairytale. The PR Fairy Godmother who waves the big wand around and gets me everything I want. Big fast expensive cars, amiable women with long straight legs, champagne breakfasts, autograph books, cameras, lights, homage, fancy apartments, genuflecting headwaiters, the right clothes. (CSFN 193)

Finch's biographer, Elaine Dundy, believes that this is prob-ably authentic Finch talk, and that he often went on in this vein to his agent, Olive Harding, complaining of being trap-ped in the phoney world of success, and insisting that he wanted to go back to stage acting, which is precisely what Johnston's Archie Calverton says. Then, says Dundy, another film offer would come along, offering big money, and Finch would inevitably accept it, and the dreams of the stage would once more vanish.

The Literary Guild money was not actually payable, John-ston discovered, until January 1962, but because of the crucial state of their finances it was arranged that William Morrow would send them cheques from time to time in the form of advances. $2000 came in May, but debts quickly swallowed that, and another $2000 was requested and paid in July. The casual way in which Johnston made these requests worried Harold Ober Inc. a little, and they wrote somewhat advisedly that Morrow 'understand your precarious economic situation. Let us hope it is now relieved for all time.'[17] Both Morrow and Collins were fussing over the typescript of The Far Road, which they wanted to publish, but were behaving cautiously over. Peeved, Johnston complained that this showed lack of confidence in the book, and that it did not augur well for their promotion of it. After several epistolary skirmishes, Morrow's editor, Helen King, finally conceded to Johnston that 'she liked it very much', and offered a $1500 advance. So now the money was positively rolling in.

In October 1961 Johnston replied, after almost a year, to a letter Elsie had written to him when he was in England. After apologising and filling her in on the lows and highs of his fortunes in the interim, he surprised her with the news that he had written to Gae suggesting to her that she could, when she finished at University, come to stay with them for 'a year or two's experience in Europe', which he was sure they would all enjoy. 'Martin and Shane talk endlessly about their half-sister (her photographs are framed in Shane's room),' he said, and added that it would be 'most valuable for her, I think, especially if she wants to continue on foreign lan-guages, or wishes to be a writer'.[18] In fact Gae had not shown any positive inclinations to be a writer, or anything else at that stage; she had a talent for painting, but this was still undeveloped then.

Copying his tardiness, it took Elsie a whole year to get around to replying to this suggestion, and when she did it was to deliver some strong reprimands. The years of struggle as a single mother had caused her to bottle up a great deal of resentment, and the thought that he could now send for Gae when all the hard work had been done rankled. 'It must be wonderful to put your hand in the hat and pull out something as glamorous and refreshing as Gae . . . Am I to step aside now that my job is no longer important? Pardon me if I sound a little bitter, but I'm sure any mother in similar circumstances would feel the same,' she wrote him.[19] Of course, Gae was excited at the prospect, but before Elsie would agree she wanted assurances that his offers of help to find her a job in Paris or London were realistic, and not mere pipe dreams that would cause disappointment. Her vehemence took him back a little, so he let the matter rest for another four months before he replied.

When Johnston first raised the subject, the atmosphere on Hydra was good, and relations between George and Charmian were relaxed; he would never have invited Gae into a situation such as the one that had prevailed in the summer of 1959. And although his weight was still at a low 53 kilograms (8 stone 6 pounds), and he was complaining of a lack of energy, he nevertheless did 'feel pretty fit', was enjoying 'the joys of peace', and believed he had 'some pretty good books coming up'.[20] Only *The Far Road* deserved this description. The only other book in the hands of the publishers was *A Wake for Mourning*, which was, he knew, one of his worst 'Shane Martin' efforts, for which he could not find enough interest to make the changes Collins were demanding; in the end they gave up and published it anyway. It was to be the last of his 'Shane Martin' books. On the other hand, his conviction about *The Far Road* was vindicated by an excellent review in the *Times Literary Supplement* in February 1962, although Collins's feeble efforts to promote it were still annoying him, and he wrote to Billy Collins asking him to ginger them up in the office. He also did some heavy name-dropping by asking Collins for ten extra copies to send 'to old friends in the USA – Eleanor Roosevelt, Brooks Atkinson, John Hersey, Ed Murrow, because they might be willing to provide useful endorsements'.[21]

It was another sign of harmony between them at this time that Johnston and Clift entered into one more collaborative venture in the early months of 1962. Their interest in the Hydra tourist market had increased to the point where they now set out specifically to write something for it, this time a factually based history of the island mixed with gossip about the fashionable visitors who graced its quayside every summer. It was to be called, with a certain mockery of their own source of misery in the recent past, 'The Serpent in the Rock'. This marked the fourth piece of work by them that made use of Hydra for its material, but this was really scraping the bottom of the barrel, and was certainly the least imaginative attempt. Elizabeth Jane Howard had told Johnston that she thought a writer 'could get one good book out of a place like Hydra',[22] but he and Clift persisted well beyond this sensible limitation, and were now apparently prepared to resort to writing tourist guides in order to make use of every last scrap of print the place could offer. It could no longer give them the stuff of exotic adventure fiction that they'd written in the past, although they had both reached the stage when their hearts were not in this sort of writing anyway. The only source of fresh material available to them now was within themselves, and within their relationship, but they were not ready to see this yet, though Johnston almost was, and had in *Closer to the Sun* and *The Far Road* come near to realising it. Books such as 'The Serpent in the Rock' were going to get them nowhere, and fortunately Higham and the publishers were astute enough to perceive this, even when Johnston was insisting that they might be able to repeat their luck and catch another book club selection. The typescript for the new venture was sent direct to Harold Ober Inc. in New York on 28 May 1962, with an urgent request that it be published in time for the following year's summer tourist trade. But it met with total lack of interest, and Ober wrote that they were unable to get it accepted by a single publisher. The general opinion was that American interest in Hydra was 'at best, fleeting' and that the place 'was not worth a whole book'.[23]

While this was happening, William Morrow were cavilling about making further payments of the Literary Guild money. They had paid over a further $500 the previous December, and then in March 1962 Johnston had asked for $4000, which would make the total advances paid during the year $8500, a larger annual income than they had ever had. Morrow had themselves received the money from the Guild, but now they advised Johnston that they would give him no more of it until the next quarterly royalty payments were made — about October. Their excuse was bookkeeping practice, but the real reason was mistrust of Johnston. Ivan von Auw from Harold Ober Inc. wrote to Higham in March:

> *I didn't know exactly what to say to George. The truth is that we're all worried here about how fast he is going through all this money and are afraid he'll spend it all and then come back on Morrow for more when there isn't any in the kitty.*[24]

Higham, behind Johnston's back, agreed that he, too, was 'puzzled about how George gets through his money so quickly, unless it is that his health has failed him again'.[25] Morrow then offered to pay $2500 immediately, but after further protest from Johnston agreed to the $4000 on the proviso that no more would be paid until after October. Well meant as their arguments were, they were nevertheless patronising and self-interested. They were right to be concerned about where the money was going to, but since no contractual arrangements for the timing of the payments seem to have been made, they appear to have had no legal right to withhold the outstanding sum. As to what the Johnstons were doing with the money, this is not evident. There were debts carried over from England, but these should have easily been settled, as should the account at the Katsikas store. Nothing in any of the Johnston correspondence suggests unusual spending around this time.

For all the relative affluence and calm they had experienced in the fourteen months following their return from England, the Johnstons' more serious problems had not been solved. Financial security distracted them from matters of personal importance, but really they were travelling on thin ice. Over this summer of 1962 a hole was to open up once again, and this time their plight was to become almost hopeless. Sexually, his illness had all but broken Johnston. He and Clift were rarely lovers, and this was exacerbated by the fact that Clift, at thirty-nine, was desperate to prove that she had not lost her sex appeal. It seems that the American Chadwick returned, and the old agonies were lived through all over again — jealousy, public rows, drunken scenes, friends dragged in to take sides — except that this time it was so much worse, the confrontations were that much more bitter, and at times violent. Grace Edwards learned that Clift had cut Johnston's face with a broken glass on one occasion; on another Johnston went berserk and tried to take on the world, ending up in the local cell for the night;[26] Chadwick seems to have kept a remarkably low profile through all of this, and none of the survivors from those days can recall him. For the children it all had, said Martin, 'a nightmare quality', in which sequences of events, and who was blaming who for what, all became a total confusion. Martin and Shane found themselves taking sides with different parents from one week to the next, and sadly the relationship between the two of them, which had not been close since they were very small anyway, became one of unrelieved conflict and dislike.[27]

The confusion was made worse by what had become a general deterioration in the social climate on Hydra. There were sexual and intellectual jealousies going on everywhere, not so much within the expatriate colony, as between colonists and newcomers, foreign visitors who came to question or scoff, or in other ways to provoke trouble. For the Johnstons, the whole place had become a chaotic and destructive mess, and by the end of that summer their emotional stability as a family was in tatters. It is difficult to put one's finger on the precise nature of it, or over what period of time it had developed, but by the late months of 1962 Johnston was a changed man. He had become remote, withdrawn and uncharacteristically indifferent to other people, including Clift, who later recalled: 'Perhaps he thought he had nothing to lose any more. Perhaps he thought if people didn't like what he was and what he thought and what he felt they could bloody well lump him. The necessity to charm, to please, to entertain, to be approved ... dropped out of him like so much unwanted baggage.'[28] He told Clift he wanted to leave her; he had said this in the past, and had even made attempts to do so, but now it was not said as a dramatic gesture, but with an inner conviction. He had to change himself and his circumstances if he was to cope with life. It was a question of finding the right moment and the right circumstances to separate. Poor Colin Simpson arrived in the midst of all this to write his chapter on Hydra for the large travel book on Greece that he was writing. The passages dealing with the Johnstons in Simpson's book say very little about the current circumstances — not that he would have delved into matters of personal disharmony anyway — but it is interesting that in order to relate a set of happy events to Simpson, George and Charmian focused attention on the recent triumphant past — their bad experiences in England followed by their welcome home to Hydra and the success with the Literary Guild selection. This was because there was little of anything especially good going on at that time that they could tell Simpson.

Perhaps the most vivid evidence that Johnston had changed can be found in his work. He began making curious notes on the characters of Meredith and his wife, with an at-that-stage-unnamed novel in mind. The notes are disorganised, obsessional and intensely self-directed, for which he did some pointed reading and some careful quote-lifting. From Arthur Mizener's Introduction to Scott Fitzgerald pieces, titled *Afternoon of An Author*, Johnston selected passages that discussed the past and the expiration of passion. He singled out the phrases 'the *pastness of* the past in Fitzgerald's work' and Henry James's term 'the visitable past' from Mizener's book, and a quote from Scott Fitzgerald's story 'One Trip Abroad':

> 'It's just that we don't understand what's the matter,' she said. 'Why did we lose peace and love and health, one after the other? If we knew, if there was anybody to tell us, I believe we could try. I'd try so hard'.[29]

There is a particular aptness in this plea for some outside help, for some figure of authority to set the wayward 'children' on the right path again, for in cutting themselves off from their families and community in Australia, Johnston and Clift had condemned themselves to lack of support and emotional isolation. Johnston found as so many others have found, that Scott Fitzgerald's understanding of the process of human breakdown had a great deal to teach him about himself and about his writing on the same subject.

In the notes on Emma Bovary, Johnston is looking to

Flaubert as a guide to his portrayal of Meredith's unfaithful wife, who at this stage is still called Kate. The notes have various headings: 'Notes For the Study of a Woman', 'Observations from the Romantic Malady', 'Elements of Jealousy', for which he had plundered Eric Hoffer's *The Passionate State of Mind*. It all whiffs of an anxious search for insights, supporting observations, companionship in writing about these particular sources of suffering. He typed out such Flaubert passages as:

> Yet she must go on smiling all the time, all the time must hear herself saying over and over again that she was happy, must somehow contrive the appearance of happiness and make him believe in its reality. There were moments, all the same, when such hypocrisy disgusted her.

and then again:

> 'You must get hold of yourself, Monsieur Bovary — it'll pass!'[30]

Johnston also cast his mind back to an unforgettable moment when Clift had come to visit him during his recuperation in Athens:

> Kate Meredith had never loved her husband so deeply or so truly as when, to rejoin him in his sickness after several weeks, she stepped off the little steamer escorted on the one side by her lover and on the other by an admirer even younger and equally ardent. She arrived in a new grey suit, looking very beautiful: she had done her hair the way her husband liked it and had made a point of wearing some little ornament 'especially for him'.[31]

From *The Passionate State of Mind* he typed out several extracts, including

> It is an evil thing to expect too much either from ourselves or from others. Disappointment with ourselves does not moderate our expectations from others: on the contrary, it raises them. It is as if we wish to be disappointed in our fellow men.[32]

The peculiar mixture of psychological and literary quotations Johnston has typed out suggest some confusion in his own mind about whether he was doing research for a novel or trying to make sense of his own anguish. In the event, he made little use of any of them in print. The quotations are relevant to parts of *Clean Straw for Nothing*, but Johnston was still some time away from a clear conception of that novel; there were many stages to go through before then. He had made a beginning, with these notes, in thinking of himself and his experience, which so far he had mostly ignored, at least in any serious way. In thinking seriously of his past he was demanding of himself a rigour and an honesty that had previously been missing. Clift hardly knew him any more, she later said, and it made her uncomfortable:

> ... as he fined down alarmingly in weight (for a man six feet tall a weight of seven stone is alarming) he also fined down in character, persona or whatever you call it. And, of course, this in a way was alarming too — for a wife, that is, who found she was married to somebody else entirely.[33]

His new insoucience at times had an abrasive edge. When Collins said they did not like the rewritten typescript of *The Far Face of the Moon*, Johnston said he wasn't surprised, because their editor Robert Knittel harboured 'some little animosity to me', and he suggested to Higham that they ought to try dealing with another publishing house because 'Collins generally have not been altogether good for me',[34] which suggests that Collins were somehow to blame for the unsatisfactory state of *The Far Face of the Moon*. The fact was that Johnston had hardly rewritten it at all, so it was practically identical to the version they had rejected early in 1960. He had lost interest in going over all that stuff about nymphomania and impotence, and really just wanted to get rid of the book and let it try to make a little money. Higham diplomatically did not pursue the book with Collins, and fortunately managed to get Morrow to take it for an American edition, which took the pressure off the issue of relations with Collins. Johnston's unbenign mood was not helped when someone sent him a copy of a recent story by Charles Sriber in the *Bulletin* called 'We'll Never Go Back', a thinly fictionalised portrayal of the Johnstons, showing their professed satisfaction with living in Greece to be hollow and desperate. Johnston took this as an act of betrayal by an old friend, but Sriber's reaction was 'it is all right for George to write about others, but not for anyone to do it to *him*'.[35]

A number of things now conspired to focus Johnston's attention on Australia. He had received Elsie's belated letter in September, criticising him for inviting Gae to Europe; this did not both him because everything had changed now, and there was no thought of having Gae stay with them. He delayed telling Elsie this for some four months, during which time he was in deep retreat from the world, 'a semi-invalid and housebound',[36] in a bad state of physical deterioration and low spirits, not at all helped by an enormous Greek tax demand that had to be paid before the end of the year, leaving the coffers practically empty once again. When he wrote to Elsie in January 1963, he tried to explain, without losing too much face, the circumstances that were forcing him to withdraw the invitation to Gae:

> The fact is that Charmian and I have been grappling with a domestic and emotional crisis for some little time and although for the sake of the kids we are desperately trying to see it through for a bit longer it is all rather difficult and in a sense (to me, at least) there doesn't seem to be much hope of it being resolved. (Maybe it's just me who can't make these things work out!) Anyway, at the moment the atmosphere is hardly one in which I would like Gae to be involved.[37]

The tendency here to blame himself is entirely characteristic of Johnston's reaction to the crisis; again and again he sought within himself the cause of all the unhappiness and distrust. The tone of melancholy regret that he uses here to Elsie is typical of that time.

> I assure you, Else, I never have and I never will want to come between you and Gae, but surely it is not strange that I should have developed a very deep and very sad love for this child, whom, in a sense, I betrayed, and whom I have not seen since she was five or six.[38]

Once again there is that term 'betrayed', a term he would hardly have applied to himself a few years earlier, but which now he uses with a firm conviction that it properly describes the lack of interest he has shown in his family and friends back in Australia for the past twelve or more years. He had recently received a letter from his niece, Joy Russo, in Australia, which had also prompted his conscience. She had read an article on Johnston in *Woman's Day*, which had played up the glamour and success of his life, and wrote to point out the fine values and humility that his brother, Jack, possessed, but for which Jack sought no credit.

So, confined to the house, ill and despairing, but nevertheless determined to keep going and to try to make some sense
out of it all, Johnston clung to his writing. Australia, his
childhood, the different members of his family, the dim shaping forces of those times, intruded repeatedly upon his
thoughts, and he began to feel the power of an irresistible
nostalgia for it all, so that he was compelled to make it the
subject of his work. As he later recalled:

> *I was homesick for my native land. As a way of trying to*
> *overcome the long dragging hours of confinement in a sick-*
> *bed, I set myself the task of trying to remember a street in*
> *Melbourne I used to walk along in the early nineteen-*
> *twenties, when I was a ten-year-old schoolboy. Although I*
> *had no distractions, it did not come easy. However, I per-*
> *sisted, and gradually − I thought at the time miraculously −*
> *the street assembled itself in my mind, bit by bit, shop by*
> *shop, house by house, the most minute detail, people and*
> *things I had not thought about for forty years.*[39]

He wrote a whole chapter about his childhood, starting with
the first memories of his grandmother caring for him while
his father was away at the war and his mother was nursing.
Along the way, details got changed in the cause of greater
thematic and aesthetic considerations. His mother's role was
made more heroic, his father's verbal violence was turned
into physical cruelty, his brother's character was inflated to
heroic proportions and simplified to an Australian stereotype,
the 'culture' of wartime was given prominence, his beginnings as a writer dramatised to suggest a deeper identifica-
tion with the artists against the philistines in his youth than
was the case, his own healthy activities, such as football and
yachting, were suppressed to create the impression of a
hypersensitive misfit. When the first chapter was completed
he could see where it was leading. He knew immediately
he had a real novel within his grasp. With very little of it
written, he wrote to Robert Knittel at Collins in December
1962: 'All I can say to you [is] that the present novel − for the
moment entitled *My Brother Jack* − is immeasurably the best
thing I have ever done, and it is certainly the novel on which
I would be prepared to stake my writing future.'[40]

Unlike his previous books, this one was written slowly and

with great care. Initially, Johnston told Higham it would be 'three months or so' before it was finished, but it took seven. Clift played an important role in its creation. Never less than generous in her willingness to help him write, as indeed he was with her, she could see that with illness and the effects of the drugs reducing his stamina and powers of concentration, he would need assistance in the exacting business of recalling the past and transforming it into readable form. 'I sat on the steps by his desk every day for seven months so that I would be there when I was wanted for discussion or suggestion or maybe only to listen.'[41] At the same time, she had her own work to be going on with — she was taking another crack at *Honour's Mimic* — though she gave Johnston priority when he needed her. There is no better example of Clift's sublime integrity than this: she would insist (she had long given up denying her past affairs) on her right to personal freedom, even if it meant hurting George, and yet she was fiercely loyal and unstintingly generous to him. She was, reflected her son Martin, 'anarchistic in the best sense', having total disregard for conventional morals, and at the same time devoid of petty egotism.

Although it began as an exercise in memory, prompted by intense nostalgia, *My Brother Jack*, as it developed, soon became a much more analytical quest than these terms would suggest, and the subject of analysis was his own character. It should not be forgotten that Johnston wrote the novel in the bitter conviction that he was a failure — that sense of himself as a 'betrayer' that he confided to Elsie — in practically everything he had attempted. As a writer, he was neither a literary nor a financial success; as a journalist he had failed to get to the top; in the war he had played what he saw as an ignoble role; as a husband he was a cuckold; and as a parent he was neglectful. His health and sexual drive had left him, and he no longer belonged to a community that provided him with any social satisfaction. Whether or not all of these failings were strictly true, he certainly felt that they were. Notes he made for the construction of *My Brother Jack* indicate that David Meredith was conceived as the very expression of this catalogue of character faults:

> *It is important, I think, to point out that he [Meredith] was,*
> *like many of us, a man whose talents never quite reached the*
> *mark of his ambitions. He was that everlastingly lamentable*
> *figure, the man who never quite comes off, the near-miss, the*
> *also-ran.*[42]

The notes suggest that Meredith's faults were not just the
failures of his adult life, but had their roots in childhood —
not as an inherited condition, but virtually imbibed as a
disease of mediocrity from the very atmosphere of his dreary
Australian suburban boyhood:

> *His mind, perhaps, had been in some way twisted strangely*
> *by a childhood which he had not come to understand — or*
> *even been prepared to try to understand — until he was a*
> *man of middle age. Only then did he come to see the geog-*
> *raphical flatness of the suburbs, the emptiness of the sky, the*
> *hollow places where companionship should have been, and*
> *the imperfections that had surrounded him.*[43]

So for all Johnston's nostalgia, and all the good things that
Australia now represented to his stricken expatriate spirit,
Australia was not without its faults, and had a large share of
the blame in the formation of his flawed personality.

In this, and in Meredith's account of his growing up under
a cruel father, and Meredith's boyhood tendency to resort to
treachery in getting his own way, Johnston is building a case
in *My Brother Jack* for the child being the father to the man.
This is, of course, a fairly common novelist's means of creating the 'illusion' of character development, but there is in this
an element of deception, legitimate though it is, when the
author already knows the outcome of that development before he even begins. This was precisely the frame of mind in
which Johnston conceived Meredith — he knew he was to be
a treacherous failure as an adult, so he constructed the childhood that would be consistent with, and give rise to, that
particular adult. In this sense, because we know that Johnston
at the time of writing thought of himself as possessing these
flaws, Meredith is obviously a repository for Johnston's own
sense of failure.

Meredith also has some of Johnston's good qualities, and to
convey this was another part of Johnston's plan for the novel,
as his notes indicate:

*He was neither Icarus flamboyantly falling into the Aegean
nor Dedalus making a cautious landing in Sicily. Yet, in his
way, he was a good trier — and for this he should be
respected.*[44]

To be 'a good trier' — not to give in, not to succumb to the
forces of death or conformity (another kind of death) — is the
point that brings Meredith and Johnston into a union that
insists on the moral dimension in life: to succeed is not as
important as to fail with honour, and honour is gained by
trying with courage. Johnston was honest enough to avoid
false modesty and to represent his own courage, and his
desire to *be* honest, in Meredith, though these qualities are
more evident in the two final volumes of the trilogy than in
My Brother Jack.

It is clear that the design of *My Brother Jack* is based on the
'novel of success' — the rags-to-riches story — that Dickens so
often made use of. Also like Dickens, Johnston criticises that
success myth by telling us about (but not, I think, successfully
showing us) the acts of treachery that accompany Meredith's
rise from obscurity to fame as a war correspondent. Against
this, Meredith's brother, Jack, is held up as a model of heroic
Australian virtues, with his belief in mateship, honesty,
toughness and loyalty: in effect, the Australian stereotype,
which, contrary to what some critics have said, Johnston
treats with total lack of irony.

The point to be grasped here is that Johnston, in designing
the novel in this way, is in conscious control of his material,
selecting and shaping it in order to construct a unified work of
art. The fact that that material was closely related to the autobiographical source should not blind us to this reality. Nor
does this deny that Johnston's intention was to tell the truth; the
truth was precisely what he thought he was telling in shaping
David Meredith's 'development' towards the inevitable end of
revealing his character, in all its worst aspects. It is just that he
believed, when writing this novel, that 'development' was the
best way of understanding character, that the chronological
progression from one set of events to the next, showing the
central character emerging more definitely formed from each

event, was the way in which 'reality' worked, and to use that form in the novel was, in effect, to be faithful to reality. What he did not then perceive was that 'development' as the only means of understanding human character is in itself a myth, or at least merely one possible approach to the problem. We do not understand something merely by showing what it came before and what it came after. When a novel is tied to this chronological approach to understanding, it is usual to give it the label 'realism', although it is no less an art form for that, and no less subject to limitations in what it can achieve as a means of understanding human nature. Later, when beginning to think about the second volume (he planned right from the start to write a trilogy), Johnston saw the trick he had played on himself by assuming a necessary relation between understanding and 'development' in strict chronological sequence, and decided to experiment with a more appropriate form for that novel in an interesting way. But this was not until he had finished *My Brother Jack*, and had had a chance to reflect on its distortions and limitations.

In an ABC talk in 1970 Johnston stated that his depiction of David Meredith's defections was a deliberate exaggeration of his own faults in order to make Jack's virtues more apparent:

> *I honestly do not believe that I was quite so treacherous a young man, so gifted for betrayal and self-interest and opportunism. But it was necessary to draw the Davy character in this way to build up the almost tragic irony of the final situation, where Davy becomes his brother Jack's hero, and also to point up the contrast with Jack's honesty, guts and, in a real sense, his uncomplicated nobility. The real difficulty of the book was to do this while still retaining sympathy for Davy and understanding of his character.*[45]

The evidence of his childhood would support him here. He was *not* so treacherous a young man as Meredith is supposed to be, and which *was* a consciously designed feature of the novel. Yet notice in the final sentence of his ABC talk that the 'real difficulty' was in 'retaining sympathy' for Davy, while showing him to be deeply flawed. Johnston's most troubling concern is with Davy's complexity, against which, as I have said, Jack, for all his warmth and nobility, is a simple stereotype. But there is an inner struggle explored in Davy, which is marked by the paradox that he is 'too acute and too complex to accept the straight-forward code of beliefs of Jack, yet he is too imbued with the same myths not to castigate himself for failing to subscribe to them'.[46] In other words, he has the utmost admiration for Jack's qualities, yet there is something in him that rejects them as too simple. Much of his inner conflict springs from the irreconcilable nature of that paradox.

The odd thing is that in the actual reading of the novel I do not believe that we truly feel this 'treachery' of Davy's to be very real. He is *supposed* to be a betrayer and an opportunist, as Johnston tells us, and Meredith himself never tires of telling us of his own 'defections' in his guilty, brooding manner, with its overtones of self-laceration. But can we agree with Meredith's criticism of his own character? Do we ever see any of those defections? What actions does he perform that make him reprehensible to us as readers? The answer is, very few. Meredith cites examples such as his boyhood cruelty to Harry Meares, the selling of his parents' war memorabilia, pretending Steiner's paintings were his, and his lack of bravery as a war correspondent. But, as failings, these feel too ordinary for the intense degree of shame they arouse in him, and in any case when people tell us how bad they are, we are inclined to take the opposite view, so their self-criticism becomes a virtue. The consequence of reading Meredith's 'confessions', then, is − as Johnston said in his ABC talk he intended it to be − our 'retaining sympathy' for Davy.

The reason for his disparity between Meredith's sense of shame and what actually occurs is that the real source of the shame lies outside the period of Johnston's life covered in *My Brother Jack*, which takes us only as far as the end of the war, when Meredith and Cressida begin their relationship. The source of shame and guilt lies, as we know, in the last years of their life together on Hydra, referred to in the trilogy as simply 'the island'. It is in writing about these years in the second volume, *Clean Straw for Nothing*, that Johnston can convincingly show why Meredith is so riddled with self-hatred. In that novel there is no plea for sympathy for Meredith.

There is another point to be made on the subject of Meredith's 'defections', and that is in relation to Johnston's marriage to Elsie. Here was an opportunity to give Meredith some genuine fault based on his own actions as Elsie's husband. As we have already seen, it was he who was unfaithful to Elsie; it was he, as dominant partner in their marriage, who dictated their social life in such a way as to rob Elsie of confidence, and he who selfishly used and abused her. Instead there is a disturbing reversal of roles: Helen is made the dominant one, using him for her own social ambitions, and there are hints that she may have been unfaithful with American officers in Meredith's absence abroad.

If Helen Meredith is *not* a version of Elsie (as Johnston stated), where does she come from? Olga Reid is the source only of the Helen of the naked encounters in the room behind the subscription library, and possibly of the Helen of political and intellectual interests. What of the tall, blonde appearance, her four-year seniority to David, her domination of the marriage, her interest in writing and her unfaithfulness? She may have been pure invention, of course, designed as an attack on bourgeois Melbourne values. But consider the following details: it was Johnston who was the dominant partner in that marriage; it was he who made the domestic and social running; it was he who was interested in writing; it was he who was tall and blond; it was he who was four years older than Elsie; and it was he who was the unfaithful one. Looked at in this light, Helen is much closer to Johnston himself than to Elsie. Is it not possible that in the odd transpositions that take place in the creative imagination, not always in the full conscious control of the author, a desire to tell the truth about himself without confessing the facts, if the distinction be allowed, can bring to the surface such distortions as role reversals and sex changes?

This in no way reduces the effectiveness of the character of Helen as an attack on bourgeois Melbourne; it simply locates Johnston's anguish about it not in external social forces, but in internal biographical ones inflamed and intensified by guilt. This would explain why Helen feels too powerful to be a mere social type based on observation. Why would Johnston do this? Possibly to avoid accusations of culpability in the first marriage; by making Meredith an innocent victim he might have been hoping to appear that way himself. Johnston's letter to Elsie, putting her on her guard not to take Helen as herself, also claimed that in writing the novel he had come to the view that it was 'time I was honest, even if it meant hurting myself'.[47] The path that that honesty and self-punishment took was so indirect, so bizarre, that at times in *My Brother Jack* it is almost unrecognisable.

From the time Johnston began writing *My Brother Jack*, his correspondence with friends and family back in Australia increased, especially with Elsie, in whom he began to confide matters of personal concern. He wrote to her in January 1963 in terms that suggest he was now speaking for himself alone, and not for the rest of his family:

> ... *if I can pull off what I am doing I think it might make everything worthwhile. If not I shall sell up here, which should give me enough money to clear up what debts I have and get back to Australia.*[48]

This sounds as if he was still planning to leave Clift, and that nothing had been repaired in their relationship, despite the co-operation between them on *My Brother Jack*. He finished it in June, and was so exhausted and ill that he had to go into hospital in Athens for six weeks to recuperate. When he came out, the news from Collins was everything he had hoped for. Billy Collins told him he had 'finally written the Great Australian Novel',[49] which had been a half-joke between them for years. In September, Johnston wrote to George Ferguson of Angus & Robertson, after years of silence between them, introducing 'a young writer well worth watching' to them in Redmond Wallis, the New Zealand novelist, and mentioning that Collins was 'going to town in a big way' on *My Brother Jack*, with Sidney Nolan doing the cover, and publication planned for January 1964. He also said that he and Charmian were trying 'to get back on a visit next year', and that his desire to see Australia again was increasing all the time.

A letter from Elsie in October contained the news that Gae was to be married on 21 December. Although she had mentioned an engagement in an earlier letter, this came as 'rather startling news' to Johnston, who unhappily pointed out that although he was returning to Australia for the launching of *My Brother Jack*, he would not be there in time for the wedding. This reply from George was a long one, confiding in Elsie a number of interesting matters. It stated, among other things, that his American publishers (Morrow) were delaying the US edition of *My Brother Jack* until late in 1964 (it did not appear until 1965), and were releasing *The Far Face of the Moon* in March 1964, because they thought it 'a superb American novel', an astonishing view after the flak it had received over a period of two years from Collins. Even in its rewritten form it was still no more than an adventure story about American air force flights over 'the hump', spiced with the sexual extremities of nymphomania and impotence. The American publishers obviously thought he had made a decent job of it, and planned to promote it enthusiastically.

The letter to Elsie also contains comments about *My Brother Jack* being 'an honest self-examination, shall we say, and not a very pretty one as far as I am concerned', although he had 'taken very great fictional liberties with characters, incident and so on'. It is here that he makes his disclaimer about Helen Meredith being a portrait of Elsie, insisting that it is himself he is hurting most by depicting his acts of betrayal through Meredith. Johnston ends the letter on a note of breathtaking presumptuousness:

> You gather from this I am not particularly happy. I don't at all want you to think I am making suggestions, but perhaps it would interest you to know that I now often find myself thinking how nice it would be just to go back to you.[50]

By this time, November, Johnston and Clift had decided on a separation; the trip being arranged back to Australia was now for him alone, and Clift would remain on Hydra with the children.

In the intervening months, between the time *My Brother Jack* was finished and the time of Johnston's departure at a still unspecified date, a mood of paralysing uncertainty de-house at Charity Farm, Worcestershire, England

'A semi-invalid and housebound', Hydra, 1963

In a taverna with friends, Hydra

The Johnston family on Hydra, 1963

...nston and her husband, Ross,
...er 1963 *(Photo courtesy of Gae Johnston)*

Clift with Anthony Kingsmill, 1964

Johnston and Clift at Eulaba in New South Wales, 1964

The day of Clift's departure from Hydra, 1964. *Left to right:* Martin, Clift, unknown child, Gordon Merrick, Jason

Johnston back on familiar ground, Sydney, 1964

scended over the household, as they waited for events to take their course. Exhausted anyway by the huge creative effort he had just completed, Johnston could do no more by way of work than jot down ideas and disconnected notes for the second volume of the trilogy. Some of the thoughts in them are nevertheless of considerable interest:

> Neither of them works any more. Not really. They are waiting for something. The apocalypse, perhaps? A stroke of luck well deserved? Or something that will surprise them and yet be expected in a way, a kind of reward? A sort of accolade to mark with respect the years of their expatriation.[51]

Expatriation was an idea he was turning over and over in his head, 'trying to answer the question, What makes an Australian an expatriate and what makes an Australian an Australian',[52] as he wrote to Elsie. His notes show him moving towards some degree of definition:

> After ten years of expatriation ... fifteen if you count the London time. No, ten is more precise. The London time was more a state of suspended animation, suspended agitation if you like, at the end of a long broom, ten thousand miles long ...[53]

By this he may mean that London was an extension of Australia, which at that point he had not in any significant way left — that is, as an act of deliberate and permanent exile. This is consistent with the view he had of his departure when he left Australia in 1951: he did not think of himself as an expatriate then. But in the course of writing *My Brother Jack* he had come to the view that it was more than merely a geographical displacement, it was a state of being. In one of the central passages in *My Brother Jack*, Meredith undergoes an experience in wartime Italy that makes this brilliantly clear:

> It is not just curiosity that makes an expatriate, there must also be something that happens in the very soul of him. Gradually I began to sense that already, and deliberately, I had begun proceedings of divorcement from my country and my people, and it was at this point that I got up and walked down the room to the huge baroque mirror at the far end, and the glass had the same cloudy, muddy opacity of the mirror in Gavin Turley's house, and I stared very intently at the indistinct reflection that looked back at me through the clouded

> *darkness and the pin-spots of time. I saw change in it at once.*
> *I saw it as older than I had realised, and becoming a little*
> *world-weary, and a shade too cynical around the deep-set*
> *eyes, and then I looked closer and I realised that it was not at*
> *all the same face as those other faces under the broad-*
> *brimmed hats ... not the same, for instance, as my brother*
> *Jack's face. A difference had grown into it, or developed out*
> *of it. I turned my head this way and that, studying it, and*
> *suddenly I realised that there was a sort of calculation in it,*
> *that this was a face watching for opportunities, that what*
> *was lacking in it was the truth those other faces had for the*
> *passionate regard for the adventure in itself, and I knew then*
> *that I was not quite one of them, that I never had been, and*
> *that I never would be.* (MBJ 353)

Expatriation is not 'outer', it is 'inner'; not geographical but existential. It is a particular form of alienation, in which one feels displaced anywhere, and estranged from all others, who are recognised as 'normal'. This is a beautiful and painful perception, one of the profounder insights that Johnston produced in the writing of *My Brother Jack*.

By late November 1963 he was trying every possible ploy to get the fare back to Australia for the book launching in January. Collins had suggested Johnston try to get Qantas to fly him out free, and this resulted in him writing a most sycophantic letter to their publicity officer, promising that in his next book, *Clean Straw for Nothing*, he would 'guarantee to include a substantial portion of the story content which relates in a favourable manner to the name of Qantas, its emblem, its role in the history and development of Australia'.[54] A long prognosis followed of how he imagined slotting the Qantas references in, such as showing the effect of a boatload of tourists carrying the familiar red Qantas bag on Meredith's nostalgic longings. In exchange, he wanted Qantas to pay his fare out to Australia and back to Hydra. Qantas agreed to the scheme, though Johnston never did keep to his side of the bargain, at least not in the terms he proposed: he did later write two film scripts for them, which may have satisfied their requirements. We can only be thankful that he did not carry out his proposal to pepper *Clean Straw for Nothing* with blatant commercial symbols.

Late in the piece, in December, Collins changed the publication date from January to March, so arrangements were made for Johnston to fly to Sydney in February. By this time there had been further developments of plan. He was no longer intending to return to Hydra. He wrote to Gae: 'we shall *all* be returning to Australia next year ... I'll go out around the end of February and will stay out there, and the three kids will follow with their mother about June'.[55] So the separation was now to be only a temporary one. Clift had grown homesick too, though not to the same degree as he had, and she was also uncertain about cutting off finally from Hydra.

The letter to Gae was written to reach her before her wedding on the 21 December, and it contained some touching fatherly words:

> I suppose I should have solemn and fatherly things to say to you, but in a sense I have rather defaulted on this privilege and dignity — so will you simply accept the fact, Gae, that your father does wish you every happiness in the world ... in all the years of my absence I have thought about you very much and loved you very deeply ...[56]

He also had some praise for her mother:

> I would also like you to know, at this vital moment in your own life, how very deep my admiration is for all that your mother has done. I think you know that I have never not had respect for Else — I think perhaps she knows this too — but the solitary and very tough burden she has borne, alone and to a very great degree unaided, in getting you to the fulfilment of your womanhood should never be underestimated or forgotten.[57]

The letter included a handsomely written Christmas greeting from seven-year-old Jason.

Indeed, efforts had to be made over that Christmas to look on the bright side of coming events, with the family about to be split up in a way that had never happened before. Charmian organised a party for all their friends, and as part of the festivities everyone was to bring along something to read aloud. A relative newcome to the island then, painter William Pownall, to whom Johnston had been helpful in organising an exhibition in London, recalled the occasion:

> George got up and read some Conrad. Charmian read something from T. S. Eliot. Then an American poet called Bill — a

227

nice chap, with a deep resonant voice — asked to read a passage of prose. It was a deeply felt, circumstantial passage from an unpublished novel describing the early years of a writer's life. After he'd finished no one spoke, we were so carried away. I looked across at George and tears were streaming down his face. It was a passage from My Brother Jack.[58]

A cable from Collins arrived in January foreshadowing the kind of publicity orgy in which Johnston was about to become embroiled, though he did not yet know it:

PUBLISHING IN AUSTRALIA 5TH MARCH STOP IN PROCESS ARRANGING YOUR STAR BILLING WITH ALAN MOOREHEAD PATRICK WHITE NOLAN ADELAIDE FESTIVAL WHICH BEGINS MARCH 7TH STOP VERY DESIRABLE YOU ARRIVE SYDNEY LATE FEBRUARY.

He wrote to Higham telling him about all this, and clearing up details about royalty payments, which were in future to be paid in Australia because of the more favourable tax conditions. Other arrangements had to be tied up, such as the postponements until she got to Australia of the advance on Clift's *Honour's Mimic*, her recently completed novel going over the sponge-diving theme again. It was also decided to withdraw 'The Serpent in the Rock' completely as a hopeless prospect. These all had the feel of final instructions to Higham about them, for suddenly he was to be no longer centrally involved in their writing affairs, no longer their chief salesman, though there would still be small items of service he would perform from time to time.

Publication of *My Brother Jack* in Britain took place on the scheduled date in January, and this was partly to act as advance publicity for the Australian release two months later. Billy Collins wrote to Johnston late in January that the response to it had been wonderful. Reviews were excellent — the *Illustrated London News* went so far as to call it 'one of the greatest books written this century', and even the more temperate reviews recognised its exceptional quality, without always using the condescending qualifier 'Australian' in doing so. There was even fan mail for Johnston from British readers. In the light of all this, Collins doubled the number of copies they were shipping to Australia from 4000 to 8000.

It was all set for the great Welcome Home and Media

Extravaganza, into which Johnston was to be dropped direct from years of living in virtual retreat. He wrote to friends and family letters filled with optimism and excitement:

> ... *while in Melbourne I'll probably stay either with Mum and Jean or with Jack and Pat. It's all become quite exciting to me, although a bit scarey also, because apparently I'm booked for TV appearances and all sorts of things which sound rather alarming after 9½ years of quiet island living ... only a few weeks really. Gee!*[59]

John Hetherington wrote a full page spread in the *Age Literary Supplement*, based on a ten-page questionnaire he had sent Johnston, and announcing his return as an important cultural event. The essential theme of the article is that Johnston was returning, not in any spirit of rejection of Greece, but as part of a calculated decision to turn his attention as a writer on Australia, which rather gives the impression that the experiences abroad were undergone for the specific purpose of writing the trilogy: 'he spent 17 years thinking about the theme before starting to write it':[60] says Hetherington, under the guidance no doubt of Johnston's replies to his questionnaire. 'It is the first of a trilogy and also the first novel he has ever attempted with a completely Australian setting', he adds. Obviously, Johnston did not tell him about 'The Piping Cry'. The article, like all the other publicity being promoted by Collins, was directed towards the single end of showing that Johnston, after years of having earned his colours as an international novelist abroad, was making a considered choice to return to an Australia that had grown in sophistication, and was now a worthy place for an established novelist and his family to live in. This was not wholly wrong, of course, but it does leave a great deal of the failure and suffering out of the picture, not to mention the degree to which his personal life on Hydra had disintegrated, so much so that he had become an emotional refugee, desperately anxious for sanctuary and a warm welcome. He was terrified of appearing to be coming home a failure, with his tail between his legs. He told this to Clift and several friends over and over again.

Johnston departed from Greece on 24 February 1964. He

was fifty-one years old, alone, unsure of what lay ahead of him, anxious about what he was leaving behind. William Pownall remembers him leaving the island on the ferry: 'He was hunched up in a coat. A small group of us stood and waved. We knew we'd never see him again.'[61] Clift went with him to the airport; the children stayed in the care of friends.

In *Clean Straw for Nothing* Meredith, too, flies home after his fourteen years of absence. He feels less excitement than fear. As he looks down from his seat in the aircraft he is 'seized by a shiver of uneasiness' and a 'spasm of panic' as he glimpses the brown Australian continent below:

> *Meredith looked down upon a country quite foreign to him. You are alien here, too, he told himself. You are an alien everywhere, because alienation is something you carry inside yourself, and all you can do is fashion little enclaves and try to live inside them. You are an alien because there is no one you will ever really know, not even yourself.* (CSFN 318)

This was written after Johnston had been back in Australia some four years. Did it have more relevance for him then, one wonders, than when he was actually on the aircraft back home? Did he become *more* alienated, withdrawn and afraid after his return? This may be so, for at least on the flight back there were things to be hopeful about, and a feeling that he was someone important again, a necessary comfort after what he'd recently been through. I believe that Johnston, in contrast to Meredith, was his characteristically optimistic self on his return, uncertain, no doubt, but looking forward to the reception of *My Brother Jack*, about which he felt such satisfaction. Meredith is never given that pride in his achievements; indeed, he appears to have no achievements.

This is not the only difference between Meredith and his creator. Looking back over the events in Johnston's life since about 1958, one can summarise the particular forces that came together to produce him, for that was his period of gestation and birth — the years of shattered hopes, when Johnston's worst fears about Clift were confirmed, when his illness burdened him with the mammoth task of keeping going, when his dreams of becoming a successful writer were replaced by the grinding reality of much hard work for little reward, and with none of the security of a steady job or a sudden lucky strike of life-changing proportions. All of these things fell in on him at the very time of his life — his late forties, when he could least cope with failure, and yet here it was rearing up at him on all sides. The result was that out of sheer self-preservation he had to find a way of literally 'getting hold of himself', of taking a psychic step back in order to get himself into better perspective and hope to understand, if not change, himself. David Meredith is this 'other self', his *alter ego*, and his brooding, nostalgic, isolated, self-pitying, courageous, moralising and perceptive nature is a direct reflection of the disintegrated environment that produced him.

However, Meredith is not the whole George Johnston, not the boy and man who lived through the rich and varied events of George Johnston's life. That man was only partly a David Meredith; he was also a healthy, fun-loving boy, who was good at sport and socialising, and as a man was always gregarious and popular — never a loner — and though his sensitivity and vivid imagination made him easily afraid, he also drew loyalty and much admiration from his friends. He had faults, too, including the capacity for cruelty and deceit to which Meredith confesses, as well as some to which he does not: Johnston's unfaithfulness to Elsie and his dishonest use of other journalists' stories are two obvious examples, and there are others dotted throughout his life. Essentially, however, what separates Johnston from Meredith is a manifest exuberance that regardless of the circumstances never left Johnston's nature for long. His close friends (Sidney Nolan, Cedric Flower, Bruce Kneale, Grace Edwards) and other friends (Neil Hutchison, Storry Walton, Hazel Tulley, Geoffrey Hutton) all testify to the ebullience and energy, the appetite for fun and life, with which he swept up everyone who entered his circle, especially in the days before things went wrong on Hydra. We get no sense of this exuberance in Meredith. Nor do we get an adequate idea of Johnston's impulsiveness; his characteristic way was to leap into situations with naïve optimism, often to find himself floundering and struggling to stay in his depth. Nolan's description 'innocent' again comes to mind for that side of Johnston's nature that was not wise to the world's sophistry. Meredith, on the other hand, is more calculating: he knows the dark side of life only too well, and most of the time it usurps his capacity to celebrate life's joys. In short, Meredith is Johnston's inner voice of disillusion, especially in *My Brother Jack*, where he describes how he learned to exploit the world. The voice that Johnston himself used publicly was characteristically the voice of constructive communication, of dogged aspiration, of continual creation of illusion, making use of the past and the present to form something new or interesting to share with others, urgently pressing on with life as if fortune was about to arrive any minute in the next post.

Journalists, photographers, television crews, publishers' representatives, friends and family turned out at Sydney airport to greet him. The fuss and confusion overwhelmed him as he stood in the midst of it all, frail and haggard, but smiling. Everyone was shocked by the change in his appearance, somewhat dampening the pleasure of seeing him again. 'He looked simply awful,' recalled Mungo MacCallum.[62] 'Like something out of Belsen,' thought Sidney Nolan.[63] MacCallum's first resolve, after taking him back to his flat, was to get him some proper medical treatment.

CHAPTER XI

Home

Well, now they gave him prizes. Cash prizes. The prizes were big enough, too, but he could never quite get rid of the suspicion that they might turn out to be brummy . . . (CofC 146)

Although Johnston had sounded definite when he wrote to Elsie: 'we're selling up here and returning to Australia permanently',[1] the matter of permanency was by no means settled. In particular, Clift was not sure about coming back. Despite all the bad times she still loved Hydra, and whatever they decided to do with themselves, neither she nor the children wanted to sell the house. In fact Martin, now sixteen, and old enough to feel the full impact of what was happening to his parents, though not to have much say in decisions, always understood that the house was unquestionably to be kept as a holiday house, wherever they lived. In the last weeks before Johnston left for Australia, there were endless debates and changes of mind about their plans, but in the end nothing was firmly resolved.

The fact was that both of them knew they needed this separation. They had hardly been out of each other's sight since they were married, and in the current climate of feeling, remaining close only locked them into a cage of worsening resentment. Clift said he had become 'bitter and hating and difficult to live with'.[2] And Johnston, if we are to judge by the sentiments in his letters to Elsie, had had enough of her for the time being. Moreover, Clift did not want to go back to Australia,

233

forsaking a life she loved, merely to be a part of Johnston's media triumph. For her to move, there would have to be a stronger reason than that. So the separation was a test to see if they could live apart, and for Johnston to report on what the possibilities were for Clift in Australia.

It is not altogether surprising, in these circumstances, that Clift formed a relationship with another man. Anthony Kingsmill was an English writer who met Clift one day in February 1964, in an Athens taverna, where she had gone with Jean-Claude Maurice. 'She was wearing an Eva Bartok hat,' recalled Kingsmill, 'and she looked magnificent. Straight away I knew I had to see her again.'[3] Clift had seen Johnston off at the airport the night before, and had run into Maurice, according to Kingsmill, 'by sheer accident'. Kingsmill arranged to meet Clift in an Athens café some days later, but when he turned up she did not seem to be there. He waited ten or fifteen minutes and was about to leave when she stood up for him to see her: she'd been watching him. She told him to come to Hydra, and after about a week he did. Clift met him on the port, took him to the house, and there he lived with her for the remainder of her time on Hydra. The situation was never explained to Martin or Shane, who for a time understood Kingsmill to be a 'friend',[4] but they soon grew to understand what was happening. Martin resented it deeply, and disliked Kingsmill as a threat to his parents' relationship. Shane felt differently about it. At this time Shane and Martin were in habitual disagreement about almost everything, and on this matter she took her mother's side, because she thought it might keep them on Hydra. Martin was able to get away from the discomfort of the situation when he took up an invitation from a long-standing friend of Johnston and Clift, Gilbert Horobin, to stay with him and his family in Beirut for some months. It was a golden opportunity for Martin to see Syria and the Lebanon, to fall in love with an English girl in Beirut, and to have something else in his life than classifying animals and translating classical poetry for school. During this time Jason was largely left to run wild, although he was a healthy and happy enough boy. With the family scattered far and wide about the world for these months, there was a real threat of disintegration. When Martin eventually returned to Hydra, it was with pleasure and relief that he learned they would be going to Australia after all, and that his curiosity to see that much-mentioned place, as well as his father, was to be satisfied.

Johnston was counting on Australia being the panacea he so badly needed. He knew only a large stroke of luck could save him now – his work, his family, perhaps even his life depended on it. How important, then, and how gratifying, was the warmth with which the whole country, it seemed, welcomed him back. It was a sound move by Collins to publish *My Brother Jack* in England first, and then make use of the favourable notices in a generally high-powered PR effort, creating the impression that Johnston was coming home as a conquering hero. And that is exactly how he was treated; he was in demand everywhere, and barely had time to gather his wits. Mungo MacCallum had taken his immediate care in hand, put him up at his Edgecliff flat and put himself at his old friend's disposal. On his second night back he went to a party at the home of Jill Porter, where he had a reunion with Ruth Park and D'Arcy Niland, among a host of others who had not seen him for thirteen years.

At the Adelaide Festival he was so busy that he had time to see only the Nolan exhibition and a dress rehearsal of a Robert Helpmann ballet. Patrick White was there, but Johnston never mentions having spoken to him either then or at any other time. He would have been extremely wary of a novelist of such high standing, and in need of lots of matey overtures of the kind White would probably eschew. He did meet Hal Porter for the only time, and told him that reading *Watcher on the Cast-Iron Balcony* in 1963 had 'inspired him to write *My Brother Jack*'.[5] That was about the extent of their literary discussion: Johnston got on better with painters than with other writers.

As he watched Johnston cope with all this, MacCallum noted some marked changes in the man he had known back in the 1940s, not just physical changes, but personality ones as well. Gone was the brash journalist determined to get to the top, and in his place was a far less confident figure who 'realized that things were a lot less simple'.[6] He had an immense fear, he confessed to MacCallum, that people would say that he had only come back 'because he had not been a success abroad'. In some respects this was an improved George Johnston, thought MacCallum, who watched his performances on the media and was impressed by his 'modest, sensible and penetrating' responses to questions thrown at him. He still had all the old facility to pour it onto the page when he needed to: he borrowed MacCallum's typewriter and wrote letter after letter at the same old frantic speed, mostly to Clift, filling her in on everything that was happening to him. MacCallum also sent him to a chest specialist, who gave him drugs and strict instructions about taking them. 'He got better for a while,' said MacCallum, 'but then he forgot to keep up the medicines.'[7]

As soon as he could, Johnston went to Melbourne to see his family. They were as shocked by his appearance as his Sydney friends had been.

> *He had no socks to wear, and his shoes were awful ... he was desperately ill, he hadn't made the success he wanted ... and it didn't mean a thing to his family, they were all so happy to see him back, and we all thought we'd be able to nurse him back to health.[8]*

So said Pat Johnston. His mother, now eighty-five, was beside herself with excitement. 'I don't think Mrs Johnston slept from the night she heard he was coming until he arrived,' recalled Pat. 'She had his bed all made up in his room ... and she had this huge family party arranged for him, with all his friends there ...'[9] Johnston, just as he had in previous times, quickly grew bored with family occasions, and to everyone's disappointment he made excuses to go. 'He stayed, I suppose, two hours, and shot through,' said Pat, 'and [Mrs Johnston] didn't see him again for months.'[10]

Jack perceived anguish in this behaviour, however, and, believing he could discern the cause, he made a kindly and totally characteristic gesture:

> *I knew he had nothing because his clothing was threadbare; he was down as low as he could get. I got the shock of my life, and I got him aside and I said 'How're you fixed for*

money?'. And he started to cry, and he said, 'You're the only
one in my life who's ever thought of asking me that'. He had
nothing, but he wouldn't take anything. He would never
admit to the family that he was broke.[11]

Johnston spent part of that evening with Elsie and Gae, and
Gae's new husband, Ross, presenting them with his promised wedding gift of Mycenaean cups. It was a brief and far
from satisfactory meeting after so long, especially for Gae, for
whom her father had been scarcely a memory — more like a
heavy absence — for most of her life. He promised her that
when he was settled in Sydney she could come to stay
whenever she liked, and she did this on a couple of occasions. Johnston wrote to Elsie a week or so later congratulat-
ing himself on remembering their wedding anniversary of 19
March, and promising to see her again when next in Melbourne.

All Johnston's high expectations of *My Brother Jack* were
justified. The first 8000 copies were sold out in less than three
weeks, and Collins had to order more from England. The
financial rewards would, of course, be gratifying, but because
he'd been starved of it for so long, the critical praise that was
coming from all quarters was even better. 'What is most
important to me', he wrote to Higham, 'is that the book is
accepted critically as one of the best and most important
Australian novels yet written.'[12] At the same time he was not
averse to using the success of *My Brother Jack* as a means to
rekindle interest in previous books, and he suggested to
Higham that *The Sponge Divers* and *The Far Road* might be
published as paperbacks.

At the end of April 1964 he left MacCallum's flat and went
to stay with an acquaintance from the old days in Sydney,
Matt Carroll, and his wife, Sheila, who now owned a grazing
property called Eulaba at Coolah in northern New South
Wales. Carroll had stayed with the Johnstons on Hydra for a
time, and now was returning the favour. This was an opportunity for Johnston to relax, to do as he liked, and to get away
from the barrage of media people and others making exhausting demands on his time and energy. It also gave him just the
strong dose of classical Australian outback living that he

craved, so he could feel that it was the whole country he was returning to, and not just the Sydney push. He wrote to Elsie:

> The place is marvellous for me, high and dry and there's absolutely nothing to do except ride a bit and shoot a bit and write a lot and go to bed early and get up early ... I have a study-bedroom all my own, with heating and everything, and great kangaroo skin rugs on the floor, and they never come near me when I am working and wait on me hand and foot.[13]

In this atmosphere Johnston was able in the next couple of months to get on with some work. The correspondence flowed between him and Clift, mainly from him, urging her to come home, and assuring her that she, too, would be a celebrity and could take advantage of numerous opportunities that were being offered, especially in radio and television.[14] He wrote an article for the Melbourne *Age* that he cast in the form of an open letter to his wife and children, and in which he expressed his surprise and delight at the changes he had found since returning. Gone, he said, was the old resentment of those who had been abroad and liked it ('if you like it so much over there why the bloody hell did you come back'), and in its place was a new spirit of self-criticism and confidence.

> After the tired, cynical, disillusioned Old World one sees so much in this country to be truly thankful for. It is a nation walking onwards briskly, but not feverishly, high-stepping and with the head well up. The kids are marvellous, the women are beautiful, space is free, and there's a high sky above a wide country.[15]

Slowly Clift was coming round, but she angered him with the suggestion that she bring Anthony Kingsmill with her. By May, however, it was settled that she and the children would be making the journey in the following August. She would not be able to sell the house in time, and with cash still short, it was decided that they should apply for assisted passages under the migrant scheme, and come home on a Greek migrant boat. Johnston was trying to get some money out of Collins: he advised Higham to tell them that he would not be able to work on the second volume of the trilogy unless they gave him a substantial enough advance — say £1000 — to reject all the smaller but quicker-paying commissions he was receiving from journals and the ABC.[16] Sir William Collins responded positively and offered him the money if he would get straight on with the book and have it finished by the end of the year. Johnston agreed, and in the comfort and quiet of Eulaba he settled down to work on the second volume of the trilogy.

Johnston found it tough going. In a chatty letter to Elsie he complained that his muse 'day by day becomes a more fugitive and fleeting bitch' as he tried 'wrestling with this bloody novel . . . I am rather depressed by the thought that perhaps *My Brother Jack* was the ONE book I had to write, and I can't do another'.[17] One suspects that in his current mood of satisfaction it was proving stale and tiresome to recall his unpleasant experiences and that he was finding it difficult to motivate himself. Once again he made notes that focused his attention on the thematic issues, and set down some sketchy details of the main characters. He knew for some time that he wanted to call it *Clean Straw for Nothing*, after that sign in Hogarth's picture 'Gin Lane' that he had seen in a New York bar twenty years earlier. He had made some notes on Hydra, discussed in the previous chapter, after reading Scott Fitzgerald and Flaubert; now he wanted to come to grips with the treatment of David and Cressida Meredith's relationship, and to develop the themes of betrayal and jealousy. In 'Particular Notes on Cressida'[18] he traces the conflict between them back to her resentment at being trapped in marriage when she had had her first child, and to the role she had been forced to play in London as the dutiful executive's wife and mother of two children. This role, say the notes, was in conflict with Cressida's previous self, the 'pagan, free-living creature of the golden beaches'. But Cressida's character is further complicated by another important quality within her, which is that of possessing 'a strong sense of loyalty and honesty', especially towards Meredith. Put together, these two elements of her personality create an almost schizoid Cressida, who actually invents a third personality, that of a wife brutally determined upon her right to freedom 'almost at any cost', and who is aided and abetted by the careless, morally lax foreign community among whom they find themselves when they move

239

to Greece. This Cressida is a mixture of 'suffragist' and betrayer. Meredith, however, 'is not lax, is not gay, is not careless. He is watchful. He is suspicious. He is jealous.' Because of their irreconcilable attitudes to life in Greece, the marriage is in trouble and the foundations for tragedy are laid.

While considering the character of Cressida, he must have taken the decision, either at this stage or at some other, that Cressida would not reflect the literary or artistic side of Clift. Cressida's role, from her appearance in the closing chapters of *My Brother Jack*, through *Clean Straw for Nothing* and up to her death in *A Cartload of Clay*, is almost exclusively sexual, either as a wife and mother or as a betrayer. Many Clift devotees have found this to be a degradation of an immensely talented woman writer, and believed it could only have been motivated by Johnston's malice or envy. This view rests heavily on the assumption that Cressida is intended to be a literal portrait of Charmian Clift, an assumption that has little to recommend it. The overwhelmingly central concern in the trilogy is David Meredith's passionate egocentricity, the very stuff of autobiographical writing. All characters, including Cressida, exist only in relation to him and not as characters in their own right whose lives we follow with interest independently of his view of them. Even Meredith is only a partial view of Johnston, so it is not surprising that Cressida is only a partial view of Clift, and her role is essentially that of drawing Meredith's emotional and moral ebb and flow. The decision to give her this role was artistic, not personal, and the one public comment that Johnston made on the matter is perfectly consistent with this: 'Cressida was fictional, and for this reason [I] would not make her a writer.'[19]

There are no grounds for believing that personal animosity influenced his decision. Johnston and Clift were both remarkably free from professional jealousy, and indeed all the evidence points to just the opposite in their support of each other's professional reputations. Moreover, the idea that Johnston ought to have represented Clift's writing life is itself presumptuous — she was capable of doing that perfectly well, and indeed she did. My own guess is that Clift was pleased that George steered clear of that side of herself, and relieved

Johnston making a friend at Circular Quay, Sydney, 1964

The house at Kirkoswald Avenue, Mosman

Shane Johnston, late 1960s

Clift with Sidney Nolan in Central Australia, 1967

Clift, c. 1968 (Photo: Jill Crossley)

The house at Raglan Street, Mosman – a recent photograph (Photo: Richard Toms)

Johnston. Ray
Crooke's portrait
won the Archibald
Prize in 1969
*(Photo: Art Gallery of
New South Wales)*

Clift, *c.* 1968, with Russell Drysdale's
portrait of Johnston in the background
(Photo: Lance Nelson)

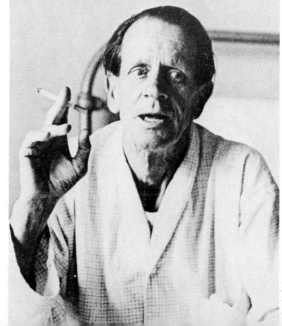

Johnston in hospital, 1969 *(Photo:
courtesy of Australian Tourism Industry
Association)*

Clift, 1969

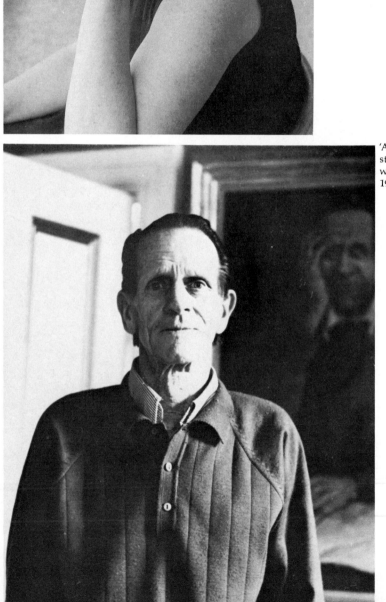
'A tattered coat upon a stick...' Johnston a few weeks before his death, 1970

that he made the rather two-dimensional figure of Cressida that much unlike herself.

On the matter of their sexual relations, however, there is every reason to believe that Meredith and Cressida are a close likeness to Johnston and Clift, seen, of course, very much from his point of view. The notes typed out on Hydra show a sense of confusion between 'objective' ideas for the creation of the characters of Meredith and Cressida, and a therapeutic attempt to put himself and Clift into perspective. For instance, when the notes make reference to Meredith's sex life, none of which went into the published novel, the tone of intimacy and self-disgust have a distinct suggestion of Johnston's own confessional:

> *all his sexual experiences have in some way been casual, inexperienced, worthless, distorted, cheap, contrived, makeshift. Always falling short of what he feels himself to deserve. . . . In their lovemaking there is the role to be played, the willingness to submit, the acting out of sexual satisfaction . . .*[20]

He is describing the early days here: sexual satisfaction is not an issue in the later life of either Meredith or Johnston, although of course this is no disqualification for sexual jealousy.

Other strategies in these notes suggest a more single-minded concern with art, such as the quotation from Henry James:

> *There is no more nutritive or suggestive truth than that of the perfect dependence of the moral sense of a work of art on the amount of felt life concerned in producing it.*[21]

This expresses precisely Johnston's sense of his task in writing the trilogy. However, his most persistent and difficult problem was not in making what he wrote dependent on 'felt life', but in transforming that felt life into detached, self-contained art – fiction rather than autobiography. It is evident throughout the preparatory notes for *Clean Straw for Nothing* that he was struggling valiantly to do this – searching for models among the works of others, spelling out to himself the issues that must be faced, but, so far, failing to get the novel into an artistically satisfying state, because, try as he did, he was still unable to detach himself from his obsessive private anguish about the reality on which his writing was based. Perhaps he was hoping that the act of writing would resolve the anguish.

In June 1964 Johnston returned to Sydney, where he stayed on his own in Sheila Carroll's flat in Woollahra. Whether he had fallen out with Matt Carroll is not certain, but he did find the grazier's company depressing after a time, and needed to get away from him.[22] Carroll was later hurt to find himself represented in the early pages of *Clean Straw for Nothing* as 'Peter the grazier who had once stayed on the Greek island with us and who dreamt melancholically of selling everything up and going back to Europe to live' (*CSFN* 10). It continues on in a not very flattering vein, and is hardly just payment for Carroll's hospitality.

From the Woollahra flat Johnston made several journeys, including an ambitious fortnight to the Kimberleys, Cape York and Darwin for a film on Australia he was writing for Geoff and Dahl Collings, who were making a series for Qantas. Then he had to make a less enjoyable return to Melbourne, where his mother had become seriously ill after a stroke. She never recovered from this, and within a few weeks she passed away. Throughout his childhood they had been close, and though as an adult his thoughtlessness must often have caused her pain, he never said or wrote a word of disrespect for her.

By July the details of the return of Charmian and the children were settled. Their application for assisted passages was successful: they would sail as migrants on the Chandris lines vessel *Ellinis*, which would dock in Sydney on 28 August. Johnston immediately began to cast around for a suitable house to rent. He was greatly excited at the prospect of reunion, and felt pleased and more than a little proud that, after his months of relaxation, good food, travel and sunshine his weight had now gone up to 63 kilograms (10 stone), and he would be able to greet them looking something like his old self again.

Leaving Hydra was a wrench for Clift. Apart from the packing and filling-in of forms and medical examinations, there

was also the heartrending business of choosing which possessions could be taken and which were to be abandoned.
She and Johnston had collected many loved and valuable
items that they were prevented by Greek law from taking out
of the country, so Clift had tearfully to give away antique
pistols, Byzantine ikons, amphoras and other treasured
pieces, and all this with Kingsmill amorously pressing her to
stay, and her feeling anyway that she might be doing the
wrong thing for herself in leaving. Two things probably kept
her to her decision: it would be better in the long run for the
children, and her loyalty to Johnston. Kingsmill, when it came
down to it, was unimportant. She had neither the time nor
the will to undertake selling the house, which she eventually
left in Kingsmill's charge.[23] In the chaos of leaving, she managed to set fire to the kitchen one evening, though the damage was small. The children were still divided over what they
wanted: Martin was now desperate to leave, and Shane — and
probably Jason — wanted to stay. Even the journey itself, as
Clift was later to describe it, was riddled with doubts and
fears:

> ... the ship on which we travelled was a migrant ship, and
> filled with other families also travelling hopefully or
> apprehensively from one world to another. It was a queer
> feeling to be part of a nomadic horde ...
> Anyway, there we all were, our worldly possessions re-
> duced to what was portable, but still tied emotionally to what
> we had abandoned. By the time a migrant — and I am
> including myself and my Australian-born children in the term
> — actually boards the ship that is to carry him to his brave
> new world the audacious bite of decision has long since been
> blunted, if not altogether gummed up, on the toffee-apple of
> bureaucracy. The freshness of adventure has worn off and
> uncertainty, alas, is practically all that remains.
> There were times when it was necessary to support each
> other in sadly faltering convictions. In a special sense it
> seemed actually miraculous to arrive. 'I can't believe we're
> here', was a literal statement. Australia did in fact exist, and
> we were one family under one roof again.[24]

The *Ellinis* arrived as scheduled on 28 August 1964. Once
again there was that shock among the friends and family at
what they saw: the children were a bit scruffy and barefoot,
which was not surprising, though some made too much of it.

Clift was a different matter. Friends such as Toni Burgess and Cedric Flower could hardly believe the change in her. It was not simply that she was older, but that she seemed to be a different woman. The beautiful, confident, stylish Clift who had gone abroad with such hubris thirteen years earlier had vanished and been supplanted by a flaccid, overweight, terrified matron with scraggy hair and no stockings. The huge, white smiling teeth were now brown and rotting. Moreover, as was soon to become apparent to all, she had returned with a drinking problem. Cedric Flower recalls her fingering her hair over her face in a defensive, nervous measure, and looking as though she wanted to become invisible.

Johnston had managed to rent a house in Kirkoswald Avenue, Mosman, in what Mungo MacCallum thought was

> the perfect spot for somebody who'd been living on Hydra
> . . . a wonderful rambling old bungalow in a very jungly
> Australian garden which looked straight out between the
> heads, and you had this view of sea, rocks, trees — ideal for
> someone who had lived on a Greek island.[25]

At the house, Johnston had arranged a welcome home party, with all the old friends — Arthur and Monica Polkinghorne, many other journalists, the Flowers, the Nolans, the Drysdales, the MacCallums, Alan Moorehead, Toni Burgess. When Johnston and Clift entered the room, MacCallum recalls, it was obvious that the whole occasion was a disaster — she was so afraid and nervous that she could not, or would not, smile at all, and she 'just stood there quivering',[26] looking as if she'd been bound up in some dreadful corset. For some time the overwhelming feeling was one of embarrassment, though eventually people rallied round and tried to make the best of the situation. Just to ensure the worst memories of the evening, however, somebody broke one of their priceless big amphoras — shattered it to pieces on the floor. With typical doggedness Johnston spent months of painstaking work gluing it all together again.

The Johnstons were back, ragged and bruised, like refugees from some disaster, but together and unbeaten. Friends helped enormously, especially Russell and Maisie Drysdale. In fact, this was to be the beginning of a friendship between

Johnston and 'Tass' Drysdale, which was to be extremely important to them both. They had first met in Sydney in the late 1940s, though their acquaintance was then slight. This time they took to each other instantly. Around this time Drysdale built a splendid house called Bouddie Farm in the hills at Kilcare Heights north of Sydney, and he loved nothing better than to pick up Johnston in his car — George's driving days were over — and have him stay for a few days of long, beer-lubricated debates far into the early hours of the morning. They found they had a host of common interests, from ancient civilisations to Western movies. Maisie Drysdale recalls that George might ring up and say 'O.K. Corral tonight on TV — be there buddy'[27] or some such nonsense, part of a cheery mateship they had going between them, which was undoubtedly a great boost to Johnston's spirits in times of need. They saw each other regularly, and did some outback travelling together.

There was a repeat for Clift of all the media 'hype' that Johnston had been through, but one thing that soon became happily obvious was that there was going to be plenty of work for both of them. Clift's novel *Honour's Mimic* had come out in London and Australia in July, with excellent reviews and promising sales. By September, approaches had come from two separate sources, American and European, to make it into a film, which Clift was hoping might be directed by either Jules Dassin or Michael Cacoyannis. All of this helped her local reputation, and John Douglas Pringle, editor of the *Sydney Morning Herald*, asked her to write a weekly column for the paper's women's pages. Pringle made it clear to her that she had a free hand to write what she liked, but that he had approached her because he specifically wanted a writer, as a distinct from a journalist, who could maintain a good literary tone while at the same time finding something interesting to say each week.[28] He was never to regret his choice of Clift, who over the next several years turned the column into a great personal success.

Clift soon got the chance to reveal another side of her writing ability. Their old friend Neil Hutchison was now head of Television and Radio Drama at the ABC, and was keen to make a television serial of *My Brother Jack*. The job of producing it was given to Storry Walton, whose first thought for scriptwriter was Johnston himself. Johnston told Walton that he could not muster the interest required to go through it all again, struggling as he was with the sequel. So Clift agreed to take responsibility for the script adaptation, and she did so with relish, displaying, recalls Walton 'a great natural flair for screenwriting because of her superb ability to visualize'.[29] These two tasks — the column and the TV script — were to keep her frantically busy in these first months after her return, and Johnston's renewed efforts on *Clean Straw for Nothing* were to occupy his time and energy. With the children installed in schools, the family now had cohesion and purpose, making, as Johnston wrote to Grace Edwards, in February 1965, 'an awful lot of money . . . Already Greece seems so far away and in a sense unreal, as if it all happened in some dream that goes on fading and fading.'

To some extent too much was happening too quickly, 'some good and some nightmarish', wrote Johnston to Elsie, in a letter foreshadowing a visit to Melbourne in April 1965. Johnston was to give a talk to the Victorian Fabian Society there, and Clift was to go into a huddle with her Melbourne *Herald* editors, one of the several interstate newspapers to which her column was being syndicated. The 'nightmarish' things included another bout of bacterial pneumonia, which he had contracted while travelling about in northern New South Wales around Christmas. He had to be rushed to Mudgee Hospital, where he was kept for a couple of weeks.[30] He had feared it might be the signal for a return of the tuberculosis, but that turned out not to be the case. The health of both was fragile, and not helped by the heavy pressures they had been under since their return. According to Toni Burgess, Clift had 'almost permanent bronchitis', and she, too, came down with pneumonia around Easter. Neither of them made any serious attempt to control their drinking and smoking: Johnston was up to about eighty cigarettes a day.

Alcohol was still the catalyst for bitter rows between them, when back to the surface came all the old accusations and venom. Being word-spinners, both had wounding tongues, nor did they spare their friends the spectacle of some of their worst performances. 'Virginia Woolf scenes', Cedric Flower called them, and he and Pat began to lose the desire to be with them, because it was so painful. More than once Johnston was heard to proclaim 'the trouble is I can't fuck her any more',[31] as if the only thing left was their mutual humiliation before those who most cared for them. There were times when it all had the reek of self-destruction about it — in both of them — and it seemed only a matter of time before a tragedy would occur.

At least the coffers were for the moment nicely swelled. On their Melbourne visit they stayed in a VIP penthouse provided by Sir John Williams of the *Herald*. George took Jack, Pat, Jean and Bert to Florentino's for a meal, which, according to Jack, cost him over £100. Not that Jack was impressed: 'They gave me spatchcock, no bigger than sparrow, a spoonful of spinach and half a potato,' he said, and as far as he was concerned it was a 'clip joint'.[32]

The success of *My Brother Jack* continued when it won the Miles Franklin Award in April of that year. Johnston was still working hard when he got the satirical story 'Vale, Pollini!' written and sent off abroad. He felt that its elaborate joke against the Hydra 'existentialists' would be lost on Australian readers, so he asked Higham to find a home for it in the UK. This was promptly done, and the story appeared later that year in a collection called *Voices II*, published by Michael Joseph. Also in the first half of 1965 he began work on a 'high prestige documentary book' with American photographer Robert Goodman, which was to be called *The Australians*. It was just the right time to engage Johnston in such a project, because he was still flushed with boundless optimism about the country, and this enabled him to attack the task with energy and conviction. Goodman's photographs were intended to provide the main interest, but it could be argued that Johnston's 50,000-word text outshines Goodman's photographs. Contrary to what one might expect, the text does not consist of an unrelieved string of eulogies: for the coffee-table book that it undeniably is, it is well researched and literary in its approach, including references to such commentators on

Australia as D. H. Lawrence and Mark Twain, and its lively style gets much of its feeling of authenticity from the personal anecdotes and memories that are sprinkled throughout. One such conveys the atmosphere of the Victorian gold districts by recalling that farm at Dereel near Ballarat where he holidayed as a boy (he calls it here 'Uncle Wattie's; his full name was Wattie Whittle):

> When I was a schoolboy my Uncle Wattie used to tell us stories of the great drought, eight years long, that broke in 1903. It killed, he said, half of the animals grazed and pastured in Australia. Wattie was only a courtesy uncle, a 'Geordie' from Tyneside with grey flannel bands sewn round rheumaticky fingers which were always tamping stubby broken pipes. He had a scrubby, quartzy little selection farm in old diggings near Corindhap in Victoria.
>
> We never really believed these stark dramatic tales because he always told them in good or idle times, when we were fishing for eels or perch in the Battery Dam below Chinner's woolshed, when the wheat was high and green and the clay paddock-dam yellow-full and lively with yabbies and his own meagre wool-clip was selling at 20 pence a pound at the Ballarat or Geelong wool sales. This was all years ago, and these were an old man's cautionary tales told in fat seasons as touchstones against the lean.
>
> We listened wide-eyed, not realizing that it had all been true until years afterwards, when Old Wattie's selection was no more than a fire-charred memento overgrown with bracken. He was dead, his sons gone from the place, and the rabbits back in their sandy squats.³³

For a writer brought up in the Melbourne suburbs, and not usually thought of as a depicter of rural Australia, this is engaging and sinewy and full of bush flavour. Terms such as 'scrubby, quartzy little selection', and 'yellow-full and lively with yabbies' and 'fat seasons as touchstones against the lean' not only sound well, but they make us see the life and people vividly and accurately. It also has the feel of having been written with great enjoyment.

Once again, however, the energy expended on writing sapped his health, and by July 1965 it was evident that the tuberculosis was back again, despite his gain in weight. He was admitted to Royal North Shore hospital on 10 July, suffering from 'moderately advanced' tuberculosis of the lung, breathlessness and anorexia.[34] Suddenly the family was in confusion again. With Clift busy on the television serial of *My Brother Jack*, which required her presence at the studio for long periods of the day, Johnston had been able to work at home and keep an eye on the children, which mainly meant nine-year-old Jason these days (Martin was studying for matriculation, and Shane had left school and was working in a film studio). With Johnston in hospital, Clift would have to manage somehow on her own. Friends and family rallied round, sent cards and letters of support and encouragement. Jack had been cavilling for some months about signing an agreement not to sue over any aspect of the ABC serial, much to Johnston's exasperation. Now Jack and Pat signed, and family attention was focused on George, who celebrated his fifty-third birthday in the thoracic ward. Mainly, Jack and Pat were anxious to help in some practical way. Clift wrote to them thanking them for their concern, and attempting at the same time to reassure them about the television serial:

> *I think the Jack and Sheila that the viewers will come to know are the nicest people in the world . . . it's strange and unprecedented on this that we've had people bawling like babies in rehearsal, and even the producer, Storry (whom you met) was in tears as the last episode was put on tape.*[35]

It turned out that there *was* something practical the family could do. Jack's daughter, Joy Russo, a mother of six, offered to have Jason to stay with them in their home near Euroa in Victoria. Johnston and Clift were deeply touched by this gesture, and each wrote an emotional letter of thanks, George adding details about Jason that he thought might be helpful:

> *. . . he's a very charming and loveable character . . . it would be a wonderful break for him to be with other kids and an organized family life during what is bound to be a pretty confused and difficult time over here. Particularly such a cheerful and happy and loving family as yours is. This would give Charm a bit more mobility and independence to cope with the domestic and economic problems while we get over this little crisis. As we shall. On the religious side, Jason was actually baptized Greek Orthodox (which is more related to Catholic than anything else) but hasn't been to church or sunday school since coming here: Probably he could go along with your kids.*[36]

He might have warned them about Jason's passion for tampering with washing machines, which Maisie Drysdale, who spoke from experience, claims he still had. Clift wrote: 'Joy and Felix have been so kind about Jason that I am close to tears when I think of it.'[37] Their gratitude may have been intensified by an awareness of their neglect of both sides of the family, not only in the years they had been away, but also since their return. Jack and Pat felt that his Melbourne journeys were always brief and concerned with more glamorous activities than visiting the family, and all had been hurt by the dearth of letters from Greece during all those years. Joy Russo formed the opinion that 'he thought himself too good for them', and that *My Brother Jack* had been written partly to expiate his guilt about this. Yet, however prodigal George appeared, his family proudly insists that it never rejected him, and the generosity of the Russos is proof of the justness of their claim.

Clift had occasion to reflect on her own family feelings around this time, too, when her brother Barré, aged only forty-two, died suddenly of a heart attack. Through her column Clift shared her sadness, and a degree of self-reproach, with her readers:

> He was my first and best friend. Being, as we were, a year apart in age, an inch apart in height, and a class apart in school, we were almost like twins.
>
> We were frowzled, freckled children, skinny and hard, with our front teeth coming down like half-lowered blinds. We had the same long bony arms and legs bruised and scarred and scored and scratched from the violence of our games . . .
>
> . . . He was wiser than I. Under the defensive savagery of our childhood games he was a peculiarly gentle boy, more-than-average good at everything if he had a chance to work on it laboriously and in secret, but excelling in nothing except his instinct for what was kind and generous and brave and true. He was sick with apprehension before any competition, and when he came first it was by virtue of will and endurance and to please us, who valued such things . . .
>
> . . . I lost him somewhere there, obsessed as I was by my own feverish impatience to get on to the first prizes that he didn't seem to care about.[38]

The diagnosis of Johnston's condition while in hospital was

not good. He was therefore discharged on 22 July, in order to make whatever domestic arrangements were necessary in what was going to be a prolonged absence from home, and on the understanding that he would be re-admitted in four weeks' time. A bad attack of pleurisy on 16 August, however, saw his re-admission a week early.

In the meantime, Clift had the consolation of seeing her adaptation of *My Brother Jack* achieve great success, and become compulsive viewing over the weeks of August and September. It was the first time viewers had seen the lives of working-class Australians portrayed sympathetically and realistically on the small screen. Storry Walton believes that the programme contributed significantly to the wave of nationalistic feeling that grew steadily in the mid-1960s, and the enthusiasm of Johnston's and Clift's personal rediscovery of Australia came through in the series in a most forceful and infectious way. Not everyone liked it: objections were raised in Parliament that it was 'dirty, and the work of a leftist writer who was receiving the favours of a leftist cell in the ABC'.[39] The crew who worked on it were full of praise for the belief in the Australian character of the programme that Johnston and Clift showed, and this, according to Storry Walton, fired their confidence and dedication to the task. The fact that it ran over six times its estimated budget seemed unimportant compared with the effect the project had on the morale of the ABC, staff and administration alike. Again according to Storry Walton, it inspired a new commitment by the ABC to Australian television subjects. He has the highest praise for Clift's adaptation, too, and insists that in this, her first effort at writing for the medium, she showed that she was 'potentially one of Australia's best screen writers'.[40] Her own bubbling satisfaction is obvious in a newsy letter she wrote to Higham during September 1965:

> *Sorry about the long silence. This has been all so invigorating in a mad sort of way. I think I like it. At least it is a country where you can still make things happen instead of waiting for them to happen. I have been making my own sneaky little revolutions, first, by writing essays for the weekly presses to be read by people who don't know an essay from a form guide, but absolutely love it, and second by barging into*

> *television with a ten-part serial of* My Brother Jack *that is
> getting rave notices from astonished critics who didn't seem
> to know that we could make good television in Australia. All
> this has been tremendous fun and tremendous hard work and
> all in the first year back, so at the moment I am taking stock
> and considering what to do next. Here I am high-priced help
> and greatly valued and I suppose I could go on writing
> television or start pushing a film, or turn to straight theatre
> (which I'd love to do, actually). On the other hand I have a
> half-finished novel which I'd like to get done — excepting
> that there is so little from novel-writing in the way of daily
> bread, let alone jam or gravy, that I don't know whether I can
> afford to.*[41]

Clift's reservations about novel-writing came as a result of
Honour's Mimic, which had started so well in England, but
had disappointed her hopes. Hutchinson 'were going to
abandon [it] to a cheap edition to get rid of them',[42] a matter
for which she largely blamed the publisher's failure to cap-
italise on her growing Australian reputation — as if that
would have counted overseas. Furthermore, the film negotiations for *Honour's Mimic* had fallen through. But none of this
mattered a great deal now that more lucrative work was on
offer. She closed her letter to Higham with news of Johnston's
condition — 'they say they can cure him really this time' —
and of the children, who had

> *adjusted rather well (excepting perhaps for my daughter who
> thinks Australian men crude beyond belief and swears she's
> going back to Europe as soon as she can raise the fare). But
> the eldest is on his way to Sydney University with (on
> present marks) a Commonwealth Scholarship to see him
> through, and the youngest is as happy and busy as a small
> boy should be, and nobody is really pining.*[43]

Not even Johnston, she could have added, for he found
enough energy 'dibbling at it an hour or two each morning'
to get the text of *The Australians* completed and off to Rigby,
the publisher. Foolishly, he had accepted Robert Goodman's
offer of a flat fee instead of royalties for the job, and was to
feel bitter towards Goodman when the lavish production and
promotion of the book brought its sales to around 35,000 in
Australia alone, with overseas promotion going ahead, meaning that he missed out on a great deal of money.

Johnston also tried to get on with *Clean Straw for Nothing* in hospital, but its problems were infernal, and his strength was not up to it. By November the promised date of delivery had passed, and all he had to show for two years of work on it were 120 pages of first draft. Ignorant of his hospitalisation, the Collins administrative staff in England took the astonishing step of debiting the £1000 advance on *Clean Straw for Nothing* against the earnings of *My Brother Jack*. Johnston was angry. He wrote to Higham pleading with him to do something about Collins's 'disturbing and improper' action, insisting that it was partly his efforts to get the novel written in time that had landed him in hospital, and pointing out how his efforts to promote *My Brother Jack*, from which Collins were benefiting handsomely, were also activities that had distracted him from working on the sequel:

> ... it was not coming well, partly because I was physically and mentally exhausted by the tremendous running about on the home-coming production of My Brother Jack, partly because the unsettlement was not conducive to thoughtful creative writing, and mostly because, quite unknown to me at the time, I had developed active TB and a new and large cavity in my previously sound lung.
> ... when I came into hospital I tried to tackle the novel again, but this proved hopeless, in an eight-bed ward with a typewriter balanced on the edge of the bed, and under constant heavy drugs and sedation. In these circumstances I could not have tackled even a 'Shane Martin', let alone a deep and serious novel which has to be at least better than My Brother Jack ... I think I have, while in here, worked the novel out in my mind now, and will go at it full spate as soon as I am discharged ... But I cannot write Clean Straw for Nothing unless I can give it my best. It MUST be the best thing I have ever done.[44]

There is no better example than this of his changed attitude to his writing. Not a word about best-sellers, none of the rush and talk about films being made of it as in the days before *My Brother Jack*. Now it is all 'thoughtful creative writing' and anguish about the quality of what he was doing. Indeed he was probably getting over-anxious, to the point where it was having a paralysing effect, because the standard he had achieved in *My Brother Jack* was before him as something he

dare not lower for fear of damaging his newly won reputation. This is another reason why *Clean Straw for Nothing*
was so slow in coming, though he does not mention it here.
When he re-read what he had so far written, he decided that
after his discharge from hospital he would scrap the lot and
begin all over again.

A happy outcome to his dispute with Collins was en-
gineered, once again, by Sir William Collins. Always Johnston's champion, he stepped in and prevented the offsetting
of the advance against other royalties, and insisted that Johnston be allowed, under the circumstances, the freedom to let
his book come in its own time.

In September 1965 Clift and the children moved out of the
house at Kirkoswald Avenue into a modern three-bedroomed
flat in Neutral Bay. This was cheaper to rent, easier to manage
and more conveniently placed than the ramshackle old Mosman house. Clift was now very much in the position of
breadwinner, and played her role conscientiously. She saw
Toni Burgess more often these days, and during Johnston's
stay in hospital Burgess managed to 'wean her off whisky'.[45]
If Clift paused to reflect, as she did to some extent in the letter
to Higham on 10 September, she had reason to be satisfied
with their first two years back in Australia. There was more
work and money than ever before — and fame, which they
had always wanted, though they knew that they would now
have to be content with only the local share of that. The
family was back together, and the children making the difficult cultural adjustments with reasonable ease.

It was not all rosy, however. Despite the truce while Johnston was in hospital, he and Clift were not fundamentally
happy together, still being plagued by the recent traumatic
past, still drinking too much, still falling into malicious rows,
still waging a war of destruction on their own and each
other's spiritual and physical health. The truce perhaps promised to become a lasting peace when it was found, during
December, that Johnston's condition had deteriorated so far
that surgery was necessary. Depressed and apprehensive,
they saw Christmas through, and in the second week of
January Johnston had the upper lobe of his right lung re-

sected, and a tracheostomy to clear the blocked airways. When Storry Walton visited him afterwards, he saw a 'fragile and almost transparent figure', cheerful and laconic as ever, 'surrounded by a mass of masonry that dwarfed him'.[46] It was going to be some considerable time before he would be strong enough to get back to serious work.

CHAPTER XII

Release

> There was a story Meredith liked of a voyager who, decid-
> ing to quit the sea, shouldered an oar and set off inland from
> the coast, walking and walking until he encountered a man
> who asked him, 'What is that thing you're carrying?'. He
> knew that was where he had to throw away his oar and stop.
> (CofC 65-6)

His 'shark bite', as Johnston called it, was not an unqualified
success. It left him weak and depressed for a year afterwards,
short of strength and short of breath, and still underweight.
He was discharged on 21 April 1966, after a stretch of eight
months in the thoracic ward, with restricted movement in his
fingers and an inability to climb stairs.

Strange, therefore, that soon after Johnston was discharged,
they bought an Edwardian villa that was two-storeyed, situated in Raglan Street, Mosman, and which cost around
$12,000. The three upstairs rooms were to be occupied by the
children. Johnston was to use the front lounge room as his
bedroom and study, and this adjoined a sitting-room. Clift
had a small bedroom-study towards the rear of the house. It
was nothing like as spacious or beautiful as their Hydra
house, but it was adequate and convenient.

Johnston continued to see a great deal of Tassie Drysdale,
mostly up at Bouddie Farm. There was more than just jokey
talk between them — Drysdale had had his personal
tragedies, too, after the deaths of his son and first wife — and
the experience of suffering was part of their bond. Bouddie

had a constant stream of colourful visitors — artists, writers, politicians — and one time when Jack and Pat were visiting him in Sydney, Johnston decided to take them along to Bouddie to meet the Drysdales. It proved not to be a good idea. Under the influence of alcohol, Johnston behaved obnoxiously to his brother, discussing him with Thomas Keneally and others as an example of Australian working-class culture, listing his virtues and his 'ocker' weaknesses as if Jack was not even in the room. '. . . they drove me mad, analysing people,' recalled Jack. 'You'd think they were the only brains, the only decent people, the only good people themselves, you know . . . I felt dirty amongst 'em. I was glad to get away . . .'[1] Jack was insistent that Drysdale himself was not a party to the discussion, and seemed to him 'a decent sort of bloke'. But it cut him that George led others in the assault.

Johnston's strength returned sufficiently for him to take on a commission from ABC Television to write the script for a profile of Drysdale, which he began during the last months of 1966. It was filmed at Bouddie early in 1967, woven around Drysdale painting a portrait of Johnston, and in some respects it conveys as much about Johnston as about the painter. While Drysdale paints, Johnston's voice-over speaks the narrative in his husky, light tenor, or talks with Drysdale or Hal Missingham, who is also in the film. Johnston moves about on camera, angular, emaciated, graceful, as if his body is weightless. At one point he discusses the sequel to *My Brother Jack*, saying that the 120 pages are all wrong and have to be done again.

That 120 pages of draft did in fact bring Johnston significantly closer to the finished version of *Clean Straw for Nothing*. The forty-one pages that survive show that he was at this stage trying to pick up from where *My Brother Jack* left off, and create in chronological order the events of Meredith leaving Helen and taking up with Cressida Morley in a serious way. It gives an account of their meeting very like the one Clift was to write in her unfinished novel 'Greener Grows the Grass', discussed in Chapter IV.

This draft of *Clean Straw for Nothing* has a more detailed account of the first meeting between Meredith, Cressida

George Johnston — A Biography

and Archie Calverton than in the published version. Calverton, prior to becoming a dedicated actor, is working in tandem with a character called Beazley as gag-writers for a radio comedian, and they generously give up their room at Riordan's Hotel, next to the 'old tin shed' by the Post Office in Melbourne, so that the young lovers may spend their first night together. Since in other parts of the novel Calverton appears to be loosely based on Peter Finch, it has been suggested that Johnston and Clift met Finch in this way. It is remotely possible: Finch did travel about a good deal in the mid-1940s, and did mix with comedy writers such as Fred Parsons and Lenny Lower, who wrote radio shows. It is more likely, however, that Johnston and Finch met in Sydney in 1946 or 1947, perhaps in the Journalists' Club, where Finch often went.

Once again, in this draft of *Clean of Straw for Nothing*, he returned to the memory of those hundreds of thousands of Chinese refugees returning to their Eastern provincial towns at the end of the war, some of them after nine years of exile. As with the memory of the refugees from Kweilin earlier in the war, the staggering sight exerted a peculiar power over Johnston. Now, in his present state of illness, and feeling himself in his worst moments to be an 'exile' from humankind, he began to look for an affinity, to connect himself to suffering that occurred on a massive scale, and to seek in that journey a reflection, and perhaps a meaning, for his own:

> He had convinced himself that everything fitted into a persisting continuity in which nothing had seemed quite real since China — since he had flown out of Chungking from the grassy, treacherous strip beside the Chialing, climbing up and over worn rocks and laboriously terraced paddies to look down at the fringe of the plains beyond the confluence of two ravined rivers, and to see below them an ant-horde of uncountable people disgorging from a central mat of human blackness ... a million exiles setting out after nearly nine years of war to walk back to homes in distant provinces across a devastated land bigger again than his own Australia ... nine years ... He had felt a great pity for them and for their journey, then eased the heaviness in his soul by remembering that the Chinese, like their earth, had infinite capacity for renewal. (Thinking back on this in later years, he

*realized that nine years after that time he had far from
finished his own journey; indeed, had traversed only half the
distance to disaster, with the worst for him still to come.)*[2]

Several ideas here were to be developed into important
motifs in the final version — the linking of suffering on an
historical scale with his own private experience of it; the idea
of the *journey* as one answer to the search for a pattern in life.
The expression 'We are still out on the long journey from
Szechwan' recurs throughout *Clean Straw for Nothing* like a
refrain that acts as a touchstone for Meredith in his fight
against despair; finally, the period of nine years links the
period of exile for the Chinese with Meredith's own period of
expatriation on Hydra. This is the kind of coincidence that
Johnston was continually digging up. It was clear that whatever else it might be, *Clean Straw for Nothing* was going to be
a highly self-conscious novel, with Meredith's character and
problems right at the centre of things, and no longer sharing
the limelight with a contrasting figure such as Jack was in the
first volume. For the moment he was not satisfied with what
he had written, and was allowing himself to become distracted by less taxing projects, such as the Drysdale film.

The rows between Johnston and Clift were if anything
getting worse as he slowly got his strength back, and felt less
concerned about how much he drank. The public humili-
ations went on. At Toni Burgess's house Johnston said of
Clift: 'Look at her standing there like a fucking great praying
mantis',[3] implying, says Burgess, that she had devoured her
mate. Clift would simply weep quietly after such attacks.
'George had persuaded her that *she* was responsible for his
tuberculosis,' says Burgess, who winced at the way he could
torment her over the loss of her looks. 'She was never a match
for him in the Virginia Woolf stakes.'[4]

Burgess became Clift's closest friend in these years. Appalled by what had happened to Clift since the days in the
1940s when they were young mothers together, Burgess remained loyal, affectionate and admiring. But she disapproved
of Clift's neglect of her children, especially Shane and Jason:
'... she returned from Greece addled', Burgess insists.

... one moment full of wit and joy, another moment in

despair. I remember getting up at six a.m. one morning and going to the market with her. It was a wonderful morning. We had breakfast in a 'truckie' café. At one point we saw a Greek or Italian woman walking along in front of us and Charmian said [imitating her rich, educated contralto] 'Isn't it marvellous: they just let all their pubic hair grow. Everybody here shaves it off and disinfects themselves. You know what we should do, darling? We should let all our underarm hair grow very long, like seaweed, stand in the wind and let it blow'. She was a peculiar mixture of the fanciful and the real.[5]

In a different sense it was also true that there were two Charmian Clifts developing — the one of public success who wrote novels, television plays and a newspaper column, and with a public image of great ease and grace and a degree of wisdom that she passed on to grateful readers. And there was the unhappy, alcoholic wife, loathing her coarsened body, in a state of terror every week at the prospect of writing the column, forcing herself out of bed at 4 a.m. to get it written before the distractions of the day overwhelmed her. The public and distant relatives saw only the first Charmian Clift: close friends and family watched, helpless and saddened, the decline of the second.

For Christmas 1966 Jason returned from his long stay with the Russos in Victoria. Charmian wrote them a warm letter of thanks, saying, 'He will always have two families now and be richer to that extent.'[6] The Russos were also coming to stay with them over the summer, and Charmian was hoping to have renovations to the house finished before they arrived, and that George would be able to get away at times from his involvement with the Drysdale film, which was occupying his time in these early months of 1967.

In February, Johnston wrote to Higham after a gap of about a year in their correspondence, and explained why he had been out of touch and doing so little serious writing. The operation, he pointed out, had gone 'rather worse than we had expected', and 'difficulties of accommodation', until they bought the house in Raglan Street, had made him indolent and depressed. He had not contacted Higham because, he said, 'I couldn't bring myself to write when I had nothing to

say that wasn't dispiriting.'[7] Clift also had found it impossible to get any writing done apart from her column. Indeed
this period after Johnston's operation was a disillusioning
one generally, in which much of the gloss of their return and
their optimism about Australia changed. It was probably a
reflection of their own physical and mental depression, for
the most part, but they looked on Australian life from their
position of familiarity with Sydney affluence with an increasingly critical eye.

However, Johnston was cheered during this year by a visit
from Sidney Nolan, for whom Hal Missingham had arranged
a large retrospective exhibition at the New South Wales Gallery to celebrate Nolan's fiftieth year. These days the Nolans
lived mostly in London, where his reputation had soared, but
they came to Australia from time to time. It was an important
exhibition for Nolan, who used it as an occasion to make a
searching assessment of himself and question whether or not
his painting had ceased to make progress. Johnston and Clift
saw a great deal of him (less so of Cynthia), and Nolan talked
to Johnston seriously again about art, as he had not been able
to do for six years. Nolan later explained the kind of thing
he'd told Johnston.

> I'd never been completely convinced that I was born to be a
> painter, and with this exhibition I felt I was putting myself on
> the line; I was fifty, therefore I could toss it away and do
> something else — I'd no idea what, but still the last thing I
> wanted to be was a failed painter, and I wasn't going to be. If
> it didn't work I was just going to quit. When I went in I was
> going to say yes or no. Actually what happened, I became
> interested, not in that kind of moral or aesthetic question of
> whether I was going to continue to be a painter, but in the
> progress of my brain over the thirty years . . . as if I was an
> outsider looking at someone else's exhibition.[8]

The occasion of this retrospective, and a subsequent journey to Central Australia, which the three of them made in
connection with an ABC film being made on Nolan, is represented in *Clean Straw for Nothing*, where similar events and
conversations about art and life take place between the Merediths and Tom Kiernan, who is described as,

> . . . a big success now, but this, besides making him fairly

> *wealthy after all the years of battling, his made him wiser and*
> *gentler ... It seems that a kind of intense humility keeps*
> *driving him back over the old ground. (CSFN 63)*

Johnston's admiration and affection for Nolan, which had always been reciprocated, is evident here, as it is throughout *Clean Straw for Nothing*. Their lives, if not their art, had followed such similar paths that they talked each other's language and were totally relaxed together, just as Johnston and Tassie Drysdale were.

April of 1967 was the time of the *coup* that brought the Colonels to power in Greece, and naturally the Johnstons took an interest in developments. Clift used her column as a voice of protest against the Colonels at a time when the Australian Press generally was not giving events in Greece much coverage. Her interest was appreciated by many among the Greek community, and she was made honorary vice-president of the Committee For the Restoration of Democracy in Greece. Her public speeches of opposition ensured that she would not be allowed back in to Greece so long as the Colonels remained in power.

From this time on, Johnston and Clift became more politically minded than they had ever been before. This was partly under the influence of Martin, who was now a nineteen-year-old student at Sydney University, and deeply involved in the politics of protest that marked the 1960s. There was the particular issue of Vietnam, and Johnston and Clift were among the early protesters against Australian involvement, again brought into the debates by Martin's being the right age to be included in the conscription ballot. Johnston's experience of World War II, and his belief in the rightness of its cause, did not blind him to the evils of the Vietnam situation.

> *I'm not a total pacifist [he said in an interview], I'm still*
> *schoolboyish enough to read of battles and derring-do. But I*
> *object to the Vietnam war on its inhumanity and stupidity; its*
> *desecration of mankind ... I think, for me, the critical period*
> *was with the first party that went down to Hiroshima. This*
> *left, as it obviously would, a very profound impression on me.*
> *From that point I suppose I became very anti-war.*[9]

Clift felt much the same way:

> *I would fight to the very death for my kids, for my home, for*

*my everything. But Vietnam, no. Because I think it has
nothing to do with us ... At the moment there is a movement
going on about abortion. Now I say what sort of morality is
this? If you can carry on about the life of an unborn, unwanted foetus, and then put the lives of wanted, loved,
dearly-loved, 20-year-olds in a lottery barrel, this is
immoral.*[10]

On one occasion she spoke at a protest rally in the Sydney
stadium and 'held several thousand people spellbound,'
wrote journalist Allan Ashbolt, 'not by any political appraisal
of the Vietnam conflict, but simply by speaking as a mother
on behalf of her sons and of other mothers' sons everywhere'.[11]
She also publicly supported Aboriginal radical groups, and
became firm friends with Aboriginal writers such as Faith
Bandler and Kath Walker.

To some extent this new political awakening in Johnston
and Clift was a second youth, but of the kind they had missed
out on the first time. In her column Clift was constantly
raising matters concerning the youth of the day, contrasting
them with her own generation and that of the immediate
post-war decades, and she writes not as a parent but as a
participant, attempting to learn from the behaviour of the
young people around her. She had come to the view that the
previous generations had been neurotic, self-centred and
totally uncommitted to causes in a way that had during those
years both attracted and repulsed her (one thinks of Jean-
Claude Maurice). But this new generation of the mid-1960s
was, she was pleased to say, utterly unlike that:

*Students meet and march. Banners are snatched and torn like
battle trophies. Political rallies are stormy and even physically violent. Mothers of sons march for one cause and outraged
architects for another while another group vigorously demands racial equality. Dissension spreads. Hostility also.
Vigils, protests, sit-ins, teach-ins and even freedom rides are
becoming usual. ...*

*One thing is certain. No state of affairs was ever bettered
by putting up with it, no wrongs ever righted by passively
accepting them. A cause, a purpose, a goal, a creed, an idea, a
cherished attachment is the stuff all human evolution is made
of. Without some belief most passionately held we would
expire for want of vitality.*[12]

The 1960s offered causes that even the middle-aged middle-class could support, providing they were daring enough. Clift, in her public stand on a range of issues, was influential enough to persuade many such people into supporting her causes, and so she undoubtedly played a vital role in Australian public life during those years. The great cause of her own and Johnston's youth had been World War II, which had whetted their appetites for experience and action, making peacetime routine and dull. The 1950s especially had been a time of political starvation, offering no great causes to its youth, as that spokesman of the era Jimmy Porter in *Look Back in Anger* so vehemently asserts. Clift and Johnston were happy to leave that era behind, and throw in their lot with Martin's generation, when it came to matters of principle.

All the same, while politics could develop their beliefs, it could not pervade their lives deeply enough to bring about a complete revaluation or change of direction. It was not going to alter the bouts of depression, the physical deterioration, nor the terrible self-destructive spiral that their relationship had fallen into in recent years. That was now too ingrained, too habitual to be affected by what was happening around them. It was the same with their optimism about Australia: that came and went, hardly touching their individual selves or their relationship. It was infectious and encouraged others, but it did not cause them to take a grip on themselves, nor to stop drinking and smoking so much, nor to stop their rows, nor to look after their health, nor did it affect their work. They wrote as hard as they could whether life about them was wonderful or terrible, so long as they had the strength and energy, because they were driven by inner motivations and compulsions, not socio-political ones. The fact that they were in this way expending themselves without proper regard for the need for renewal and sustenance, burning themselves out with an inevitability that was painful for their friends and family to witness was as mysterious as it was irretrievable. Their lives were out of balance, and they were incapable of bringing about a correction.

Later in 1967, Tassie Drysdale became concerned about Clift's physical and mental condition. He had just returned from a trip north with Alan Moorehead, including a visit to

his painter friend Ray Crooke in Cairns, and observing that
Clift badly needed a break from her obsession with her loss
of beauty and her terror of meeting the weekly deadline, he
suggested she make a journey to Cairns that would furnish
her with material for an article or two.[13] She could, he suggested, stay with the Crookes, whom the Johnstons had met
briefly at the Drysdales' a year or two earlier. So Clift was
persuaded to go. Clift's sophisticated reputation had created
in the Crookes expectations of great self-assuredness, and
they were not sure they would be high-powered enough for
her. But when Clift arrived in Cairns they found her nervous,
timid and incapable of taking any sort of initiative, and entirely and gratefully dependent on them. June Crooke suggested to her that since she had already come 1500 miles she
might as well go the extra 500 and visit Thursday Island,
where the Crookes had lived a dozen years earlier. Clift was
fascinated but terrified by the idea, and insisted she could
not go unless June went with her. So while Ray went off on a
trip to Western Australia, paying Johnston a visit in Sydney
on the way, the two women spent several weeks exploring
life on Thursday Island. It turned out to be one of the happiest times of Clift's life. She was totally absorbed by everything she saw, responded strongly to the island people, in
particular their pearl divers, whom she naturally kept liken-
ing to the Kalymnian sponge divers, and told June Crooke
about the plan to bring Kalymnians to Darwin that was the
catalyst in their going to Greece. 'Young gods', she called
them, and, caught up in everything about the place that
seemed so healthy, strange or beautiful, she began to get
some of her old spark and vitality back. She and June Crooke
went on a lugger trip to observe the Japanese pearlers, and to
the mainly native-patronised Royal Hotel night club, where
they enjoyed themselves dancing and mixing with the locals.
In one of the pieces eventually published in her column about
the trip, Clift notes the aura of the colonial past that still hung
about, mingling with the carefree present, on Thursday Island:

> The days of the Assemblies, China boats, shell traders, pearl
> buyers, and the reign of Burns Philp might be gone but

> *something still lingers, a smell and a taste and an essence, half*
> *squalid and half romantic, something indolent, excessive,*
> *irresponsible, shameless and happy. One responds instinc-*
> *tively, and I suppose atavistically.*[14]

'It was a charmed trip from the start,' recalls June Crooke,
reflecting on how everything went well and Clift's confidence
returned. She even managed to boost her self-esteem by a
brief affair with a naval officer — the old Clift was not
finished yet! When it was time to leave she wept like a child,
but returned to Sydney sun-tanned, smiling and bubbling
with stories. Her editor, John Douglas Pringle, arranged for
all her considerable expenses to be met and gave her a free
hand to write as many pieces on Thursday Island for the
column as she wished, which she proceeded to do. At home,
George was astonished to see the change in her, and he
immediately dashed off a letter of thanks to June Crooke:

> *I am so grateful that you were with her to give her this rare*
> *and I think extremely special interlude in her life. She doesn't*
> *know that I'm writing this letter to you, but I have been so*
> *moved by her obvious and immensely deep feeling and love*
> *for you that I feel it would be churlish of me not to thank you*
> *for all your warmth and kindness to her. Charm. is a rather*
> *special sort of person, I think, but she always has been a bit*
> *of a 'loner', very particularly where other women are con-*
> *cerned, and in all the 21 years I have been with her I have*
> *never known her to have such rapport and compatibility and*
> *love with another woman as she clearly has with you. She*
> *came back looking ten years younger, walking on air, and still*
> *bubbling over with* joie de vivre *... The whole trip up north*
> *seems to have flicked some switch in Charm. and given her*
> *back so much that is real and valuable and tender and mar-*
> *vellous — she has had a pretty shitty time of it in these last*
> *few years — that it is almost as if she has been re-born.*[15]

Three days later Clift also wrote to June Crooke that it was
'an incomparable time' and that it had produced in her

> *splendid resolutions about public platforms and charitable*
> *luncheons and television interviews, also about losing a stone*
> *of weight, and brisk walks and keeping fit. I wonder how*
> *long it will last before sloth and muddle overtake me again. I*
> *feel so good that I would like to go on feeling good, and*
> *feeling private too and not public property ... I can't thank*
> *you, because there aren't any words for that. But we will*

never lose each other now, and I will love you very truly and dearly always.[16]

In her absence, Johnston had reorganised her study, 'filled the shelves with Folio Society books, all sombre and glowing and rich with red and blue and gold bindings', and reframed and hung her personal Nolan, Drysdale and Gauguin paintings so that her study, she said, was 'so rich and lush that I probably won't be able to do any work here at all'.[17] Ray Crooke had also made her a gift of one of his fine Thursday Island paintings, and this, too, was newly hung in the sitting-room.

When Storry Walton heard the details of the Thursday Island trip, he immediately wanted to do a documentary series for ABC Television, but lack of funds forced it into the future and eventually to oblivion. But Clift was not especially concerned to write for television at this time: she had applied for and received a Literature Board Fellowship to help her to write another novel, the autobiographical 'Greener Grows the Grass', with which she had been tinkering on and off for years. It was Johnston who was at this time more interested in film and television work. He had done some more of *Clean Straw for Nothing*, of which Clift said: 'I have read it and liked it very much indeed.'[18] But he had also been commissioned and given an advance of $2000 to write the ABC film on Sidney Nolan, which had been in the pipeline for some time, called *The Seven Day Bicycle Rider*. He began it about August 1967, and it was shown in February 1968. More than this, however, since coming out of hospital eighteen months earlier, Johnston had completed scripts for some half-a-dozen television plays, including a dramatisation of the early drafts of *Clean Straw for Nothing* and a play about the bushranger Ben Hall, none of which went into production. A glance through them suggests that he was making the mistake of returning to his earlier, spurious fictions of the days before *My Brother Jack*, which once found their way into print if they were lucky, but which were unlikely to survive the close scrutiny of television company accountants.

Over the summer of 1967–68 life in the Johnston household was relatively settled. Clift's bouyant mood continued for a

time, though she was gradually coming down to earth. Martin
completed his first-year University exams, but was tending to
live farther apart from the family. Clift found this difficult to
handle, and she wrote to June Crooke:

> ... *something or other is making him evasive, dishonest and
> really rather shoddy. I wish he could tell us. I wish he would
> go to the dentist and have his teeth scraped, I wish he would
> cut his hair. I wish I knew what he was up to. I feel ashamed
> of him and for him and ashamed of myself for feeling this.
> The only good thing he's done lately was to sell a poem to the
> book pages of the S.M.H.*[19]

Shane was in love, and had found herself a job as circulation manager for the *Hellenic Herald*. In February, Jason began his first term at high school. Johnston had recently had
most of his teeth extracted and replaced with dentures; Clift
had had hers expensively recapped and had lately taken to
wearing a wig in public.

On 9 February 1968 Johnston gave an interesting paper to
the Australian Society of Authors titled 'Aspects of the
Novel'. Generally it is commonsensical advice about keeping
one's writing style simple and not expecting to make much
money. Among some quotations from his favourite, Conrad,
and new discoveries such as Jorge Luis Borges, he imparts
one from Eugene Ionesco that has a ring of distinct aptness to
himself:

> *Being unaware of the purpose of life, I am not quite sure
> either why I write. Yet I have always been a writer, just as I
> have always been alive for as long as I can remember, and
> wondering about the meaning of life. I am impelled to write,
> that is, to ask myself questions and to look around me and to
> describe what I see.*[20]

Adds Johnston: 'To me, this will do. This is a splendid statement ... not at all a bad *credo* for a creative writer.' He
continues the talk with some forthright judgements on
Australian novelists: there is 'no Herman Melville' of Australian writing, therefore it has not yet fully matured. Thomas
Keneally seems a better novelist to him than either Randolph
Stow or Patrick White, who 'has an over-obsession with what
we loosely define as "style"'. He concludes his address with
an exhortation to writers to be original at all costs, repeating

Ionesco's comment that 'It is novelty which is the true sign of sincerity, which is truth. What is original is true. What resembles everything else being done is false, because convention is an impersonal falsehood.'[21] It is a scrappy but ,stimulating paper, and happily quite unacademic.

In April 1968 Johnston was devastated to learn that the tuberculosis had become active again. He and Clift must have suspected it for some time, and in the weeks after it was diagnosed they both fell into a black depression. Clift wrote to June Crooke, apologising for her long silence:

> Things have been going badly for quite some time now. I think I am pulling out of it, but still have relapses into panic and desolation and have to force myself to see people or go out at all. We've had a bitter blow in these last couple of weeks to find that George is positive again. It's hard after nearly eleven years of sickness and brutal surgery to be back again at the beginning. Everyone is being very cheerful and reassuring, and they are doing everything they can to make it easier for him, even to the extent of letting him stay at home for treatment instead of hauling him in again, but the new drugs make him sick and depressed and he has to force himself to work, and this is disappointing when the novel was going so well. Anyway, I suppose we'll get through this lot eventually. We've got through worse before.[22]

In fact Johnston's condition did require hospitalisation, and he was re-admitted to Royal North Shore on 28 May 1968. This was to be another protracted stay – almost five months – but since it involved drug treatment and not surgery, he was not nearly so sick as before and therefore able to be a great deal more active. People who visited him found him cheerful, surrounded by books, flowers, get-well cards, his typewriter, and more often than not some smuggled-in cigarettes and whisky. It was here that he was able to get to grips with the final version of *Clean Straw for Nothing*.

The problem of the novel's form had been a persistent headache. There were several factors against repeating the straight chronological narrative of *My Brother Jack*. The 'development' idea, suitable for showing growth from childhood to adulthood, would not serve to capture the distinctively adult, nightmarish circularities that characterised the post-war material. Also, he wanted to create something psychologically stronger, closer to the narrator than in the first volume, because again the material was as much 'inner' as 'outer', and the significance of the events is largely that which Meredith's own discriminating consciousness gives them as he struggles to understand the forces that shaped his life. Finally there was the artistic need to do something new, to find an appropriately new form for new content. He suddenly remembered a remark Sidney Nolan had made to him at the time of his retrospective exhibition the previous year. They had gone together around midnight into the empty gallery where the pictures were hung. 'What you do', said Nolan, 'is lay on the colours underneath. But then you have to cut into them.'[23] At the time Johnston did not quite understand the point, but now, wrestling with his own problems of method, it made sense as an example of finding liberation from looking at the problem as the spectator or reader sees it. It drove home that the artist is free to work his material in any order, to achieve his effects by even reversing what would appear to be the logically sequential way to go. He later told an interviewer that he got the idea of a kaleidoscope, where one shakes the material and *then* discerns the pattern, and that the shaping of it should follow 'an emotional rather than a chronological sequence'.[24] The concept, he confessed, was exciting, but dangerous, because it threatened to undermine the tension by removing the element of suspense. This meant that he was thrown back onto the quality of his writing, its handling of themes and characters, if he was going to make a success of it. If it worked, however, it would be a far more sophisticated literary approach than anything he had brought off before. He went ahead, scrambling the order of his chapters, though nevertheless keeping a semblance of chronology, and changing the narrative from first to third person wherever he saw fit.

The novel begins by taking up the question of Meredith's inability to write it: 'I'll tell you why I'm not writing,' says Meredith to Jeremy at a party, and proceeds immediately to hedge around the answer, which eventually emerges as a loss of faith in himself and his ability to find the words to get at the truth. Meredith reflects: 'Once you've traded in memory for experience there's no difference any longer between the lies and the actualities' (*CSFN* 12). This beginning is, of course, a classic means of a writer to clear his creative block by writing about the reasons why he cannot write.

In his depressed mood Meredith decides that keeping 'a random journal' won't really be going back to writing: 'Just trying to work it out, rather, to get it straight before it is too late' (*CSFN* 13). By this means Johnston is hoping he has found a way of giving his material shape without falsifying it, as a consciously controlling narrator or strict chronology might be inclined to do: 'getting it straight' does not mean ordering the events of his life into the correct sequence, but understanding the truth about himself. The novel proceeds in an apparently random manner, with out-of-sequence chapters identified by place and year, such as 'Melbourne, 1945', 'London, 1954' and the recurring section 'Sydney, 1968', representing the time of Meredith's (and Johnston's) writing of the journal in hospital, making a unity of time and place between author and narrator. (This complex relation between author and narrator/character is one explored with great effect by Conrad himself in several works, but especially in *Heart of Darkness*.) It is only an 'apparent' randomness in *Clean Straw for Nothing*, because there is a rough chronology: its early chapters tend to be concerned with immediate post-war matters and the later ones with returning from Greece to Australia. Also, there is an occasional connection by thematic association between chapters. For instance, the chapter headed 'Lebanon Bay, 1946' ends on page 62 in a depiction of Meredith and Cressida's honeymoon Paradise, and this is immediately followed by the chapter 'Central Australia, 1965', in which they discuss with Tom Kiernan the feeling of Paradise in the Australian desert. The moments are almost twenty years apart, but they connect instantly in Meredith's imagination. In another case, 'London, 1950' on page 85 ends with Meredith wondering 'whether we got away [from Australia] in time', and this is followed by the section 'Sydney, 1949, that is, the year *before*, and Meredith admonishing himself with 'No, no . . . you can't get away like that', and then taking the reader back over some of the unhappier events in Sydney that encouraged them to leave. There is also a very curious shift from first person to third person in these chapters, creating an effect of the author 'catching out' the narrator, and correcting his memories with a wiser voice. Other similar shifts of person, and the narrator's habit of commenting on his own narrative, contribute to a self-consciousness that is part of the novel's psychological complexity, as if Meredith is looking over his own shoulder as he writes. Moreover, standing above and controlling him, is the creator himself, Johnston, half-confessing half-denying the truth of what he creates. So clearly a great deal of tricky labour has gone into the construction of *Clean Straw for Nothing*, and the 'random journal' idea is only an illusion of artlessness for the purpose of making Meredith's memories seem spontaneous and therefore 'honest', a necessary condition for Meredith's successful rendering of the truth about himself.

The central theme of the novel is personal betrayal, whereas in *My Brother Jack* it was family and patriotic betrayal as well. In this second volume, however, the theme is more relentlessly analysed and is more unforgiving of Meredith. The dramatic climax of the novel comes towards the end where, on 'the island', there is a sequence of confrontations between the four main participants: Meredith, Cressida, her lover Jim Galloway, and Archie Calverton. The issue between them is unfaithfulness, with Cressida cast in the role of her literary namesake, Galloway playing Diomedes, and Meredith a less-than-heroic Troilus. Meredith wrings a confession out of Cressida, and then confronts Galloway, who is about to leave the island, and bitterly urges him to take Cressida with him since he has virtually destroyed their marriage. Galloway insists that she would not abandon Meredith, and departs from the island alone. He leaves behind a legacy of mistrust between the Merediths that rankles for two years, until Meredith, unable to cope with it any longer, decides that he, too, will quietly slip away to live with a friend in Athens. He fails to get away because Archie Calverton, by a deft combination of trickery and physical force, prevents Meredith from catching the boat. Acting as a wise friend and counsellor, Calverton is emphatic that Meredith must try to understand Cressida and recognise his own role in their unhappiness.

It is the view of many of their friends, and many who have simply read the published novel, that Johnston was in *Clean Straw for Nothing* undertaking a callous exposition of Clift's behaviour on Hydra, either out of revenge or out of a selfish desire to reveal all in the cause of truth, or, worse, to create a sensational novel. Indeed, Clift herself came to believe some of these things, and after reading those early drafts and liking them, eventually began to realise that the version he was now writing in hospital dealt with those traumatic last three or so years on Hydra. She began to believe that George was going to cut her down, both emotionally in relation to him, and professionally in what the world would think of her in taking her as the adulterous Cressida. For this reason she found herself totally unable to give him any help in the writing by acting as his sounding-board, as she had done almost without exception for his previous books. 'With *Clean Straw For Nothing* I have had a complete emotional block, and not all my deep and genuine sympathy at the sight of him struggling and fighting with what was obviously proving to be recalcitrant (sometimes I thought intractable) could force me into the old familiar step-sitting role', she later wrote.[25]

Is it true that Johnston was using the novel to malign her? My answer is an emphatic 'No'. There can be no doubt that if he had chosen to give a full account of her affairs and the consequences, the picture could have been one of squalid drunkenness, public love-making, violent quarrels, beatings, all of which are still the subject of gossip among people who were on Hydra in those days. The novel depicts nothing of this kind. On the contrary, Cressida emerges from it with considerable dignity and with her sexual powers fully within her own control. She is made to insist on her right not to be reduced to a possession of her husband: 'I am dreadfully sorry that you have to be hurt', she tells Meredith, 'but I can't stand here now and be a liar and say that I'm sorry that it happened . . . I am not ashamed' (*CSFN 268*). As elsewhere in the novel, she keeps a part of herself inaccessible to others, and this adds to her mystery and dignity. It is also a source of irritation to the jealousy-minded Meredith.

Against this Meredith's reactions are self-righteous and unforgiving. He replies in terms of 'sin' and 'adultery', attempts to cheapen Cressida's feelings and finally walks away from her in a tacit admission of the ineffectuality of his outrage in the face of her simple honesty. Immediately afterwards he visits Galloway and adopts a similar meanspiritedness, couched in similarly pompous terms. He is 'incensed to observe that the American's conscience was less troubled by the enormity of his adultery than by the injustice and crudeness of his having played a dirty trick on someone weaker than himself, a sick man unable to assert his rights, a friend, too; the transgression a social solecism rather than a moral crime' (*CSFN* 272). Put like this, it is difficult not to prefer Galloway's humane guilt to Meredith's lofty moral principles.

In contrast with Meredith's physical frailty and tendency to hysteria, Galloway is strong, generous-minded and contrite. Despite his name, he is not just a stud; indeed, he is shown to be a fully rounded man, a sensitive artist, a close observer of nature, a lover of life: 'He sang, talked, laughed, jested, drank, gave parties, swam and walked the length and breadth of the little island with no stint to his exuberance. If he was sometimes exhausting he was always kind and generous and outgiving ...' (*CSFN* 256). Meredith's approving description comes, of course, before he discovers he has been cuckolded by Galloway.

Galloway does not appear to be a characterisation of any of Clift's lovers: there may be something of the shadowy Chadwick in him, but Galloway's gregarious and exuberant personality seems not to fit the little-known Chadwick — none of the Hydra friends of those days remembers him in any but the vaguest terms. And certainly there seems nothing in him of Jean-Claude Maurice, or of Anthony Kingsmill, whom Johnston did not meet.

Galloway is not recognisable by any of Johnston's friends from those days — Grace Edwards, for example, or Patrick Greer, although Greer had admittedly departed from Hydra by 1959. Galloway would seem to be a fictionalised substitute for, rather than an amalgamation of, the several men in Clift's life. Johnston has designed him as an idealised lover for the double purpose of dignifying Cressida's affair and degrading Meredith's character.

This purpose is underlined in the scene between Meredith and Archie Calverton. It is possible that Calverton is here representing Peter Finch at the time of his visit to Hydra in 1961, but it is not likely that Finch took part in a dramatic scene of the order depicted in this part of the novel. The wise counsel Calverton gives to Meredith to look to his own faults and to recognise the unfair demands for perfection he has always made on Cressida is no piece of memorised advice that Johnston may have received from friends such as Finch. It is produced by a stretch of sustained fictional polemic that began with the scene between Meredith and Galloway, developed in the scene with Cressida, until now with Calverton the purpose of exposing Meredith's crippling limitations has been achieved. 'People want mercy and escape', says Calverton, 'they're not looking for justice and truth' (*CSFN* 308). Meredith's response is exactly the same as when he confronted Cressida: he lays the blame on her and her habit of keeping a part of herself out of his reach. Calverton's reply is unanswerable:

> '... it's what makes her Cressida ... it's her soul if you like, her belief, her poetry ... it doesn't matter really what you call it ... it doesn't really matter whether it's right or wrong. It's the music she hears. It's hers ... Do you ever hear it?' Calverton asked softly ... 'this music of hers'. 'How can I? I told you, I'm barred'. (*CSFN* 309)

This last comment by the embittered Meredith suggests the extent to which he has given up the struggle to understand Cressida, and has fallen back onto his self-righteous despair. Incidentally, Johnston uses the same 'music of life' idea that Clift herself used in her 1953 story 'Three Old Men of Lerici', where on that occasion it is the woman who has to discover her partner's openness to the 'music of life'. In each case a gesture is being made in praise of the other.

We must be clear that this important section of *Clean Straw for Nothing* is not really autobiographical: it is the organised work of a novelist in full control of his material, shaping his characters and their dialogue according to his overall design, which is primarily to isolate Meredith and expose him as a morally unbalanced man. While this degrades Meredith, it actually represents a moral and artistic triumph for Johnston, for he, like his *alter ego*, had in the course of the trilogy come to see his task as a *quest*. Meredith's persistent attempts to forge links with the past, between himself and Chinese exiles, with Odysseus's twenty years of wanderings, with the Australia and Europe of his own experience, are, as A. E. Goodwin has argued, a quest to find a *pattern* in his life, something that will give it meaning.[26]

For Johnston himself the quest is for more than a pattern: it is for self-knowledge as a prerequisite to self-reconstruction. Simply, he is hoping, in his indefatigable optimism, that by transcending his morally smaller self in David Meredith, in the act of writing *Clean Straw for Nothing* he will become a wiser, better George Johnston. It is a kind of exorcism, and Meredith is the evil that must be expelled. Self-purification is part of it, but not all: Johnston was not preparing himself for death when he wrote this novel — he fully intended to get well again and go on living to complete the trilogy and many other things as well. It is self re-construction that lay behind his determination to overcome the massive obstacles presented by this novel, and the foundation for it is laid by showing Clift's attitude to life to be dignified and right, and his own, in its threadbare David Meredith garb, to be degraded and wrong.

How bitterly ironic it is, therefore, that Clift would not read the typescript. She continued in ignorance of the truth of Johnston's generous treatment of those bad times, totally convinced that it was a vengeful attack on her. John Douglas Pringle recalls Cynthia Nolan coming to his house and declaring: 'Poor Charm. George is killing her with that book!'[27] By this time the rift between the two women had been largely healed, though Cynthia retained her dislike of George, and was prepared to take Charmian's side in any dispute, as indeed was Toni Burgess, to whom Clift looked frequently for support in these days. Neither of them knew what Johnston was doing with the novel: they simply believed Clift's worst fears, and presumed that Johnston was indulging his malice.

In the last weeks of this hospitalisation, in September 1968, Johnston got the script of *Clean Straw for Nothing* to 'within 20 or 30 pages of completion'.[28] During this time he was interviewed in his hospital bed for *Walkabout* magazine by Clifford Tolchard, who also interviewed Clift at home and combined the two into one article. A significant feature of the article is the degree to which both of them had changed their views of Australia since their lavish praise and infectious optimism of 1965. Clift is quoted as saying:

> ... when I came back here I was terribly enthusiastic. I wanted to love it ... but three-and-a-half years later I am still *saying, oh, there is an imminence here, and this sort of worries me. There is a complacency, an apathy. In Europe you're living with this sense of hazard that has gone on for centuries, and people are indoctrinated, and there's so much more liveliness. There's so much more agony, too. There's no real agony here.*[29]

Johnston saw a more positive kind of danger:

> ... unadventurous, conformist and, I think, veering towards a fascist style of authoritarianism which people are accepting: in other words, the good life, the easy life.[30]

These are familiar criticisms of Australia, and while they carry no less weight coming from Johnston and Clift, it is also difficult not to sense the personal disillusionment behind them, just as their wild eulogies of four years earlier were equally influenced by their personal circumstances.

Johnson and Clift had no professional grounds for complaint, since they were both still in demand by publishers, television, radio and film people. However, it was becoming increasingly difficult to produce the goods, harder to find the energy to keep going. *Clean Straw for Nothing* took so much out of Johnston that he could not do anything else for weeks, but simply 'lay for a month on the green couch in the sunny living room and worried'.[31] His worry was over what kind of judgement would be passed on the novel, and he expressed enormous relief when Sir William Collins phoned from London to tell him how much he liked and admired it. Clift was having the same problem of keeping going. She had complained to Tolchard that there was 'no real agony' in Australia, but of course she had her own full share of it in trying to

meet the deadline for her *Sydney Morning Herald* pieces every
Thursday. She frequently phoned her editor excusing her
failure to get it done because of 'pneumonia' or 'flu'.[32] Sometimes she did have such ailments, but that was often itself a
consequence of prolonged drinking bouts, insufficient sleep
and poor diet. Her binges were now frequent and disturbing.
'She preferred whisky,' said John Douglas Pringle, 'but she
would drink anything. One night she came round and I had
nothing but a cask of wine, and she drank the lot by
herself.'[33] Toni Burgess, too, often had to sit with her all night
while she drank and talked out her fear of doing the weekly
article.

Clift had, friends observed, a tendency towards jealousy of
Shane now that her daughter was grown up and exceedingly
attractive, and was often intent upon putting her down in
front of others, especially boy-friends. Shane was in many
respects the most neglected of the children. The boys had
fared better: Martin was always the focus of attention, as is
common in the eldest, and Jason received special interest
always as the baby, though as he grew up in a household
increasingly riddled with illness and emotional struggle, he
came in for considerable neglect. In 1969 he was placed in
Cranbrook private school as a boarder, where he was, Martin
observed, much happier than before. Martin himself had by
this time given up full-time study and had taken a journalism
cadetship with the *Sydney Morning Herald*, and had his own
pursuits, which kept him away from home much of the time.
Shane had suffered from being the middle child and a female
– surprising perhaps from such unconventional parents –
and was more severely disturbed than any of the others by
being wrenched away from her life on Hydra. She had found
it very difficult to adapt to Australian life, and therefore the
family was hoping that marriage would make the difference,
for in February 1969 Shane was married to Robert O'Connor.
Clift wrote a piece in her column called 'Betrothing a Daughter', in which she joked about her own inexperience of formal
weddings and her mild disapproval of the conformity of it all.
' "Look," I said, "why don't you two elope?" '[34] she wrote and
could easily have added '*I* did'. Shane and Robert opened a

little antique shop in Mosman, called 'Shane's Shop', soon after their wedding.

Around this time Johnston persuaded Ray and June Crooke to move from Cairns to Sydney, and to find a house near them in Mosman. The four had grown close since the Thursday Island trip, and this was important to Johnston and Clift at a time when, apart from the Drysdales and one or two others, many of their friends rarely saw them: illness and rows were not the most inviting prospects for friendly visits. Ray Crooke stayed with them for a few days while house-hunting, and then, he recalls, he suddenly saw 'the other side of their Sydney lives'.[35] The house was in a mess, Charmian had stopped bothering to cook meals, and the sink was piled with dishes from days past. They did little but drink and argue and, observed Crooke, were obviously 'two rather sick people'.

The Crookes did buy a house near by and continued to see them often, though they were increasingly apprehensive about going to Raglan Street 'not knowing what to expect'.[36] If they arrived 'after they'd started their session', it could prove to be a nightmare. On one occasion, in a drunken hysteria, Johnston and Clift were playing the final movement of Beethoven's Ninth Symphony on the record player when the Crookes arrived, and they simply went on playing it over and over again, insistently shouting that it was 'the greatest thing ever done', as if they had personally discovered it. For years Ray and June Crooke had lived relatively quiet lives, mainly in the country. Now, knowing the Johnstons suddenly dragged them into a supercharged style of living that they at times found bewildering, and at other times depressing. There was, in these weeks approaching mid-1969, an air of disaster in the house at Raglan Street.

Clift had for some time been involved in a serious love affair with a married Sydney man. She confided in Toni Burgess, who knew that Johnston knew of it. 'He taunted her savagely about it,' Burgess recalls.[37] Some time towards the middle of the year the affair collapsed, and Clift went into a black depression. It was, according to Burgess, an affair that meant a great deal to Clift, 'the only serious affair I've ever had', she told her friend. Burgess offered support, but felt utterly useless in the face of Clift's desolation. She asked Burgess round for breakfast one morning, and Clift had nothing but whisky. She went on a television talk show appearing and sounding manifestly drunk, and with her wig on embarrassingly crooked. Then one Monday morning in July she came round to Burgess's flat in a terrible state — not so much drunk as deeply depressed and weeping incessantly. She wanted Burgess to go away with her to Fiji, or New Guinea, or Thursday Island, just the two of them, to leave everything in Sydney behind immediately. Of course, Burgess, who had her own commitments, could hardly agree to go like that. 'She cried all night,' said Burgess, 'and said nobody in the world loved her except me.'[38] She left early in the morning in despair.

Clift still had the publication of *Clean Straw for Nothing* weighing on her mind. It was due to be issued this very month — July — and she still had not read the typescript but was fearing the worst. She had, a week or two earlier, sent off an article to *POL* magazine telling of her inability to come to terms with it by acting as Johnston's sounding-board:

> ... Not all my professionalism could lure me into listening dispassionately. I do believe that novelists must be free to write what they like, in any way they liked to write it (and after all who but myself had urged and nagged him into it?), but the stuff of which Clean Straw for Nothing is made is largely experience in which I, too, have shared and ... have felt differently because I am a different person ...
>
> But what was troubling too was that when the novel was finished at last he wouldn't — or couldn't — give it up. For weeks he tinkered and polished and fiddled and re-wrote until, watching him, I felt that the wisest thing to do was to ring his publisher and get rid of the damn thing. For better or for worse. Which I did. I think he was relieved by this action, but nervous, too, more nervous than I have ever seen him. That waiting time is always jittery for a writer, but usually you have some idea of what sort of a job you've done, and this time he evidently had none at all. He only knew he had committed himself absolutely, as a professional and as a person too, and it had been the hardest piece of writing he'd ever done in a long writing life ...
>
> Whatever anybody says, I will read that book myself one

*day. When I'm brave enough. Or when I feel I've earned my
own small bundle of clean straw.*[39]

This is, as we have come to expect from any public statement that either made about the other, honest and generous.
But it barely masks the state of tension that existed between
Clift and Johnston over the book, and in this atmosphere the
slightest ill-judged remark could spark off a row. On Tuesday
8 July — the day after she had spent that harrowing night
with Toni Burgess — Johnston and Clift had an argument, the
cause or subject of which is unknown, since nobody else was
in the house. They had both had a great deal to drink during
that afternoon — there is talk of Clift having finished a bottle
of whisky on her own — and the argument grew increasingly
bitter and unremitting. Vile accusations were topped by viler
ones, reaching a pitch of terrible hysteria until they each
made their way, exhausted, to bed — he to the front room of
the house, she in her small study-bedroom at the back.

In the morning Johnston got up, surprised to find the house
in quietness because Clift was usually up first, working. Presuming she was sleeping in, he went to the kitchen, squeezed
her an orange juice, and took it in to her. She was dead.
Beside her bed was a barbiturate bottle — his own — and a
note:

> Darling please forgive me — I can't bear it any longer, it had
> all become too much, and this way 'I shall cease upon the
> midnight with no pain'.[40]

The doctor confirmed that she died somewhere around the
middle of the night.

Johnston rang Toni Burgess, who came at once. He was agitated, wanted to talk to her about it, to blame himself for the
things he'd said the previous night. By the time Martin and
friends such as Arthur and Monica Polkinghorne and Geoff
and Dahl Collings arrived, he was giving every sign of making a huge effort to control himself. There was little anyone
could say, and people moved about the house in numb disbe-
lief. Later that morning Johnston got angry with Toni
Burgess, because, she believes, 'in a moment of weakness he
had told her about the fight and blamed himself'.[41] Burgess

moved into the house for the next two weeks to keep the place going and look after George and Jason, and to organise the Press and funeral arrangements, jobs he was in the circumstances not capable of doing.

The news of Clift's death — not announced as suicide — shocked not only family and friends, but affected people throughout the country. Tributes poured in from newspaper writers, but more touching were the many responses from readers in every State where her column was syndicated, which in itself was a testimony to the success she had been able to make of it. 'I am the best damned essayist in the country,' she was heard to say more than once, and there were many who would have agreed with her. One reader wrote:

> Not only was Charmian Clift, in my opinion, the best woman columnist, if not the best columnist, Australia has ever produced, but she had a quality in her writing that left her readers feeling they had not so much read an article, as spent a few minutes with a valued friend.[42]

Another said:

> For all the sense of loss and the tragedy of a life cut short there is also a profound surge of thankfulness for her life. From one small voice in the wilderness that is suburbia comes the heartfelt prayer that her family, who are mourning her death, will permit us to grieve a little too ...
> She had courage, humour, compassion, honesty. And love. How she loved her country and its people! Otherwise, why bother to take us to task?[43]

Few of her readers could have guessed that behind the weekly voice of sanity and grace that she managed to sustain for over four years, there was an increasingly desperate woman who at times had to drink, talk, weep and go through hell before she could drive herself to the typewriter and get those words into shape in time to meet the deadline. One of the best tributes came a little later from Johnston himself, in his Introduction to the collection of her essays published the following year under the title *The World of Charmian Clift*:

> She ... put guts and sinew into what had been the bland formularies of the women's pages. She wrote with a graceful and highly personal style, but she wrote to no formula. One never knew from week to week what she would come up

*with, yet she always had something to say that was different
and original and fresh. Sometimes she was very funny, sometimes very angry, sometimes very truculent — for she took up
causes, often unpopular causes, if she deeply and sincerely
believed in them, although she was never a professional
'crusader'. But whatever she had to say she said it with great
panache.*[44]

Charmian Clift was almost forty-six years old when she
died. The City Coroner at his inquest in October found that
she had died 'from the effects of poisoning by pentobarbi-
tone, self-administered while in a state of severe mental depression and while considerably affected by alcohol'.[45] Johnston had told the inquest of his complete shock at her action,
because 'she had never done anything to indicate she would
take her own life'. A story emerged, possibly from Johnston,
that she feared she might have had cancer. There is no evidence of grounds for such fears, but her health had been bad
for so long she might well have feared she had numerous
illnesses.

It is easy to share Toni Burgess's view that Clift saved
herself a great deal of further pain and degradation by taking
her own life. Her decline, Burgess feels, had gone to the point
of no return; she was deeply and irreconcilably unhappy, and
this was the tidiest, most dignified way she could end it. In a
way she was going through two agonising deaths — her own,
and Johnston's relentless decline, suffering along with him
and from him, acting as his object of anger at life for what it
was doing to him: 'there were times when he was affronted
and outraged by the corruption working in his lungs,' she
wrote. 'He raged against it for years, despaired, became bitter
and hating and not easy to live with.'[46] She could no longer
take that hatred. Why should she bear the burden of two
tragedies? His death would now have to be his business,
something he must face alone, with no one else to punish for
it: she had done all she could, and it was time to retire from
the field with as much grace as she could. All the same, she
still had considerable ability, such good work left in her to
do, all wasted now. Those who had known her in her best
days felt saddened by that waste, recalling — as her old
admirer from London days, Nan Hutton, did a few years after

Clift's death — the power of her personality at its height. At the Journalists' Club in London, Nan Hutton recalls,

> ... *we saw Charmian the instant she swept in, with husband George behind.*
>
> *I had never seen her before, but when the Canadian correspondent breathed 'Quick! Who is she?' I said instantly 'That's Charmian. George Johnston's wife.'*
>
> *George looked thin and elusive as ever, but Charmian looked like the Queen of Sheba. I forget what she wore — something long and simple with a gold band about her full throat. It was her face, strong boned and mobile, the set of her firm shoulders and her voice, talking to George low and throaty but penetrating ... she died with her talent still burning and her work unfinished.[47]*

Clean Straw for Nothing duly came out in the month after Clift's death. Reviews were mixed, sometimes confused, but generally admiring. Old friends such as John Moses and Harry Kippax knew something of the background of the novel and were able to recognise the courage and seriousness that lay within its jumbled chapters. Alan Trengrove in the Melbourne *Herald* thought it was a 'modern classic', but did not seem to be able to say why, and Owen Webster in the *Age* found it unreadable, a disability that he proved in every paragraph of his longish review. Its departure from conventional form made most reviewers scuttle for safety, and except for Brian Kiernan in the *Australian*, who identified its strengths and weaknesses readily, and understood the point of its fragmentary approach, it was not until some years later, when critics such as Alan Lawson and A. E. Goodwin examined it, that it received the careful attention that its complexity and literary daring deserved.[48]

It was a slow process for Johnston to gather himself together again. He had 'hundreds of letters to answer', he wrote to Elsie,[49] who had sent a warm note of commiseration, and he was grateful to have tasks to perform to keep his mind occupied. He wasted no time in attempting to make a start on the third volume of the trilogy. Friends were generous with help — he took Jason and Shane and stayed with the Drysdales for a few days. He spent time with the Crookes, and Ray began studies for a portrait of him. But there was no bridging the terrible gap that was left in his life. 'Charmian and I lived for many years with the idea of sudden death,' he reflected. 'But it was to be my death, not hers . . . Now she's gone, and nothing can replace her. But you have to push on.'[50] Push on he did, but in the absolute certainty that the main event was over.

'But Charm's death hasn't bowled me over completely,' he told Elizabeth Riddell. 'As Scott Fitzgerald said when in the lowest physical and mental depths, "work, boy, work. It's therapy." '[51] Johnston gradually built himself a routine of writing in the morning, lunch, a nap in the afternoon, and then in the evening friends or perhaps Shane or Martin would drop in. In this way he dragged his life back onto an even keel. In particular, his devotion to Jason, who was again living at home and attending school as a day student, was of great importance to them both. Now a tall, handsome and affectionate thirteen-year-old, Jason grew very close to his father during this time. To a degree it was moot as to who was looking after whom — George prepared the meals and so on, but Jason kept a protective eye on his father, whose health was getting no better. Maisie Drysdale remembers Jason stealing the cigarettes and matches from George's pockets and hiding them, as a tactic to stop him smoking.

Johnston saw more of Martin from this time on, too. They talked more as friends now than as father and son, with a common interest in literature. He was no doubt pleased to see Martin following a path similar to his own, and with promise: Martin was reviewing for the *Bulletin* and the *Sydney Morning Herald*, and had started a poetry press at Sydney University, where he was again studying, part-time. In fact Martin's prodigious reading enabled him to pass on several authors of interest to his father: not only Borges and Ionesco (whom Johnston had referred to in his 'Aspects of the Novel' lecture), but also Seferis, Camus and Nabokov were among those who were to prove of use in his current writing.

There is evidence of this increased interest in modern writers of what might loosely be called the existentialist school in Johnston's working notes for the third volume of the trilogy. There are references to several of the authors mentioned, as well as to Kafka, Cavafy and Carlo Levi. As he had done when approaching *Clean Straw for Nothing*, he typed out extracts from the works of others, and in most cases they read more like wise maxims addressed to himself than like material that he could put to specific use in a novel. For instance, he copied out the quotation from T. S. Eliot:

> *There is only the fight to recover what has been lost*
> *And found and lost again and again.*[52]

and from Nabokov's *Pale Fire*:

> *One gets so accustomed to another's life running alongside one's own that a sudden turn off on the part of the parallel satellite causes in one a feeling of stupefaction, emptiness and injustice.*

and a very pithy quotation from Orwell on the subject of autobiography, which is

> *only to be trusted when it reveals something disgraceful. A man who gives a good account of himself is probably lying, since any life viewed from the inside is simply a series of defeats.*

And getting closer to David Meredith's mental functions, he produces a quotation from Roger Shattock's *The Banquet Years*:

> *Given the courage, we live by moments of interference between past and present, moments in which time comes back into phase with itself. It is the only meaning of history. We search the past not for other creatures, but for our own lost selves.*

Difficult as it is to find any particular connection between these quotations and what emerged in the third volume of the trilogy, the general air of introspection, and theme of gaining what has been lost, whether it is Cressida or his own youth or the society he once knew, are all consistent with Meredith's continuing quest for a shape and a meaning to his life.

With family and friends drawing closer to him, Johnston was never short of companionship in this last year of his life. He even managed a new relationship with a woman. He had known Jill Porter since just after his return from Greece, when he went to her home for a reunion party with Ruth Park and

D'Arcy Niland. She had always found Johnston interesting and attractive, and he had liked her. She had been separated from her husband for some years, so there was no reason why they should not seek comfort in each other, and this is what they did. She stayed often at Raglan Street, and George came to rely on her as a 'security blanket', as she termed it. His health put sex out of the question, but he did eventually ask her to marry him, a proposition that Porter felt neither of them took seriously, because they both knew he was dying. She was a loving friend, who got on well with the children, particularly Jason, who told her: 'You can come here as much as you want, but you can't be my mother.'[53]

The new year of 1970 brought slices of fortune. In January, Ray Crooke's portrait of Johnston won the Archibald prize. Crooke had painted Clift also, but this one was better, and better also than Drysdale's portrait of George. It has him sitting at a table with his hands in front of him and a book near by. The simplified but strongly sculptured head and hands are lit by a pale glow and suggest an inner, radiant energy, while the arms and torso are insubstantial and merge into the dark-green background. It is a ghostly but wonderful picture of Johnston, capturing several aspects of his person – strength, fragility, grace, fear and his unique body language.

Then in February *Clean Straw for Nothing* won the $1000 Moomba Book Prize in Melbourne, and followed it up by winning the Miles Franklin award, emulating the first volume. 'I have a really swollen-headed ambition now to do the hat trick,'[54] he wrote to Pat Johnston. Around this time he was appointed by Prime Minister John Gorton to the Australian Council for the Arts. He had met Gorton recently at Russell Drysdale's house, where Gorton was staying while having his portrait painted. The luck continued when he was awarded the OBE, and went along to Canberra on 1 May 1970 to have it formally presented by Her Majesty in person. Finally, it was all capped off when Shane gave him the news that he was to be a grandfather.

He was sufficiently aware of the realities of his situation to have a new Will drawn up, which made Russell Drysdale and Ray Crooke executors, and Shane and the Drysdales

appointed legal guardians of Jason. Not that this meant Johnston was giving up the fight: he continued on as he always
had, so far as his strength would allow. Jill Porter insists that
he was 'never morose', that he never complained, even when
the pain was obvious, but remained cheerfully himself, still
smoking, drinking and biting his nails, still garrulous as ever,
still capable of topping anyone else's story. He did make
some effort to give up smoking: a friend of Porter subjected
him to hypnosis, but Johnston complained that it was no use
because if he could not smoke he could not write. So nothing
changed. He did at times discuss death with Porter, and told
her he had for a long time been interested 'in the process of
dying',[55] by which he presumably meant that he was very
conscious of what was happening to him, and from time to
time he could observe himself in a detached way, as if he
were looking at someone else. His prolonged focusing on the
character of David Meredith might well have been a mental
training ground for this. Yet, even when taking an interest in
his own death, it would seem that he never allowed himself
to descend into self-pity or morbidity. His old colleague from
Argus days, Greeba Jamison, paid him a visit in April 1970,
and found him looking 'sick, tired, but somewhere faintly
was the George Johnston of the *Argus* days'.[56] Jack and Pat
Johnston saw him soon after, and were concerned at the
deterioration.

The main problem was still lack of breath. Tuberculosis and
surgery had reduced his lung function drastically, but as well
as this he had chronically obstructed airways from the years
of heavy smoking, and this made it impossible for him to
walk far. He had not been able to go upstairs in the house for
pretty well the whole time they lived there, but realising the
need for exercise he forced himself to take brief journeys
along Raglan Street, resting often on the way. These modest
excursions to the world outside became important to him,
partly because they supplied him with the structural idea for
the final volume of the trilogy. And whatever else was happening to him, it was this task that was now the most important thing in his life, and he was determined to last out long
enough to complete it.

Johnston decided to call this volume *A Cartload of Clay*, a title appropriate for Meredith's final act, in which his own mortality and insignificance occupy much of his mental time. He was of the firm belief now that 'any serious work of creative fiction must be autobiographical in a lesser or greater degree, since the author's most reliable touchstone and yardstick to experience and to emotion must always be himself', a view he expounded in March of that year in an ABC talk for schools.[57] Adhering strictly to this belief, he now fashioned Meredith's movements around his own brief walks, thus continuing on a reduced level the idea of the journey that runs on a grander scale through *Clean Straw for Nothing*. Although his physical journeys are short, they serve to stimulate long range 'journeys' of his memory, so that there is a continual shifting in the narrative between his immediate experiences as he trudges his suburban street, and the soaring flights of his mind as it freely ranges into the past. When the particular memory ends, we are brought back to the present with Meredith sitting on a bus-stop seat or pottering about the house. Often these memories are of his time in China, a time oddly neglected in the previous two volumes, and yet one that contains significant moments in Meredith's (and Johnston's) life: his meeting with the poet Wen Yi-tuo, and his affair with 'Phoebe' (of the hogs' bristles), his memory of the dead babies wedged in the trees along the Pan Lung river, the sight of the gum-trees that might have been taken from Australia in the last century by Chinese miners at Bendigo, where his family came from. Meredith's task, as he sees it, is to find links between the disparate moments of time and space in his life: 'To try to plot the arabesque that linked everything together' (*CofC* 37).

The striking difference between *A Cartload of Clay* and the previous volumes is the inclusion of the existing events of Meredith's life, not just the walks, but his activities around the house and his discussions with his son, Julian (Meredith has only two children). He is lonely, but he nevertheless battles on doggedly, attempting to sustain an interest in the world about him, a world that increasingly eludes his understanding. There is a distinct sense of Meredith attempting to

'tidy up' the remaining threads of his life in order to push on
to something else. Thus, the links with the past have to be
forged, and certain painful obstructions cleared away — the
death of Cressida, for instance, which he describes in its
slightly theatrical grimness with its note bearing the Keats
quotation, being of course, largely a re-enactment of his
memory of Clift's death. Meredith's reading of Camus and
others has helped him to make sense of his own life and
death, but he is a loss to understand Cressida's:

> *In the end, he had come to believe, with Camus (during this*
> *period he did much reading and re-reading of Camus, espe-*
> *cially* Le Mythe de Sisyphe)*, that if existence was, in the*
> *final result, without meaning, the true revolt against its*
> *absurdity was not in suicide but in continuing to live; in, as*
> *Camus put it, 'dying unreconciled and not of one's own free*
> *will'.*
>
> *But this offered no explanation of the haunting and terrible*
> *enigma of Cressida's death. What had prompted her action?*
> *Which philosophy did she support? What writer was she*
> *reading? (It was* The Possessed, Dostoyevsky, *that was the*
> *book open — that was still open — upon her desk).* (CofC
> 124)

This little indictment of Dostoevsky (the suggestion is un-
mistakable that Cressida has been influenced by the novel)
may be based on Clift's actual reading at the time of her death
— evidence is not available — but one is reminded of Johnston's lifelong hatred of Dostoevsky, and of what he used to
call 'the Dostoyevsky thing' when he spoke to Patrick Greer
about it on Hydra on many occasions. Just what he meant by
this phrase is a mystery; a rough guess would put it down as
Dostoevsky's belief in the irrational soul, but I doubt that
Johnston read him thoroughly enough to grasp this element
in his work.

Once the enigmas of the past have been accounted for or
mentioned, there is left the fearful matter of Meredith attempting to come to terms with the dark and final experience that
threatens to engulf him. In writing of such things, Johnston
produces clear, intelligent imagery and cool, objective self-
representation:

> *If at this stage you were to imagine the scene being presented*
> *on the stretched-out oblong of the modern cinema screen it*

*would be most interesting to visualize it through whatever is
the opposite to a zoom lens; the retreating viewpoint, that is,
soaring higher and higher like an escaped balloon: focused at
the figure of Meredith huddled lonely and solitary on his
mundane suburban bus seat, diminishing him to an unidenti-
fied man, to a foreshortened pigmy, to a speck, to a nothing,
the surroundings of his suburb rushing in on all sides to fill
the screen . . .*

*You might say that this, in a symbolic sense, is one of his
basic problems. Not all of his problems, for he has sickness to
contend with, and grief and loneliness and certain guilts and
other fears, but certainly* one *of his problems. He is, in a
word, frightened. He is frightened of what surrounds him. He
has been frightened by what has happened to him, but he is
even more frightened by what might yet be in store for him
. . . he is genuinely afraid (with, you might admit, some
reason) that these surroundings which you have just observed
will take him, or what is left of him, and swallow it all down
— the ageing, scrawny residual bone and flesh and gristle and
humours and passions and fears and hopes and emotions of
David Meredith — yes, and the fingernails too, or what is left
of them — and it will all mean no more than one gulp in the
crowded clanging of the preoccupied helter-skelter world, and
afterwards no echo left, no trace, nothing. Nothing at all.*

This is what frightens him. (CofC 126–8)

This extract is characteristic of the tone and subject-matter
of *A Cartload of Clay*: the tortuous intensities of relationships
between Meredith, other people and his country are gone,
and along with them the accusations of betrayal and the
striving after meaning that dominate the first two volumes.
Instead, the mood of *A Cartload of Clay*, even in dealing with
his fear of death, is reflective and philosophical, appropriate
to its frequent references to China, and indeed Meredith's
physical and mental journeys might even be called meditations, conducted as they are without passion, without moralising, without optimism. 'The chief thing was to keep on
living,' he quotes from the poet Rilke (*CofC* 73). This is rather
forced on him by his physical condition, but there is a glim-
mer of sageness running through the narrative of this novel,
which suggests that the attempt at self-reconstruction in
Clean Straw for Nothing was beginning to pay dividends for
Johnston himself.

Gradually Meredith's memories fade in prominence and are replaced by his immediate experiences: the present is over-taking the past. While drowsing on his bus-stop seat, he is suddenly brought face to face with a particular representative of this immediate present: the 'Ocker',[58] a coarse-minded conformist, whose values are contrasted in Meredith's mind with those of his son, Julian, who with his 'shyness and sensitivity, his bewildered gropings for a place in a society concerned with things and not ideas' (*CofC* 72), has no place in the 'Ocker's' scheme of things. Meredith, however, stands between the 'Ocker' and Julian, as a man who knows both sides, a legacy of his broad experience going back over years of travel, war and Depression. For Meredith knows that if Australia is to be understood then the 'Ocker' must somehow be accepted as part of it, albeit the worst part. He rises from his seat and walks together with the 'Ocker', until they even-tually return to Meredith's house. There follows a sustained scene where the two men attempt to talk intelligently, although there is an unbridgeable gap of experience between them. Despite his companion's fatuity and racism, Meredith neither judges nor patronises, nor attempts to accommodate his narrowness. Meredith tells him that he and his family have lived in Greece:

> '*Shit, eh! With all them bloody dagoes. How did you go?*'
> '*Greeks, not dagoes.*'
> '*All the same. All wogs. But how did you go. I mean actually livin' with 'em?*'
> '*Fine. We loved it.*'
> '*But ... didn't you tell me you got kids? Were they with you?*'
> '*Oh sure.*'
> '*But what about their schoolin'? What did they do about ...*'
> '*They went to school with the Greek kids. At the Greek school.*'
> '*You don't say!*' *He shook his head in admiring wonder.*
> (CofC 157)

Johnston told his brother, Jack, and Pat that he detested the 'ocker' in Australian life, and yet they saw the irony that in many respects Jack, whom he had idealised so much in *My Brother Jack*, was exactly the kind of man he would label an 'ocker' in different circumstances.[59] I think Johnston found himself in two minds about this kind of stereotype 'plain Aussie', because not only did he understand it well through his brother and father and the life he had grown up in, but he was, and always remained, a little 'ockerish' himself. The film-maker Geoff Collings, with whom Johnston made a long trip through the Kimberleys and elsewhere soon after returning from Greece, said that Johnston was constantly filled with wonder at the beauty they saw in the outback, but that equally constantly his most characteristic response to it all was 'Shit, eh',[60] which is stereotypical Australian understatement, or non-statement, but which Johnston used with great enjoyment, and a little play-acting. Like many Australian artists, writers and intellectuals, he liked the 'ocker' style, but not its cultural implications. The ambivalence is to a degree evident in his handling of the 'ocker' figure in *A Cartload of Clay*.

The novel stops, unfinished, before this scene ends. Martin Johnston believes that his father intended to make Meredith go on a final walk with his son, Julian, in a protest march, and that to save his breath he was to take a short cut across King's Cross. It is here that Meredith was to meet his death, beaten up in an alley by a gang of young toughs ('ockers'?), and unable in his frail condition to survive the ordeal. 'So much', Martin wrote in an article, 'for [Meredith's] attempt to understand the young.'[61]

A Cartload of Clay is a difficult novel to evaluate, not only because it remains unfinished. It is simpler and more spare than either of the previous two volumes, although its central interest in Meredith's humble actions and meditations keeps it sufficiently consistent with these novels to be a true completion of the trilogy. It contains a large proportion of Johnston's best and most mature prose, written with great care and more discipline than in any previous novel. In this work his days of the purple passage and the overworked adjective were well behind him.

Some friends of Johnston found its melancholy tone and its preoccupation with death depressing, Nancy Keesing among them. But she also found it to be a fitting finale to a highly impressive achievement. In fact Keesing makes some valuable comments on the trilogy as a whole work. She argues that David Meredith's public and private life from childhood to death is representative of a whole generation of Australians who were children during World War I:

> *Many retain insecurities even in success . . . It may be this very insecurity which leads to the further paradox that most of these artists are fiercely Australian and have interpreted their country in books and on canvas more diversely, truthfully, and on the whole more symbolically, than most who came before them. Their manner, too, seems more distinctively Australian than that of their immediate predecessors or their present juniors. They are represented by numerous thinly disguised characters in Johnston's trilogy.*[62]

This is certainly the case, and it is also true that, like Meredith, this generation had its character formed in the Depression and World War II, leaving them with a further understanding of the fragility of this country's identity, and making them more determined to shoulder the responsibility of establishing that identity. This goal was complicated by, and to some degree in conflict with, an appetite for a larger experience, awakened in them by the violent international experience that the conflicts gave them, so that when peace came it felt dull and routine to many Australians, who saw nothing to look forward to but a quiet life unnoticed by the rest of the world. Thus many of them, like Meredith and Cressida, like Johnston and Clift, became expatriates of one sort or another, either in a spirit of rejection or just drifting into it, both as physical and imaginative exiles, torn in a love/hate relationship with their country of origin.

The Meredith trilogy is, then, the expression of an era in Australian life. Like its great predecessor *The Fortunes of Richard Mahony*, the Meredith trilogy begins on the broad canvas of relations between the central character and his society, goes through a period of disillusioning absence from Australia, and finally focuses closely and sharply and more exclusively on the personality of its central character. And just as Richardson's novel is what Dame Leonie Kramer calls a 'memorial' to those who 'failed' in their struggle in the last century to come to terms with Australian society,[63] so is

Johnston's trilogy a testimony to the same struggle, and to a similar kind of failure, for those in the first half of this century.

As David Meredith and George Johnston grow closer together in *A Cartload of Clay*, their identities become indistinguishable. In this state, the only fitting, indeed the only possible end to Meredith's journey is the end of his creator. Just as in autobiography, the most complete form of ending in autobiographical fiction is the unfinished work, in which the final interruption to the self-exploration has been made by death itself.

Around May or June 1970 an X-Ray failed to confirm the suspicion that TB was active again, but Johnston had often to fight for breath for some minutes, and was left exhausted by the effort. He refused, however, to go to hospital. He told Jill Porter that he could not bear to end with his life ebbing away in a ward, and was determined to go on as normally as possible. This at times caused Porter concern: one evening when he did not come home at the expected time, she had visions of him lying in a gutter somewhere. When she checked with the people he was with, he was cheerfully drinking and smoking as ever, and had been delayed only by his inability to stop one-upping the yarns of his friends. He was still writing as much as he could, and in June he published a review in the *Sydney Morning Herald*, in which he reminisced engagingly about his acquaintance with Arthur Waley, and heaped uncarping praise on the book under discussion.[64]

On Monday 20 July he turned fifty-eight. On the Wednesday morning after, the 22nd, Jill Porter received a phone call from Jason: 'Can you come over? I think dad's dead.' Jason had gone in to give his father his morning kiss, and found him still, lying half out of bed.[65] When Jill arrived, the doctor and Ray Crooke were already there. It was exactly a year and a fortnight, to the day, after the death of Charmian Clift. The doctor who had treated him throughout most of his illness since 1964 described the cause of death as

> *tuberculosis ... a major contributor, but heavy smoking I believe also played a big part in his developing severe chronic obstructive lung disease — in other words both were involved*

*in his increasingly depleted breathing reserve. His tuberculo-
sis was probably not active when he died, although he was
still having treatment.*[66]

The newspapers carried many fine tributes. Elizabeth Riddell in the *Australian* recalled a recent party:

*About halfway through the evening a pretty young girl
joined the party and it got through to her that George was a
celebrity on her medium, television.*

*'Are you that George Johnston?' she breathed, and sat at
his feet for the rest of the evening. Those of us who weren't
jealous felt like cheering.*[67]

Elsewhere in the article, Riddell emphasised her knowledge
of Johnston's irrepressible energy and courage, and his un-
pretentiousness. John Moses in the *Sunday Telegraph* claimed
him for journalists: 'one of us', he said, and described his
generation's image of Johnston as

*... the reporter all reporters wanted romantically to be:
lean-faced, tough, trench-coated, covering wars, rebellion,
earth-quake, pestilence and famine, passport a palimpsest of
indecipherable, rubber-stamped symbols.*[68]

This description would have secretly pleased Johnston,
though his outward reaction would probably have been deri-
sive laughter. After all, he had already demolished that picture of himself in David Meredith.

Johnston's old colleague Geoffrey Hutton, who had never
had an unqualified liking for Johnston, wrote a piece in the
Age praising his 'inexhaustible talent for making friends' and
his irresistible energy.[69] Johnston knew, well before he died,
that he had achieved a place in the minds of Australian
readers and in the history of Australian literature, although
the exact importance of that place was unsettled. It was one
ambition, among many, fulfilled: to receive the praise and
admiration of his profession, of his friends and of his readers.
David Meredith was to die lonely, unsung and with the bitter
taste of failure in his mouth. George Johnston did not: he
died with a host of friends praising him and in the knowledge that he had lived richly and that some of that richness
had been transformed into art that would give generations
after him much pleasure and insight.

Johnston was cremated at Chatswood in Sydney on 24 July.

At the funeral service the Reverend Ted Noffs called him 'a giant of a man' before a crowd of 150 mourners. His ashes were taken in charge by Ray and June Crooke, and what became of them is a delightful story.[70] Some months before this, Crooke had bought a house and some land near Yerinbool some miles south of Sydney. The name of the property was Little Forest, and it is a beautiful and secluded place, to which the Crookes were constantly inviting Johnston, but his health prevented him from making the journey. He was, however, excited by Crooke's descriptions, and somewhere tucked away in that extraordinary memory a bell rang of an account of a pastoral retreat somewhere in Horace. Soon he had it, and 'bright-eyed like an excited little boy at a party' he read it out to Ray and June Crooke. 'We were stunned and moved by its uncanny and detailed aptness — a kind of *déjà vu* in reverse — on the part of Horace AND George! In utterance it became a timeless, stateless evocation of the goodness and the satisfaction of the simple life.' It read:

> This used to be among my prayers — a portion of land not so very large but which should contain a garden and near the homestead a spring of ever-flowing water and a little forest to complete it.

So when they gathered George's ashes, the Crookes decided that he should at last get his visit to Little Forest, for they would bury the ashes there, close to the spring, not far from the homestead, and near the bush. Jill Porter and her son, Richard, Shane and her husband, Bob, Geoff and Dahl Collings and the Crookes all gathered together in what was far from being a solemn occasion. Unfortunately, Charmian Clift's ashes had been lost, so they could not bury them together. Lightheartedly they dug a hole. The first thing that came up was a rabbit trap. Then they placed the ashes in an Arnott's biscuit tin, buried it, and together proceeded to plant over a thousand daffodils, a flower they chose because 'more than once he recalled his U.K. days in the Cotswolds and the sight there he loved most — the scattered mass of daffodils flowering on the hillside'.[71] Later, Jill Porter became the owner of Little Forest, and she had a stone laid at the burial spot inscribed with the Horace quotation as an epitaph. The final

words of the story may best be left to June Crooke, the close
friend of both Johnston and Clift:

> *Since then the daffodils have bloomed, though the dry years
> have not been kind to them. It is always surprising in a good
> year how successfully the nodding, shimmering patches of
> gold, cream and green can hold their own image yet also
> merge fittingly into the scraggy Australian landscape. George
> I know would have voiced the most appropriate eloquent
> words of approval and appreciation.*[72]

Notes

Chapter I

1. This is confirmed in two independent interviews: Jack and Patricia Johnston, interview with Chester Eagle, 29 July 1980; and Marjorie Quinton (Johnston's sister), interview with GK, 1982.
2. Patricia Johnston, interview with Chester Eagle, 29 July 1980.
3. GJ to Jack and Patricia Johnston, 3 March 1965 (all three quotations).
4. Elsie Johnston, interview with GK, 1983.
5. Johnston exaggerates the social gap between the two families in *MBJ*, where he has Minnie 'Having grown up with governesses, pony carts, riding instructors, music teachers and private lessons in oils and pen-painting', and her father is the *owner* of several newspapers, as well as a goldmine. The Editor of the Bendigo *Advertiser* was never so well off. There are many details of the nineteenth-century ancestors of the Merediths given in the novel that cannot be checked against the Johnston family background. Where Johnston got them from is unknown.
6. Some years after the war the name was changed to Avalon, its name in *MBJ*.
7. In *MBJ* David Meredith describes his father as a hypochondriac who 'imagines that the gas he swallowed at Vimy Ridge was the cause of his severe bronchitis'. Both Jack and Marjorie, in the interviews cited above, insist on their father's reluctance to talk about his war injuries. One might imagine that mustard-gas poisoning

would not help severe bronchitis, if that is what his chest complaint was.

8. Jack Johnston, interview with Chester Eagle, 29 July 1980.
9. Minnie Johnston was not a qualified nursing sister, as is Minnie Meredith in *MBJ*. Her duties as a VAD nurse would have been mainly caring for convalescents, and not the casualty and surgery duties of her fictional counterpart. Mrs Johnston gave up nursing after the war.
10. Jack and Patricia Johnston, interview with Chester Eagle, 29 July 1980.
11. *Closer to the Sun* 17. (Publication details for this and other works of Johnston are given in the Bibliography, as are the works of Clift and the works of which they were joint authors.)
12. *Journey through Tomorrow* 112.
13. Student records of Brighton Technical School.
14. The school magazine *Sea Spray* 1:4 (1926) 27.
15. Ron Ridge, interview with GK, 1982.
16. Employment details from the Wages Register of Troedel & Cooper (La Trobe Library). Fully qualified artists received £8 per week. An interesting detail from these records is that there was a male Offset Machinist called H. Midgeley working there at the same time as Johnston. In *MBJ* Meredith's first wife is called Helen Midgeley.
17. Enrolment records of the National Gallery School for 1927.
18. Richard Haese, *Rebels and Precursors*, Allen Lane, Melbourne, 1981, p. 16.
19. Ron Ridge, interview with GK, 1982.
20. Haese, op. cit. 20.
21. Sam Atyeo, interview with GK, 1984. For an outline of Atyeo's life and work, see Jennifer Phipps, 'Sam Atyeo', *Art and Australia* 19:2 (1981) 182–9.
22. See Chapter VI for the account of a Melbourne murder that Johnston used in the novel.
23. Haese, op. cit. 20.
24. Jack and Patricia Johnston, interview with Chester Eagle, 29 July 1980.
25. Ron Ridge, interview with GK, 1982.
26. Jack and Patricia Johnston, interview with Chester Eagle,

29 July 1980.
27. Ron Ridge, interview with GK, 1982.
28. Jack and Patricia Johnston, interview with Chester Eagle, 29 July 1980.
29. Hartley (Bill) Watson, interview with GK, 1983. Watson is a former president of the Shiplovers' Society of Victoria, and a former Olympic yachtsman.
30. The personnel records of the *Argus* show that he began work with the paper on 2 October 1933.
31. Geoffrey Hutton, interview with GK, 1981.
32. Elsie Johnston, interview with GK, 1984.

Chapter II

1. Patricia Johnston, interview with Chester Eagle, 29 July 1980.
2. The affair with Olga is based on confident surmising by Elsie Johnston, interview with GK, 1984.
3. Elsie Johnston, interview with GK, 1984.
4. Ibid. Though she later qualified it to GK as 'normal bride's nerves'. According to Patricia Johnston, interview with Chester Eagle, 29 July 1980, George whispered to her as he left the Church that he 'wished the roof would fall on him' to save him from a fate worse than death. This, however, may be a case of reality confused with fiction, because the idea occurs to David Meredith on page 245 of *MBJ*.
5. Elsie Johnston, interview with GK, 1984.
6. This is a mistake, and probably refers to Mackie Grove, East Brighton, which they moved to some time in 1939.
7. Letter from Rosalind Landells to GK, 29 Aug. 1981 (possession GK).
8. Both incidents from Bruce Kneale, interview with GK, 1985.

9. Elsie Johnston, interview with GK, 1984.
10. Patricia Johnston, interview with Chester Eagle, 29 July 1980.
11. Elsie Johnston, interview with GK, 1984.
12. Letter from GJ to Elsie Johnston, 7 Nov. 1963 (possession GK).
13. Letter from Rosalind Landells to GK, 29 Aug. 1981.
14. Bruce Kneale, interview with GK, 1985.
15. Bruce Kneale, interview with GK, 1985.
16. Patricia Johnston, interview with Chester Eagle, 29 July 1980.
17. Elsie Johnston, interview with GK, 1985.
18. Introduction to *Grey Gladiator*.
19. Ibid. 84.
20. The Commander of *Sydney*, Captain J. A. Collins, co-operated warmly with Johnston's research, and later commented, somewhat reservedly, that the book was 'a fair survey of the activities in the Mediterranean while *Sydney* was there'. HMAS *Sydney* was sunk in 1941 in action against the German Raider *Steiermark* in the Indian Ocean.
21. Letter from W. G. Cousins (editor at Angus & Robertson) to GJ, 5 April 1941 (Mitchell Library).
22. Letter from GJ to W. G. Cousins, 30 May 1941 (Mitchell Library).
23. Ibid.
24. Jack Johnston, interview with Chester Eagle, 29 July 1980.
25. Jack Johnston, interview with Chester Eagle, 29 July 1980.
26. Bruce Kneale, interview with GK, 1985.
27. Letter from GJ to W. G. Cousins, n.d. (Mitchell Library).
28. Bruce Kneale, interview with GK, 1985.
29. Elsie Johnston, interview with GK, 1985.
30. Bruce Kneale, interview with GK, 1985.

Chapter III

1. This succession of *Argus* editors was compiled from *Who's Who in Australia*.
2. Bruce Kneale, interview with GK, 1985.
3. W. G. Cousins to GJ, 26 Nov. 1941 (Mitchell Library).
4. *Australia at War* 5, 275.
5. Ibid. 227—8.
6. Ibid. 4.
7. See George Johnston, 'Gallipoli Paintings' in *Art and Australia*, Sept. 1967, pp. 466—9. Nolan confirmed this in an interview with GK, 1982.
8. Osmar White, interview with GK, 1983.
9. Personnel records of the *Argus* and *Australasian* Limited.
10. The notebook was begun on Friday, 13 February, but he backdated entries to 3 January, based on 'enquiries, examinations of reports etc., of earlier activity'. The notebook, a simple exercise book, was discovered in an American rare book catalogue and purchased in 1981 by the National Library, Canberra, who published it in 1985 as *War Diary 1942*.
11. This account of the state of Port Moresby when they arrived was given by Osmar White, interview with GK, 1983.
12. Sidney Nolan recalls Johnston telling him these things in Greece in the 1950s: interview with GK, 1982.
13. Bruce Kneale, interview with GK, 1985.
14. Osmar White, interview with GK, 1983.
15. Osmar White, interview with GK, 1983.
16. Elsie Johnston, interview with GK, 1984.
17. Geoffrey Hutton, interview with GK, 1981.
18. *Life,* 5 July 1943, pp. 104—12.
19. Geoffrey Hutton, interview with GK, 1981.
20. Geoffrey Hutton, interview with GK, 1981.
21. Elsie Johnston, interview with GK, 1984.
22. Greeba Jamison to GK, 13 Feb. 1983.

23. Geoffrey Hutton, 'He Died Alive', *Age*, 23 July 1970.
24. Bruce Kneale, interview with GK, 1985.
25. *Skyscrapers in the Mist* 99.
26. GJ to W. G. Cousins, 28 Jan. 1944 (Mitchell Library).
27. *Journey through Tomorrow* 379.
28. Ibid. 84.
29. Ibid. 100−1.
30. *Argus*, 25 Aug. 1944, p. 2.
31. 'Battle Looms in Kwangsi Province', *Argus*, 23 Sept. 1944, p. 2.
32. 'Communism Spreads in Southern Europe', *Argus*, 4 Dec. 1944, p. 2.
33. K. E. I. Wallace-Crabbe, 'Pens and Yarns, Wings and Wheels' (unpublished MS).
34. Elsie Johnston to W. G. Cousins, 28 March 1945 (Mitchell Library).
35. Bruce Kneale, interview with GK, 1985.
36. Bruce Kneale, interview with GK, 1985.
37. *Journey through Tomorrow* 97−8.
38. Ibid. 117−18.
39. Ibid. 120.
40. Ibid. 218.
41. Ibid. 223−4.
42. Ibid. 284.
43. Ibid. 288.
44. Ibid. 291−2.
45. Ibid. 296.
46. 'End of the War Brings Big Problems', *Argus*, 20 Aug. 1945.
47. *Journey through Tomorrow* 399.
48. Ibid. 389.
49. Ibid. 396.
50. Ibid. 397.
51. Geoffrey Hutton, 'He died Alive'.
52. Bruce Kneale, interview with GK, 1985.
53. Greeba Jamison to GK, 13 Feb. 1983.
54. *The Far Road* 47.
55. Ibid. 75.

Chapter IV

1. GJ to W. G. Cousins of Angus & Robertson, 22 Feb. 1946 (Mitchell Library).
2. Elsie Johnston, interview with GK, 1983.
3. W. G. Cousins to GJ, 18 June 1946 (Mitchell Library).
4. Greeba Jamison to GK 13 Feb. 1983.
5. Hume Dow, interview with GK, 1982.
6. Bruce Kneale, interview with GK, 1985.
7. Margaret Backhouse (*née* Clift), interview with GK, 1982, supplied most of the information about the Clift family background.
8. Charmian Clift, interview with Hazel Deberg, 3 June 1965, National Library, Canberra.
9. It has not been possible to verify this information, which came from Toni Burgess, interview with GK, 1982, and supported by Grace Edwards, interview with GK, 1983. Edwards heard Johnston and Clift refer to the adopted child on several occasions, and Johnston told Edwards that Clift's deep regret over the matter might have explained her frequent retreats into silence and her often otherwise inexplicable tears. Bruce Kneale also recalls hearing about the child, which he believes was born when Clift was about fifteen years old. There is mention of an unspecified 'disaster' in her life when she was eighteen (see 'Taking the Wrong Road' in *The World of Charmian Clift* 20). Against all this it should be pointed out that Margaret Backhouse seriously doubts the truth of the story of an illegitimate child.
10. In the possession of Martin Johnston.
11. Edward Heffernan, interview with GK, 1982.
12. Leo Kenney to Edward Heffernan, 26 May 1946.
13. Edward Heffernan, interview with GK, 1982.
14. 'Greener Grows the Grass', n.d., TS, National Library, Canberra. I do not mean that Clift's criticism applied to Kneale, just the physical appearance. 'Eaton' suggests

Kneale's English style of dressing and talking. Kneale has read the typescript and agrees.
15. Ibid.
16. Ibid.
17. Quoted by Clifford Tolchard, in 'My Husband George: My Wife Charmian', *Walkabout*, Jan. 1969, pp. 26–9.
18. Bruce Kneale, interview with GK, 1985.
19. Greeba Jamison to GK, 13 Feb. 1983.
20. Bruce Kneale, interview with GK, 1985.
21. Elsie Johnston, interview with GK, 1983.
22. Bruce Kneale, interview with GK, 1985.
23. Elsie Johnston, interview with GK, 1983.
24. Gae Johnston, interview with GK, 1982.
25. 'The Meredith Papers', n.d., typed notes, National Library, Canberra.
26. Ibid.
27. Hume Dow, interview with GK, 1985.
28. Elsie Johnston, interview with GK, 1983.
29. Several colleagues of Johnston confirm this story, told to GK by Greeba Jamison, letter 13 Feb. 1983.
30. Bruce Kneale, interview with GK, 1985.

Chapter V

1. Margaret Backhouse, interview with GK, 1982.
2. Elsie Johnston, interview with GK, 1983.
3. GJ to David Higham, 8 July 1954.
4. Ibid.
5. Margaret Backhouse, interview with GK, 1982.
6. Arthur Polkinghorne, interview with GK, 1982.
7. 'Why Write a Book?' *Sun*, 28 Nov. 1948.
8. 'Sydney Diary', *Sun*, 5 April 1948.
9. Charles Sriber, interview with GK, 1982.
10. Charles Sriber, interview with GK, 1982.

11. Albert Arlen to GK, 20 July 1984.
12. Ibid.
13. Mungo MacCallum, interview with GK, 1982.
14. Mungo MacCallum, interview with GK, 1982.
15. Johnston stated that 'Gavin Turley is really a composite of three separate newspaper reporters I once knew', in 'My Brother Jack', an ABC radio broadcast in *English for School Certificate* series, 6 March 1970.
16. Charles Sriber, interview with GK, 1982.
17. Neil Hutchison, interview with GK, 1982.
18. Biographical questionnaire, Bobbs-Merrill MSS, Lilly Library, University of Indiana, USA.
19. Neil Hutchison, interview with GK, 1982.
20. Neil Hutchison, interview with GK, 1982.
21. Toni Burgess, interview with GK, 1982.
22. Mungo MacCallum, interview with GK, 1982.
23. John Moses, 'George Johnston', *Sydney Telegraph*, 26 July 1970, p. 33.
24. Charles Sriber, interview with GK, 1982.
25. 'Why Write a Book?' *Sun*, 28 Nov. 1948.
26. Biographical questionnaire for GJ, Bobbs-Merrill MSS, Lilly Library, University of Indiana, USA.
27. Review of *High Valley* in *Argus*, 3 Sept. 1949.
28. Patricia Johnston, interview with Chester Eagle, 29 July 1980.
29. Patricia Johnston, interview with Chester Eagle, 29 July 1980. Marjorie, it must be said, has no memory of this event.
30. Hazel Tulley, interview with GK, 1982.
31. Toni Burgess, interview with GK, 1982.
32. Biographical questionnaire, Bobbs-Merrill MSS, Lilly Library, University of Indiana, USA.
33. Greeba Jamison to GK, 13 Feb. 1983.
34. Ibid.

Chapter VI

1. Sheila Saint Lawrence, of Ann Watkins Inc. (Higham's US representative) to GJ, 11 May 1951.
2. GJ To George Ferguson of Angus & Robertson, 21 Aug. 1951 (Mitchell Library).
3. David Higham to Ann Watkins Inc., 3 April 1951.
4. Ibid.
5. Ibid.
6. Toni Burgess, interview with GK, 1982.
7. Toni Burgess, interview with GK, 1982.
8. Nan Hutton, 'Dipping into the World of Charmian', *Age*, 16 Aug. 1973.
9. Arlen had gone to London in 1951, but returned with Johnston's libretto still not done. He wrote the following year, pressing Johnston for the script, and this time Johnston advised that he was too busy working on *The Big Chariot*, and that Arlen should find another librettist. He did.
10. 'News of Earls Court — Fifteen Years Ago', in *The World of Charmian Clift* 55. The title echoes a Scott Fitzgerald story titled: 'News of Paris — Fifteen Years Ago'.
11. Sidney Nolan, interview with GK, 1982. See Chapter I.
12. Jennifer Phipps, 'Sam Atyeo', *Art and Australia* 19:2 (1981) 182—7.
13. Colin Colahan to GK, n.d., March 1982.
14. Ibid.
15. Colin Colahan, interview with GK, 1983. The portrait is in the possession of GK.
16. Reports on the death of Mary (Mollie) Dean in the *Argus*, 21 Nov. 1930 to March 1931.
17. Colin Colahan, interview with GK, 1983.
18. Colin Colahan, interview with GK, 1983.
19. Hazel Tulley, interview with GK, 1982.
20. GJ to George Ferguson, 21 Aug. 1951 (Mitchell Library).
21. Ibid.

22. GJ to Albert Arlen, 17 Sept, 1952.
23. Albert Arlen to GK, 20 July 1984, quoting GJ to Albert Arlen, 17 Sept. 1952.
24. GJ to George Ferguson, 8 Jan. 1953 (Mitchell Library).
25. 'Poet of Zen: George Johnston on Arthur Waley', *Sydney Morning Herald*, 6 June 1970, p. 20.
26. Charmian Clift's journal, typed notes in black 8vo folder, n.d., National Library, Canberra.
27. Ibid.
28. Ibid.
29. *The Big Chariot* 29 (both quotations).
30. Hazel Tulley, interview with GK, 1982.
31. Internal memo at Bobbs-Merrill, 13 Feb. 1953 (both review quotes).
32. Internal memo at Bobbs-Merrill, 22 March 1955.
33. GJ to Aubrey Cousins of Angus & Robertson, 8 April 1953 (Mitchell Library).
34. GJ to Morley Kennerley of Faber & Faber, 19 May 1953.
35. Sidney Nolan, interview with GK, 1982.
36. Sidney Nolan, interview with GK, 1982.
37. Hazel Tulley, interview with GK, 1982.
38. GJ to Gae Johnston, 26 Jan. 1954.
39. GJ to Aubrey Cousins, 17 Sept. 1953 (Mitchell Library).
40. Anthony Whitlock, interview with GK, 1982.
41. Medical records, Royal North Shore Hospital, Sydney.
42. GJ to Gae Johnston, 29 Jan. 1954.
43. GJ to David Higham, 25 April 1954.
44. *Mermaid Singing* 17.
45. Internal memo at Bobbs-Merrill, April 1954.
46. Ibid.
47. Hazel Tulley, interview with GK, 1982; confirmed independently by Anthony Whitlock, interview with GK, 1982.
48. Cynthia Nolan to Pat Flower, n.d. [March 1956].
49. Donald Horne, interview with GK, 1982.
50. Anthony Whitlock, interview with GK, 1982.
51. Neil Whitlock, interview with GK, 1982.
52. GJ to David Higham, 19 Oct. 1954.
53. GJ to David Higham, 19 Sept. 1955.

54. GJ to Paul Scott of Pearn, Pollinger & Higham, 28 Oct. 1954.
55. This story appears in *CSFN*, p. 138, but Anthony Whitlock thinks it could be true.
56. Anthony Whitlock, interview with GK, 1982.
57. Hazel Tulley, interview with GK, 1982.
58. Wilfred Thomas, interview with GK, 1983.
59. Wilfred Thomas, interview with GK, 1983.
60. Anthony Whitlock, interview with GK, 1982.
61. GJ to David Higham, 14 Sept. 1954.
62. Cedric Flower, interview with GK, 1982.
63. Cedric Flower, interview with GK, 1982.
64. Neil Whitlock, interview with GK, 1982.
65. Neil Whitlock, interview with GK, 1982.
66. Wilfred Thomas, interview with GK, 1983.
67. Cressida says this privately to Meredith in *CSFN*, p. 124, but Clift also said it at this moment at the party, according to Wilfred Thomas, interview with GK, 1983.

Chapter VII

1. GJ to David Higham, 30 Nov. 1954.
2. Cedric Flower, interview with GK, 1982.
3. Details of day-to-day life on Kalymnos are taken from *Mermaid Singing*, which is a reasonably reliable account of the way things were. The fact that Clift chose not to fictionalise it strongly indicates her intention that it be faithful to actualities.
4. Ibid.
5. GJ to David Higham, 29 Dec. 1954.
6. GJ to Gae Johnston, 16 Feb. 1960.
7. Internal memo at Bobbs-Merrill, n.d.
8. GJ to George Ferguson of Angus & Robertson, 29 March 1955 (Mitchell Library).

9. Ibid.
10. *Mermaid Singing* 42–3.
11. Cedric Flower, interview with GK, 1982.
12. David Higham to GJ, 8 July 1955.
13. GJ to George Ferguson, 29 March 1955 (Mitchell Library).
14. Cedric Flower, interview with GK, 1982.
15. David Higham to GJ, 8 July 1955.
16. GJ to David Higham, 28 July 1955.
17. Cedric Flower, interview with GK, 1982.
18. *Mermaid Singing* 151.
19. Martin Johnston, interview with GK, 1981.

Chapter VIII

1. V. Mingos, 'Island of Writers', *Pictures From Greece* (Athens), no. 29 (June 1958) 4–11.
2. Patrick Greer, interview with GK, 1983.
3. Sidney Nolan, interview with GK, 1982.
4. Sidney Nolan, interview with GK, 1982.
5. George Johnston, 'Gallipoli Paintings', *Art and Australia*, Sept. 1967, pp. 466–9.
6. 'With this book I am trying to develop a new character in Professor Challis, which I plan to use in subsequent thrillers of a similar nature, but with different settings.' GJ to David Higham, 13 March 1956.
7. Ibid.
8. Cedric Flower, 'The background to the letter from Cynthia Nolan to Pat Flower', Mitchell Library.
9. *Flaws in the Glass*, Jonathan Cape, London, 1981, p. 235.
10. Original letter in Mitchell Library.
11. Sidney Nolan, interview with GK, 1982.
12. Flower, op. cit.
13. Sidney Nolan, interview with GK, 1982.
14. Martin Johnston, interview with GK, 1981.

15. Cedric Flower, interview with GK, 1982.
16. Sidney Nolan, interview with GK, 1982.
17. Martin Johnston, interview with GK, 1981.
18. GJ to David Higham, 1 May 1957.
19. Grace Edwards, interview with GK, 1983.
20. GJ to David Higham, 1 May 1957.
21. Harold Ober Associates Inc. to Charmian (Johnston), 4 June 1957.
22. Grace Edwards, interview with GK, 1983.
23. *Peel me a Lotus* 116.
24. Charles Sriber, interview with GK, 1982.
25. *Peel me a Lotus* 37, 68.
26. Ibid. 90.
27. Anthony Kingsmill, interview with GK, 1983.

Chapter IX

1. *Peel me a Lotus* 163.
2. Patrick Greer, interview with GK, 1983.
3. Patrick Greer, 'George Johnston in Hydra', *London Magazine*, Nov./Dec. 1980, pp. 109–15.
4. Ibid.
5. Ibid.
6. Ibid.
7. Neil Hutchison, interview with GK, 1982.
8. Neil Hutchison, interview with GK, 1982.
9. Elizabeth Jane Howard, interview with GK, 1983.
10. Elizabeth Jane Howard, interview with GK, 1983.
11. Grace Edwards, interview with GK, 1983.
12. Charles Sriber, interview with GK, 1982.
13. Sidney Nolan, interview with GK, 1982.
14. Martin, then about eleven years old, would often have to go down to the Katsikas store and bring his parents home, he remembers, somewhat in the spirit of the Victo-

rian song 'Father, dear father, come home with me now'. Later, when he was in his teens, he would stay and listen to their talk. Interview with GK, 1981.

15. 'Perhaps the finest statement ever made on the art of fiction', he called it in 'Aspects of the Novel', a paper by GJ at an Australian Society of Authors' seminar, 9 Feb. 1968.
16. *The Darkness Outside* 162.
17. Grace Edwards, interview with GK, 1983.
18. GJ to David Higham, 20 Jan. 1959.
19. Ibid.
20. Charmian Clift to David Higham, 27 Jan. 1959.
21. *Closer to the Sun* 17.
22. Ibid. 18.
23. Ibid. 9.
24. *Peel me a Lotus* 127.
25. *Closer to the Sun* 39.
26. *Peel me a Lotus* 165.
27. *Closer to the Sun* 170.
28. Ibid. 319.
29. Charmian Clift, 'My Husband George', *POL* magazine, July 1969, p. 83.
30. Ibid.
31. GJ to David Higham, 23 March 1959.
32. *Closer to the Sun* 171.
33. GJ to David Higham, 23 July 1959.
34. Ibid.
35. Charmian Clift to David Higham, 23 July 1959.
36. Clift, 'My Husband George'.
37. Charles Sriber, interview with GK, 1982.
38. Janette Read, interview with GK, 1983.
39. Martin Johnston, interview with GK, 1981.
40. Charles Sriber, interview with GK, 1982.
41. Charles Sriber, interview with GK, 1982.
42. These details were included when he broke the news to Higham, saying that 'after much proscrastination I was finally leg-roped last week to a doctor in Athens, where X-Rays revealed that I've got TB'. GJ to David Higham, 26 Oct. 1959.

43. 'The Verdict', in *Strong Man from Piraeus and other stories*, Nelson, Melbourne, 1984, p. 156.
44. Ibid. 165.
45. Ibid. 172.
46. Grace Edwards, interview with GK, 1983.
47. Grace Edwards, interview with GK, 1983.
48. Grace Edwards, interview with GK, 1983.
49. GJ to Monica Preston, of David Higham Associates, 26 Oct. 1959.
50. David Higham to GJ, 30 Oct. 1959.
51. GJ to Gae Johnston, 16 Feb. 1960.
52. Ibid.
53. Ibid.
54. Clift, 'My Husband George'.
55. Ibid.
56. Ibid.
57. Susan Clilverd, interview with GK, 1982.
58. Didy Cameron, interview with GK, 1983.
59. Didy Cameron, interview with GK, 1983.
60. Clift, 'My Husband George'.
61. *The Far Road* 246.
62. Clift, 'My Husband George'.
63. Ibid.

Chapter X

1. Martin Johnston, interview with GK, 1982.
2. John Ryland, interview with GK, 1983.
3. Colin Simpson, *Greece*, Angus & Robertson, Sydney, 1968, ch. 4, pp. 105–6. Johnston was in fact forty-eight at that time.
4. Sidney Nolan, interview with GK, 1982.
5. George Johnston, 'Gallipoli Paintings', *Art and Australia* Sept. 1967, pp. 466–9.

6. David Higham to GJ, 10 Feb. 1961.
7. GJ to David Higham, 1 April 1961.
8. Elaine Dundy, *Finch, Bloody Finch*, Michael Joseph, London, 1980, pp. 274—5.
9. GJ to Elsie Johnston, 5 Oct. 1961.
10. Reprinted in *The World of Charmian Clift*, Ure Smith, Sydney, 1970, pp. 33—5.
11. Didy Cameron, interview with GK, 1983.
12. Simpson, *Greece* 106.
13. Ibid.
14. GJ to David Higham, 1 May 1961.
15. David Higham to GJ, 27 April 1961.
16. Charmian Clift to David Higham, 9 June 1961.
17. Harold Ober Inc. to GJ, 22 May 1961.
18. GJ to Elsie Johnston, 5 Oct. 1961.
19. Elsie Johnston to GJ, 13 Sept. 1962.
20. GJ to Elsie Johnston, 5 Oct. 1961.
21. GJ to David Higham, 3 Feb. 1962.
22. Elizabeth Jane Howard, interview with GK, 1983.
23. Harold Ober Inc. to GJ, 20 Aug. 1962.
24. Harold Ober Inc. to David Higham, 21 March 1962.
25. David Higham to Harold Ober Inc. 29 March 1962.
26. Grace Edwards, interview with GK, 1983. Meredith also spends a night in gaol in *CSFN* for striking a policeman during a public row with Cressida (pp. 274—82). The two incidents may well be connected, but the novel dates its version 1961, *before* they go on their visit to England in 1961—2. Grace Edwards is uncertain of the time, so Johnston may have had his run-in with the police in 1959, as part of the catastrophic events of that year.
27. Martin Johnston, interview with GK, 1982.
28. Charmian Clift, 'My Husband George', *POL* magazine, July 1969, p. 83.
29. TS, untitled, n.d., Johnston Estate Papers, National Library, Canberra.
30. Ibid.
31. Ibid.
32. Ibid.
33. Clift, 'My Husband George'.

34. GJ to David Higham, 11 Nov. 1962.
35. Charles Sriber, interview with GK, 1982.
36. GJ to Elsie Johnston, 15 Jan. 1963.
37. Ibid.
38. Ibid.
39. 'My Brother Jack', an ABC radio broadcast in *English for School Certificate* series, 6 March 1970.
40. GJ to Robert Knittel of William Collins Publishers, 3 Dec. 1962.
41. Clift, 'My Husband George'.
42. 'The Meredith Papers', TS, n.d., Johnston Estate Papers, National Library, Canberra.
43. 'Childhood — the Dollikos', typed notes, n.d., Johnston Estate Papers, National Library, Canberra.
44. 'The Meredith Papers'.
45. 'My Brother Jack'.
46. Greer Johnson and Chris Tiffin, 'The Evolution of George Johnston's David Meredith', *Australian Literary Studies* 2:2 (Oct. 1983) 170.
47. GJ to Elsie Johnston, 7 Nov. 1963.
48. GJ to Elsie Johnston, 15 Jan. 1963.
49. Ibid.
50. GJ to Elsie Johnston, 7 Nov. 1963.
51. 'Clean Straw for Nothing', typed notes, n.d., p. 1, Johnston Estate Papers, National Library, Canberra.
52. GJ to Elsie Johnston, 7 Nov. 1963.
53. 'Clean Straw for Nothing', p. 1.
54. GJ to John Ulm, Qantas Airlines, 19 Nov. 1963.
55. GJ to Gae Johnston, 12 Dec. 1963.
56. Ibid.
57. Ibid.
58. William Pownall, interview with GK, 1983.
59. GJ to Elsie Johnston, 5 Feb. 1964.
60. John Hetherington, 'An Australian Author in Greece Returns to His Native Land', *Age* Literary Supplement, 8 Feb. 1964, p. 21.
61. William Pownall, interview with GK, 1983.
62. Mungo MacCallum, interview with GK, 1982.
63. Sidney Nolan, interview with GK, 1982.

Chapter XI

1. GJ to Elsie Johnston, 5 Feb. 1964.
2. Charmian Clift, 'My Husband George', *POL* Magazine, July 1969, p. 85.
3. Anthony Kingsmill, interview with GK, 1983.
4. Martin Johnston, interview with GK, 1982.
5. Hal Porter, *The Extra*, Nelson, Melbourne, 1975, p. 115.
6. Mungo MacCallum, interview with GK, 1982.
7. Mungo MacCallum, interview with GK, 1982.
8. Patricia Johnston, interview with Chester Eagle, 29 July 1980.
9. Patricia Johnston, interview with Chester Eagle, 29 July 1980.
10. Patricia Johnston, interview with Chester Eagle, 29 July 1980.
11. Jack Johnston, interview with Chester Eagle, 29 July 1980.
12. GJ to David Higham, 25 March 1964.
13. GJ to Elsie Johnston, 30 April 1964.
14. Martin Johnston, interview with GK, 1982.
15. 'Terra Incognita Revisited', *Age*, 25 April 1964, p. 15.
16. GJ to David Higham, 1 May 1964.
17. GJ to Elsie Johnston, 7 June 1964.
18. The quotations in the rest of this paragraph are all taken from these notes, titled 'Clean Straw for Nothing', n.d., Johnston Estate Papers, National Library, Canberra.
19. Quoted by Kay Keavney in 'From George with Sadness', *Australian Women's Weekly*, 3 Sept. 1969, p. 13.
20. 'Clean Straw for Nothing'.
21. Ibid.
22. Sheila Carroll, interview (by telephone) with GK, 1985.
23. Anthony Kingsmill, interview with GK, 1983.
24. 'Coming Home', in *Images in Aspic*, ed. George Johnston, Horwitz, Sydney, 1965, pp. 13–18.
25. Mungo MacCallum, interview with GK, 1982.
26. Mungo MacCallum, interview with GK, 1982.

27. Maisie Drysdale, interview with GK, 1982.
28. John Douglas Pringle, interview with GK, 1982.
29. Storry Walton, interview with GK, 1984.
30. GJ to Elsie Johnston, 1 April 1965.
31. Arthur Polkinghorne, interview with GK, 1982.
32. Jack Johnston, interview with Chester Eagle, 29 July 1980.
33. *The Australians*, photographs by Robert Goodman, text by George Johnston, Rigby, Sydney, 1966, p. 45.
34. Medical records, Royal North Shore Hospital, Sydney.
35. Charmian Clift to Patricia and Jack Johnston, 17 Aug. 1965.
36. GJ to Joy and Felix Russo, 3 Aug. 1965.
37. Charmian Clift to Jack and Patricia Johnston, 17 Aug. 1965.
38. 'A Death in the Family', in *Images in Aspic* 115–18.
39. Storry Walton, interview with GK, 1984.
40. Storry Walton, interview with GK, 1984.
41. Charmian Clift to David Higham, 27 Nov. 1965.
42. Ibid.
43. Ibid.
44. GJ to David Higham, 27 Nov. 1965.
45. Toni Burgess, interview with GK, 1982.
46. Storry Walton, interview with GK, 1984.

Chapter XII

1. Jack and Patricia Johnston, interview with Chester Eagle, 29 July 1980.
2. 'Clean Straw For Nothing', typed notes, n.d., Johnston Estate Papers, National Library, Canberra.
3. Toni Burgess, interview with GK, 1982.
4. Toni Burgess, interview with GK, 1982.
5. Toni Burgess, interview with GK, 1982.
6. Charmian Clift to Joy and Felix Russo, 1 Jan. 1967.

7. GJ to David Higham, 25 Feb. 1957.
8. Sidney Nolan, interview with GK, 1982.
9. Quoted by Clifford Tolchard in 'My Husband George: My Wife Charmian', *Walkabout*, Jan. 1969, p. 28.
10. Ibid. 29.
11. 'A Writer Who Believed in Human Dignity', *Sydney Morning Herald*, 10 July 1969, p. 8.
12. 'Banners, Causes and Convictions', *The World of Charmian Clift* 255.
13. Ray and June Crooke, interview with GK, 1982.
14. 'Half Squalid and Yet Half Romantic', *Sydney Morning Herald* Women's Section, 9 Nov. 1967, p. 2.
15. GJ to June Crooke, 6 Nov. 1967.
16. Charmian Clift to June Crooke, 8 Nov. 1967.
17. Ibid.
18. Ibid.
19. Charmian Clift to June Crooke, n.d. (probably April 1968).
20. Quoted in 'Aspects of the Novel', a paper delivered to an Australian Society of Authors' seminar, 9 Feb. 1968.
21. Ibid. for all quotations in this papragraph.
22. Charmian Clift to June Crooke, n.d. (probably April 1968).
23. Quoted by Kay Keavney in 'From George with Sadness', *Australian Women's Weekly*, 3 Sept. 1969, p. 13.
24. Ibid.
25. Charmian Clift, 'My Husband George', *POL* magazine, July 1969, p. 85.
26. See A. E. Goodwin, 'Voyage and Kaleidoscope in George Johnston's Trilogy', *Australian Literary Studies* 6:2 (Oct. 1973) 143–51.
27. John Douglas Pringle, interview with GK, 1981.
28. GJ to Joy and Felix Russo and family, 30 Sept. 1968.
29. Quoted by Tolchard in 'My Husband George: My Wife Charmian', p. 28.
30. Ibid. 27.
31. Quoted by Keavney in 'From George With Sadness'.
32. John Douglas Pringle, interview with GK, 1981.
33. John Douglas Pringle, interview with GK, 1981.
34. *The World of Charmian Clift* 79.
35. Ray Crooke, interview with GK, 1982.

36. All quotations and information in this paragraph come from Ray Crooke, interview with GK, 1982.
37. Toni Burgess, interview with GK, 1982.
38. Toni Burgess, interview with GK, 1982.
39. 'My Husband George', p. 85.
40. This account is based on independent information from Martin Johnston, interview with GK, 1982, and Toni Burgess, interview with GK, 1982. It is difficult to confirm the precise wording of the note, since the City Coroner took the unusual step of placing it along with some other papers in a sealed envelope marked 'never to be opened'. This wording is how Toni Burgess remembers it.
41. Toni Burgess, interview with GK, 1982.
42. Letter column, *Sydney Morning Herald*, 12 July 1969, p. 12.
43. Ibid.
44. *The World of Charmian Clift* 11–12.
45. Quoted in an obituary in the *Age*, 8 Oct. 1969, p. 14.
46. 'My Husband George', p. 83.
47. Nan Hutton, 'Dipping into the World of Charmian', *Age*, 16 Aug. 1973, p. 17.
48. See Alan Lawson, 'Where a Man Belongs', in *Studies in the Recent Australian Novel*, ed. K. G. Hamilton, University of Queensland Press, 1978, pp. 168–93; and Goodwin, op. cit.
49. GJ to Elsie Johnston, 19 July 1969.
50. Keavney, 'From George with Sadness'.
51. 'George, for Whom Working is Therapy', *Australian*, 16 Aug. 1969, p. 18.
52. This and the following three quotations are in handwriting on loose sheets in the Johnston Estate Papers, National Library, Canberra.
53. Jill Porter, interview with GK, 1982.
54. GJ to Jack and Patricia Johnston, 22 April 1970.
55. Jill Porter, interview with GK, 1982.
56. Greeba Jamison to GK, 13 Feb. 1983.
57. 'My Brother Jack' an ABC radio broadcast in *English for School Certificate* series, 6 March 1970.
58. The Supplement to the *Oxford English Dictionary* credits Johnston with being the first to use this term in print.

59. Patricia Johnston believes 'he had a horror of the Australian ocker, and his brother was the epitome of the Australian ocker': interview with Chester Eagle, 29 July 1980.
60. Geoff and Dahl Collings, interview with GK, 1982.
61. See 'The Final Cartload of Clay', by Martin Johnston, *Age*, 2 Oct. 1971.
62. Nancy Keesing, 'The Mischiefs of Time', *Bulletin*, 23 Oct. 1971, pp. 62–3.
63. Introduction to *The Fortunes of Richard Mahony*, Penguin, Ringwood, 1971, p. xxvii.
64. 'Poet of Zen: George Johnston on Arthur Waley', *Sydney Morning Herald*, 6 June 1970, p. 20.
65. Jill Porter, interview with GK, 1982.
66. The surgeon's name is withheld at his request: information conveyed in a letter to GK, 19 July 1982.
67. Elizabeth Riddell, 'Writing Near the Brink', *Australian*, 23 July 1970, p. 11.
68. John Moses, 'George Johnston: who could forget such talent . . . such kindness', *Sunday Telegraph*, 26 July 1970, p. 33.
69. Geoffrey Hutton, 'He Died Alive', *Age* 23 July 1970, p. 6.
70. The story is contained in a letter of 5 April 1983 from June Crooke to John Thompson of the National Library, Canberra, with whose permission it is drawn upon and quoted here. Additional details, such as the rabbit trap and biscuit tin, were supplied by Jill Porter, interview with GK, 1982.
71. June Crooke to John Thompson, 5 April 1983.
72. Ibid.

˜˜˜˜˜˜˜ B I B L I O G R A P H Y ˜˜˜˜˜˜˜

Editions of the Works of Johnston and Clift referred to in the text

By George Johnston

Grey Gladiator, Angus & Robertson, Sydney, 1941.
Battle of the Seaways, Angus & Robertson, Sydney, 1941.
Australia at War, Angus & Robertson, Sydney, 1942.
New Guinea Diary, Angus & Robertson, Sydney, 1943.
Pacific Partner, World Book Co., New York, 1944.
Skyscrapers in the Mist, Angus & Robertson, Sydney, 1946.
Journey through Tomorrow, Cheshire, Melbourne, 1947.
Death Takes Small Bites, Dodd, Mead & Co., New York, 1948.
Moon at Perigee, Angus & Robertson, Sydney, 1948.
The Cyprian Woman, Collins, London, 1955.
The Darkness Outside, Collins, London, 1959.
Closer to the Sun, Collins, London, 1960.
The Far Road, Collins, London, 1962.
My Brother Jack, Collins, London, 1964.
The Far Face of the Moon, Collins, London, 1965.
The Australians (with Robert Goodman), Rigby, Sydney, 1966.
Clean Straw for Nothing, Collins, London, 1969.
A Cartload of Clay, Collins, London, 1971.

By 'Shane Martin' (pseudonym of George Johnston)

Twelve Girls in the Garden, Collins, London, 1957.
The Saracen Shadow, Collins, London, 1957.
The Man Made of Tin, Collins, London, 1958.
The Myth is Murder, Collins, London, 1959.
A Wake for Mourning, Collins, London, 1962.

In Collaboration with Charmian Clift

High Valley, Augus & Robertson, Sydney, 1949.
The Big Chariot, Faber, London, 1953.
The Sponge Divers, Collins, London, 1956.

By Charmian Clift

Mermaid Singing, Michael Joseph, London, 1958.
Peel me a Lotus, Hutchinson, London, 1959.
Walk to the Paradise Gardens, Harper, New York, 1960.
Honour's Mimic, Hutchinson, London, 1964.
Images in Aspic, Horwitz, Sydney, 1965.
The World of Charmian Clift, Ure Smith, Sydney, 1970.

Selected Stories by George Johnston and Charmian Clift

Strong Man from Piraeus and other stories, selected by Garry
Kinnane, Nelson, Melbourne, 1984.

Some Useful Articles on George Johnston

A. E. Goodwin, 'Voyage and Kaleidoscope in George John-
ston's Trilogy', *Australian Literary Studies* 6:2 (Oct. 1973)
143–51.
Geoffrey Thurley, '*My Brother Jack*: an Australian Master-
piece?', *Ariel* 5:3 (July 1974) 61–80.
F. H. Mares, 'A Review of *My Brother Jack*', *Southerly* 24:4
(1964) 244–8.
Alan Lawson, 'Where a Man Belongs', in *Studies in the Recent
Australian Novel*, ed. K. G. Hamilton, University of Queens-
land Press, 1978, pp. 168–93.
Richard N. Coe, 'Portrait of the Artist as a Young Australian',
Southerly, no. 2 (1981) 126–62.
Greer Johnson and Chris Tiffin, 'The Evolution of George
Johnston's David Meredith', *Australian Literary Studies* 2:2
(Oct. 1983) 162–70.

Index

324

Index

Index

marriage, 29, 30, 83; meets 'Cressida', 71, 76; pseudonym, 18; relationship, father, 8–9; relationship, wife, 239, 275; relationship, women, 58; views on 'ocker', 292; war correspondent, 67; *see also My Brother Jack,*
'Meredith, Helen' (*née* 'Midgeley', 29–31, 97, 222–3
'Meredith, Jack' (senior), 1, 3, 14
'Meredith, Jack', 1, 8, 14, 22, 25, 36
'Meredith, Sheila', 21, 25
'Meredith' trilogy (GJ), x, 68, 294–5
  see also MBJ, CSFN, CoC
Mermaid Singing (Clift), 145, 146, 155, 162, 163, 164
Miles Franklin Award, viii, 287
Missingham, Hal, 257, 261
Monk, Noel, 35
Monsoon (GJ), 87
Moomba Book Prize (1970), 287
Moon at Perigee (GJ), 87
Moorehead, Alan, 153, 244, 264
'Morley, Cressida', 71
Moses, John, 284, 296
'Murder By Horoscope' (GJ), 108, 112
My Brother Jack (GJ), viii, 106, 125, 224
  attitudes to war, 8; autobiographical sources, 219; awards, 247; biographical aspects, 3, 29–31; Chapter One, 216; promotion of, 228, 235; reviews of, 228; sales, 237; television adaptation, 246, 251–2; writing of, 216–20
Myth is Murder, The (GJ as 'Shane Martin'), 174, 175

National Gallery School (Vic.), 16, 28, 75, 115
New Guinea Diary (GJ), 42, 45, 46
'Night of Horror' (GJ), 12–13
Niland, D'Arcy, 99, 100, 235
Nolan, Cynthia (*née* Reed), 114, 130, 133, 152, 155–9, 244, 276
  attitude to GJ, 157–60
Nolan, Sir Sidney, 19, 28, 40, 94, 114, 127, 133, 158, 160–2, 166, 261–2
  friendship with GJ, 160; Gallipoli paintings, 40, 152–4, 201
'Notes From an Expatriate's Journal' (GJ), 123

O'Connor, James, 59, 63, 64
O'Connor, Robert, 278
O'Grady, Desmond, ix
Olsen, Axel, 59
'Other People's Houses' (Clift), 203

Pacific Partner (GJ), 46
'Pagoda' (GJ), 112, 118, 130
Palethorpe, Nigel, 64, 111, 133, 138
Palmer, Howard, 71
Parer, Damien, 43
Park, Ruth, 99, 100, 235
Pearn, Pollinger & Higham (GJ's agents), 108

Peel me a Lotus (Clift), 160, 162, 163–4, 165, 166, 169, 179–80, 184
Peterson, Frederick, 111
Petit Feu, A (GJ) (French edition of *Death Takes Small Bites*), 92
philistinism, Australian, 104, 117
'Piping Cry, The' (GJ & Clift), 104–5, 106, 108, 112, 118, 229
Plate, Carl, 127
Polkinghorne, Arthur, 93, 94, 99, 101, 244
Polkinghorne, Monica, 93, 244
Pollard, Jack, 111
Porter, Barney, 36
Porter, Hal, 235
Porter, Jill, 235, 286–7, 295, 297
Pownall, William, 227, 230
'Press the Rue for Wine' (GJ as 'Shane Martin'), 162
Pringle, John Douglas, 245, 278
pseudonyms,
  'David Meredith', 18; George Johnston, 155

radio, GJ and Clift writing for, 101, 108
Rasmussen, Jack, 81
Reed, John, 19, 114
Reid, Alan, 94
Reid, Olga, 26, 28, 30, 190, 222
'Requiem Mass' (GJ), 117
Riddell, Elizabeth, 296
Ridge, Ron, 13, 17, 20, 22, 23
'Roman Mosaic' (GJ), 53–4, 55, 56
Russo, Joy (*née* Johnston), 215, 249, 260
Russo, Felix, 260
Ryland, John, 198

Sainthill, Loudon, 114
Saracen Shadow, The (GJ as 'Shane Martin'), 163, 169
Saturday Evening Post, 46, 54
Sea and the Stone, The (GJ & Clift), 143, 144, 147, 152
Sea Breezes (Pacific Steamship Navigation Company), 18
Sea Change, The (E.J. Howard), 171
Sea Spray (Brighton Technical School), 12
Sentimental Bloke, The 96, 104, 108, 112, 119
'Serpent in the Rock, The' (GJ & Clift), 209, 228
Seven Day Bicycle Rider, The 267
'Shane Martin', GJ's pseudonym, 155
Shiplovers' Society of Victoria, 22
Simione, Patricia, 130, 139
Simpson, Colin, 203, 204, 212
Skyscrapers in the Mist (GJ), 49, 55, 91
Slessor, Kenneth, 94, 99
Speight, Danny, 99
Spencer, Gwen Morton, 75
Sponge Divers, The (GJ & Clift), 147, 152, 160, 162, 163
Squadrons Up (Noel Monk), 35
Sriber, Charles, 96, 103, 165, 172, 182, 184, 185, 189, 214